De Gaulle
and the World

W. W. KULSKI

De Gaulle
and the World

*The Foreign Policy of the
Fifth French Republic*

SYRACUSE UNIVERSITY PRESS

To my princess in the fairy tales

Preface

General Charles de Gaulle was reelected on December 19, 1965, to another seven-year term as President of the French Republic. Unless death, illness, or overt loss of support in his own country ends his public career prior to January 1973, he will remain an absolute master of French foreign policy until then. Since 1958 the external policy of the French Republic has been the policy which he himself has molded. The same will be true as long as he is President.

It is far from certain that a post-Gaullist France, if governed by his present domestic opponents, would abandon all the main aspects of his foreign policy. Contrary to views frequently held abroad, the effects of his policy might survive a long time.

General de Gaulle formulates his policy without regard for the wishes or pressures of the other major powers. He determines the path France follows in international affairs. As this path does not run parallel to but often crosses the paths of other nations, French external moves at times have startled foreign capitals and often have had worldwide repercussions. A few aspects of de Gaulle's foreign policy indicate its importance for other nations: the French attitude toward the Atlantic Alliance and the recent decision to withdraw from NATO; the joining of the nuclear club with China and, like China, despite lack of assistance or encouragement by any of the three initial members of that club; the firm opposition to any supranational institutions in the European Economic Community (Common Market) and the veto which barred British access to that Community; the policy of close friendship with the German Federal Republic followed in 1963 by a notable deterioration in the relations with this neighbor and by the warming-up in French-Soviet relations; the establishment of diplomatic relations with China; an open challenge to United States policy in Europe and in the other parts of the world, including Latin America; a complete disapproval of American policy in Southeast Asia, in particular in Vietnam; the liquidation of the former French colonial empire within the amazingly short period of four years, followed by a persistent effort to extend French influence in the underdeveloped continents in general and to maintain it in the former French colonial possessions in particular.

Every major power, Western or Communist, and most other nations simply may not overlook de Gaulle's actual moves or probable intentions in formulating their own foreign policy. It is not only France but he himself who is one of the major factors in contemporary international politics. This is the main reason why this book has been written.

After long meditation and research I feel that I may address a word of caution to the non-French critics of President de Gaulle's policy. In the first place, one should never lose sight of the rather self-evident fact that the office of President of the French Republic compels him to protect principally French national interests as he understands them, even if foreign national interests are hurt in the process. No other president or prime minister is expected to act otherwise, although traditionally some effort is made to convince foreign nations that one's own external policy is beneficial to their well-being and security. The only legitimate quarrel with General de Gaulle would consist of points yet to be proved: that his policy would eventually endanger French national interests or that his estimates of international conditions are erroneous. However, even this sort of dispute should not be distorted by the personal dislike and mistrust of the French President common in several Western countries. After all, his long record of political activities, opened by his famous broadcast on June 18, 1940, is not made up of mistakes. Like other human beings, he is sometimes right and sometimes wrong. Moreover, one lacks the necessary historical perspective to evaluate correctly certain of his "unorthodox" views. In any event, prejudice in this, as in other cases, is a poor guide in evaluating the policies pursued by a foreign statesman, especially if they conflict with one's own objectives.

I might have unintentionally failed in following my own advice but have honestly tried to evaluate General de Gaulle's foreign policy mainly from the point of view of its concordance with French national interests and only secondarily from the point of view of its meaning for other nations. This book reviews all aspects of his policy and covers the whole period of his Presidency, beginning with his return to power in 1958 and ending with the most recent events, such as the presidential election in France in December 1965, the revival of the Common Market, French withdrawal from NATO, de Gaulle's statements regarding Vietnam, and his present attitudes toward Britain, Germany, and the Soviet Union.

The research for the present book was begun without any preconceived ideas, except for my general interpretation of international politics, which was formulated in my *International Politics in a Revolutionary Age* (Philadelphia, Pa.: J. B. Lippincott Co., 1964). This research was tantamount to a rediscovery of France, which I had intimately known during the interwar period, when I was a student at the Paris School of Law and a very frequent visitor or resident in that country.

It was a rediscovery, because the France of today is very different from the France of yesterday.

I spent twelve months in France during the troubled years of 1961 and 1962. I returned there in 1965. Those contacts with Frenchmen of all classes, including active politicians, high dignitaries of both the Fourth and Fifth Republics, and distinguished university professors, instilled life in the French printed words.

I do not want to name my French friends and acquaintances who graciously helped me to understand the intricacies of French domestic and external politics. To print their names would be disobliging, because some of my own views could be illegitimately ascribed to them. I assume the exclusive responsibility for every word in this book. However, this obligation does not extend to the printed word, which is the property of everyone.

I decided that the best and most effective way to enable the reader to form his own opinion was to include as many quotations from the French sources as seemed useful and was feasible. I wanted the reader to hear the many and sometimes discordant French voices tell him what they thought of the foreign policy of the Fifth Republic. My privilege was to analyze their views and provide my own comments.

A large space was reserved for quotations from General de Gaulle's statements and writings. His is the most important French voice at the present time. If I often disagreed with him, this disagreement should not be interpreted as a lack of respect; for me de Gaulle will always remain the man of June 18, 1940, who refused to surrender to the Nazi victors. But I have never been a worshiper of any man, as great as he might be. I felt free to criticize what I found wanting in de Gaulle's foreign policy, as I would have done in any other case. This does not mean at all that I do not recognize in the French President a great man whose name will forever remain in history.

My critical attitude extended to France herself; even loyalty to my adoptive country has never blinded me to certain shortcomings in the foreign policy of the United States. Frenchmen, including my personal friends, cannot ask for more. They would be wrong in thinking that my sincere friendship for their country has disappeared. It is there, but "magnus amicus Plato, sed maius veritas." Of course, I do not claim that my truth is *the* truth, because I have no divine key for unlocking the door to an absolute truth. Like other men I have only my own truth, which might be denied by others, but which results from a careful research and the intention to remain intellectually honest with myself.

I owe words of deep gratitude to those Frenchmen who talked to me and in this way helped me, and also to the following institutions without whose financial assistance I would have been unable to make two long visits to France. I received a Fulbright research grant and a John Simon Guggenheim Memorial Foundation fellowship for a twelve-month visit in 1961–62. I should like to express particularly warm appreciation to the president of that foundation, Dr. Gordon N. Ray. My second visit, in 1965, was made possible by the generosity of Duke University. I am glad to pay homage here to its president, Dr. Douglas Knight, to its provost, Dr. Taylor R. Cole, and to my distinguished colleague, Dr. Robert R. Wilson, to all of whom I am indebted for Duke University's help.

The acknowledgments for any of my books would not be complete if I did not mention the helpful assistance and warm encouragement which I have always received from my wife.

W. W. K.

Durham, North Carolina
July 5, 1966

Acknowledgments

The author gratefully acknowledges the copyright permissions for the use of quotations from the books and periodicals (their titles and other reference data are reproduced in the footnotes and the *Bibliography*) printed by the following publishers:

The Bodley Head Ltd., 9 Bow Street, London, England.

Calmann-Lévy, 3 rue Auber, Paris, France.

F. W. Cheshire Pty. Ltd., 338 Little Collins Street, Melbourne, Australia.

Librairie Armand Colin, 103 Boulevard Saint-Michel, Paris, France.

College of Europe, Bruges, Belgium.

Les Editions John Didier, 6 rue Garancière, Paris, France.

Doubleday and Co., 277 Park Avenue, New York, N.Y.

Librairie Arthème Fayard, 18 rue du Saint-Gothard, Paris, France.

Librairie Ernest Flammarion, 26 rue Racine, Paris, France.

Librairie Gedalge, 75 rue des Saints-Pères, Paris, France.

Editions Bernard Grasset, 61 rue des Saints-Pères, Paris, France.

Harvard University Press, 79 Garden Street, Cambridge, Mass.

René Julliard, 30 rue de l'Université, Paris, France.

Little, Brown and Co., 34 Beacon Street, Boston, Mass.

Editions G.-P. Maisonneuve et Larose, 11 rue Victor-Cousin, Paris, France.

Le Monde, 5 rue des Italiens, Paris, France.

R. Pichon et R. Durand-Auzias, 20 rue Soufflot, Paris, France.

Librairie Plon, 8 rue Garancière, Paris, France.

Presses Universitaires de France, 108 Boulevard Saint-Germain, Paris, France.

Editions du Seuil, 27 rue Jacob, Paris, France.

Simon and Schuster, 630 Fifth Avenue, New York, N.Y.

Sondages, Revue Française de l'Opinion Publique, 20 rue d'Aumale, Paris, France.

Editions Stock, 6 rue Casimir-Delavigne, Paris, France.

Contents

She [the French nation] is logical in her discourses, but she is sometimes surprising in her actions.

PAUL VALÉRY, *Regards sur le Monde Actuel*

I The Charismatic Leader

His historical mission and his myths

"It is General de Gaulle undoubtedly who makes the decisions concerning foreign policy."[1] De Gaulle himself readily admits this.

Looking back at his seven years as President of the Republic, he said:

> During the last seven years he [the President] was determining the orientation of French domestic and external policies; he steadily supervised their implementation; he was making the supreme decisions relating to problems which committed our destiny and which required, therefore, the cutting of an equal number of Gordian knots. This was true regarding the institutions, State security, national defense, the general development of the country, the economic, financial and monetary stability, etc., etc., as well as the Algerian problem, Europe, the decolonization, the African cooperation, our attitude toward Germany, the United States, England, Russia, China, Latin America, the Orient, etc., etc.[2]

General de Gaulle has reserved for himself the power to make decisions regarding all matters he considers important. Foreign policy and national defense are among them.

Therefore, the foreign policy of the Fifth Republic is his foreign policy. This is even more true because of his concept of historical mission; he is the leader predestined to be responsible for the fate of France. He derives the moral right to speak on behalf of France from this supernatural mission; only his legal right to do so is founded on his powers as President of the Republic. The image he has of himself is not that of another Richelieu or of a French Pitt or Bismarck. He sees himself as being much more than a statesman to whom only chance and his own talent have given the opportunity to formulate national policies. He is what he is owing to a supernatural call, but not because the French people or their representatives vested in him the powers of government. In brief, he claims to be the incarnation of immortal France.

He is a charismatic leader, i.e., a man who, together with his followers, believes that he has been called upon by God or by history or

1

destiny (in any event by a supernatural force) to carry out great feats for the benefit of his nation. His vocation is independent of the will of other men. The only rational proof of this vocation is the success of his mission. The failure would end in the dispersal of believers. Savonarola's career came to a tragic conclusion after his Florentine followers began to doubt the veracity of his prophecies.

De Gaulle's career has been amazingly successful. His French followers, the so-called unconditional Gaullists, might at times fail to understand some of his decisions; but they take comfort in the thought that the General was so often right that they safely may trust in his superior wisdom.

It is an amazing spectacle to see a nation that prides herself on her Cartesian rationalism and is usually hypercritical assenting in several votes to rule by a charismatic leader. His presence at the helm indicates that Frenchmen are inclined in times of stress to entrust their fate to a "providential man."[3] Joan of Arc was the prototype of this savior of the country. In this century Frenchmen have given their support to three "providential" men: Clemenceau from 1917 to 1918, Marshal Pétain from 1940 to 1942, and lastly de Gaulle.

De Gaulle's personality has two seemingly contradictory features: mysticism and realism. He is a stark and coldly calculating realist in his views of the world and of foreign nations, in his determination of objectives, and in his choice of means. Assuming that he is not infallible, he acts in accordance with at least his own interpretation of political reality. His images of France and of his own mission are, by contrast, mystically based on faith; he does not even consider it necessary to adduce rational proofs of their validity.

Like most of his contemporaries, whatever their nationality, he sees the world from one and only one center: his own country. To use a Chinese expression, his France is the Kingdom of the Middle. She is unique among all nations. He wrote: "Any large-scale human edifice will be arbitrary and ephemeral if the seal of France is not affixed to it."[4]

France should not be confused with Frenchmen. He said in 1961: "I believe that the French nation is [now] truly worthy of France."[5] De Gaulle could not have been clearer: the French nation should not be equated with France; it may or may not be worthy of France, who exists, so to speak, independently of Frenchmen. He gave his own description of France in the following oft-quoted words:

All my life I have thought of France in a certain way. This is inspired by sentiment as much as by reason. The emotional side of me tends to imagine France, like the princess in the fairy stories or the Madonna in the frescoes, as dedicated to an exalted and exceptional destiny. Instinctively I have the feeling that Providence has created her either for complete successes or for exemplary misfortunes. If, in spite of this, mediocrity shows in her acts and deeds, it strikes me as an absurd anomaly, to be imputed to the faults of Frenchmen, not to the genius of the land. But the positive side of my mind also assures me that France is not really herself unless in the front rank; that only vast enterprises are capable of counterbalancing the ferments of dispersal which are inherent in her people; that our country, as it is, surrounded by the others, as they are, must aim high and hold itself straight, on pain of mortal danger. In short, to my mind, France cannot be France without greatness.[6]

This hymn to France is moving in its sincerity. It is an act of faith. Yet it strikes a non-Frenchman as naive. Any fervent patriot might be tempted to dream of his own country as "the princess in the fairy tales" and "the Madonna in the frescoes," and also imagine that Providence has created his people for greatness. De Gaulle, however, would probably find these thoughts pretentious if applied to a country other than France.

In fact, history does not seem to support his claim that France has been marked for an exceptional destiny. There have been periods in the history of European civilization when France occupied the first rank and others when she did not. It was Italy that was the teacher of Europe during the Renaissance, while France was only one of the eager disciples. In 1940 it was Britain who did not doubt of her great destiny rather than the France of Pétain. De Gaulle evades the historical record, as checkered for France as for all other nations, by declaring that the periods of mediocrity were due to the fault of Frenchmen but not to the genius of the Fatherland. At this point no one but an equally mystical French patriot may follow his argument. His France, existing apart from the Frenchmen living at any given time, becomes a supernatural being, a divinity. However, common sense indicates that the great French achievements—political, military, intellectual, and artistic, everything that has made up France—have been the product of efforts by many generations of Frenchmen. France is those generations of Frenchmen, and hence not only their successes but also their failures and mediocrities make up the true image of France. It is amazing that a man of de Gaulle's brilliant intellect could conceive this absurd dualism between the pure soul of France and the sinful body of Frenchmen. Yet this axiom is his first article of faith. A French opponent phrased it this way: "France is not in his eyes all Frenchmen, but an entity that does not participate in their mediocrity."[7]

The second article is that since June 18, 1940, General de Gaulle has been the embodiment of French legitimacy. On that memorable day he undoubtedly entered history. A brigadier general who had scandalized his superiors with his "heretical" views on the crucial role of armored divisions in the future war and who was sadly vindicated by the German victories, an undersecretary for war in the ministry of Paul Reynaud, he was known to the military hierarchy and to the politicians of the Third Republic, but in June 1940 his name was not familiar to the mass of Frenchmen. In his breach of military discipline and his rebellion against the government of Marshal Pétain he was practically alone. When he fled to London in protest against Pétain's decision to seek an armistice, de Gaulle had no companions among high-ranking French military or political figures. French people closed their ranks behind their old Marshal, who offered them what they wanted most: the termination of hostilities. De Gaulle's was a lone voice when on June 18 he proclaimed from B.B.C. radio stations: "France is not alone. . . . This war is not ended by the battle of France; this is a world war. . . . Whatever might happen, the flame of French resistance must not be extinguished; it shall not be extinguished!" In July of the same year his proclamation pasted on the walls of London proudly affirmed: "France has lost a battle but not the war."[8]

This relatively unknown brigadier general, who dared to contest the legitimacy of his political and military superiors and who disagreed with the views of the great majority of his countrymen, needed an article of faith to sustain him, to give him the authority which would allow him to speak on behalf of France. His fervent admirer François Mauriac says of him, "He does not confuse the French with France. . . . The opinion of the French that he accepts is the opinion that agrees with his own. The opinion of France, for de Gaulle, is always the opinion France will receive (is receiving) from him."[9] This is as true today as it was in that fateful summer of 1940. If Frenchmen are not France, and if they especially are not France when they disagree with him on crucial issues, then he is France. He has had the courage to say it. During one of his debates with Sir Winston Churchill in 1942 the British Prime Minister impatiently asked: "After all, are you France?" De Gaulle replied: "If I am not France, why do you discuss with me?"[10] Similar statements have abounded from 1940 to the present. On June 19, 1940, he said: "I, General de Gaulle, French soldier and leader, am aware that I speak in the name of France."[11]

He clearly considers his historic broadcast of June 18, 1940, as the beginning of a mission which will end only with his death. He wrote in his *Memoirs*: "As the irrevocable words flew out upon their way, I felt within myself a life coming to an end—the life I had lived within the framework of a solid France and an indivisible army. At the age of forty-nine I was entering upon adventure, like a man thrown by fate outside all terms of reference."[12] On that day his career as a professional military officer terminated and that as a statesman began. For him that day meant much more; he has felt since then that he was "annointed" as the predestined leader of Frenchmen, as the providential man who had the right to speak in the name of France. His proud prophecy that 1940 marked only the end of the French battle, but not the end of the war, was vindicated by later events. Owing to him, France, crushed in 1940, recovered in 1945 the diplomatic rank of a victorious power. The German defeat was for him and a great number of his countrymen a proof of his providential vocation. He was right, not Pétain and the great majority of Frenchmen who followed the old Marshal in 1940. By the same token he provided an alibi for Frenchmen who neither heard him in June 1940, nor wanted to follow him in the years 1940–42. It flattered French pride to think that France had not been in Vichy then but with de Gaulle in London. One of the most distinguished French political scientists wrote after the last war: "He would have the right to say like Sertorius: 'Rome is no longer in Rome; she is here where I am.' "[13] De Gaulle himself has had no doubt since 1940 that France is always where he is. During his retirement she dwelled with him in his private residence at Colombey-les-Deux-Eglises.

Being the incarnation of eternal France, de Gaulle may not appear to the world as an ordinary human being. A great actor, like all men who successfully perform in public, he molded for himself a mask of solemn and dignified aloofness; by now this mask, worn for so many years, has probably become his true face. As he said: "In short, limited and alone though I was, and precisely because I was so, I had to climb to the heights and never then to come down."[14]

Legitimacy versus legality

Since 1940 he has had to face the problem of conflict between himself, the voice of France, and the actual holders of power in the France that existed not in his dreams but on earth. During the last war it was the Vichy regime and from 1946 to 1958 the successive governments of the Fourth Republic that actually governed Frenchmen. Those were the periods of mediocrity which de Gaulle deplored. But at those times the man who claimed to be the only authentic voice of eternal France was living either abroad or in his private retreat. The soul of France no longer resided in the sinful body of Frenchmen.

De Gaulle found the solution to this puzzling problem in contrasting French legitimacy with French legality. Pétain's government and the governments of the Fourth Republic were legal, but illegitimate, because since 1940 the true French legitimacy had rested in de Gaulle's hands. Frenchmen could recover peace of mind and true happiness only when legality and legitimacy were reconciled by the return of de Gaulle to power.

All this might at first glance seem to be an impossible story except that this is the story which he never tires of telling. Writing about his resignation in 1946, he says:

> Gone was that atmosphere of exaltation, that hope of success, that ambition for France, which supported the national soul. Every Frenchman, whatever his tendencies, had the troubling suspicion that with the General vanished something primordial, permanent and necessary which he incarnated in history and which the regime of parties could not represent. In the sidetracked leader, men persisted in seeing a kind of capital of sovereignty, a last resort selected in advance. They supposed such legitimacy could remain latent in a period without anxiety. But they knew it could be invoked by common consent as soon as a new laceration threatened the nation.[15]

Since he came back in 1958 he has often repeated the same thought. On June 18, 1940, history vested in him the mission to be the voice of eternal France and hence the anointed leader of Frenchmen. He is the President of the Republic not only because such is the will of the majority of Frenchmen but principally because history has given him the right, that no one may annul, to rule France and lead her to greatness. It is the good luck of Frenchmen that the legitimacy and legality of power are now merged in his person.

A careful scrutiny of his statements makes it clear that he exercises his almost unlimited powers by virtue of these two titles: his incarnation of the true French legitimacy and the support of the majority of French voters. If he were a monarch, he would say of himself: "By the grace of history and the will of Frenchmen." In other words, history has conferred on him the right to rule France, but he consents to exercise it only with the assent of the majority of his countrymen. It would be unfair to him to doubt whether he would step down and once again retire, as he did in 1946, were that majority to refuse him their support.

In a televised speech made on January 29, 1960, the time of the uprising of Algerian Frenchmen, de Gaulle asked for the support of the French people. He formulated his theory in one sentence of that speech: "By virtue of the mandate that the people has [sic] given me and of the national legitimacy that I have embodied for twenty years, I ask all men and women to support me, no matter what happens."[16] Everything is there: the embodiment of French legitimacy, the year of anointment by history, and the mandate from the people. He reiterated this on April 23, 1961, in a message to the French people on the occasion of the generals' revolt in Algeria: "I assert myself, for today and for tomorrow, in the French and republican legitimacy which the nation has conferred on me."[17] On January 6, 1961, he referred to the fateful year of 1940: "For more than twenty years, events have willed that I serve as the guide of the country in the grave crises we have lived through."[18] In his oration at the funeral of René Coty, the last President of the Fourth Republic, de Gaulle said of him: "He beseeched the cornered regime to entrust its fate, as he himself had done, to the ultimate legitimacy."[19] What he meant was that in 1958 President Coty asked him, de Gaulle, to save the Republic by returning to power; but what he praised the late President for was his decision to turn to the providential man who embodied French legitimacy independently of any legal mandate. On September 20, 1962, addressing Frenchmen on television, he was no more secretive about the true source of his power, his historical vocation, which Frenchmen could only confirm by their vote but certainly might not cancel: "Ever since the French people called me to take my place again officially [sic] at its head . . ."[20]

"His personality is marked by an immense pride . . . because de Gaulle is France," says one French writer.[21] Who would not be proud if he thought himself the incarnation of the eternal genius of his country? This pride is so natural for de Gaulle that it is not offensive. It is reflected in his frequent way of speaking of himself in the third person, "General de Gaulle . . . ," as though he were speaking as France, who has chosen to dwell in the body of a French general and to borrow his voice for her messages. The same unruffled pride may be seen in his letter of January 18, 1947, to Léon Blum, then Prime Minister of France. Refusing to accept the highest military decoration, which Blum intended to confer on him, he wrote: "Indeed, what I accomplished between June 18, 1940, and January 22, 1946 [the date of his resignation as the head of French government], was done at a time when, as you know, I exercised, by virtue of necessity, the functions of the head of State and those of the head of government. It is, of course, unimaginable that the State or the government ever decorate themselves in the person of him who has personified and directed them and for the manner in which he has done it."[22] With the same pride he rejected the offer to elect him to the French Academy in 1944; he told the representatives of that august body: "As you know, de Gaulle cannot belong to any category, nor receive any distinction."[23]

If one is neither a mystic nor an unconditional Gaullist, he need only make one comparison to appreciate the enormity of de Gaulle's claim. In many respects he resembles Sir Winston Churchill. Like Churchill, he is a great national leader, a man whose stature is fully seen only against the background of tragic events, a master of spoken and written word, a statesman who, like Pericles, rules by the word but not by the sword. Yet Churchill never claimed, even in 1940, to be the holder of British legitimacy or to be the embodiment of Britain; this claim is inconceivable in Great Britain. Churchill modestly said that he was only the voice of the British lion. He certainly was not a mystic. Moreover, an old parliamentarian, he would have been unable to conceive of a divorce between legitimacy and legality. After his electoral defeat in 1945 he gracefully stepped down and accepted the Labour government as legitimate because it had the support of the majority of British voters and was duly appointed by the sovereign.

De Gaulle has never answered several questions a nonbeliever might ask: Is the holder of French legitimacy infallible because of his charisma? Which Frenchmen were previously the incarnation of that legitimacy? Was it all the French kings or only those de Gaulle would consider great? Was it Joan of Arc? Was it Clemenceau in 1917–18? Were there long periods of "mediocrity" in French history when legitimacy was absent altogether and when France had to be satisfied with mere legality? What sign of heaven reveals to Frenchmen the existence of an authentic holder of legitimacy? An unconditional Gaullist can say with Pascal: "Credo quia absurdum."

Will de Gaulle have an heir to French legitimacy? He once expressed doubt whether France would ever have another de Gaulle: "Perhaps my mission consists in being the last flight toward the summits in our history. Perhaps I shall have written the last pages in the book of our greatness."[24] In any event one decision is beyond his power, namely, to anoint the person that would replace him after his demise and that would have the support of the French people. Even his enthusiastic admirer concedes this: "What he is not responsible for is the choice of the man who doubtless already exists and who will succeed him."[25] There is no Frenchman who has or claims to have his stature. Nobody in France today is capable of inheriting the purple mantle of that elected, nonhereditary monarch. The nearly unlimited powers he has as President would probably crush a lesser man if he tried to be a second de Gaulle. On January 31, 1964, he said:

> Indeed, the President, who in accordance with our Constitution, is the man of the nation, placed in his position by the nation itself in order to answer for its destiny; the President, who selects the Prime Minister, who appoints him and the other members of the government, who has the right to change the Prime Minister, either because the task which he assigned to him has been fulfilled and he wishes to keep him in reserve for a later stage, or because he no longer approves of him; the President, who sanctions the decisions taken in the councils, promulgates the laws, negotiates the treaties, enacts or does not enact the measures proposed to him, who is the commander-in-chief of the armed forces, who appoints the public officials; the President, who, in the event of peril, must take it upon himself to do all that is necessary; the President is obviously the one to hold and to delegate the authority of the State. . . . The President distributes public powers as he deems it necessary. But, while it should obviously be understood that the indivisible authority of the State is entrusted entirely to the President by the people who elected him, that there is no other authority, either ministerial, civilian, military or judiciary which is not conferred and maintained by him; finally that it is his right to adjust the supreme jurisdiction which is his own with the jurisdictions which he assigns to others; nevertheless everything requires in ordinary times to maintain the distinction between the office and the field of action of the Head of State and those of the Prime Minister.[26]

This description of powers of the President of the Republic is contrary to the provisions of the Constitution of the Fifth Republic. The regime he describes is neither parliamentary nor presidential. His President is truly an absolute monarch but an elective monarch whom the people may dismiss after seven years in office. His rejection of the separation of powers goes so far that even the judiciary is said to derive its authority from the President, who seems to be, like French kings, the fountainhead of justice.

Only his charisma allows de Gaulle to expound this extravagant theory of government publicly. Fortunately for France no other Frenchman could claim those exorbitant powers and still hope to be elected President of the Republic. No other Frenchman would dare "to have dissociated once and for all the ephemeral French from eternal France"[27] and yet enjoy popularity among those "ephemeral" Frenchmen.

The pragmatic statesman

If one steps down from the charismatic heights and looks at de Gaulle as a mortal and fallible human being, he cannot remain blind to the greatness of his personality and achievements. The man who refused to accept French defeat in 1940 as a final verdict of history, who in 1945 skillfully regained for his defeated country the diplomatic rank of one of the four victorious powers, who ensured a peaceful transition from the Vichy regime and the enemy occupation to the democracy of the Fourth Republic, who in 1958 saved France from the danger of a threatening military putsch, who freed his country from the burden of an obsolete colonial empire, who had the courage to terminate the Algerian war which, like cancer, was eating deep into the French body politic, and who provided France with a respite from governmental instability—obviously such a man is not made of ordinary clay. He belongs in the ranks of the great men who have left an indelible mark on our century. His actions have had fewer universal repercussions than those of a Churchill, a Lenin, or a Stalin, but they have profoundly influenced the fate of his own country.

Like those of other statesmen, his public actions are not guided by Christian morality although he is a practicing Catholic. As early as 1932 he wrote in his *Fil de l'Epée*: "Evangelical perfection does not lead to Empire." In the same book he sketched an image of the leader which he has not forgotten since: "The man of action is inconceivable without a strong dose of egoism, pride, hardheartedness, and guile."[28] Many years later, he paid a tribute to Churchill, but this tribute was also his own self-portrait: "On top of everything, he was fitted by his character to act, take risks, play the part out-and-out and without scruple. In short, I found him well in the saddle as guide and chief."[29] The following image of de Gaulle could just as well be of Churchill: "His destiny is to be the man of catastrophic epochs. . . . His authority imposes itself only at a time when the events are so dramatic that they become commensurate with his haughty and solitary genius."[30] In the same tragic year, 1940, both Churchill and de Gaulle proved to be the men who were needed in periods of national catastrophe. De Gaulle proved it once again during the grave crisis of 1958.

It is not easy to paint a portrait of the man who wants to remain aloof and keeps secret his innermost thoughts. His best biographer mentions the difficulties:

> It is difficult to talk about a contemporary person. Lack of necessary perspective prevents the finding out of what is essential among so many events which modify the visible contour of a man's life. . . . Related to all national upheavals and to all historical dramas of our time, he has aroused the most conflicting passions, bringing forth in each of us either admiration or indignation, either enthusiasm or resentment, but never indifference.[31]

This is only too true. Neither Frenchmen nor foreigners who observe his policies remain indifferent. Usually, they divide between two poles: admiration and dislike, if not hatred. This emotional aura which surrounds him increases the difficulty of seeing him in his true proportions. "The best known Frenchman remains the least known."[32]

Nevertheless, his actions reveal certain outstanding features of his mind and character. Unlike most other Frenchmen, who tend to show their emotions, he displays English-like self-control. Even in 1944–45, his greatest hour, he remained master of his emotions while landing on his beloved native soil after four years of exile and while making his triumphal entry into a liberated Paris. Yet a French commentator concludes too hastily that "sentiments have no place in the politics of General de Gaulle."[33] An Englishman could tell him that a man who is reluctant to show his emotions might harbor feelings as deep, if not deeper, than another who gesticulates or sheds tears at the slightest provocation. None of de Gaulle's actions can be understood without realizing his profound love of France. There is true compassion in his many statements regarding the moral obligation of rich nations to offer aid to the proletarian peoples of the underdeveloped world. One has the impression that this calculating politician who does not seek evangelical perfection has been deeply distressed by the contrast between the prosperity of developed nations and the utter misery of the underdeveloped continents and is affected by the feeling of Christian charity. What is true is that he is not sentimental in the cheaper sense of the word.

We have said that he is a mystic and a realist. He firmly believes in the two myths of his own creation: eternal France and his own historic vocation. At the same time all his countrymen, friends and fierce opponents alike, agree that he is above all a pragmatist in politics. If he has a political doctrine it is that of having none. He wrote himself: "In economy as in politics or strategy, there exists, I believe, no absolute truth. There are only the circumstances. It was my conception of the latter which was responsible for my decision."[34] When one calls him a realist he must not forget that there are as many "realities" as there are men who discover them. A realist in politics is the man who acts in accordance with his own vision of reality. This is what de Gaulle means when he refers to his conception of circumstances that determines his decisions.

His opinion of himself is supported by the views of others. A French political scientist says: "This great empiricist, who has few preconceived ideas, seems to make decisions as events occur."[35] André Siegfried wrote: "His whole political career proves that, while he knows how to make decisions, he is also a remarkable tactician."[36] His Socialist opponent, Guy Mollet, agrees: "The general orientation of his policy remains fixed, but he pays attention to obstacles with his own pragmatism and very readily follows each forward step with a pause."[37] Finally, a Communist leader voices the same opinion: "De Gaulle is, above all, a pragmatist determined to succeed in his venture at any price, but ready to maneuver and, if necessary, take recourse in all sorts of methods if they seem likely to enable him to reach the objective he wants to attain.[38] De Gaulle's pragmatism is reflected in his favorite expression: "Things being as they are . . ." In other words, if you cannot change external circumstances, make the best of them.

His own life-career is testimony to his openmindedness and willingness to accept things as they are. However, this acceptance of things as they are is not passive; it is the starting point for action. De Gaulle, a professional military officer inculcated with the spirit of discipline and respect for superiors, raised the standard of rebellion in 1940. Scion of an old and highly respectable bourgeois family, he had no qualms about accepting Communist cooperation in the resistance movement or later about associating Communist leaders with his government; it was not he but a Socialist Prime Minister who later compelled the Communist ministers to resign. A man of order, he presided over the drastic purge of Frenchmen guilty of collaboration with the enemy, men who mostly belonged to his own social class and with whom he had much in common prior to the war. Impatient of the party game and a severe critic of parliamentary intrigues, he was never attracted by the antiparliamentary Vichy regime. An apostle of French greatness, he was the artisan of liquidation of the French colonial empire. His Catholicism has never affected his domestic or foreign policies. But there is a constant factor in all these adjustments and seeming contradictions: his total devotion to France.

This is why he is accused of being an outmoded nationalist. This reproach is rather hypocritical in our age of triumphant nationalism. The two world wars, recent developments within the Communist movement, the emancipation of former colonial peoples, and the re-birth of Israel are proof that love of one's people is, in the last analysis, the strongest social bond. One may, if one wants, indulge in semantic acrobatics and call one's own love of country patriotism while calling the same feeling in foreigners nationalism, but the sub-stance of that social phenomenon is not affected by manipulation of words. Moreover, the citizen of any country expects his government to take good care of national interests. De Gaulle is the President of the French Republic; it would be amazing if he were not a French patriot and did not protect French national interests to the best of his abilities. Neither the President of the United States nor the Prime Minister of Great Britain would feel flattered if told that he is less patriotic than de Gaulle. It is a manifestation of national ethnocen-trism to consider one's own patriotism enlightened and to stigmatize the same feeling in other men as a narrow or outmoded nationalism. De Gaulle is at least honest enough not to hide his fervent patriotism. One comparison demonstrates that his kind of nationalism might not necessarily be unenlightened. The Socialist Prime Minister, Guy Mollet, never short of humanitarian phrases, condoned the ruthless repression of the Algerian insurrection and was one of the master-minds of the old-fashioned imperialist expedition against Egypt; de Gaulle gave freedom to the Algerians.

Nations, the only realities in history

What can truly be ascribed to de Gaulle is a distinctive philosophy of international reality. His biographer says: "De Gaulle has adopted a certain conception of history. For him, history is in the last analysis the history of nations. Regimes might succeed each other as the consequence of crises or revolutions. . . . Nevertheless nations remain. They are the supreme driving force of history."[39] De Gaulle is not a professional historian, and his interpretation is a gross oversimplification. In different historical periods men gave their supreme allegiance to entities other than the nation—the tribe, the city-state, the Roman Empire, the Church, the feudal lord, if we consider only the history of European civilization. For long stretches of time loyalty to one's linguistic-ethnic group was not the highest. But de Gaulle is right as far as our own time and the last few centuries are concerned. For him and for many of his contemporaries "the nation is the supreme value, one could almost say a unique value."[40] Two French political scientists thus sum up his outlook:

> What counts is the role of the nation, conceived as a person in international life; this life itself is viewed as only a confrontation between nation-states. The ideological conflicts are either transitory or only make-believe. . . . In this perspective external policy dominates domestic policies or, more precisely, it is the only true policy. The only objective of domestic policies is to ensure stability and increase power, both stability and power being the means of external policy.[41]

The conflict between the Soviet Union and Communist China supports this view. But it is a simplification. The religious wars cannot be understood only by a reference to his interpretation of history. In our time, if ideology played no role in the formulation of policies, the Soviet Union would be an ally of the United States in the struggle against China. While it is true that all ideologies eventually are differentiated in various national environments, they nevertheless play a role in the formulation of foreign policy as long as policy-makers believe in their ideological creed. In this respect, de Gaulle the realist is blind to an important aspect of present reality.

He further distorts this reality when he says: "Yes, international life, like life in general, is a struggle."[42] Nations, like individuals, compete but also cooperate. After all, he himself cooperates when he grants aid to developing nations. Knowing his outlook, however, one can better understand his distrust of French allies and partners.

France is de Gaulle's supreme value. One can easily picture his dream of perfect happiness. This would be a France with a population of 100 million people (he sometimes wistfully says: "Ah, if we were 100 million Frenchmen"), the most powerful country economically, the only nation armed with nuclear weapons, dominating the international stage, united domestically—composed of 100 million Gaullists. But things are as they are!

There is no doubt that his main preoccupation is France's place in the world. Domestic problems must be subordinated to this main preoccupation. This is why he is irritated by quarrels and conflicts among Frenchmen, which appear to him unnatural. This is another oversimplification of reality.

He is no more a prophet than any other mortal man. But he has the gift of quick perception of new historical trends and the ability to analyze present events astutely as the forerunners of future developments. It is a gross exaggeration to say: "De Gaulle, as someone has claimed, is a political presbyopic: he does not see well at a short distance, but sees very well from afar."[43] When one analyzes his predictions, he realizes that they were not prophecies but very intelligent forecasts founded on close observation of contemporary developments. Writing in 1928, he predicted German expansion, including the *Anschluss* with Austria, the recapture of former German territory from Poland, and the claim to Alsace. He saw better than his contemporaries that Germany, once again economically powerful and rearming, would not remain forever resigned to the territorial losses inflicted at Versailles. During the interwar period he was aware of the change in military tactics brought about by the appearance of armored units, although he did not foresee the joint use of armor and planes. Unlike the French military leaders, he refused to overlook progress in military technology and envisage the future war as a repetition of the war of trenches and fortifications. In 1940 he did not need prophetic gifts to realize that two great powers, the United States and the Soviet Union, were still neutral and that their might could tilt the balance of war against Germany.[44]

The same perspicacity has made him aware of the awakening of the Third World of underdeveloped continents with its unavoidable consequences: the end of colonial empires and the ambition of underdeveloped countries to become modern. When he detects a new historical trend that he considers irreversible, he adjusts his policies accordingly.

It is because he sees well at short range that he is able to foresee future developments. François Mauriac's opinion is true: "It is what he already sees that enables de Gaulle to foresee."[45]

His tactics

De Gaulle's tactics bear the mark of military training; he is not one to compromise. He prefers surprise, ruse, *faits accomplis,* even threats, as the means of confusing his partners and adversaries alike. In negotiations he believes that "intransigence pays off,"[46] because he expects that eventually the other party will have to make concessions greater than initially intended. If his intransigence is met with equal obstinacy by the other party and there is no way out, he retreats. The history of his Algerian policy provides the best illustration of his willingness to retreat when he finds out that he is unable to impose his views on the other party. During 1959 and 1960 he said firmly that the best solution was internal autonomy for Algeria in close association with France and no less firmly refused to negotiate with the Algerian rebels. ("This I will never do," he said on January 29, 1960.) Over two years later he granted independence in an agreement negotiated and signed with the official representatives of the same rebels: the provisional Algerian government in exile.

One of the Prime Ministers of the Fourth Republic, Edgar Faure, compares him to "the knight in a game of chess, who advances by leaping along a broken line."[47] An opponent expressed the same thought in another manner: "One of de Gaulle's assets consists in his ability to set only one objective at a time and advance toward it always by following two paths."[48] He quoted from de Gaulle's early work, *Vers l'Armée de Métier*: "One must have recourse to stratagems in order to make [the adversary] believe that one is there where one is not and that one intends to do something which one does not intend at all."[49] De Gaulle's tactical flexibility is so great that one may at times wonder whether he does not change his strategic objectives while seeming to modify only his tactics.

In any event his tactics are those of a military commander rather than of a diplomat. He is not inclined to sugarcoat bitter pills. He is also too loquacious for a statesman. His speeches are seldom free of barbs, which cause irritation abroad without benefiting France. He often forgets that telling a truth that is distasteful to another government might wound its pride more than a deliberate insult. His mastery of the word is a perpetual temptation to say things which often should not be said at all, or said in a less aggressive manner.

Another weakness of de Gaulle, especially in relation to the United States, is that he bears grudges. He seems to have neither forgiven nor forgotten his quarrels with President Roosevelt. His manner of handling French relations with America (manner, not necessarily the substance of his policies) seems to justify the view that he wants to chastise Roosevelt's ghost by being publicly hostile toward Washington.

A man of the Great Century or a modern man?

It is too easy to confuse his style in manners, writing, and speaking with the substance of his ideas. When he moves majestically among other men or speaks in elegant phrases, he seems to have come to us straight from the Great Century, the century of Louis XIV when France dominated European politics and culture. The solemnity of his manners is also of another age. However, his mind is modern. One of his most intelligent critics notes these two aspects of his personality: "He truly bears the mark of that century [the seventeenth]; he shares with that century its love of order and grandeur. . . . Charles de Gaulle has many times demonstrated correct intuition about great political trends."[50] Another adversary, the brilliant former Prime Minister, Mendès-France, says the same: "His intelligent understanding of great historical trends is well known."[51] We shall have many occasions for illustrating this point. It suffices, for the time being, to recall his appeal to the French people on December 20, 1960: "She [France] must espouse her times and adapt herself to the circumstances, full of hope but brutal, that are reshaping the universe."[52] This brief extract contains two thoughts: on the one hand, the world is undergoing a profound change, and on the other hand, France must accept this change and adapt to it. The man who is able to speak in this vein in spite of his own advanced age is not only intellectually vigorous but aware of his time.

De Gaulle is wise and experienced enough not to expect total victories in international politics. He knows that there is no such thing as a perfect policy which would produce only beneficial results without any harmful consequences. He said: "To govern is to choose between inconvenient alternatives."[53]

France in the contemporary international setting

Frenchmen are not the most logical people in politics. They have the capacity for perceptive analysis of complex problems but also the inclination to act without regard for their own intellectual conclusions.

The view their specialists have of the contemporary world is not startlingly new but is correct:

> International life is made up of the sum total of complex relations, feelings and resentments, calculations and fortuitous events, all of which determine the physiognomy of nation-states in their mutual intercourse. . . . Its essence consists in mutual relations and constant interaction. It has been subject for the last several years to an accelerated rhythm of history which we all recognize and in which we all participate. An unexpected series of sudden transformations constantly upsets international life. . . . All countries realized after the First World War that they henceforth had to pay attention to the problem of international relations as a whole and could no longer limit their concern to relations with more or less immediate neighbors. . . . Intercontinental solidarity, inconceivable in days gone by when civilizations were born, developed, and died unaware of each other, is now an established fact. . . . The problems of the whole world concern each state and, vice versa, the

problems of each state involve the whole world. But this interdependence exists in a most fluid environment, where political constellations emerge, are transformed, and die at a very rapid pace. . . . The profile of the world is essentially ever changing and hence undecipherable. Any upheaval or metamorphosis is possible.[54]

De Gaulle's view of the contemporary world is strikingly similar: "We are in a century that has reached the two-thirds mark in its course, no more. However, since the beginning of this century, the world has undergone changes unprecedented in their pace and their scope. Everything leads one to think that the trend is going to continue. For a whole series of facts of far-reaching significance is now reshaping the world."[55]

This image of a world undergoing great transformations, which in turn might bring in their wake unexpected international alignments, is borne out each day. Who in the middle thirties would have expected the rapid disintegration of the British, French, Dutch, and Belgian colonial empires, or in 1945 would have dared to whisper that Germany and Japan would have become the trusted allies of the United States, or in 1950 would have predicted the Sino-Soviet dispute and the rise of polycentrism within the Communist movement?

French specialists thus define the place of France in this ever-changing world:

Situated at the end of the European Continent and wide open to the Atlantic and the Mediterranean, France belongs simultaneously to several spheres of interest; the coincidence of those interests is by no means a priori assured. She belongs to Europe by virtue of her geography and history. . . . She belongs to a wider group of liberal-democratic countries by virtue of her humanistic tradition and of her fundamental political concepts, which express that tradition. She is linked by a particular bond to all the French-speaking overseas countries because of the responsibilities she had directly assumed for a long time in Asia and in Black Africa and the responsibilities she continues to assume, as well as the extensive interests of all sorts she has on the African Continent. Finally, France is a power with worldwide interests because of the means at her disposal, the relations she maintains with numerous countries bearing the mark of her influence, and her large contribution to the great trends in cultural, commercial, and technical exchanges.[56]

The order in which the four spheres of French interest are enumerated deserves attention. First, French national interests are in Europe because French security depends primarily on the course of European events. She is one of the great European powers. Second, whatever de Gaulle might say, ideology plays a role in the formulation of French foreign policy. France belongs to the Western liberal-capitalist world. This is why the President of the Fifth Republic, who quarrels with his senior ally, nevertheless stresses the necessity of the Atlantic Alliance as long as there is even a remote possibility of an armed crusade by the Soviet Union. A Communist president would immediately denounce the North Atlantic Treaty; de Gaulle would do it only if he were sure that the Soviet Union could not possibly endanger the present system in France—a system that embodies his own fundamental values. The third sphere of interest is the surviving consequence of the former French colonial empire. French political, economic, and, above all, cultural influence has remained strong in those newly independent states where the educated class speaks French. This is especially true of the African Continent from Algeria down to tropical Africa, but it is also true, though to a much lesser extent, of the Indochinese peninsula. The fourth and last sphere exists owing to the fact that for many centuries France has been one of the main cultural centers of our civilization; her cultural influence in the world has declined in correlation to the growing impact of two other centers of the same civilization—the United States and the Soviet Union—but is still important.

What is the view of the French government regarding the world in full transformation? Georges Pompidou, the Prime Minister, gave a frank answer on February 24, 1964, in his address to the American Club in Paris:

> The important thing is that there were [in the years which followed the end of the last war] two masses and that there was in each a head, an uncontested and solitary head. Since that time the world has moved on. And first of all we gradually saw the emergence of a third mass. . . . Little by little a certain number of countries, for the most part, in any case many of which had formerly been colonized by Europe or by different European or even American powers . . . , affirmed the will to form, on the edge of the two blocs, a third world, neutral or neutralist, it is said, whose principal concern is its own development, the effort to embark on industrial civilization and industrial prosperity. For this, moreover, it counts indiscriminately, we must admit it, on the aid of one or the other bloc, at least of the one that wants to give this aid, and it fundamentally claims the right not to take sides. This is the first change.

A second change came about when, within one of these groups (I am referring to the Communist group) divergencies, shades of opinion began to appear. . . . We find ourselves in the presence of a Communist bloc which is at the very least cut in two; not, of course, that we should overestimate these divergencies and maintain that tomorrow these countries will clash directly and violently, but henceforth they march separately and their policy is independent. . . .

And then, something has also happened within the Western bloc which is very different but nevertheless worthy of note: the countries of Europe . . . have little by little regained their strength. . . .

And so the old division into somewhat monolithic groups is outmoded, hence the shades and oppositions within certain groups, the shades within others, hence policies which cannot be exactly the same.[57]

It is impossible to disagree with this diagnosis. The bipolar system which dominated world affairs in the postwar years has disintegrated for several reasons. Perhaps the main reason was the appearance of the nuclear stalemate between the two Super-Powers, neither of which would dare to use nuclear weapons against the other for fear of committing suicide. The respective allies of these Super-Powers drew two conclusions from the stalemate. First, they could no longer be sure that their most powerful ally would have recourse to its nuclear weapons in their defense if other means were to fail. Alliances with the Super-Powers did not lose their value but ceased to provide fully dependable guarantees. Second, fear of nuclear escalation, shared by Washington and Moscow, engendered a feeling of security; a third world war, which could mean the utter ruin of all belligerents, was held improbable. These two conclusions lessened feelings of dependence on the major powers. France and China adjusted their policies accordingly.

China went much further than de Gaulle's France. Her open challenge to Moscow casts a dark shadow on the Sino-Soviet alliance, which neither party has, however, denounced. Are the two Communist powers quarreling allies or enemies? What is certain is the absence of any generally acknowledged international Communist leader. The two most powerful parties have been engaged in the sixties in an open competition for the first but not the dominant place within the Communist movement and among the radical nationalists in the underdeveloped countries. Until Khrushchev's fall the Chinese seemed to have had the upper hand in this competition but since then have been losing to the rival party owing to clever Soviet tactics. The Soviet leaders have avoided responding to the Chinese with insults of their own, as was Khrushchev's habit, and have been regaining prestige among the other Communist parties with their restraint, constant appeals to unity, and outward willingness to readmit the Chinese to their friendship. The stubborn refusal of the Chinese to settle their differences with the Russians has visibly alienated the other parties.

While the Chinese were accusing the Soviet leaders of having betrayed Marxism-Leninism and having become the concealed accomplices of American "imperialists," the other Communist parties demonstrated their trust in Moscow by sending their delegations to the Soviet Party's Twenty-Third Congress held in March and April 1966. In spite of the boycott by the Chinese, Japanese, and Albanian parties and a minuscule New Zealand party, all the other parties as well as the ruling non-Communist parties of such countries as the United Arab Republic, Mali, and Guinea were present. The greatest moment of Soviet triumph came when the principal North Vietnamese delegate exclaimed that every Vietnamese had two Fatherlands: Vietnam and the Soviet Union! The Soviet party regained its former prestige, but not the dominant position it had in Stalin's time, at the price of manifesting its revolutionary zeal by giving economic and military assistance to North Vietnam and by its political support to the South Vietnamese National Liberation Front. However, there is now no uncontested head of the Communist movement; there are only two powerful parties engaged in a hostile competition for first place among the Communist parties which all claim that they are equal.

These other parties align themselves with one or the other of the rivals. They tend to benefit from the split between Moscow and Peking in that it gives them opportunity to assert their own autonomy. In other words, the Communist threat to the West is lesser than it would be if Moscow and Peking were staunch allies.

This increases the feeling of security among the United States' allies. This feeling is even stronger because of the two Communist powers China is more militant. The Western European nations are not vitally affected by Chinese militancy, but the United States is. The rise of China has shed light on the fundamental difference in geographical perspectives between the United States and its European allies. The United States is compelled to safeguard its security both in the Atlantic and in the Pacific. Depending on circumstances American attention may shift from one ocean to another. The problems of Southeast Asia have riveted the eyes of the United States on China. On both sides of the Atlantic the opinion that the Soviet Union is no longer an immediate menace is shared. However, the North Atlantic Alliance was formed against Russia, not against China. The more the United States considers China the main threat to its vital interests, the less the European allies, who (except for Britain) have no great interest in Asia, feel the bond of Atlantic solidarity. The Alliance, they believe, must be preserved for the bad days which might come, but its significance is no longer the same as in 1949. France says it openly, while the others begin to think so.

Finally, Western Europe in the sixties is not what it was in the forties. Rehabilitated after the war, it is now economically stable. Prosperous and dynamic, it is no longer in need of a new Marshall Plan. Its main currencies are as hard as the dollar. This too makes European nations feel less dependent on the United States.

In brief, the distribution of power between the United States and Western Europe has undergone a drastic change. This cannot help but have repercussions on the formulation of Western European foreign policy, which becomes more or less different from American policy. De Gaulle, like Mao Tse-tung, feels that the time has come to assert the national independence of the major ally. He is more cautious than Mao and thinks that the nuclear umbrella, which the major ally holds open over the heads of junior allies, continues to be required for French security. This is why he always repeats that the Atlantic Alliance is necessary for France. Western Europe would be almost defenseless if the Americans truly went home and left it alone to face the nuclear giant in the East. The Chinese too would come to appreciate the value of the Soviet nuclear umbrella if they ever found themselves in a direct confrontation with the United States.

The French Prime Minister was right in stressing the importance of emergence of the Third World of underdeveloped continents of Asia, Africa, and Latin America. There lies the main battlefield where all the great powers vie for influence and try to modify the *status quo*. France plays her own role there, especially in her former colonial possessions. This Third World tends increasingly to be uncommitted.

The two hegemonies

In de Gaulle's view the main phenomenon of our time is the worldwide revolt against the bipolar system, or, as he says, against the two hegemonies. He detects this revolt within the Communist group and within the Third World, and would like to lead it in Western Europe. Actually his present ambition is greater. He wants France to become at least the rallying center, if not the leader, for all those who resent the existence of the two hegemonies. His statements in the last few years leave little doubt on this point. When he talked, for instance, in June 1965, to his countrymen on a tour of places around Paris, and in each short speech never failed to mention the two hegemonies, he was addressing himself less to the cheering French crowds than to Peking and Eastern European capitals, to Latin America as well as to Asia and Africa, and, obviously, to Western Europe.

Does he want to reduce the power of the United States and the Soviet Union by encouraging dissidence among their allies and thus, by virtue of the relativity of international power, increase the French ratio of power, or does he intend to build a sort of Third Force of nations who have different regimes but who would find a common denominator in their assertion of independence of both Super-Powers? In any event, Mao expressed a somewhat similar idea, dictated by his animosity toward both the United States and the Soviet Union; he suggested that the medium powers such as Britain, France, Germany, Japan, and China should cooperate in order to free themselves of the two hegemons whom he suspects of being ready to unite against his own country.

The temptation to find an independent place in between the two giants is ably presented by the French specialists on foreign policy:

> The temptation to form a Third Force always exists in a world dominated by the two Super-Powers. Certain states hope that their cooperation would allow them to play the useful role of intermediary and even of counterweight which could apply a brake alternately to that of the two adversaries who would exceed the limits. . . . The oscillation between conditional alliance and an unavowed neutrality will probably dominate international life as long as the balance of terror, created between the two Super-Powers by their nuclear armaments, lasts.[58]

It is rather improbable that a Third Force truly united in its objectives could be formed to counterbalance the two gigantic powers. But there is no doubt that the trend toward greater assertion of independence by the other states is constantly growing and expressing itself in conditional alliance or neutrality. The dividing line between these two latter conditions is blurred, as the policies of France and Pakistan amply demonstrate. A new international phenomenon makes its appearance: an uncommitted ally.

It is only natural that assertion of independence is not welcomed by the major ally. De Gaulle is no more popular in Washington than Mao is in Moscow. The former is accused of wanting to establish his own hegemony in Western Europe, while the latter is castigated for his supposed intention of dominating the Communist movement. Frenchmen bitterly remark: "At the time when she [France] was the victim of frequent domestic crises, she was called the sick man of Europe. Now, when her domestic situation is stable and her finances are prosperous, she is accused of harboring hegemonic ambitions."[59]

Although a government may denounce the two hegemonies, it is rare that its interests are affected equally by the policies of both Super-Powers. This is the situation of China, which considers the United States as the main enemy but which also distrusts the Soviet Union and harbors designs on Soviet territory. Usually a government wants to increase its independence of only one of the Super-Powers, the one dominating that part of the international stage where the nation concerned is located. De Gaulle talks of the two hegemonies, but in fact asserts French independence of the major ally, the United States. The Rumanians try to do the same with the Soviet Union. The movement of dissidence always takes place within the camp to which a nation belongs.

De Gaulle's attitude, moreover, stems from remembrance of the French past. During the interwar period Great Britain exerted strong influence on the formulation of French policies. A Gaullist writer is not entirely wrong when he says: "The fate of France, prior to the Second World War, was decided at crucial moments in most cases by Whitehall rather than by Matignon, and, since 1945, by the White House rather than by the Elysée."[60] British advice contributed to the French policy of reconciliation with Germany from 1924 to 1932, to French nonresistance to the German violations of the Treaty of Versailles in the thirties, and to the French decision to declare war on Germany in September 1939. European diplomats were inclined to think that the road to Paris went through London. One cannot deny the existence of United States influence in Paris in the postwar years. Resistance to that influence did not begin in 1958, but only de Gaulle made it a signpost of his foreign policy.

De Gaulle has stronger feelings on this matter than other Frenchmen. He cannot help but be haunted by memories of his own past. Whenever he proudly remembers June 18, 1940, can he forget that his fateful appeal was broadcast by the B.B.C. with the permission of the British government? On that day and for several months later he, the embodiment of French legitimacy, had no means of communication but what was provided by a foreign power. When he returned in 1944, acclaimed as a savior by his countrymen, he knew that his beloved France was again free only because the "Anglo-Saxons" had liberated her. During the decisive and most dramatic years of his life, both he and his country were dependent on foreign help.

French "grandeur"

De Gaulle's revolt against the bipolar system is one aspect of his policy, but an independent formulation of policy must have an objective. De Gaulle's objective, the "grandeur" of France, means a constant increase of French influence in the world. His key statement is: "France, because she can do so, because everything invites her to do so, because she is France, must conduct in the world a world policy."[61] This is another Gaullist axiom, which its author does not justify by any argument. There is no visible reason why France should or should not have a worldwide policy simply because she is France. If he means that she is powerful and hence is able to make her influence felt everywhere, his claim is no better founded than if voiced by a German, a Chinese, or a Japanese. Even so, this sort of statement should always be qualified in light of the geopolitical position of a country. The impact of a Super-Power is not the same in every part of the world. This is even more true of lesser powers. To say that France must have a worldwide policy is almost meaningless, as obviously her role may not have the same weight in Europe and in French-speaking Africa or in Latin America and the Indian peninsula.

If de Gaulle wanted to say (this is less probable) that the nature of contemporary international politics is such that events in a distant part of the world might eventually affect France, and that France must watch the whole international stage, his argument would be a truism applicable to all governments. For example, President Nasser too would need a worldwide policy, because any important shift in the distribution of power between the United States and the Soviet Union, the evolution of Sino-Soviet relations, the policies of the Common Market, or the trends within the Third World could produce important repercussions for the security and the well-being of the United Arab Republic.

Although de Gaulle's statement is not as clear as it might be, it is important as a declaration of intention. France must be present everywhere. His enthusiastic supporter anxiously asks at this point, "Has France the means to implement de Gaulle's policy?"[62] He adds sadly, "The best gambler can play only with the cards he has in his hand: in de Gaulle's, neither kings nor aces are abundant."[63]

De Gaulle's first Prime Minister, Michel Debré, takes a similar view of the limited means at France's disposal: "France is no longer one of the first-rank powers. . . . The contemporary era is dominated by non-

European states, and their power is such that we cannot equal it. In other words, France is henceforth a nation of second rank with all the shortcomings and all the risks which this rank entails in view of her geographical situation and the political downgrading of old Europe."[64] The opinion of one of the most distinguished opponents of de Gaulle, former Prime Minister Paul Reynaud, is identical: "However, she [France] is no longer France of Louis XIV or of Napoleon. . . . Like England, who understands it, France cannot have the same rank as the two giants, each of whom has a continent at its disposal."[65]

De Gaulle himself does not contest the validity of the principle that a successful policy depends upon achieving a balance between objectives and available means. His praise of the policies of prerevolutionary France fully acknowledges this principle: "The policy of the Royal regime was that of circumstances; it avoided abstractions, but liked realities; it preferred what was useful to what was sublime, what was opportune to what was resounding; for each particular problem it sought a solution which was by no means ideal but practical; it had few scruples regarding choice of means, but its greatness consisted in keeping an exact balance between the desired objective and the power of the state."[66]

This statement is a concise formulation of criteria by which any foreign policy, including his own, may be validly evaluated. It is his pragmatic creed. It also sheds light on one of de Gaulle's weaknesses: his propensity for making sweeping generalizations. This particular generalization certainly is not wholly supported by the long history of Royalist France. There were periods when France practiced a policy such as described by de Gaulle, for instance during the reign of Louis XI or during the ministries of Richelieu and Mazarin; but there were other times when she pursued objectives beyond her means, for instance during the invasions of Italy (late fifteenth and early sixteenth century) or during the reign of Louis XIV.

In any event, if he wants to practice a worldwide policy, he must constantly try to increase the range of means at his disposal. He does it in two ways. On the one hand, he increases French national power by modernizing its armed forces, by ensuring governmental stability, and by encouraging domestic economic and technological development. France of the sixties is undoubtedly stronger than France of the fifties. However, she cannot hope, as Debré says, ever to become an equal of the two Super-Powers. Hence de Gaulle tries to increase the range of his means through a foreign policy designed to attract the support of other nations.

He attempts to convince other governments that French objectives and their own coincide and that it is in their own national interest to join in French battles. His crusade against the two hegemonies, his appeals to Western European solidarity, his courtship of the Third World—all these aim at gaining supporters for French policies. He certainly is rewarded for his efforts by the personal and national prestige he enjoys in the world. Those nations which share his antipathy for one or both hegemons repay him with cordial cheers; all governments follow with keen interest the independent course of Gaullist France and calculate its probable effect on their own national policies. Does the popularity Gaullist France enjoys in many countries and the interest she evokes everywhere ensure her of active foreign support? De Gaulle, who is a pragmatist, should know that no nation is inclined to pull another's chestnuts out of the fire.

Balance-of-power combinations

If her objectives are high, France must act in conjunction with other states. De Gaulle's mind operates in this respect within the framework of balance of power. If France is to play a role greater than her own power would allow, she must compete with more powerful nations by joining forces with other states grouped around France. This fundamental concept is a constant factor in his policy. The various combinations he has envisaged have changed like the pieces in a kaleidoscope, moved by changing circumstances and by his own hopes and disappointments.

During the war his problem was simple: his Free French movement had to cooperate with the United States, Britain, and the Soviet Union to tilt the balance against Nazi Germany. Toward the end of the war and in the period immediately following, his mind was preoccupied with the problem of finding a counterweight against two threats: possible new aggression by Germany and American dominance over Western Europe. His first reaction was to seek the cooperation of Britain and the Soviet Union. In November 1944 he proposed to Churchill that they jointly assert their weight against the United States and the Soviet Union. Churchill declined this offer in a way characteristic of British-American relations. He said that Britain might better protect her interests by remaining friendly to the United States. By advising the United States she could influence American policies more effectively before they were formulated rather than by open opposition later.[67] De Gaulle was not discouraged; on September 10, 1945, in an interview granted to the London *Times,* he suggested close cooperation of Western Europe under joint British-French leadership. As late as July 28, 1946, he said: "Nations of the old West . . . what would be their weight if they succeeded in coordinating their policies . . . ! This kind of harmony implies, first of all, an understanding between London and Paris."[68] Disappointed by the lack of response in London, he deduced the conclusion which has continued to be a part of his political creed: "When all is said and done, Great Britain is an island; France, the cape of a continent; America, another world."[69] While the United States has always belonged to another world,[70] Britain is an island which may have either an Atlantic or a European orientation. In spite of his later veto barring British accession to the Common Market, he said on June 17, 1962, that a Europe-oriented Britain might one day be allowed to join the Western European union: "First the union and probably later the unity of Europe must be achieved; England and the English people might one day join it."[71] For the time being, Britain looks across the Atlantic. De Gaulle acknowledged this on September 25, 1949, thus excluding Britain from his balance-of-power combinations: "England turns away, attracted by the mass on the other side of the Atlantic."[72]

In the middle forties he looked not only toward Britain but also toward the Soviet Union. In 1944 the Soviet Union was for him the same old Russia in a new ideological guise. He went to Moscow to sign a bilateral treaty of mutual assistance with Stalin, renewing the former French-Russian alliance. He expected in return to have Soviet support for his designs on Germany, which he wanted to dismember into several quasi-independent states only loosely confederated. The Rhineland, the Ruhr, and the Saar were to be placed under Allied or French control. His plan was to erase the effects of the Franco-Prussian War, forgetting that the pages of history might never be turned back. Stalin, who already had amputated Germany's eastern territories, was uninterested in de Gaulle's plan to further dismember the defeated foe. Perhaps he did not take de Gaulle very seriously, expecting Communist seizure of power in France in the near future. He certainly had little respect for France since events of 1940 and probably did not consider her a reliable international partner. De Gaulle's concept of a balance-of-power system built around London, Paris, and Moscow proved a vain dream.

His Grand Design for Europe

In the late forties his mind turned to a different concept. France would organize Western Europe into a political union that would become a counterpart to the "Anglo-Saxons" and the Soviets. He realistically accepted the necessary implication of this new concept, namely close French-German cooperation. Abandoning his plans for dismembering the former enemy, he was now ready to enter into partnership with Western Germany. The axis of Europe was to be Paris-Bonn instead of Paris-London-Moscow.

On November 22, 1944, he formulated his first Grand Design in the following words: "We are convinced that . . . this European unity, in which we believe, will be built up, and we hope that it will be expressed in definite actions binding together these three poles: Moscow, London, and Paris."[73] On March 16, 1950, Germany took the place of Britain and the Soviet Union as one of the poles of European unity: "I am convinced that the whole European atmosphere would be transformed if France . . . took the initiative of calling on Europe to become a [united] Europe, in particular, with German participation."[74] Europe was reduced in this context to its Western part.

The united Western Europe, built up around the German-French cooperation, was to supply the counterweight to both the Anglo-Saxons and the Russians. On June 29, 1947, he called for: "[Europe] organized as a whole, capable of containing any possible ambition of hegemony and of creating between the two rival masses a factor of equilibrium indispensable for peace."[75] The two rival masses were the United States with its British "satellite" and the Soviet Union. Thirteen years later, on April 7, 1960, when he addressed the British Parliament, he stressed another aspect of Western European unity: "She [France] hopes that . . . the future will allow Europe to lead its own life thanks to an equilibrium established between its two parts, which have different regimes."[76] Western Europe of the future was to be strong enough not only to become a factor of international equilibrium between the two Super-Powers, but also to be a counterweight to the Soviet Union. This Europe of his distant vision would be neatly balanced between its Western and Eastern parts, and the need for alliance with the United States would at last disappear. In the meantime Western Europe would play the role of "arbiter between the Soviet and Anglo-Saxon camps."[77] In spite of the difficulties he has encountered, he still clings to this second Grand Design, which would eventually terminate American interference in European affairs.

His ambition to make of Western Europe "a third planetary power," as he likes to say, has the defect of oversimplification. Western Europe has the potential to become a third Super-Power only if the six states merge into one federal state. A Super-Power, like any other unit in international life, must speak with one voice. However, de Gaulle cherishes French independence so much that he would never consent to delegate national powers to a supranational government. His Western

European union would be a coalition of six sovereign states which would only coordinate their external policies. In fact, it would continue to speak with six voices which would not necessarily be concordant. This is a contradiction surprising in a pragmatist.

He overlooks another difficulty. His Western Europe should assert its independence of the United States, but his five partners are not inclined to follow him in this direction. He thinks only Britain, if admitted to the Common Market, would be an American Trojan horse. Experience should have taught him that the five states which, with France, belong to the Common Market are all Trojan horses, because they all intend to maintain close relations with both the United States and Great Britain.

Also, he does not pay enough attention to the problems involved in cooperation with Western Germany, which was to become one of the two cornerstones of a united Western Europe. He would like to see the Common Market evolve into a protectionist economic unit, while the Germans prefer it to be largely open to trade with outsiders, including Britain and the United States. He intends to transform the Atlantic Alliance into a loose coalition and to put an end to its military integration, but the Germans see in that integration the guarantee of American commitment to protect their security. France has no quarrel with the Soviet Union, while German claims (unification and return to the 1937 frontiers) designate it as the main adversary. The two outlooks are so different that one can hardly see how France and Germany could practice identical policies.

The result is de Gaulle's bitter disappointment, which he has expressed openly since the summer of 1963. The Germans may feel disappointed too; de Gaulle was the only Western statesman to recognize publicly, on March 25, 1959, the finality of the German-Polish frontier along the line of the Oder and Neisse rivers.

He seems never to have understood the German problem of today. He expected that Western Germany would conclude a monogamous marriage with France and not indulge in any extramarital love affairs. But the Germans prefer political bigamy. They need France as a partner in the Common Market and also as the holder of veto if ever the United States and Britain were inclined to seek a rapprochement with the Soviet Union at their expense. They know that whenever the two Anglo-Saxon powers seemed to envisage such rapprochement at the price of modifying the status of West Berlin or their attitude toward the German Democratic Republic (their fears might be unfounded, but they manifest themselves from time to time), de Gaulle has remained adamant in refusing any concession. But they also know only too well that the only guarantee of their free survival is the alliance with the United States. They want to have two wives, French and American, and, if forced to choose, they would contract a monogamous marriage with America rather than with France. De Gaulle could have seen this earlier, but in any event he is learning it now.

He also overlooked another point. In this respect he is in the company of all the North Atlantic allies. France is, like all of them, resigned to the survival of the *status quo* in Europe, including the partition of Germany into two separate states. Western Germany is the only member of the Atlantic Alliance who is and cannot help but be revisionist. She cannot abandon her claim to be reunited with East Germany. Has de Gaulle asked himself what foreign policy a united Western Europe would have? Would it press for unification of Germany and for the return to the 1937 frontiers or at least a revision of present boundaries? Would it be in the interest of France to see a powerful united Germany emerge on the Rhine and dominate the Western European union? Is he ready to espouse German claims? His recognition of the Oder-Neisse frontier gives a partly negative answer. Does he really believe that the Germans would sacrifice their unity for the sake of a Western European union? It would be unfair to him to think that he is blind to the existence of these problems. But then his Western European union could not speak with one voice and become a "third planetary power."

His Grand Design has obvious flaws. However, his French opponents, who clamor for a supranational Europe, do not escape the same criticism. They too never stop to examine the difficulty of defining one foreign policy for a federal Europe, in which five states would be *status quo* powers and the sixth, Western Germany, a revisionist power. In this respect they, like de Gaulle, live in an unreal world.

De Gaulle's Grand Design gravitates around his concepts of Europe. When he talks about Europe, one thing is certain, namely that the United States belongs to a different world. His Europe is either Western Europe or Europe from the Atlantic to the Urals. America is conceded the modest place of a daughter of Europe, but a daughter that is on her own. The larger image of Europe is strictly geographical, because the Soviet Union does not end at the Urals but extends to the Pacific. This larger concept does not coincide with the frontiers of our civilization, which embraces the whole of the Soviet Union, Britain, the Western Hemisphere, Australia and New Zealand—all the countries which share the same heritage.

As we have seen, his vision of distant Europe from the Atlantic to the Urals is founded on the hope that a united Western Europe would become strong enough to be a counterweight to the might of Russia. Then the whole of geographical Europe would live its own life independent of the United States and would regain its former place in the international politics. This distant vision is of necessity vague. Paul Reynaud writes: "The Russians say: 'De Gaulle has never told us clearly what he means by: Europe from the Atlantic to the Urals.' "[78] What is certain is that they would warmly welcome an understanding with de Gaulle at the expense of Germany, but de Gaulle may be able to afford only friendly gestures toward Moscow, not much more. Friendly gestures are calculated to frighten the Western Germans with the ghost of a Franco-Soviet Rapallo and incline them to be more amenable to French policy in Europe, but he may hardly go further in his flirtation with the Soviets. Any understanding with the Soviet Union would destroy his plan for a Western European union and is, moreover, inconceivable so long as France and Germany are tied together by the Common Market.

His Grand Design for the Third World

The slowdown in the realization of the European Grand Design forced de Gaulle to seek non-European partners within the Third World. Since the termination of Algerian war in 1962 his hands have been freed of colonial chains. France is no longer a colonial power. De Gaulle personally is popular as the man who emancipated the former colonies and who has favored the policy of economic and technical aid. He is the most trusted among Western statesmen for these two reasons and also because he advocates noninterference in the domestic affairs of other states. Since the emancipation of the former French colonies he has intervened militarily only once, restoring a pro-French government in Gabon. In all other cases of violent changes of government, he has maintained the attitude of neutral observer ready to cooperate with any government interested in cooperation with France.

His popularity in the Third World is certain, because his attitudes toward it are genuinely friendly. Were all his other policies since 1958 to end in failure, his Presidency of the Fifth Republic would be remembered for courageous decolonization and for fidelity to the idea that the West should help developing countries to modernize.

Although he has not abandoned his European Grand Design, in the last few years he seems to have constructed another Grand Design, which would make France the spokesman of uncommitment for the Third World. France, the rebel against the two hegemonies, would be the voice of Asians, Africans, and Latin Americans who want to assert their national independence. Will he reap a better harvest there than in Western Europe?

In any event his courtship of the Third World is not without contradictions. These are medium-sized or small nations, a few of whom might hope to attain one day the status of true great powers. They are jealous of their hard-won or still contested independence and certainly would not relish a future where the world would be ruled, it is true, not by the two hegemons but by a concert of great powers. The logic of de Gaulle's flirtation with the Third World should lead him to advocate an international democracy where France would be the spokesman for that multitude of weak peoples. Speaking on behalf of the vast majority of mankind, France could aspire to speak as an equal to the great of this world. But de Gaulle is not logical. He has an undisguised predilection for rule by a concert of great powers on the condition that France be a member of it.

It is difficult to imagine that this concept of a concert of great powers could seduce the underdeveloped nations. The concept itself is fluid. De Gaulle has proposed various candidates for the directorate of great powers, depending on times and the nature of problems. Only France should be a member of each directorate. He proposed in September 1958 to form an American-British-French directorate for the Western world. The Europe of Six should follow the German-French lead. All international life should be placed under the management of France, the United States, the Soviet Union, Britain, and China. Each formula begs questions on the part of those who would be excluded, among whom there are important nations. Germany and Italy would never agree to a Western directorate of which they would not be members. Italy, Belgium, Holland, and Luxembourg made it clear that they would not stay in a Western European union ruled by France and Germany. Finally, one can imagine the reactions of the French European partners, of India and Japan, of other Asian states, of Latin Americans, and of Africans when they hear of the proposal to entrust the government of the world to the five permanent members of the Security Council, most of whom, by the way, are at loggerheads.

This predilection for a concert of great powers is irreconcilable with the vision of Western-European unity and with efforts to gain favors in the Third World.

His main objectives

Which objectives does de Gaulle emphasize? Perhaps he answered this question in a broadcast speech on April 16, 1964. He addressed that speech to his own people on the eve of entering the hospital for serious surgery. An old man, he could not be sure whether he would survive the operation. That speech might have been his last. One might conjecture that on that day he mentioned only those aspects of his foreign policy which he considered most important. He pointed out three topics: the Common Market, a French nuclear force, and aid to underdeveloped nations.[79] He said that the Common Market "is gradually becoming essential for our prosperity"; he admitted by implication that it was next to impossible for France to withdraw from it. Insistence on the need for an independent French nuclear force is his most cherished idea. He condensed all his arguments in these few sentences:

> So long as the ambition of the Soviets and the nature of their regime brings the threat of a terrible conflict to bear on the free world, on this side and on the other side of the Atlantic, France is in danger of destruction and invasion without having any certainty that her American allies, themselves directly exposed to death, would be able to protect her against this danger. For France, to deny herself the means capable to dissuade the adversary from a possible attack, while she is in the position to have these means, would amount to the attraction of the lightning and, at the same time, the self-denial of a lightning rod. Moreover, that would mean that she would entirely rely for her defense and, thereby, for her existence and, finally, for her policy on a foreign protectorate which is anyway uncertain.

We shall later examine the validity of arguments for and against a French nuclear force. For the time being, we may note another of de Gaulle's contradictions. He does not attach any real importance to the ideological factor in international politics, but in this particular speech he partly attributed the Soviet threat to the nature of the regime.

When he claims that France, deprived of her own nuclear force, would be an American protectorate, he overlooks the fact that he himself has been proving every day since 1958 that France is able to follow a policy independent of the United States. He has not needed nuclear weapons to disengage France from the United States and to make vital decisions without regard for American wishes.

The most surprising part of his speech was his emphasis on the problem of underdeveloped countries. It is amazing that the man for whom France and France alone is the supreme value should stress this problem as one of three main aspects of French foreign policy in a speech which might have been his last. He said:

> As for terminating the friendly, reciprocal, and planned cooperation which we practise in relatio nto a number of developing states, that would mean, in the first place, turning away from them, while

leaving our place to others. . . . Last but not least, that would be tantamount to denying the role which is ours as regards the evolution which induces so many peoples of Africa, Asia and Latin America to develop themselves, in their turn, without surrendering to one or the other of the two hegemonies which are tending to share the world so long as Western Europe is unable or is unwilling to organize itself so that an equilibrium be established.

This paragraph is full of implications. As long as Western Europe is not organized as a third Super-Power, France alone must fly the flag of revolt against the two hegemonies. She will win friends among the peoples of the underdeveloped continents, including Latin America, which resent the existence of one or the other hegemony. French aid should serve as proof of French sincerity and as a means of asserting French influence on a worldwide scale. A skeptic among the nationals of the underdeveloped countries could ask whether France does not intend to establish her own political hegemony (preponderant influence) by rallying the malcontent nations together under her flag of struggle against the American and Soviet hegemonies. He could also express some doubt as to whether France has sufficient means for waging a worldwide campaign against both the United States and the Soviet Union.

A Gaullist Frenchman once compared de Gaulle to a train engineer who keeps all the switches open and, depending on his changing evaluation of the situation, drives his train east one day, west the next, and south the next. There is something true in that image of his flexibility always attuned to the things as they are and as they change. The risk is that of arriving nowhere. His assessment of objectives does not remain constant. For instance, his speeches in 1962 dramatically stressed the need for construction of a Western European political union, while the same objective received only a passing mention in his speech of April 26, 1964.[80]

The man who keeps all the switches open does not believe any political alignment eternal. He is basically right because international life is always changing. History is on his side, offering many illustrations of drastic and sometimes unexpected shifts in international friendships and animosities. De Gaulle could make his own the famous statement of Palmerston that Britain had no permanent friends or enemies but only permanent interests. This is also de Gaulle's philosophy, which his Prime Minister formulated in the following words:

> France, member of the European Community and of the Atlantic Alliance, for this reason does not intend to perpetuate the policy

of blocs. . . . We hope that relations between East and West might one day be normalized and founded, in spite of the differences between regimes, on respect for the rights of all and for the independence of everyone. Situated as she is geographically and supported by her historical traditions, France will be able to assume her own role in the necessary reestablishment of good relations, at least on the day when the totalitarian world sincerely renounces any inclination to commit aggression.[81]

His French critics

De Gaulle's French opponents naturally denounce his foreign policy most vehemently. This does not necessarily mean that if they or their parties were to return to power after de Gaulle they would abandon all his objectives. But there is some truth in what they say. A moderate leftist and de Gaulle's main opponent in the 1965 presidential election writes:

One day he points out a grandiose objective to France: European reconciliation across ideological frontiers, from the Atlantic to the Urals, a rally of the white race face to face with the yellow multitudes. The following year he negotiates with Peking and tells the peoples of the Third World that France intends to lead them against Moscow and Washington in the name of their claim to true economic and political independence. Sometimes they dream in Paris of a north-south Paris-Madrid-Rabat axis and why not Dakar; sometimes they fancy to relieve Castro in prompting the emancipation of Latin-American masses. Sometimes he revives the age-old friendship with the Slavs, the traditional counterweight against German expansion; sometimes he becomes a Teutonic knight ready to halt the Slavic thrust and laments at the foot of the Berlin Wall. One cannot say that de Gaulle has no foreign policy; he has all of them, one after another, or sometimes simultaneously. Which road has not been open in five years? Only the road to the White House has been closed. No dissertation will be as eloquent as this brief summary: in 1958 de Gaulle, leader of an unstable France exhausted by the Algerian war, wants to subordinate the Western alliance to the will of a General Staff composed of the United States, Great Britain, and France. He fails. In 1960 he turns around toward Europe and tries to impose the Fouchet plan which keeps off Great Britain and weakens the Atlantic Pact. He fails. In 1962 he proposes the Paris-Bonn Axis; he wishes to organize the European structure on the foundation of that Axis and to use this expedient in an attempt at cutting off the ties to Great Britain and at separating Germany from America. He fails. In the same year 1962 he invites the Soviet Union to a crusade against the yellow peril. The rest is well known.[82]

The moderate conservative, Paul Reynaud, whose protégé de Gaulle was at the time of the Third Republic, writes no less bitterly:

> There is no foreign policy of Gaullism that would be inspired by a principle. There are successive and contradictory policies, all of them inspired, in the first place, by idle dreams and, secondly, by resentments. It is an idle dream to believe that France may take a first-rank place beside the American and Russian giants. It is an idle dream to imagine that mutilated Western Europe may alone ensure its security in the face of Soviet Russia. It is an even madder dream to believe that Europe may act as an arbiter between the American and Soviet giants. It is a stubborn dream, this dream of a Europe from the Atlantic to the Urals, America having been discarded. Resentment against the "Anglo-Saxons" due to bitter wartime personal recollections and to the fact that France may not be in the first rank while America is there.[83]

The source of his power

Public opinion polls leave no doubt that his foreign policy has qualified popular support.[84] Mitterand admits it: "No doubt the popular enthusiasm that supports him allows him to do as he pleases."[85] His opponent's explanation of this support is close to the mark: "People like those who exalt them."[86] This is especially true of the French people, deeply humiliated by the crushing defeat in 1940 and the failure of its colonial wars in Indochina and Algeria. De Gaulle's foreign policy provides them with psychological compensation. His France, boldly challenging the United States and displaying her independence each day, is the France they want to have. Their national pride is flattered.

The most amazing aspect of de Gaulle's dominant position in France is that he does not have the usual instruments of power at his disposal. The traditional political parties oppose him. Most of the French notables, great and small, dislike him. He has few friends among the intellectuals. He has said more than once: "The Army? It has never liked me."[87] Prior to the last war he was a heretic among French military officers. In 1940 he gave them the difficult choice of fidelity to their oath of allegiance to the legal government or answering his call to rebellion in the name of supreme interests of France. He quelled their revolt in Algeria, where they in turn believed they had opted for the supreme interests of France against his legal government. He purged their ranks twice: at the time of liberation, and again after his return to power. Eventually he tamed them, but he is not popular among them. The Army is not the mainstay of his power. His own political organization, the Union for the New Republic, is his own creation and owes its existence to his popularity. It helps him in governing the country, but it did not bring him to power and may or may not survive him.

He rules France like an absolute monarch, but only through personal prestige and the magic of his word.[88] It is hard to find historical analogy. Perhaps he governs the French democracy as Pericles did democratic Athens, or perhaps as Lorenzo the Magnificent ruled Florence in the fifteenth century. In any event, it is true that "the French people are bound to General de Gaulle by a personal allegiance independent of his policies."[89] They trust in his superior wisdom. His political adversary says ironically: "It [French public opinion] prefers the myth of the father (de Gaulle takes care of everything), the myth of happiness (de Gaulle conjures fate), the myth of prestige (the world envies France who has de Gaulle), the myth of prosperity (thanks to de Gaulle we shall soon number a hundred million, the franc will overcome the dollar) to the cold reality of a balance sheet."[90]

De Gaulle fully realizes that his claim to be the incarnation of national legitimacy would not in itself give him power; his historical mission must be recognized by the French people. The problem of power is a matter between him and the people: "For more than twenty years, events have willed that I serve as the guide of the country during the grave crises we have lived through. . . . But also, I need—yes, I need—to know what is in your hearts and minds. That is why I am turning to you by-passing all intermediaries. In truth—who is not aware of it—the matter is between each woman and man of France and myself."[91]

De Gaulle knows well that no man, whatever his talents, can achieve in foreign policy more than what his own people are ready and able to support. He wrote in his *Memoirs*: "As for myself, only too well aware of my limitations and my failings, certain that no man can substitute himself for a people, how I longed to implant in every Frenchman the same convictions that inspired me!"[92]

Besides popular support, de Gaulle has other undeniable domestic assets. He presides over the destiny of a France completely different from prewar France. No longer stagnant and suffering from gradual depopulation, France today is economically dynamic, better adjusted to international commercial competition, technologically progressive, and demographically rejuvenated. It is almost unbelievable that the total increase in her population during the forties, fifties, and sixties is almost equal to the total increase between the beginning of the nineteenth century and 1939. The average age of her population is becoming lower. Being younger, she is less afraid of bold policies. The social composition of the population is changing rapidly too. The percentage of people deriving their income from agriculture and their dependents has been rapidly declining owing to the modernization of agriculture and increasing opportunities for employment in the secondary and tertiary sectors of the economy; it is now 17 per cent. Of course, the rejuvenation and modernization of France cannot be ascribed to de Gaulle, but his policies do promote economic expansion. And governmental stability, for which he is responsible, is certainly a factor in the dynamics of economic life.

Transition toward what?

Will the governmental stability survive de Gaulle? He has molded for himself the regime of elective monarchy. But his extensive and legally extravagant interpretation of the powers of the President of the Republic, incompatible with the letter of the Constitution, can hardly increase the respect of his countrymen for their new fundamental law and instill in them new political habits. He certainly does not teach respect for the Constitution, because he himself gives bad example. He does not act like a French lawgiver, like a modern Solon or Lycurgus, who wants his people to abide by his laws a long time after his death. He has a truly French skepticism concerning the durability of fundamental laws: "We know . . . the value of constitutions. We have made seventeen of them during one hundred fifty years. The nature of things is stronger than constitutional texts."[93]

France swung in 1958 from one extreme, the subservience of the executive to the parliamentary assembly, to another extreme, the omnipotence of the executive. Will she swing back to the former extreme and will the post-Gaullist Republic be a twin sister of the Fourth, or will she find, in a Hegelian way, a balanced synthesis between the extreme thesis and the no less extreme antithesis? One thing is sure, as Michel Debré says: "France will not find again, after General de Gaulle, another President of his stature; this is self-evident."[94]

An English commentator writing prior to de Gaulle's return to power said: "With one or two exceptions, all the postwar years in France were years of transition. Transition toward what? This is very difficult to say."[95] The same may be said today. De Gaulle is a meteor in the

French sky. His reign is also a period of transition. Transition toward what?

A French political scientist sadly admits: "The problem of the adaptation of the French system to the contemporary world is not thereby [by de Gaulle's constitutional practice] solved, however; it is simply postponed. In a sense, the solution may have been made still more difficult because of certain aspects of the government France has had since 1958."[96]

II His People

Love of France but dislike of the French State

The foreign policy of any country succeeds or fails for many reasons. It might be successfully counteracted by other nations, or the support expected from friendly governments might not materialize. The objectives might be too ambitious for the available means. The policy may be poorly conceived or badly executed. Above all, the ultimate results depend on the willingness and ability of the people to support a policy devised by its leaders.

It is not the imaginary "princess in the fairy tales" but, as de Gaulle knows, the "ephemeral" Frenchmen of today who are the soldiers in his international battles. He wrote: "The French people is what it is, and not anything else. If it does not want something, nothing will compel it to accept it."[1] Frenchmen might not, however, measure up to de Gaulle's ambitions; there seems to be something true in this observation by one of his biographers: "Perhaps he feels, in his innermost mind, that this country, like a bed or a suit, is too small and too shabby for him, although he probably realizes that there is no other country where a Charles de Gaulle, his person and his personality could possibly be imagined."[2] In any event the real France is not big enough for the "grandeur" that is the France of his dreams. But he is probably realistic enough to agree with his admirer who says: "The greatness of a people depends on the people itself, not on the image a great man might have."[3]

What are the Frenchmen of today?[4] If one wanted to answer this question by describing French national character and mentality, he would expose himself to two dangers. Firstly, any attempt at depicting a national mentality, whatever the nation might be, ends in a vast generalization which at best is only part of the truth. Nations are composed of millions of individuals who, unlike automobiles of the same make and year, do not resemble each other. Individuals bear the imprint of national environment but remain different from each other. Secondly, nations are changing rapidly in our time of historical acceleration. This is especially true of France, which is emerging from her former stagna-

41

tion. An image of French character, perhaps true today, might prove to be distorted in the coming decade, when the rising generation will begin to crowd the stage. The best one can safely do is to reproduce the image Frenchmen have of themselves.

They love France no less than other people love their countries. Like de Gaulle, they love the France of their dreams. He does not identify eternal France with the "ephemeral Frenchmen"; the "ephemeral Frenchmen" do not identify France with the French State they dislike. For them France is made up of French history and French culture; they regret that this "Madonna in the frescoes" painted by great Frenchmen must wear the ugly mantle of French State. For de Gaulle, on the contrary, the "princess in the fairy tales" should have the shining armor she deserves, namely a strong State. To put it otherwise, for him the French State, governed by a strong executive, should be the pedestal on which France should stand without soiling her divine feet. For his compatriots the State is not an abstract person; it is the government and its public officials, obnoxious, demanding, and interfering with the citizen's *joie de vivre*.

All French and foreign commentators agree on this point. Several quotations, selected from many others, will illustrate this French distrust of their own State:

> Frenchmen do not spontaneously feel that the existence and the power of the State are indispensable. Hence they are inclined to distrust the State. They have hardly any scruples about evading the rules which the State claims to impose on them. They conceive their participation in political life as a means of weakening the State rather than reforming it, or simply as a means of deflecting the State's action in a way that would correspond to their interests or their preferences. It seems that this hostility toward the State, this tendency to misunderstand its role and to distrust those who embody it, today manifests itself most sharply among all the characteristic symptoms of French traditional political behavior.[5]
>
> There is no civic spirit in a people if the great majority of citizens take no interest in the problems of their State and do not approach politics seriously. . . . When they [Frenchmen] mention the State, it is only to complain. They impatiently endure the State's coercion, but this does not prevent them from constantly appealing to it for help. However, the assistance they expect and receive does not increase their attachment to the State or to the remnants of its authority, which, when compelled, they reluctantly acknowledge.

Too many citizens are not at all interested in public affairs. They forget that the State in a democracy is they themselves, is every one of us, is all French men and women.[6]

People behave as though the State were a person who has nothing in common with them, a sort of foreign ruler, or, vice versa, a manager from whom one constantly demands money without paying much attention to his accounts.[7]

When I compare our country with foreign countries which I have been able to visit, I feel that France has the sad privilege of a chronic and generalized anti-state behavior. Frenchmen do not like and do not respect their State.[8]

This quasi-unanimous view of French observers is supported by a perspicacious American commentator: "The State remains the enemy . . . even though it is still the natural distributor of benefits to whom one turns at the slightest trouble and whose help is expected as a right."[9]

It is paradoxical that a nation—which is practically homogeneous—should nevertheless split up the hyphenated term "nation-state," and love France while disliking her organized expression. A Swiss observer aptly sums up this contradictory attitude:

It is difficult to find a Frenchman who does not love his country. He might tell you that he abhors French morals, institutions, and people, and without hesitation he will go as far as to declare that the government is a gang of scoundrels and the administration a pack of gangsters . . . , but this proclaimed contempt will end with a passionate statement of his conviction that France is the only country where one may live and breathe in real freedom.[10]

However, love of one's country, as profound as it might be, remains an abstraction unless manifested in willingness to carry out obligations toward the nation-state. Pierre Mendès-France is certainly not alone in complaining of the lack of civic spirit:

[The ultimate cause of French troubles] . . . resides in political morals, in the lack of civic spirit which in our time too often characterizes members of government, parliamentarians, political parties, interest groups, the press, labor unions, and even the whole electoral body. . . . Many in the governing class and in the country at large too often disregard their fundamental duty, which consists in subordinating everything, their actions, their interests, their popularity, their professional or political career, yes, everything to the national interest.[11]

Bourgès-Maunoury, one of the ephemeral Prime Ministers of the Fourth Republic, once exclaimed in despair: "A shortcoming or a quality truly French and shared by many of our citizens: critical spirit. We are against everything."[12] It is almost miraculous that de Gaulle enjoys the trust of the majority of his countrymen in spite of their hypersensitive predilection for criticism and their dislike of the State. The public opinion poll taken in October 1964, after six and a half years of his rule, disclosed that 54 per cent of the French people declared themselves to be satisfied with him, and only 33 per cent expressed dissatisfaction. "The main reasons which explain the satisfaction are related, first of all, to the feeling that the regime is stable and that the country is better governed than before. Moreover, General de Gaulle's personality as the Head of State and patriot imposes respect; he has known how to preserve, to a certain extent, French independence and to give back to France the rank of a great power."[13]

Perhaps de Gaulle has succeeded in modifying the old attitudes, and perhaps Frenchmen are beginning to take a different view of their State, which now offers them both domestic stability and international prestige.

Political indifference or disgust with the old party leaders?

Public opinion polls support the view widely held in France that Frenchmen display a great indifference to politics. To the question: "Are you interested in politics?" only 8 per cent replied, much; 24 per cent, moderately; 37 per cent, little; 30 per cent, not at all; and 1 per cent did not answer.[14] French commentators agree on this point.[15] However, what is called in France the depoliticization of citizens is perhaps less grave than it might appear. It might even be a symptom of a beneficial evolution. Frenchmen are less and less interested in the programs of traditional political parties as long as these parties are fossilized in their anachronistic attitudes, cling desperately to obsolete issues which leave the population rather indifferent, and refuse to accept the self-evident necessity of a merger into two or three large formations. It is not true that Frenchmen are uninterested in public issues, but they are tired of hearing the sterile arguments which remain so dear to the old personnel of political parties. They are becoming modern in the sense of taking a pragmatic view of politics, which for them is concerned not with past ideologies but with the current problems of their daily life. They are disappointed in the quarrelsome parties, which do not offer tangible alternative solutions to their problems. Public opinion polls clearly indicate that citizens have had enough of the old party structure, which is becoming obsolete, and desire its renovation. Asked in December 1962 whether they would favor consolidation of political parties into two or three organizations, 66 per cent replied affirmatively, 10 per cent were hostile, and 24 per cent did not answer.[16]

The party leaders remain deaf to this public demand. This is one of the reasons why de Gaulle appears to most Frenchmen as the only temporary alternative to the antiquated system of the old parties. This is not a rejection of parties as such, but a dislike of their inflexible leadership.

What this French majority seems to abhor is a return to the governmental instability of the Fourth Republic. The parties (except for the Communist party) were at that time and still are skeleton organizations of national and local staffs and had very little rank-and-file membership. Each had at its disposal a larger but still small ring of regular sympathizers willing to give a hand from time to time. The influence of party machines (which were and are what the parties amounted to) could be measured only by the electoral returns, which invariably resulted in a National Assembly composed of several parliamentary groups. The large Communist group and the usually small number of extreme-right deputies were never included in the governmental majorities, but their votes helped to overthrow the governments. (The extreme right was not so small when the Poujadist movement unexpectedly captured many seats in the 1956 elections and as suddenly lost all of them after de Gaulle's return to power.) The real differences between the parliamentary groups could have been reduced to two main orientations: left-center and right-center, but each party and each parliamentary group clung to its own identity. There never was one parliamentary majority but several, and all of them ephemeral. Such groups could agree on one issue but disagreed on another question; this other issue would have the agreement of a different combination of groups, and the solution of a third problem required still another parliamentary combination. Except for the Communist group and to a lesser extent the Socialist group, parliamentary groups had no discipline. Their members could vote as they liked. Their leaders were never sure whether their colleagues would support them on the occasion of an important parliamentary division. Each government was a temporary coalition of several parliamentary groups ready to disintegrate at the first opportunity. As long (it was never long) as the members of the government were willing to pursue the same policy regarding all current issues and their followers among the deputies remained fairly satisfied and did not cast nay votes or abstain, the government survived. It had to be cautious for fear that a bold initiative would cause an internal rift or desertion by a good portion of its parliamentary supporters. The Prime Minister had no prestige; he was only the first among his peers. Most members of his government belonged to parties other than his own and owed him no loyalty; several of them were leaders of their own parliamentary groups. The back-benchers had the ambition to win a portfolio in the next governmental crisis. They had a point. The quick succession of governments was crowding the back benches with ex-Ministers; a deputy could ask: Why them but not me?

The result of this irresponsible party game, in which the interests of France were not necessarily a major consideration, was as follows:

> If we leave out of account the years 1940–1944 (i.e., the Vichy regime which was placed in a situation abnormal in every respect), France had, since the beginning of 1876 and until the spring of 1958, 119 governments; their average life did not exceed eight months. . . . This average span of life shrank between 1920 and 1940 to six months; the same was true in the period 1945–1958. One also should calculate the time devoted, after the resignation of the Cabinet, to the formation of its successor. The total length of time taken by the three ministerial crises during the last year of the Fourth Republic (May 1957–May 1958) amounted to almost a whole quarter of a year.[17]

Many competent French commentators agree with the majority of their countrymen on the necessity of complete reform of the existing parties and their fusion into large organizations.[18] It is self-evident that no democratic system of government may satisfactorily function in France if the parties continue to be many without any practical reason and if their multiplicity prevents the emergence of stable majorities. Neither the parliamentary nor the presidential system will work in a situation where ephemeral majorities may form on one problem and immediately disintegrate when another problem is to be tackled. The writing and rewriting of constitutions will not help.

The problem is even more pressing because a large portion of the electorate vote Communist and thus make more difficult the operation of the democratic system. As long as France is a democracy, this 20 to 25 per cent of the votes is wasted politically, because a democratic government could hardly work with Communist participation. The Communist party would have to become a leftist reformist party and sincerely accept the rules of the democratic game to make its inclusion within a governmental majority safe. This may not be a utopian hypothesis in view of new trends in both the French and Italian Communist parties, but a long period of time will have to pass before the other French parties would trust the sincerity of the evolution in the Communist party's political philosophy. The present French advocates of a new Popular Front, who are not themselves Communists, consider their own wishes proof of that evolution, which is not yet visible to more cautious observers. For the time being, France, pulling along the deadweight of the Communist electorate, badly needs the merger and strengthening of her democratic parties.

It is true that the several million electors who vote for the Communist party are not in their great majority convinced Communists but malcontents who register their protest against the social *status quo* in this way.[19] The reasons for their dissatisfaction are real, namely: "the persistence in society of social-class and cultural differences and inequalities, particularly glaring in France with regard to housing and education."[20] The rapid growth of prosperity in France is only slowly affecting the material condition of small farmers and industrial workers. Measured by the high prices, their incomes are low. Their housing is often similar to slums because better apartment houses have a very high rent and public construction of inexpensive but modern housing is still inadequate for the needs of lower social classes. The percentage of children of working-class and peasant parents who receive higher education is low (around 12 per cent). Hence social mobility is low too. French parents who belong to the lower classes have not yet the consolation that their children, if talented and hard working, have a fair chance to move socially upward.

It is true that this situation is changing. Public housing is progressing; the modernization of economic life reduces the proportion of the working class and the peasantry in the population in favor of the urban lower-middle class—technicians, highly qualified workers, and people employed in the tertiary sector of the economy; eventually prosperity will percolate to all classes. The proportion of students of lower-class background in the upper grades of secondary schools is growing and with it the prospect of future larger participation of those students in the higher schools. It is rather probable that the reasons for dissatisfaction among the present Communist voters will eventually disappear. But this will not happen tomorrow. For the time being, the French democracy is burdened with this heavy Communist mortgage.

Recent public opinion polls do not indicate any decline in the influence of the Communist party. Frenchmen were asked in June 1964 whether they considered the role of the Communist party in politics beneficial or harmful; 38 per cent answered that it was beneficial; 27

per cent that it was harmful; 35 per cent did not reply.[21] Eighteen per cent expressed the wish for an increase in that role, and 32 per cent that it remain the same.[22] Thirty-one per cent were in favor of Communist participation in the government, and 25 per cent were unopposed but indifferent. Fifty per cent had friends or relatives among the Communists.[23] Forty-nine per cent thought the reason for the electoral successes of the Communist party was social discontent, while 30 per cent thought it the useful role of the Communists as an opposition party.[24]

All this does not mean that there is a danger of Communist seizure of power, because the source of the Communist electoral strength is also their weakness. People vote for their ticket because they are dissatisfied, but not because they want to support a Communist revolution. This state of mind is reflected in the polls: only 27 per cent consider it possible that the Communists might come to power within the next ten years; among those 27 per cent a good portion are not the Communist voters but their bourgeois opponents whose fear of a social revolution causes them to exaggerate its danger. Forty-two per cent declared that it was impossible, and 31 per cent did not answer the question.[25]

The French problem is not the risk of a Communist revolution, which is almost nil, but the political waste of a big portion of electoral ballots, which ensures a large Communist parliamentary representation excluded by the other parties from the governmental majorities.

Thanks to de Gaulle the extreme and antidemocratic right has been reduced to impotence following its vain efforts to destroy the Fifth Republic. But one cannot exclude the possibility that this extreme right, which is now divided into several quarreling groups, be regrouped if it finds an able leader; it would then represent more deadweight in democratic politics.

The French democracy has been compelled by the existence of the powerful extreme left and the ever-present extreme right to have governments of the center. This center may be divided, as in Britain, into the progressive left-center and the moderately conservative right-center. Unlike in Britain, the multiplicity of center parties, from the Socialist all the way to the Union for the New Republic and the so-called Independents, does not reflect this fundamental division. The emergence of two formations, one moderately progressive and the other moderately conservative, is hindered by the fact that the line of division runs partly across the present party lines. This is true especially of the Popular Republicans and the Radicals.[26] It is amazing that the party leaders, challenged by their loss of influence among the electorate and constantly prodded by de Gaulle's sarcasm, have not been able to adjust to the necessities of political life.

For the time being, de Gaulle's rule is the alternative, but not for long, in view of his advanced age. He appears in the traditional role of providential man. Raymond Aron writes:

> This is not the first time the failure of a representative regime has thrown France and Frenchmen into the arms of a savior. . . . The massive and quasi-unanimous French rally to a regime incarnated in and by a man is not a radically new phenomenon; it is a repetition of the behavior which has characterized France since 1789: the search for acceptance, in a national crisis, of a substitute for the monarch.[27]

The history of this century alone supplies the names of those saviors: Clemenceau, Pétain, de Gaulle, and, to a lesser extent, Poincaré and Doumergue. This time as before the solution is only a stopgap; the providential man is old. The problem has not disappeared and will again become acute after his political or physical demise.

France is not prepared for that day. The debates on the post-Gaullist future prove it. Some would like to maintain the present system of personal power, an impossible wish in the absence of another providential man; others would preserve the Constitution of the Fifth Republic, but they widely differ as to its "correct" interpretation; still others would amend it to accommodate the requirements of pure parliamentary or pure presidential system; finally, there is the nostalgia of the Fourth Republic. Once again there is no consensus in the political elites on what the best political institutions are. "Frenchmen almost unanimously agree regarding the criteria of happiness, but this consensus has never extended to the problem of political institutions."[28]

An unworkable Constitution

No ordinary man at the Palace of Elysée will be able to wear de Gaulle's crown of elective monarch. Assuming that the present Constitution will survive de Gaulle, his admirer is right in thinking "it is undeniable that as long as de Gaulle controls the government, we cannot arrive at a precise idea of what the present institutions are worth."[29]

The Constitution will pose an almost insolvable problem to de Gaulle's successor. It requires that the Prime Minister be appointed by the President of the Republic and probably enjoy his trust, while he should at the same time have the confidence of parliament. At the present time the problem is conjured away because de Gaulle's Prime Ministers were never seriously challenged by the political parties in the National Assembly prior to the settlement of the Algerian question. The politicians wanted de Gaulle to undertake himself the thankless task of withdrawal from Algeria—a task for which they themselves lacked the civic courage. Once the Algerian war had been terminated, they rose in the parliamentary revolt in 1962 and adopted a motion of no confidence. The dissolution of the National Assembly followed. To the general surprise the electorate returned a Gaullist majority. The problem, inherent in the Constitution, is invisible. But it is highly probable that the next President of the Republic sooner or later will face a parliamentary majority, on whose docile support he will not be able to rely. Could he remain at the Palace of Elysée, if his Prime Minister were overthrown by a vote of censure and if, following the dissolution of National Assembly, the electorate returned the same hostile majority? He could, but only on the condition of accepting his political defeat and appointing a new Prime Minister, whom he would not like but who would have parliamentary support.

The impossible triangle: the President, the Prime Minister, and the majority in the National Assembly, which the present Constitution has created, with its guiding idea of the political harmony between the three sides of the triangle, is unworkable. The Constitution bears in its womb the necessity for the President of the Republic to accept eventually the rather modest position of Presidents of the former Republics. This could be done by his not using the extensive powers vested in him by the Constitution.

This development would not endanger governmental stability if there were a prospect of stable parliamentary majorities. The many political parties would have to merge into two or three large political formations to make possible the operation of a sound British-style parliamentary regime. However, the cadres of the French political parties are like the Bourbons; they have forgotten nothing and have learned nothing. They have not forgotten the petty game of party and personal intrigue of the Fourth Republic and have not shed a nostalgia for this game. They have not learned from the bitter experience of 1958 when, but for the appearance on the stage of a *deus ex machina,* de Gaulle, they would have been engulfed in a catastrophe; the alternative to de Gaulle was the military putsch which was under way. The strength of their attachment to the old habits was demonstrated in June 1965. Faced with the proposal of the Socialist Mayor of Marseilles, Gaston Defferre, a rare politician who understood the gravity of the problem, to amalgamate the moderate progressive parties and organizations into a left-center federation, which would face the right-center Gaullist Union for the New Republic, they rejected his scheme. Guy Mollet, the leader of Defferre's Socialist party, and the Popular Republicans bore the main responsibility for the rejection. He and the other politicians opted by implication for the multiparty system of the Fourth Republic rather than for a two-party workable parliamentarism.

Will the French people accept the return to the practices of the Fourth Republic with its governmental instability and ephemeral coalitions after they have known the Gaullist stability? Have the rather short years of de Gaulle's system instilled in the French people new political habits? Will the rising young generation, who have no sentimental memories of the Fourth Republic, accept living under the unstable governments that emerge and disappear for no major reason? Will a new political personnel eventually take up the relay of the party leaders inherited from the Fourth Republic, and will they be inclined to do what their elders refuse, namely to give France two or three major political formations (excluding the Communists) which would offer clear alternatives to the voters at each election? Only the post-Gaullist future will answer these questions.

If France were again faced with a grave national emergency, the Army might not remain a passive witness of a return to governmental instability. Frenchmen prefer not to think about it, especially because de Gaulle has succeeded in forcing the Army officers to stand aloof. But events from 1958 to 1961 were not too reassuring. An astute commentator says: "In any event, apolitism [of the Army] has died and has been buried. . . . We should not delude ourselves. The army of paratroopers and the Army as a whole, having tasted the intoxication of having become for a moment 'the first party of France,' will not return by any magic to the tradition of the Great Mute."[30]

This apprehension is shared by a number of other French commentators: "The Army will weigh heavily, if the excesses of parliamentarism reappear after de Gaulle's disappearance."[31] "Today, as in 1934, 1939, and 1946, the Army remains outside the nation and represents a mortgage which each day becomes heavier, an obvious threat."[32] Two writers who have an intimate knowledge of the feelings of military officers refer to: "this bloc of resentment and bitterness that the officers' corps is today."[33]

It is true that all these comments were written during the tense period from 1958 to 1962, when the threat of a military putsch in 1958 and the rebellion of the generals in April 1961 were still fresh in people's memories. But it is hard to believe that the potentially rebellious feel-

ings of officers, repressed since the failure of the revolt in 1961, have
entirely disappeared. If the officers were to believe that France is misruled and again confronted with a major threat, would they forget that
"French officers intervened on May 13, 1958, as a political entity in a
governmental crisis and demanded the formation of a cabinet of public
salvation and national union"?[34] Would they forget that, but for
de Gaulle, the military putsch would probably have succeeded? Would
they forget that in May 1958 the population remained passive and
showed no desire to fight for the Fourth Republic against the paratroopers who were ready to descend on Paris?[35] De Gaulle's example
in 1940 is not easily forgotten: "In the name of what would one prevent the Army in the future from wishing to judge for itself at what
particular moment the legal regime would cease to be legitimate because
it allegedly did not defend, in the Army's opinion, the superior interests
of the Fatherland?"[36] It is far from certain that the spirit of rebellion
has been broken once for all by de Gaulle and his purge of officers'
corps. This potential threat to the French democracy, if France were
faced with a serious national emergency, should not be overlooked; one
can only hope it will never materialize.

One or several hundred men?

It is true that "in May 1958 the public generally held that, after all,
it could entrust to a man, to a team, the task of solving the problems
of the community, i.e., the problems of citizens themselves."[37] This continues to be true of the majority of the public, which has abdicated in
favor of the providential man. This phenomenon is easier to understand
if one recalls that the Third and the Fourth Republics accustomed the
citizens to another abdication, that time in favor of several hundred
deputies and senators. The citizen's role was considered fulfilled on
polling day. On that day he delegated his sovereign powers for the duration of the legislature to the omnipotent parliament. He had no alternative. The multiplicity of parties precluded a choice, which should
have been his, between alternative solutions for current issues or at least
between alternative groups for the next government of France. After the
elections no one could be sure which successive governmental coalitions
would emerge; it depended on the political convenience of the deputies.
The only certainty was that these coalitions would be short lived. The
choice of policies was that of the deputies, not of the electors. Unlike
the British or United States voter, the French citizen did not cast his
ballot for the next administration and by implication for a certain orientation of national policies. In consequence, it was generally held that

national sovereignty was completely delegated to the deputies for the duration of each legislature. It was characteristic that one of the eminent politicians of the Fourth Republic could exclaim in the National Assembly: "France is here!" to which de Gaulle now replies: "I am France!"

It is quite possible that the present political system might, paradoxically enough, instill a new conviction in French voters: "We are France!" De Gaulle introduced a new factor in French politics—direct participation by the mass of citizens. One may accuse him of manipulating the popular referenda in such a way that he prejudges the results. He formulates the questions, thereby narrowing the choice of answers. He makes it clear in his statements preceding the vote that he would retire if the majority of answers were unfavorable. The voter knows that no stable alternative government is visibly available. He is thus compelled to say yes. It is also true that de Gaulle has not risked a popular referendum on certain controversial questions of vital importance such as nuclear force, the Common Market, or aid to underdeveloped countries. The fact remains that individual freedoms, including freedom of expression, are respected, that the opposition is free to make anti-Gaullist propaganda, that the citizens are under no compulsion to vote yes, that the results are reported honestly, and that large minorities answer nay. For the first time Frenchmen are asked to express their views on the great issues directly.

The taste for a more active political role is also increased by the new constitutional institution, the popular election of President of the Republic. In effect, Frenchmen now elect their chief executive directly. Under the present Constitution as amended in 1962 they have the opportunity to delegate their powers separately to the President and to parliament. This gives them a new right to settle political disputes between the legislature and the executive, as they did in the fall of 1962. The exercise of sovereignty remains vested in them on the occasion of presidential and legislative elections and also on the occasion of each referendum. This is an important innovation, encouraging the citizen to feel politically more important than under the Third and Fourth Republics. This fact, now distorted by the presence of de Gaulle at the Palace of Elysée, will become fully visible after his disappearance. It might be very difficult to force citizens back into their former political obscurity. This is another reason why a return to the omnipotence of parliament might not be easy, if attempted. The growing attachment to popular election of the President is evidenced by public opinion polls. They provide a contrast with the results of the 1962 referendum on the constitutional adoption of the popular election. At that time only

46.44 per cent of the registered voters cast affirmative ballots (62 per cent of those who actually voted), 28.76 voted against, 2.04 cast invalid or blank ballots, and 22.76 per cent abstained. A poll taken in May 1964 gave different results: 74 per cent were satisfied with the new institution, only 10 per cent were against it, and 16 per cent did not reply.[38]

If this new taste for direct participation in politics were to survive and take root, it would invalidate the formerly general opinion that "the French citizen . . . prefers to deal with an authority that imposes its own solutions, because this allows him to disengage his responsibility, to remain free and to limit the extent of social compulsion."[39] A pessimist may reply that the monarchical rule of de Gaulle might outweigh the impact of the new institutions—popular referenda and the direct election of the President—and strengthen the old habit of delegating the entire responsibility for public affairs to one or several hundred men. The future will give the final answer.

One should not forget another aspect of French character. Frenchmen might patiently tolerate rule by one man or confiscation of sovereignty by a multiparty parliament, but they have proved many times that their patience is not unlimited. Insurrections, revolts, and *coups d'état* have marked many days in French history:

> July 14 and October 5 and 6, 1789; July 17, 1791; August 10, 1792; May 31 and June 2, 1793; the days of Prairial and of Vendémaire (1795); the *coup d'état* of Fructidor (1797); the *coup d'état* of Brumaire 18th; the Three Glorious Days (1830); the days of February and June 1848; December 2, 1851; September 4, 1870; the Commune of Paris; February 4, 1934; May 13, 1958; the barricades of January, 1960, in Algiers; the putsch of April 22, 1961.[40]

The reverse side of the coin is the short life of French constitutions. Frenchmen are prone to believe that their problems may be solved by enacting a new constitution. Unfortunately, political life is regulated by ingrained habits of the population rather than by the most solemn charters.

Demographic rejuvenation

It is possible that old habits will be affected by the demographic rejuvenation in France. The temperament of a population is influenced by the average age, which since 1939 has become increasingly lower in France.

Tradition dies away. This has many inconvenient aspects but also represents a gain; it makes more than one obsolete conflict disappear. Rising generations are no longer hindered by the weight of history imperfectly understood. Generally, sons do not espouse the quarrels of their fathers. The fossilized [political] watersheds tend to lose their importance.[41]

The "fathers," the political personnel of the Fourth Republic, overlook this new phenomenon. The obsolete issues, which are still dear to them, do not seem to evoke any emotional reaction among the "sons."

This demographic rejuvenation is spectacular in France, which from the beginning of the last century until the 1940's had sadly witnessed a continual fall in the birth rate. At the time of the First Empire the total population amounted to 28 million. France was the most populous nation in Europe except for Russia. While other European nations were rapidly increasing in numbers throughout the nineteenth century and while Germany and Britain were overtaking France, in 1936 the French population attained only 41 million. But even this figure hid the depopulation, because the increase of about 13 million between 1801 and 1939 was due largely to longer life expectancy and to foreign immigration, which amounted to 5 million. In the years 1935–39, as deaths exceeded births, France was threatened with gradual depopulation. The birth rate, which in 1801 stood at 32.8 per thousand, fell in 1939 to 14.6.

Nineteen forty-two marked a reversal in French demographic trends. The birth rate began to rise to attain in 1948 an impressive 20.8 per thousand. In 1964 the birth rate stood at 17.3 per thousand, which compared well with the figures for the other members of the Common Market: 20.8 for the Netherlands, 18.3 for Italy, 17.9 for West Germany, 16.7 for Belgium, and 16.0 for Luxembourg. The total French population is not much lower than that of West Germany or Italy. In 1964 France had 48 million, while West Germany had 58 million and Italy 51 million. The French natural increase stood at 315,000 in 1964 (830,000 births and 515,000 deaths). The other source of increase was foreign immigration, which amounted in 1964 to 150,000 persons.[42]

While Michel Debré is right in his melancholic observation that "France represented toward the end of the eighteenth century almost one-fifth of the European population. She represents now hardly 5 per cent,"[43] it is equally true that France is rejuvenated in her population and hence in her mentality. She is no longer the old man of Europe.

The presidential election in December 1965 failed to indicate whether demographic and other factors were producing a gradual change in the political habits of French voters.

De Gaulle's second seven-year term

General de Gaulle was reelected on December 19, 1965, for his second seven-year term as President of the Republic. French voters were asked, for the first time since the popular-vote election of Prince Louis-Napoleon Bonaparte in 1848, to elect their President themselves. They were enabled to do so by the constitutional amendment approved in the 1962 referendum. Whatever de Gaulle might have expected and his opponents might have feared, this first modern popular election of the French President did not degenerate into a sort of Bonapartist plebiscite. The election was hotly contested. If it were to be interpreted as a plebiscite for or against de Gaulle, it demonstrated a marked decline in his popularity.

Prognostications made by Gaullists and their opponents alike—at least until the sudden appearance of Jean Lecanuet's candidacy—that de Gaulle would easily win on the first ballot proved wrong. He was forced into a second ballot. He finally won, but by a rather unimpressive majority of over 55 per cent.

There were several candidates on the first ballot. Discounting two of them who had no chances and who together received less than 3 per cent of votes, three serious opponents faced de Gaulle: François Mitterand, Jean Lecanuet, and Jean-Louis Tixier-Vignancour. Mitterand had the support of the left, which for once was united, including the Communist and Socialist parties, the majority of the Radical party, and other leftist organizations. Lecanuet, a Popular Republican, appealed to the political center and to those other moderate voters who favored European integration. Tixier-Vignancour, a former Vichyite, expected to win the ballots of the extreme right and of the Algerian Europeans resettled in France; these two groups hate de Gaulle, and the former is opposed to democracy itself.

De Gaulle had known that the ballots cast for Mitterand and for Tixier-Vignancour would be lost to him. The unexpected last-minute candidacy of Lecanuet was a real blow, because this opponent could attract the moderate voters who were dissatisfied with de Gaulle's European policy but who would have cast their ballots for the General rather than for either Mitterand or Tixier-Vignancour. Farmers, who knew only too well that disintegration of the Common Market would be a major disaster for them, and other Frenchmen who favored European integration for economic or ideological reasons were given an opportunity to express their disapproval of de Gaulle's highhanded policy during the six months that preceded the election. (See Chapter V.) Other moderate voters, who feared the concentration of power in the hands of one man, also were enabled to vote against the General without rallying themselves to the leftist or the extreme-rightist candidate. If Lecanuet had not run, de Gaulle would have won on the first ballot.

The official results of the first ballot held on December 5, 1965, were as follows:[44]

Registered voters:	28,913,422	
Votes cast:	24,502,957	
Abstentions:	4,410,465	(15.25 per cent)
Invalid votes:	248,403	(0.85 per cent)
De Gaulle's votes:	10,828,523	(44.64 per cent of valid votes)
Mitterand's votes:	7,694,003	(31.72 per cent of valid votes)
Lecanuet's votes:	3,777,119	(15.57 per cent of valid votes)
Tixier-Vignancour's votes:	1,260,208	(5.19 per cent of valid votes)
Votes for the two remaining candidates:	694,691	(2.86 per cent of valid votes)

It was not surprising that strange alliances were formed in the election fought for or against de Gaulle. Mitterand was supported by a sort of Popular Front, but the moderate wing of the Radical party rallied to Lecanuet. Pierre Poujade, whose name in the middle fifties flashed in newspaper headlines because of his short-lived but at that time spectacular electoral success and who does not play any role in present-day French politics, and Jacques Soustelle, one of the leaders of the O.A.S. who now lives in exile, both publicly expressed their support for Lecanuet even though he does not share their political beliefs.

French law requires an absolute majority for election on the first ballot. If none of the candidates obtains this majority, the two who receive the largest pluralities compete on the second ballot. This rule eliminated Lecanuet and Tixier-Vignancour. The former advised his supporters either to cast invalid ballots or to vote for Mitterand. Tixier-Vignancour called on his supporters to shift to Mitterand and even to join hands with the Communists in the attempt to unseat de Gaulle. It seems that most of his voters followed his advice, while probably half of Lecanuet's voters refused to listen to their first-choice candidate and cast their ballots for de Gaulle. Approximately two million extreme-right and Algerian-European electors apparently cast their ballots for Mitterand. The Popular Front of the left received the rather unexpected support from their enemies, who visibly hated de Gaulle more than the Communists. However, antipathy felt for the same man is not a political platform.

All these strange alignments demonstrated once again that Frenchmen had no visible workable alternative to de Gaulle's regime other than the return to the tradition of the Fourth Republic with its unstable and short-lived majorities. This is the most serious French political problem; de Gaulle will not play his role of stopgap forever. For instance, if the strongest among de Gaulle's opponents, Mitterand, had won, he probably would have failed to keep his Popular Front together, united only because its component parts wished to terminate the General's rule. Behind this electoral and *ad hoc* agreement the persistent divergencies of views continued to exist. The Socialist party certainly did not intend to form a coalition government with the Communists, while the Radicals steadfastly refused, at that time and later, ever to support any government in which the Communists would participate.

A significant portion of leftist voters preferred de Gaulle's governmental stability to the prospect of Mitterand's lack of it; thus they cast their votes for the General. This becomes evident from a comparison of votes which the three parties supporting Mitterand had received in the 1962 legislative elections and the ballots cast for Mitterand in the presidential election. In 1962 the Communist, Socialist, Radical, and other small leftist parties obtained 44.50 per cent of the total popular vote. On the first ballot in 1965 Mitterand received 12.75 per cent less. This was significant even if one takes into consideration the fact that a good number of Radical voters cast their ballots for Lecanuet rather than for Mitterand in spite of their own party's appeal. The French Institute of Public Opinion estimated that on the first ballot de Gaulle received 13 per cent of the votes that were usually Communist, Socialist, and Radical and 14 per cent on the second ballot. It also calculated that 27 per cent of the electors who usually cast their ballots for the moderate-right Independents or for the Popular Republicans shifted to de Gaulle on December 5, and that this proportion rose to 71 per cent on December 19.[45]

Why was General de Gaulle confronted with a resolute though divided opposition among the French voters? This is a most difficult question to answer in any country because of the variety of reasons which decide a voter to cast his ballot one way or another. One may list here only the probable reasons. Television, which the General had used formerly with great skill, did not help him this time. Television screens reflected his old age in contrast to the still youthful appearance of his main adversaries, Mitterand and Lecanuet. His seven years of administration, whatever their merits and demerits, were long. A portion of voters in any country get tired of the government in power and want change. This factor is even more important in France, where so many people are dissatisfied with their lot (for valid reasons or not) and inclined to support the opposition in order to give vent to their frustrations. De Gaulle represented not only the government in power but also the State which Frenchmen dislike while loving France. Other voters were motivated by the traditional fear of personal power.

At his press conference held on February 21, 1966, General de Gaulle himself pointed out the last but not the least reason for his setback. He denied the validity of comparisons made between the results of popular referenda and of the legislative elections in former years (1958 to 1962), on the one hand, and the first ballot returns of December 5, 1965, on the other. He said that France was plunged in a deep crisis in those former years, and that Frenchmen had needed de Gaulle. In 1965, as normal conditions had been restored, this need was no longer felt by a large part of the electorate.

What he said was true, except that this was not the only reason for the electors' behavior. Undoubtedly, a great majority of Frenchmen believed from 1958 to 1962 that only de Gaulle would be able to surmount the crisis and solve the Algerian problem. By the time of the legislative elections in the fall of 1962 the Algerian question had been settled, but France was barely recovering from the shock of the terroristic activities of the O.A.S.

De Gaulle's observation is interesting in another respect. He has charisma only for unconditional Gaullists. For other Frenchmen, who have supported him since 1958 as Frenchmen had done in 1944 and 1945, he is not the incarnation of eternal France but "the man of the hour," as Sir Winston Churchill was in 1940 for the British people. He was thought of in periods of grave national crisis as the only man who could solve "insolvable" problems. The need for a man of the hour recedes at a time when his countrymen begin to believe that a national emergency has terminated, and that they would henceforth face only such problems which ordinary men might successfully handle. Sir Winston lost the 1945 election; de Gaulle suffered a setback on the first ballot in 1965.

In any event, Mitterand proved that the left, if united (this is a very big if), represented a great force. Over 5 per cent of the ballots cast for Tixier-Vignancour demonstrated that the extreme right, though now split into several quarreling factions, continued to be a perennial problem of French democracy.

French voters, like their counterparts in other democratic countries, are not influenced by foreign issues unless a problem appears to have a strong and immediate relation to their own well-being or to national security. Only one such issue played a role in the December election: the future of the Common Market. The crisis, opened by de Gaulle in the summer of 1965, made many Frenchmen, the farmers in particular, wonder whether the Common Market was not threatened with disintegration owing to the French challenge. Lecanuet and Mitterand sensed that this was an important question for a large part of the electorate. They both affirmed their faith in the Common Market. Mitterand's position on the Common Market was eased by the Communist party, which by September 1965 had abandoned its former opposition to it, in this respect following a similar but much earlier shift in the attitude of the Italian Communist party.

The results of the first ballot taught de Gaulle that his stringent Common Market policy did not enjoy support among the majority of his countrymen. The impressive electoral participation (only 15.25 per cent of the registered voters abstained on the first ballot and only 15.67 did on the second) destroyed the myth of the depoliticization of Frenchmen. They did not lose their interest in politics in spite of their feeble participation in the daily activities of political parties and organized interest groups. The first ballot demonstrated that a very large portion of French citizens still persevere in their old habits; if offered a choice among several candidates, they immediately split up into several groups. The multiparty system has deep roots in French soil and may be extirpated only by a change of habits. One may doubt whether any modification in the electoral laws (for instance, the adoption of the British-like one-ballot uninominal constituencies in the legislative elections) would help.

The second ballot with its two candidates compelled the voters to make a choice less sophisticated than many of them would have liked. The results of that ballot on December 19 were as follows:[46]

Registered voters:	28,902,704	
Votes cast:	24,371,647	
Abstentions:	4,531,057	(15.67 per cent)
Invalid votes:	668,213	(2.31 per cent)
De Gaulle's votes:	13,083,699	(55.19 per cent of valid ballots)
Mitterand's votes:	10,619,735	(36.74 per cent of valid ballots)

The second ballot confirmed the traditional geopolitical division of France. Southern and central France gave a majority to Mitterand, while the majority of the rest of the country voted for de Gaulle.

The first ballot suspended a question mark over General de Gaulle's second seven-year term. Elections to the National Assembly must take place at the latest in the spring of 1967 (unless the President were to dissolve the National Assembly earlier). As de Gaulle did not manage to win a clear majority on the first ballot, it is possible that his supporters might be defeated in the 1967 elections. In the 1962 legislative elections the Union for the New Republic (U.N.R.) received 31.94 per cent of the total vote on the first ballot, i.e., 12.70 per cent less than de Gaulle obtained on the first presidential ballot. On the second ballot in 1962 it got 40.5 per cent. If one adds the votes cast for those Independent and Popular-Republican candidates who had taken the pledge to support the General, total pro-Gaullist votes on the first ballot in 1962 amounted to only 37.64 per cent. However, the two ballots allowed the U.N.R. to win 229 seats in the National Assembly; it fell four seats short of an absolute majority. Support by a number of pro-Gaullist Independent and Popular-Republican deputies helped to ensure the existence of a stable majority ready to vote for de Gaulle's government.

What will de Gaulle do in 1967 if he faces a hostile though divided majority of traditional parties and if his Prime Minister fails to get a vote of confidence? In the first place, Article 12 of the Constitution forbids the dissolution of the National Assembly for a full year following the general election. Constitutionally de Gaulle would have a choice between resigning or accepting a Prime Minister imposed by the parliamentary majority. There is no other legal solution for a conflict between the President and the National Assembly. The triangle created by the present Constitution rests on the unwise assumption that the Prime Minister should simultaneously enjoy the trust of the President and of the parliamentary majority. It is hard to imagine the General in the role of a figurehead President like the Presidents of the Third and Fourth Republics. It is equally difficult to picture a de Gaulle who would defy the electorate and use unconstitutional means to perpetuate his rule. The opposition is not wrong in calling the 1967 election "the third ballot."

General de Gaulle himself seemed to concede to the opposition that the legislative elections of 1967 might become a "third ballot." At his press conference on February 21, 1966, he said of present French policy: "This policy, of course, implies that the public authorities carry it out: a Chief of State who has received from the people the mandate specifically for that purpose; a government which originates in him in order to implement this policy; a Parliament which, in order to uphold this policy, must have a majority like the one which rallied within the nation [in 1962] on the President's call and around his person. This is precisely the present French situation. The whole future depends on its duration."[47]

This prospect once again raises the question of what is a valid alternative to de Gaulle's regime. Gaston Defferre, as we have related, failed miserably in his valiant attempt to form a viable federation of the whole left-center. It would have included his own Socialist party, the Radicals, the Popular Republicans, and other left-center organizations such as the clubs; he excluded the Communists. His failure was due principally to reluctance on the part of the Popular Republicans and Socialists to dilute their parties within a larger organization.

After the presidential elections François Mitterand formed a narrower and loose federation called Left-Democratic and Socialist. It is composed mainly of the Socialist party, the majority of the Radicals, and the leftist clubs. This federation does not extend either to the Communists or the Popular Republicans. At best it can hope to get only 25 per cent of the popular vote.

The Socialist party has been inclined, since the termination of the Algerian affair and the beginning of its open opposition to de Gaulle, to conclude *ad hoc* electoral pacts in each constituency with different partners at different times depending on what is convenient. The partners in these local electoral combinations have been the Communists, the Radicals, or the Popular Republicans. Until the fall of 1962 the Socialist leader, Guy Mollet, was one of the most vocal adversaries of the Communist party. He still seems reluctant to enter into a long-term pact with that party, although the Communists never tire of proposing acceptance of a common political platform. This Popular Front would not resemble that of the thirties because the Radical party would clearly refuse to join even if the Socialists were ready. One of the major issues dividing the Communists and Socialists is the Atlantic Alliance, which the Socialists support and the Communists firmly oppose. It is interesting to note that the Communist party declared de Gaulle's move aiming at French withdrawal from NATO reasonable, and that Mitterand too, probably without Socialist approval, stated that he favored revision of military arrangements which bound France to her Allies.

On top of everything, Guy Mollet remembers that in 1958, when the party decided to support de Gaulle, its left wing deserted and formed its own small party initially called the Autonomous Socialist party and later the Unified Socialist party; this party refuses to participate in any combination that would not extend to the Communists. Today any permanent pact between the Communist and Socialist parties would probably be followed by the defection of the right wing of the Socialist party led by Gaston Defferre. The Communists refuse to join Mitterand's federation and consent only to a bilateral deal with the Socialists, who themselves are not very enthusiastic about that federation. The electoral Popular

Front in December 1965 was abortive. The prospect of a stable and united left majority is not too bright, to say the least.

Lecanuet formed another postelectoral federation called the Democratic Center which would accept association with the Socialists but not with the Communists. It is supported mainly by the Popular Republicans and the Independents. Its weakness consists in its close resemblance to the U.N.R. except that it is anti-de Gaulle and is strongly pro-"European." It could "steal" votes from the U.N.R. only if de Gaulle were unwise enough to challenge the other members of the Common Market again.

One cannot disagree with an experienced anti-Gaullist commentator who wrote: "None of the current regroupings substantiates the belief that one majority [the present Gaullist majority in the National Assembly] might be succeeded by another true majority."[48]

Foreign reactions to the first ballot were as they could be predicted. Washington, London, Bonn, Rome, Brussels, and The Hague could hardly conceal their pleasure at seeing de Gaulle defied in his own country. The Communist press was rather embarrassed. The French Communist party had supported Mitterand, but Communist governments did not relish the prospect of the demise of a man whose foreign policy they had called "reasonable." The capitals of underdeveloped countries had no reason for rejoicing, and some were frankly dismayed.

Soon after his inauguration President de Gaulle reappointed Pompidou as Prime Minister. The composition of the new government was not greatly altered, but three appointments or reappointments deserve to be noted. Maurice Couve de Murville, loyal and capable agent of de Gaulle's foreign policy, remained at his post of Foreign Minister. Michel Debré came back from semiretirement to replace the young Republican Independent, Valéry Giscard d'Estaing, as Minister of Finance and National Economy. It is possible that de Gaulle has not yet decided whether his heir should be Pompidou or Debré. The intelligent Prime Minister of the Fourth Republic, Edgar Faure, accepted the portfolio of Agriculture. In recent years he had cooperated with the General in the capacity of an unofficial emissary; he had laid the groundwork for establishing diplomatic relations with Peking and for a rapprochement with Cairo. One of his tasks will be to fight for the French point of view on agriculture in negotiations with the other members of the Common Market.

Public opinion and French foreign affairs

French experts usually agree that the mass of their compatriots do not show much interest in foreign problems:

The French public takes hardly any interest in foreign policy. Domestic problems, in particular those relating to the standard of living, attract its attention principally. . . . Besides, the public is inadequately informed on foreign problems and is hardly able to follow their complex and rapid evolution. . . . The population, taken as a whole . . . , reacts emotionally rather than intellectually, conditioned as it is by education, traditional myths, and instinctive preferences. Moreover, it manifests its existence only intermittently and makes itself known at difficult moments. On the other hand, an active opinion is represented by a small number of men who keep themselves informed and follow the development of problems, reflecting, criticizing, predicting, working out programs of action, and proposing solutions. This minority is made up of high officials, journalists, publicists, businessmen, and politicians. It acts through the press or by forming [pressure] groups. The press does not represent the general public but reflects this minority, which wants to influence the general public with its opinion.[49]

This view holds true for other nations, including democratic ones. Foreign problems are too complex for the average citizen, who has no time to study them and is therefore ill informed. Preoccupied with his daily problems, he understands domestic issues better because they seemingly affect him more directly. Public opinion regarding foreign matters is generally shaped by a small minority.

However, a French political scientist is right in drawing attention to contemporary factors which do not allow ordinary Frenchmen or citizens of other countries to forget entirely the existence of important foreign issues. He says:

The reasons for this increase [in the interest of citizens in international problems] are generally: the intrinsic importance of events, the relation—which the experience of the past quarter-century allows everyone from now on to be cognizant of—between the most remote events and his own life, and the quantitative and qualitative expansion of mass media of information.[50]

The citizen of any developed country receives daily information on foreign events from the mass media. In France this information is somewhat distorted because both the radio and television networks are State monopolies. However, the daily press and the activities of the opposition provide a certain balance. In any event, the citizen realizes that his own existence may be decisively affected by international events. He knows it from the experience of the two World Wars and from his knowledge of the existence of weapons of mass destruction. A remote event might end in worldwide catastrophe.

Recent public opinion polls indicate both the growing interest of Frenchmen in external affairs and perhaps a greater awareness of problems involved. Their attitudes are not without significance for de Gaulle's foreign policy. Asked whether France should attempt to become one of the leading world powers (de Gaulle's ambition), 42 per cent replied yes in May 1964, 42 per cent would be satisfied with a more modest international place, and 16 per cent expressed no opinion.[51] Forty per cent declared themselves satisfied with the present international role of France, thereby manifesting their support for the foreign policy of the Fifth Republic.[52] This support was also expressed in answers to the direct question: "What is your opinion of the present government's foreign policy?" Forty-seven per cent called it very good or rather good, only 24 per cent found it bad or very bad, and 29 per cent did not reply. It is interesting that three-quarters of those interviewed responded.[53]

This support of Gaullist foreign policy is not unqualified. The answers indicate that Frenchmen have doubts as to whether France should play a role in non-European affairs. Asked in September 1963 whether she should participate in Near Eastern affairs, only 17 per cent replied yes, while 46 per cent were opposed. The same question regarding Algeria, with which France maintains close economic and cultural cooperation, got only 34 per cent affirmative replies, while 40 per cent were negative. In May 1964, 52 per cent of people interviewed opposed the French role in Vietnam, while only 21 per cent approved.[54] This seems to show that Frenchmen are less ambitious than de Gaulle.

The policy of aid to underdeveloped countries, which was supported in 1962 by 73 per cent of those polled, is encountering growing resistance. Frenchmen seem to think that with decolonization should come a decrease in French expenses on former colonies and even more on other developing countries. In 1963 aid to Algeria met resistance among 64 per cent, who wanted it reduced. Only 1 per cent were in favor of an increase, while 8 per cent gave their assent to the present amount of aid. The amount of aid to underdeveloped countries in general should be reduced, according to 56 per cent, while 28 per cent were unopposed to the present level of aid, and 4 per cent favored an increase. It is interesting to note that the most educated and youngest among those questioned were most in favor of foreign aid.[55]

Frenchmen seem to be confused regarding another important aspect of de Gaulle's foreign policy: the national nuclear force. In April 1964 39 per cent were in favor; 40 per cent opposed; and 21 per cent had no opinion. A portion of those who wanted to see France armed with nuclear weapons expressed doubts concerning French financial ability to carry out nuclear armament. The percentage of people who were doubtful was greater than that of people favoring nuclear armament; it amounted to 45 per cent, while only 29 per cent thought France could pay its cost.[56]

The Western European union finds general support. Asked whether economic unification of the Six was progressing at a satisfactory pace, 40 per cent answered that the pace was too slow, 19 per cent were satisfied, only 4 per cent considered it too rapid. In other words, 59 per cent supported the Common Market. This particular poll received confirmation in the 1965 presidential election.

The more complex problem of political unification also elicited favorable reactions. Fourteen per cent thought that it was indispensable, 39 per cent that it was desirable, 11 per cent that it was unnecessary, and 5 per cent that it was dangerous. Fifty-three per cent were thus in favor of political unification, barely 6 per cent less than those supporting economic unification. No attempt was made to determine what kind of political unification (the union of sovereign states, as de Gaulle wishes, or a supranational federation) they had in mind.[57]

The support of de Gaulle's European policy is buttressed by the French attitude toward Germany. The polls indicate that Frenchmen feel reconciliation with their former enemy is final. Sympathy for Germany has been on the increase since 1956. A good opinion of Germany was held by the following percentages of Frenchmen questioned: 12 per cent in 1956, 23 per cent in 1957, 30 per cent in 1961, 39 per cent in 1963, and 53 per cent in 1964. In the year 1964, 29 per cent held neither a good nor a bad opinion, and only 9 per cent had an unfavorable opinion of Germany. Fifty-two per cent thought French-German relations had improved in the preceding year.[58] This opinion was at variance with actual facts.

The favorable attitude toward Germany seems to go so far that Frenchmen of today apparently are not afraid of German reunification. After the last war 78 per cent, as against 12 per cent, wanted Germany to be dismembered. In 1964, 55 per cent desired reunification, while 26 per cent were opposed.[59] In this respect the French public differs from de Gaulle, whose various pronouncements indicate a lack of enthusiasm for German reunification. However, one may have some doubts as to how exactly this particular poll reflects the views of Frenchmen; no vital French interest requires German reunification, and one could argue, as many politically sophisticated Frenchmen do, that a unified Germany would be too powerful for safe French cooperation. As is to be expected, the young are most sympathetic toward Germany; they have no memories of German occupation.

The polls seem to indicate that de Gaulle's foreign policy and the comments of French radio and television do not necessarily affect French attitudes toward foreign countries. Neither the United States nor Great Britain appears to be unpopular; they have been receiving growing support in the polls. The curve for the United States was as follows: 24 per cent held a good opinion in 1956, 21 per cent in 1957, 44 per cent in 1960, 49 per cent in 1961, 46 per cent in 1963, and 52 per cent in 1964. In 1964 only 11 per cent disliked the United States, and 37 per cent had no opinion. The percentage of those with a good opinion of Great Britain has been steady: 37 per cent in 1956 and 43 per cent in 1964, with small variations in the intervening years.[60]

However, it would be risky to rely on the polls too heavily for exact evaluation of French feelings toward the United States. Their results are not supported by French books or newspapers or by conversations with Frenchmen of all social classes. The same anti-American leitmotiv is heard in talk among Gaullist and non-Gaullist intellectuals, politicians, store-keepers, taxi-drivers, barbers, and passers-by. Either they dislike the Americans, among whom they have never lived, or at least severely condemn American foreign policies. The image varies in degree of sophistication, but its main features are the same: a clumsy, uncultivated giant who runs about the international stage like a bull in a china shop.

Sympathy for the Soviet Union is even more limited but it too is on the increase. Frenchmen favorably disposed increased from 12 per cent of those interviewed in 1956 to 25 per cent in 1964. As one must assume that some voters who cast their ballots for non-Communist candidates have sympathy for the Soviet Union (for instance, because they discern an improvement in the domestic regime or like some aspects of Soviet foreign policy), it is interesting to note that Communist voters do not necessarily have any particular sympathy for the Soviet Union. This becomes clearer when one compares the 11 per cent of public opinion favorable to the Soviet Union in 1957 with the large bloc, usually from 20 to 25 per cent, of Communist ballots. This is additional proof that most Communist voters are malcontents but not confirmed Communists.[61]

The polls do not support the view that Frenchmen are unaware of foreign developments. While in 1964 52 per cent allegedly held a good opinion of the United States, 49 per cent knew that relations between it and France had deteriorated.[62]

De Gaulle's preference for a loose Atlantic Alliance and his hostility to military integration did not find much support in the polls. In 1964 those in favor of even greater integration of NATO represented no less than 37 per cent, those against it amounted to only 23 per cent, while those who held no view on the matter were 40 per cent.[63]

Frenchmen are generally of the opinion that there is no great danger of a new world war. Sixty-four per cent of them hold this view, while only 13 per cent fear that danger, and 23 per cent have no opinion.[64]

What can be deduced from the public opinion polls is that de Gaulle's foreign policy is supported but not without reservations concerning some of its important aspects, such as his attitude toward the nuclear force, NATO, the United States and Britain, and aid to underdeveloped countries. His policies regarding European unification (the polls were taken prior to the 1965 crisis in the Common Market) and toward Western Germany have solid support.

The reports of these public opinion polls should be used cautiously. There is always a possibility that error will result from the choice of sample groups or from insincere answers. In any event, the polls do not indicate that de Gaulle encounters strong opposition in his foreign policy (except for the Common Market issue in 1965) or that important aspects of that policy would not survive de Gaulle.

A nostalgic status quo nation

The majority of Frenchmen support de Gaulle's foreign policy not only in its specifics, for which their support is not always unqualified, but also in its general orientation, which flatters their national pride. This is a rather natural reaction to humiliations of the recent past. However, this ambition to reassert France in the world is not an imperialist ambition to extend French rule over other countries. France is in this sense a *status quo* nation who wants to find happiness within her own frontiers. The process of decolonization is practically terminated. The former fanciful talk about 100 million Frenchmen, including the populations of the colonies, is forgotten. France is France within her European hexagon, although Frenchmen are glad to see her influence extended beyond her frontiers. One could summarize the ambition of the French people in a short formula: domestic prosperity, peace, and respect abroad.

Asked in 1964 which were the greatest achievements of the Fifth Republic, 45 per cent of those who replied assigned first place to the termination of the Algerian war, 17 per cent to governmental stability, and 8 per cent to increased prestige abroad.[65] Frenchmen are grateful to de Gaulle for giving them peace. Since 1939 they have been involved in three wars: the Second World War, the war in Indochina, and the war in Algeria. Now at last young Frenchmen are not being killed in military operations. Even if nuclear weapons did not exist, France would be a peaceful nation unwilling to be involved in any military adventure.

One can better understand the present outlook of Frenchmen if one imagines a statesman who would have dared to propose, prior to the First and even prior to the Second World War, abandoning one of the colonial possessions. His career would have been ended then and there, and his name would have been mentioned with patriotic horror and indignation. De Gaulle is praised by practically all Frenchmen, except for the lunatic fringe of the extreme right, for having almost totally liquidated the colonial empire within the short span of four years. The nation who is happy to be relieved of overseas possessions is certainly content to have her present territory confined within the European frontiers.

Michel Debré, an ardent nationalist himself, says: "Doubtless, the people were tired of the military effort required for the protection of the empire."[66] De Gaulle has held a somewhat similar view since the end of the last war: "Today, no conquest, no revenge tempted our citizens."[67] In 1961 he appealed to this hexagon mentality in order to rally Frenchmen to his side against the extreme right and rebellious officers. In a televised speech on July 12, 1961, he said: "For numerous reasons, our direct national interest demands that we unburden ourselves of costly and fruitless responsibilities and allow our former subjects to determine their own destiny."[68] In September 1961 he was even more precise: "French national interests lie, above all, within France herself."[69] A French commentator has expressed the same idea in these words:

> France is satisfied with her territorial limits in Europe. This is the spirit of the hexagon. In all political groups from the narrowest *cartierisme*[70] to the most ambitious *gaullisme,* the present territorial limits of France are absolutely not in question.[71]

Finally, French political scientists provided the following comment on the results of the referendum of January 8, 1961, which had approved by a 75 per cent majority de Gaulle's most controversial colonial retreat, that from Algeria (the policy of self-determination for Algeria): "a ballot that has revealed the country's aspiration and hope for peace."[72]

This *status quo* mentality implies that Frenchmen want their main national interests to be confined to Europe, where their hexagon is located. Satisfaction with the present extent of French territory contrasts with West German dissatisfaction with their *status quo* (the division of

Germany and Germany's eastern frontiers) and reveals the potential problem of French-German cooperation.

All this does not prevent de Gaulle and a great many of his countrymen from looking nostalgically at the days when France was one of the leading world powers and when her flag was flying in all parts of the globe. The comparison between that past and the present hexagonal reality makes them sadly aware of France's decline on the international stage.

> People say that all nations remain prisoners of the most glorious period of their history. Thus France cannot disengage herself from recollections of the *Roi-Soleil* or the image of a great nation who spread across Europe the then new symbols: liberty, equality, and fraternity.[73]

A French historian makes an almost identical statement:

> Politically, she [France] has not yet disengaged herself completely from the traditional criteria of military power and diplomatic prestige; this is costly and brings profits which are difficult to estimate. The wind of history that blew her sails turned away a long time ago. . . . France is "the smallest among the great powers and the biggest among the small powers."[74]

The quotation within the quotation is by one of the most distinguished French political scientists, Maurice Duverger. His view of the international weight of contemporary France is shared by the most sober of his countrymen. Others, however, have great nostalgia and find it difficult to accept the fact that France today is a great European power but no longer a leading world power. De Gaulle, whose policy of decolonization was a corollary and consequence of the decline in France's relative power in the world, is one of them. However, he himself provided one of the best descriptions of that decline of France in his *Memoirs*:

> At the beginning of the last century—quite recently, in historical terms—our country was the most populous in Europe, the strongest and richest in the world, with an influence unequaled. But disastrous causes had combined to drive it from this dominant position and to start it down a slope where each generation saw it stumble lower. Mutilated of the territories which nature intended her to have, grotesquely costumed in artificial frontiers, separated from a third of the population springing from her stock, France was living for a hundred and thirty years in a chronic state of infirmity, in-

security, and acrimony. While the capacity of the great nations depended chiefly on coal, France had virtually none. Subsequently, when petroleum controlled everything else, she had none. During the same period population doubled in England, tripled in Germany and in Italy, quadrupled in Russia, decupled in America; in France it remained stationary.[75]

A northern Frenchman, de Gaulle sometimes indulges in exaggerations which characterize a southern Frenchman. When he mentions that one-third of the French people live in other countries, he has in mind French-speaking Canadians, Swiss, and Belgians, who have no desire to become French citizens. Such flights of imagination disclose another aspect of his personality, which is far from pragmatic.

His lamentation over the decline of France overlooks the fact that France is not unique in this respect. Great powers have risen and fallen throughout international history. In Europe alone, Sweden, Denmark, Poland, Holland, and Spain all have been great powers at various periods. The two World Wars lowered the international status not only of France but also of Britain and Germany.

He is not the only Frenchman that finds it hard to accept the change in the relative rank of France: "One should not underestimate the importance of the feeling which is being kept alive in France by the recollection of having formerly played a great role which can no longer be played in exactly the same way."[76] He is not the only Frenchman who believes nevertheless that "France has the strength and the wish to have a great mission."[77] Nostalgia breeds ambition for equaling past greatness in a way commensurate with the present French potential. De Gaulle is in this respect the voice of a great many Frenchmen.

French influence has declined not only in politics but in culture as well.

> For several centuries France wielded a powerful instrument of [cultural] influence on foreign elites. But the evolution of societies and of international relations, owing to technical inventions, acceleration of production and trade related to industrial development and the birth of mass civilization with its quantitative aspects, has significantly altered the resonance of the French message.[78]

This change is clearly reflected in the reduced importance of the French language. In the seventeenth, eighteenth, and to some extent the nineteenth century, French was the primary foreign language spoken by the educated elites in Europe, which was at that time the center of the world. (It has since been replaced by English.)

Cultural superiority complex

However, many Frenchmen find consolation in the conviction that they are the most cultivated nation in the world. A perspicacious English commentator writes:

> It is obvious that France, caught since the war in between the two giants, fully realizes . . . that her relative weight in the world cannot be compared to what it was in the 18th or 19th century or even what it was in 1914, i.e., on the eve of the First World War. But this feeling of material inferiority goes hand in hand with a discreet but solidly rooted complex of intellectual superiority.[79]

This complex of cultural superiority, which compensates the relative decline in political power, is widespread among Frenchmen of all classes. Their national pride consists mainly in the conviction that other peoples are looking toward France for inspiration. A remarkable observer of the French scene writes: "The children . . . know that the French language is the language of Civilization and that Civilized People everywhere consider France as their second *patrie*."[80] Indoctrinated at school, Frenchmen are sure that "France was [and is] a pace-setter for the rest of the world."[81]

There is a legion of French writers who express this superiority complex in various ways. A few typical quotations will suffice:

> The [French] language is certainly among the richest and is the vehicle of incomparable philosophical thought and of poetry without peer; its political use is widespread, and its diplomatic prestige has not been impaired in spite of Anglo-Saxon attempts [to do so] at the United Nations.[82]
>
> The eyes of foreigners are turned toward the literary and artistic trends which are being born in France. This bold search and this critical spirit, always awake, belong to our tradition. One expects flares to be launched from France.[83]
>
> The French must be considered among the most beautiful human creatures; they are deeply human. . . . Those foreigners who have succeeded in discovering the man in French people are especially amazed to find this rare thing, a human being.[84]
>
> France is the freest country in the world.[85]
>
> We have legions of friends all over the world. What they ask from us is to become a model again in this unsettled world.[86]
>
> A nation that has invented freedom for citizens, the right of popular self-determination, and independence for nations.[87]

These quotations are selected from the writings of well-educated and in some cases distinguished authors, who this time have been deserted by their sense of humor and proportion. Other languages are rich too; other nations have produced a Dante, a Shakespeare, a Byron, a Goethe, a Pushkin, a Lermontov; there are other free countries; Frenchmen of the eighteenth century learned the meaning of political freedom from the English; French colonial rule was hardly compatible with the principle of self-determination; there are fine human beings all over the world; and the United States and the Soviet Union of today are much more the pace setters than France. Finally, an eminent Frenchman complained in 1956: "For twenty-one years we have not received a single Nobel prize in science."[88]

This complex of cultural superiority is a psychological device which allows Frenchmen to be reconciled with such unpleasant facts as the American and Russian outer-space exploits, the imposing power of these two countries, the long list of American Nobel prizewinners, the more advanced ways of life in the United States, or that Moscow but not Paris has been, since the October Revolution, a great center of a new ideology. A Frenchman whispers to himself: "After all, those Americans and Russians are half-barbarians, while we . . . ." This attitude does not help France find herself a new place in the world commensurate with her actual strength, which is not small at all.

A Swiss author remarks with rather cruel irony on

the claim of universality of French civilization, which wants to be considered simply as the civilization of mankind. It is conceded, however strange this fact, that there are peoples who are not French. But it is beyond the understanding of a good number of minds nourished by the best traditions that people who have a choice should refuse to become French and want to achieve human dignity in another way. . . . France has always been preoccupied exclusively with herself; this has been especially true at the time of the great trends in her life, when she believed that Christianity, the West, or mankind as a whole could be equated with herself. France has never known or understood the world except as a projection of herself.[89]

This ethnocentrism was the reason many Frenchmen were surprised to learn that Asians and Africans preferred to live their own independent lives rather than remain French subjects and enjoy the benefits of French civilization. However, Frenchmen of today have begun to travel widely, especially in Europe, and are gradually realizing that France is not the alpha and omega of mankind.

Other nations, of course, are narcissistic too. The French certainly do not understate their self-image:

> More cultivated than the American, less egocentric than the Englishman, more eclectic than other Europeans, the French newspaper reader (and listener) is certainly the one who is most interested in international life.[90]

> The Frenchman, they say, is the man of the happy medium. Refined rather than sturdy, polite rather than generous, he has more taste than many other people, but less passion. . . . These drawing-room conversationalists give principles to the world.[91]

> Our people which is one of the most educated politically. . . .[92]

> It [our political personnel] was superior on the average to American and even British political personnel.[93]

> The problem consisted in an irrevocable reconciliation between the two most gifted countries in the world, France and Germany.[94]

> France traditionally has been considered by the world to be the country of happiness.[95]

> This people is [allegedly] the most refined, the most intelligent, the most clearheaded in the world. Its teachers tell it that, by comparison, the Swiss is thickheaded, the Englishman is simple minded, the American is childlike.[96]

A group of French intellectuals provides the best comment:

> It is possible to think that Frenchmen are not the most refined, the most intelligent, etc. etc., people in the world; in fact, we are unable to understand the meaning of this sort of competition which has, in any event, no program, no examinations, and no jury. But it is equally possible to think that Frenchmen are not more stupid than other peoples.[97]

French national pride

Cassandra and the philosopher Pangloss seem to exist side by side in many Frenchmen. Cassandra bitterly denounces the true or imaginary shortcomings of French life, but Pangloss immediately replies that all is for the best in this best of possible worlds, France.

> The excellent quality of what is made in France is a dogma even in the eyes of those who say that everything is bad when they consider French achievements on their merits. This attitude, which consists in holding on the one hand that everything made in France is execrable, but on the other hand that the same things taken as a

whole are much superior to what is made abroad, also prevails regarding foreign policy.[98]

The France of these clichés is "a princess in the fairy tales." At this point de Gaulle meets his countrymen; there lies one of the reasons for his popularity. The patriotism of both de Gaulle and most other Frenchmen is nourished by these beliefs in French superiority of one kind or another. It becomes a patriotism of self-deception:

> Self-deception was fostered by the various Liberation governments to create the fiction of unanimous resistance to the Germans; in return for support they offered a general whitewash and Pétain and Laval as scapegoats. Since the self-deception could never be complete it became another source of humiliation, added to the crushing defeat of 1940, the continued presence of American troops, the colonial rebellions, the defeats in Indochina, the fund-raising trips which took Prime Ministers to Washington, the scandals affecting the faith the French had had in the justice and impartiality of the state apparatus.[99]

De Gaulle plays a contradictory role in this respect. He has fostered myths regarding the importance of the French contribution to the Allied victory in 1945; he has also partly eliminated the need for self-deception by giving Frenchmen reason to believe in themselves.

In any event, his appeals to French patriotism find echoes even among his opponents. For instance, President Johnson's criticism of his "obsolete and narrow" nationalism caused one of these opponents to come to de Gaulle's rescue:

> Nationalism may be defined (except in the U.S.S.R. and the United States) as a means of opposing the policy of blocs and resisting the hegemony of the power which dominates within either of these blocs. . . . The value of nationalism is incontrovertible: it is in a way the very expression of freedom. Whatever the differences in the forms and conditions, whatever the nature and extent of the hegemony, the struggles waged by the peoples of Asia and Africa against the colonialist states, by the people's democracies against the U.S.S.R., by the Latin-Americans and by France against the United States are one and the same. In relations between states of unequal strength, the nationalism of the stronger is an instrument of domination, while the nationalism of the others is a means of resisting domination. The former is by its nature autocratic; the latter may be called democratic to the extent that it helps to main-

tain a certain international pluralism. . . . Nationalism of the dominant state is by its nature more or less oppressive; nationalism of dominated states is more or less a factor of emancipation. . . . The resistance of the French government to the United States' efforts to dominate the Western world is not in itself either obsolete or regressive; the opposite is true. . . . For the time being, the docility of our neighbors regarding the United States is so pronounced that political integration with them could very well lead to dominance by Washington of the community thus established. Taking everything into consideration, a lonely "nay" is better than the alternative of its being strangled by five "yeses."[100]

This long quotation is taken from an article by Maurice Duverger, one of the most distinguished French intellectuals, who many times publicly opposed de Gaulle and whose orientation is toward the left. However, there is a striking similarity between his views and those of de Gaulle. This similarity is important, because it explains the qualified support that de Gaulle's foreign policy encounters in France, even among his domestic adversaries, and also because it indicates that his policy will not disappear with him. De Gaulle expresses something that exists in French minds.

Sentiments such as those expressed in the passage cited above are not rare in the world, particularly in France. The foreign critics who claim that there is not much difference between the American and Soviet aspirations to hegemony disbelieve claims from Washington that the United States is committed to stay in the Eastern Hemisphere to preserve the freedom of Europeans and Asians; instead they believe it is there to extend its dominion over foreign peoples.

The French author distinguishes between pure (democratic, liberating) and impure (hegemonic) nationalism. Unfortunately, international politics is not a contest in Christian virtue or a struggle between angels and devils. All nationalism is egoistic because it rests on the assumption that a given nation is supreme. All nations try to protect their interests and, if they can, extend their influence abroad. Some are more powerful and have greater means for achieving their ends, while others are less fortunate. One of de Gaulle's admirers frankly says: "What would de Gaulle's policy have been had he possessed the means of greatness— those of Soviet Russia or the United States? I dare not think."[101] He does not dare to speculate, but he knows well that de Gaulle's France, if she had the means, would establish a hegemony of her own. Is Chinese nationalism not carrying a new hegemony in its womb? Has President

Nasser not tried to impose his leadership on all Arabs? Did President Nkrumah not aspire to dominate sub-Saharan Africa by becoming its guide and hero?

However, the fact remains that the anti-Gaullist Duverger also sees the world dominated by the two hegemonies which are being opposed by the liberating struggle of all other peoples who form in this sense a sort of Third Force. France is on the side of the angels in her opposition to the American hegemony. Should she become the leader of the "democratic nationalists"? This question is neither asked nor answered by the French author. Her mission to fight the battle of liberation is so important that he frankly prefers not to have a politically united Western Europe if it were subservient to the United States; he wants to preserve French freedom to say no to the American hegemon. All this is almost pure Gaullism, but the Gaullism of an anti-Gaullist.

Anti-Americanism

The above quotation is not at all sympathetic to the United States. In this respect it typifies the feelings of many Frenchmen. Their patriotism today is colored by anti-Americanism, as for many past decades it was colored by a strong Germanophobia. Perhaps every nationalism needs a *bête noire* to strengthen its sense of unity and identity. In any event, Americans are not popular in France for several reasons.

First, the former relationship between France and the United States has been dramatically reversed. In the nineteenth century Americans were regarded as distant rural relatives, uncultivated, ill mannered, simple minded, but tolerated with a condescending smile. The United States did not play any role in European politics; it belonged, as de Gaulle says, to a different world. Today the same country is the greatest world power, prosperous and incessantly projecting itself as the leader of the "free world." France's power has declined. One does not like a "poor relation" suddenly to become richer and more influential than oneself. This factor of envy is undeniable.

Second, the so-called American civilization is simply the model of a contemporary industrial mass society. This model was built in the United States, which has become in this respect the pace setter for the world. The American way of life fascinates the Russians, who admit it indirectly when they say that they are engaged in economic competition with the United States, as it also fascinates the developing countries, which want to become modern, and the Western Europeans insofar as they are adjusting to the requirements of our age. This process of readjustment is more difficult in France, because prior to the last war she was economically stagnant. The modernization (one is tempted to say Americanization) of the French way of life is visible to all visitors. Frenchmen may feel proud of their rapid pace of modernization, but the rupture with old habits is painful. Older Frenchmen especially feel nostalgia for the time when they could fully enjoy the pleasures of life in a France geared to a leisurely pace. Tension caused by the rapidity of transformation and nostalgia for the France that was generate in the French a subconscious resentment against the model for modernization, the United States. A French intellectual expressed the feelings of many of his countrymen when he said: "It must be said and written that there is only one immediate threat to Europe. It is American civilization."[102]

Third, Frenchmen resent the heavy debt of gratitude they owe the United States. In this respect they are simply human. Gratitude is the rarest virtue. One dislikes one's benefactor, for it is distasteful to feel indebted. A French author recalls an old comedy in which the hero prefers to bestow the hand of his daughter on a boy he saved rather than on another young man who saved him. "Likewise, many Frenchmen like the United States because of Lafayette and resent that country because of the Marshall Plan."[103] The debt is indeed too heavy. One need only read the pathetic dispatches sent in August and September 1918 by German headquarters to the Imperial government in Berlin to discover the reason why the German military chiefs were begging their government to open negotiations with the Allies for an armistice: they feared that America ultimately would be decisive in defeating Germany. While the American contribution in human blood was relatively light by comparison to the French and British hecatombs, the Allies and the Germans exhausted their human reserves; the United States could send division after division to Europe, and American industries were essential for Allied armaments. American entry into the war was largely responsible for Germany's demise. In 1918 neither the Allies nor the Germans could win the war, but the Allies, reinforced by the United States, were able to impose their conditions of peace on the dejected Germans. France would be ruled today by a German *Gauleiter,* if she had not been liberated in consequence of enormous war effort by the United States, the Soviet Union, and Britain.

Fourth, after the last war the European Continent lay defenseless and probably would have been occupied by Soviet troops had it not been for American protection.

Fifth, France was one of the principal beneficiaries of the Marshall Plan, which contributed substantially to strengthening her. "Between April 1948 and November 1951, France received two and a half billion dollars."[104]

One could add the generosity of wealthy Americans, who did so much in helping, for instance, to restore French historical monuments. The debt is indeed too heavy. This is one of the reasons why, in the words of some Frenchmen, "the United States irritates us."[105] In all fairness, one should say that this French reaction is not exceptional. After all, Americans did not display much gratitude for France's contribution to victory in the War of Independence. Human frailty is the same in Paris and in Washington.*

Search for a place in the world

France is searching for her new place in international society. She does not yet know what this place should be. Past glories haunt her and increase her ambition. De Gaulle whets the appetite. She knows that she is not relatively so strong as she was in 1914 or even in 1939, but she also feels an accretion of strength due to her dynamic economic development and her demographic rejuvenation. This search for an appropriate place among other nations is made more difficult by the contrast between the realities of her recent past and the myths which now surround the events of the last war. Was she defeated or was she one of the principal victors? This question is deeply buried in French hearts. In this respect de Gaulle plays a dual role. With psychological insight, he restores the self-confidence of his countrymen by cultivating myths about France's contribution to the Allied victory. The thick veil of his myths prevents Frenchmen from looking rationally at their war record. The resulting confusion does not help in finding a place which is really due France.

The search for France's place in the international community began in the aftermath of the First World War.

> France is victorious in 1918 and feels, with good reason, that she was the true artisan of victory, but she does not sufficiently realize that she would have been unable to win alone. She does not realize, moreover, that the victory was for her a Pyrrhic victory. The effort was excessive, the human losses will hardly be replaced, and the economy of the country has been shattered to its foundations. The mood is that of a deceptive euphoria, while an austere rehabilitation is necessary.[106]

It was indeed a Pyrrhic victory. Threatened with depopulation, France lost 1,322,000 men during those four years of desperate fighting. Those men were young or middle-aged; many of them were promising intellectuals. The northeast of France was devastated. A large portion of invest-

* Anti-Americanism is discussed further in the following chapters.

ments abroad was either used in exchange for military supplies from the United States or confiscated in Russia by the Bolshevik government. France was exhausted by her war effort, which was truly heroic, and she preferred not to think that even that effort, beyond her true capacity, would not have been sufficient for winning victory. The fact that a French general commanded all the Allied troops blurred French eyes to the Allied nature of the victory over an enemy who had defeated France singlehandedly in 1870–71 and would have defeated her again had France not been supported by a vast coalition. "The price paid for victory in 1918 was excessively high. The extreme tension and effort to reach a level already lost and to surpass it shattered the moral strength of the country."[107]

For a few years victorious France seemed to be the dominant power on the Continent. Germany was defeated, Austria-Hungary disintegrated, and Russia for a time lost her rank of great power due to her own losses in the First World War, the civil war and foreign intervention, and Bolshevik experimentation. France had the strongest army and the support of her Eastern European allies.

The euphoria did not last long. Germany was gradually regaining her place. A decade after her defeat it was clear that she would again become the strongest European power, and Frenchmen were confused as to the policy to adopt toward their former enemy. Should they try to make concessions in order to find a stable *modus vivendi* with Germany, or should they persist in protecting the fruits of their hard-won victory and stubbornly defend the Treaty of Versailles by attempting to form a ring of anti-German states? They tried to follow both roads. Reconciliation was attempted with the Weimar Republic and with Nazi Germany, but France was reluctant to pay the price, which would have required radical departures from the *status quo* established by the Treaty of Versailles. Her efforts to muster Italian support were fruitless because she was unwilling to satisfy the ambitions of Italy's Fascist government. Her alliances with Eastern Europe required, as de Gaulle understood, an army prepared for offensive operations in case an Eastern European ally were attacked by Germany. Her generals adopted the opposite strategy of the defensive buttressed by the Maginot Line of fortifications. In effect, France had no foreign policy in spite of feverish diplomatic activities.

1940 to 1942 and its providential man

The day of retribution came after Hitler had seized power in Germany. Suddenly Frenchmen understood that they were facing the former enemy as strong as it was in 1914 but that they themselves were weaker. The old fighting spirit was gone. A new war with Germany did not seem to have much sense. Was it not true that the fruits of victory in 1918, paid for by human hecatombs, were dissipated, while the former Allies looked indifferently at the crumbling Treaty of Versailles?

France elected to retreat before Hitler. In 1935 she accepted the open rearmament of Germany, in 1936 the remilitarization of the left bank of the Rhine, in 1938 the annexation of Austria. In the fall of 1938 came the crucial test. At Munich France abandoned her most faithful ally, Czechoslovakia; Britain at least had no obligations of alliance. Both powers immolated the little Central European democracy on the altar of "peace in our time." The French Prime Minister at the time, Edouard Daladier, became the hero for a few weeks. "France saluted Munich with a sigh of immense relief."[108]

Men who could not be suspected of lack of patriotism or of pro-Nazi sympathies joined in the chorus of praise. The Socialist leader, Léon Blum, wrote on September 29, 1938: "There is not a single man or woman in France who would refuse Mr. Daladier a deserved tribute of gratitude."[109] The future chairman of the Council of French Resistance, Georges Bidault, exclaimed at that time: "Hope has revived. . . . We can breathe again."[110]

The short-lived joy of relief was bought at the price of infidelity to a solemn contract with Czechoslovakia. This breach of international agreement and another in 1940, when France concluded a separate armistice in spite of no less solemn obligations toward Britain and Poland, explain the melancholic remark made by the French Prime Minister, Georges Pompidou, on May 14, 1964, in a speech addressed to the Foreign Press Association in Paris: "We ourselves proved in the past that we sometimes recoiled before the prospect of implementing our commitments."[111]

France entered the Second World War reluctantly. She did it under British pressure, but "the dominant idea in September 1939 was: 'The First World War accomplished nothing.' "[112] The prevailing mood from 1939 to 1940 is aptly depicted in these words:

> The nation refuses to fight the war . . . , not to suffer, not to face privations. . . . If it [the defeat] were not inflicted in June by arms, it would have been the consequence a few months later of the national refusal to wage war.[113]

The crushing defeat, which followed several months of "phony war," was the result not only of superior German armaments and strategy but also of French unwillingness to resist the enemy onslaught strongly. This was the first such defeat in French history; for the first time, Frenchmen refused to sacrifice their lives in defense of their native soil.

The spectacle of May and June 1940 was most lamentable. A French writer says: "Millions of refugees on the roads, an army assumed to be invincible in full disintegration after a few days of smashing blows from the enemy, 1,500,000 prisoners of war."[114] Another Frenchman writes of "the spectacle of the material, intellectual, and moral confusion into which the whole people was plunged."[115] Half of the French army were made prisoners of war. On June 12 the President of the Republic expressed his amazement at seeing French soldiers fleeing along the roads leading toward the South, while there were not enough combatants at the front.[116] On June 17 the commander-in-chief, General Maxime Weygand, was told by his field generals that entire regiments were refusing to fight.[117] Lenin said in 1917 that the Russian soldiers were voting for peace with their feet. The same could have been said of the French soldiers deserting the front or surrendering to the advancing Germans.

The French myth began in that summer of 1940. General Weygand rather shamelessly told the French government on June 12 that the "heroic resistance" by the Army had saved the honor of France and that an armistice could now be asked for.[118]

The soldiers were refusing to fight, the population wanted peace, and the political and military elites were seized by panic. Marshal Foch said: "One is vanquished only when one admits defeat."[119] France eagerly confessed to her defeat. The generals and admirals were the first to do so. Under their pressure the decision was made to beg Germany for an armistice. On the same day, June 17, Marshal Pétain offered a myth to his unhappy country which was witnessing "a catastrophe the most complete and the most humiliating of its history."[120] In his first message as the head of the government he told his countrymen:

> I feel sure I have the affection of our admirable Army, which fights with a heroism worthy of its long military tradition against an enemy superior in numbers and in armament. I feel sure that it has fulfilled our duty in regard to our Allies by its magnificent resistance. . . . Tonight I have addressed myself to the adversary to ask him whether he is ready to seek with us, as between soldiers, honorable means to terminate hostilities.[121]

The old Marshal was thus instilling in Frenchmen a new habit of covering up unpleasant realities with myths. He was talking about the honor and the heroic resistance of an Army which was disintegrating. Yet he knew the facts; he also knew that his generals, including the commander-in-chief, were opposed to the plan for continuing the struggle from the bases in the colonial empire, for transporting the seat of government to North Africa, and for a simple cease-fire in France by the capitulation of the armies. A few days earlier General Weygand himself had told the Prime Minister, Paul Reynaud, that the capitulation of the army in France would have dishonored it, but he begged for an armistice, i.e., the complete cessation of hostilities both in France and from the colonial bases, and for official governmental recognition of the defeat as an irreversible fact; the capitulation of France herself did not dishonor his country, according to Weygand, so intent on protecting military honor only.[122]

Frenchmen at that time were not thinking of the honor of the Army or of the country; they wanted only one thing: peace! Marshal Pétain determined on fulfilling this wish, although the colonial governors of Algeria, Tunisia, Morocco, French Western and Equatorial Africa, Madagascar, and Indochina simultaneously informed him that they were ready to continue the struggle, if France were to be occupied by the Germans.[123] The Marshal was in France and knew the deep aspirations of the population. In June 1940 Frenchmen were fully aware of the cruelties of the Nazi occupation in Poland; they wanted to escape Poland's fate. Hoping she could buy Hitler's leniency by laying down her arms, France surrendered. In June 1940 Pétain represented "the only hope of the quasi-unanimous country which was going to entrust its fate to him at the time of its worst ordeal."[124]

He was the providential man on whose shoulders Frenchmen were discharging the burden of governing the defeated country. The majority of the political elite of the Third Republic rallied around him. The National Assembly (the Senate and the Chamber of Deputies sitting together) voted by an imposing majority for full powers to be given to Pétain, including the right to enact a new constitution. Five hundred and sixty-nine senators and deputies voted yes; only 80 had the courage to cast nay votes; and 17 abstained. The aye votes included the Socialists, the Radicals, and the Liberal Conservatives. Actually 80 out of 116 Socialist representatives endorsed this abdication of the Third Republic, although they knew that Marshal Pétain did not nourish any sympathy for a democratic regime.[125] Pierre Cot, at that time a young promising moderate leftist politician and since the last war an extreme leftist, expressed the prevailing opinion when he allegedly said that Pétain was the only man capable of saving France.[126]

The impulse to entrust France to a providential man in an hour of crisis is best reflected in the attitude of François Mauriac. He exclaimed in 1940: "The words of Marshal Pétain sounded on that night of June 25 [1940] almost like the voice of eternity." Eight years later he wrote: "General [de Gaulle] . . . remains today what he was since our collapse and until our liberation—a voice of eternity."[127] Most Frenchmen agreed with him both in the summer of 1940 and in May–June 1958, although not in 1948.

The history of France from 1940 to 1945 cannot be understood without reference to those two providential men, both of whom expressed the deep wishes of their country and served it. Marshal Pétain obtained peace in 1940 and protected France from the worst excesses of the Nazis by his policy of collaboration. His merit was to save his countrymen from the fate that befell other occupied nations. De Gaulle created the fiction of a France that never surrendered and that continued to fight alongside the Allies. It was his merit to ensure for his country the place of a victorious power in spite of 1940. Frenchmen should be grateful to both of them.

In 1940 the old Marshal was the legitimate spokesman of his nation. It was he, not de Gaulle, who voiced the national sentiment by asking for an armistice. "The immense rallying of support for Marshal Pétain in 1940"[128] provided the proof. All this was too easily forgotten in 1945 when the Marshal was convicted of treason, a scapegoat for the French eagerness in accepting the defeat.

The true French sentiments in 1940 are depicted in these words: "De Gaulle's appeal evokes no response. . . . The country crushed by the defeat asks for peace. . . . It refuses to follow de Gaulle. . . . Pétain . . . unquestionably represents the great majority in the country."[129]

French commentators usually agree with this opinion of one of them: "In June 1940 only an infinitesimal minority of the French people understood or even heard this appeal [de Gaulle's]. It was a time when, in the general chaos, Frenchmen were rallying to Marshal Pétain. . . . Nobody in France knew de Gaulle."[130] Even in November 1942, at a time when dark clouds began to appear on the German horizon, the total of Free Frenchmen in England amounted to only 70,000.

It is not even certain whether Pétain lost his popularity completely after the German occupation of southern France in November 1942. A French historian of occupied France describes in the following words the Marshal's visit to Paris in April 1944: "As soon as the population heard of his arrival, it was eager to arrange an enthusiastic reception for him. The official ceremony took place at Notre Dame. . . . After Mass, Pétain returned to City Hall among ovations. He made a speech from the balcony of that building, facing an immense multitude which was acclaiming him."[131] The same historian continues: "The enthusiastic reception given to the Marshal on the occasion of his last visits to French cities . . . proved that his personal prestige had survived the failure of his policy."[132]

The fidelity of the Army and the Navy to the Marshal bears the mark of utter political folly. They were ready to fight the Allies, who, after all, were engaged in the struggle against the country occupying France, rather than to disobey his orders. The British-Free French expedition sent to occupy Dakar was repulsed in September 1940 with heavy losses inflicted by the French garrison and fleet. After that failure de Gaulle did not obtain the support of any French colony except when Allied successes left no other option to the French commanders and governors. In 1941 the Vichy authorities in Syria and Lebanon were assisting the Germans who planned to occupy the Near East; after the military defeat of the French troops by the joint forces of the British and the Free French, only 127 French officers and 6,000 N.C.O.'s and privates rallied to de Gaulle; 25,000 officers and soldiers asked to be repatriated to France.[133]

The American-British landing in North Africa provided the most fantastic illustration of that political folly. The Germans responded by violating the terms of the 1940 armistice and by occupying the part of France which had been left free. Marshal Pétain became virtually a German prisoner. However, the French officers chose to fight the Americans and the Britishers, whose victory was the only hope for the liberation of France, and did not oppose any resistance to the German troops advancing toward the southern shores of France.

Following the orders of Marshal Pétain, at that time a decrepit old man, French armed forces in North Africa met the landing Americans and Britishers with fire. Several French ships were sunk and thousands of Frenchmen were killed in that senseless attempt at opposing the Allied landing. Eventually, Admiral Darlan disobeyed the Marshal's orders and stopped the French resistance to the first major Allied step toward the liberation of France! The French authorities in Tunisia in the meantime assisted the German landing and delivered to the Germans the naval base and fleet at Bizerte. The Germans thus acquired a foothold in French North Africa. This added six months to the time required by the Allies to expel the Axis Powers from Africa. The French vessels in Bizerte were later used by the Germans in their own naval operations.

French land and naval forces in France were confronted in November 1942 with advancing German troops. The fleet anchored in Toulon had plenty of time to escape and join the American-British fleets engaged in the North African operations. The French-German armistice was broken by the Germans. However, the French admiral preferred to wait until the last moment when the German troops were entering Toulon and then ordered his whole fleet to be scuttled. One battleship, five cruisers, an aircraft carrier, and thirteen destroyers were sunk, although they would have been an important contribution to the Allied liberation of France.

> As to the Army of the armistice, it had closeted itself fifteen days before in its barracks, having renounced . . . any intention to resist. On that night of November 27, when the Germans were rushing to assault the barracks, soldiers were in their beds and the officers at their homes downtown. It was child's play for the aggressor to throw out the disarmed French soldiers dressed only in nightshirts and seize their arms.[134]

Only one French commander, the future Marshal de Lattre de Tassigny, dared to disobey Pétain's orders; next day he was confined to the military prison in Toulouse. The French Army of the armistice was, however, one hundred men strong and able to make at least a show of resistance.

French officers, fighting the Allies and meekly surrendering to the Germans or even actively helping them as in Syria and in Tunisia, acted in utter disregard of common sense. In June 1940 obedience to Marshal Pétain could be excused, but in the fall of 1942 it was political folly.

Myth of France's great part in the Allied victory

After German occupation of the whole French territory, the French Resistance movement truly began. Its ranks were increased by the German error of conscripting young Frenchmen for labor in Germany. Many preferred to join the armed Resistance groups rather than leave their country. Another myth was born. The extent of French resistance was exaggerated after the war to create the image of a France that had never surrendered.

The following figures, supplied by a French historian, depict the real scope of resistance. His figures for the total of Frenchmen that died during the last war are revealing:[135]

Total	618,000
Those killed in the 1939–1940 campaign	92,000
The losses of Free-French (1940–1945)	58,000
Those killed in the Resistance	24,000
French volunteers and Alsatian conscripts killed on the Eastern Front in fighting against Russia	38,000
Deaths in the camps of prisoners-of-war in Germany	43,000
Deaths among the political deportees, French Jews, and French workers in Germany	200,000
Frenchmen executed by the Germans	30,000
Civilian victims of military operations, half of them killed in the Allied bombings	133,000

The highest figure, 200,000, includes the defenseless Jews, deported by the Germans often with the cooperation of French collaborators. More Frenchmen (either volunteers or conscripts from German-annexed Alsace) were killed by the Soviet troops than Resistance fighters by the Germans. The second largest figure is that of French civilians, passive victims of military operations. The low figures for those killed during the 1939–40 campaign as well as among the Free French and the Resistance fighters speak for themselves. They stand in flagrant contrast to 20 million Russians and 6 million Poles whom the Nazis slaughtered. The French commentator does not distort the truth while writing:

> The small share in the victory brought the humiliation of not having a really satisfactory revenge. . . . It would obviously be unjust to compare the sufferings of the French under the occupation with that of other countries, notably Poland, which lost 6 million lives. . . . Famine in France was never as great as in Greece, for example. . . . Of 620,000 victims of World War II, more than half were victims of the occupation or of the Allied bombings.[136]

The total number of French Resistance fighters armed by the Allies at the time of liberation amounted to 140,000 men and women.[137] This is not an imposing figure for a population of 40 million. It is understandable that

> the celebrations of the Allies' triumph on May 8, 1945, did not have the same air of enthusiasm as those of November 11, 1918. The French celebrated the German capitulation on this beautiful May day in a cheerless atmosphere. So the catastrophe as a whole had caused the crumbling of much of the tradition—of confidence in diplomacy and in the army, of the mistaken belief that liberty could be taken for granted, even of the idea that France was a great nation of the first rank. The French came out of the trial very bitter, also exhausted, ruined, weakened.[138]

The myths came to their rescue. Frenchmen who patiently bore the enemy occupation, those who refused to fight the Nazis, and those who collaborated with them were glad to find exculpation in a myth—"the myth, which the Resistance men gladly endorsed, that almost all of France was *résistante* in 1944."[139] Pétain, Laval, and a number of others became the scapegoats on the altar of this myth.

Another comforting myth was the allegedly important French contribution to the Allied military operations in 1944–45. The Allied landing in Normandy was effected with the support of one Free French company of

180 men. The Allied fleet included two Free French cruisers and one destroyer. One hundred Free French planes participated in the air assault on Hitler's European Fortress, while the total Allied armada numbered 9,000 planes.[140] The Free French division of General Koenig disembarked in Normandy only on August 1. France was not liberated by her own decisive contribution to the Allied war effort.

The end of the German occupation of Paris gave birth to another myth. In August 1944 (on the eve of the liberation of Paris) the French Resistance groups in Paris did not have enough weapons for their men.[141] These groups and the 3,000 Parisian policemen would have been no match for the German Army; their revolt would have ended as tragically as the Warsaw uprising. The merit of the liberation of the French capital was shared by the Allied troops pushing back the retreating Germans and the German commander, General von Choltitz, who refused to execute Hitler's order to destroy the city, giving it back to Frenchmen intact at the cost of a face-saving and desultory fight. The week of fighting inside Paris must not have been a week of cruel battles, judged by the cost of it: the city was undamaged, and according to the official figures, 901 French fighters, 582 passive civilians, and 2,788 Germans were killed; 1,455 French combatants, 2,012 civilians, and 4,911 Germans were wounded.[142] These figures include the last day of fighting when the Free French armored division entered Paris and finally cleared it of the last remnants of the German garrison (those who had not been evacuated on time).

Toward the end of the war French troops, including the colonial regiments, amounted to 10 per cent of the Anglo-American armies in Europe;[143] they could fight only because they had been armed by the United States. Was France eager in 1944–45 to join the battle? "A decree of August 23, 1944, which had ordered the acceptance of enlistment for the duration of the war by the F. F. I. [the Resistance movement] who desired to continue to fight, caused mass desertions in several F. F. I. units. On the average, the F. F. I. units then lost 35 per cent of their men."[144] De Gaulle admitted in his *Memoirs* that the French people were not in a fighting spirit. He wrote:

> There was much to be desired. Not that the French people were theoretically unaware of the merits of the men fighting in its service! But the latter too often seemed remote and almost alien to them. For many, the liberation meant the war's end, and what happened afterwards in the realm of arms offered no immediate interest.

He added an extract from a significant report received from the general commanding the French troops in Germany, de Lattre de Tassigny:

"From one end of the hierarchy to the other, particularly among the officers," the general wrote, "the impression is widespread that the nation has neglected, has abandoned us. . . . The real source of this problem is the nation's non-participation in the war."[145]

It was necessary to forge myths in order to revive the French spirit. De Gaulle undertook this task eagerly. France never accepted defeat; it fiercely resisted the invader and finally made a crucial contribution to the Allied victory. From his return to France in 1944 to the present day he has never tired of telling Frenchmen these fairy tales, which they may not believe but which they gladly listen to because these tales restore their confidence in themselves, let them forget the most painful chapter in French history, and flatter their pride. In June 1944 he visited a liberated town in Normandy and made his first speech on the free soil of France. He told his Normandy countrymen, among whom there was hardly any Resistance movement: "The country expects from you, who live behind the battle front, to continue today the struggle you have never stopped waging since the beginning of this war and since June 1940."[146] A French historian adds an ironical comment: "To tell this peaceful population, not unhappy in spite of the [enemy] occupation, that they never stopped fighting since June 1940—that was something that, under different circumstances, would have evoked a smile on the lips of those good Normans."[147]

Then and there de Gaulle began trying to cure Frenchmen of the inferiority complex implanted in them by the events of the Second World War. Believing that eternal France was incarnated in him, he felt that she never had abandoned the struggle, whatever the "ephemeral Frenchmen" might have done. Frenchmen eagerly adopted him as the symbol of what they would have liked to be. Yet he himself notes in his *Memoirs* that the German field-marshal, Wilhelm Keitel, exclaimed at the time of the signature of the German unconditional surrender in Berlin, when he discovered a French general ready to appose his signature beside those of the American, British, and Russian generals: "What? The French too!"[148] Keitel was not alone in expressing his amazement.

The myth of victorious France could appear plausible because of the British effort to ensure France the rank of one of the four great powers. At that time Britain feared quick American withdrawal and being left alone in Soviet company. France was needed diplomatically. Over American and Soviet resistance at the Yalta conference, Churchill obtained recognition of France as one of the four big victors.

France, which was not invited, obtained, however, at that conference most essential privileges: an occupation zone and a seat on the

Control Council which was to administer Germany provisionally. . . .
At the same time, France was invited to take part in the preparation
of a world conference which was to establish an "organization of the
United Nations." This latter decision ensured France a place as one
of the five permanent members of the Security Council which was to
become the principal body of the United Nations. . . . The balance
sheet of the [Yalta] conference was, therefore, remarkably advantageous for French interests.[149]

What Churchill did for France at Yalta, de Gaulle and the French government would not have been able to achieve alone.

De Gaulle has never felt grateful for this unexpected gift of the rank of
one of the five great powers at the United Nations and one of the four
victorious occupying powers in Germany. He resented the fact that he
had not been invited to Yalta, and gratitude is not his outstanding virtue.
Moreover, he accepted the gift as something due to France. His reaction
was characteristic:

> If we were invited to become, at once, a member of the council
> formed by the great powers to settle the fate of our enemies and to
> organize the peace, it was because we were regarded as one of the
> chief belligerent—and, shortly, victorious—powers. In world poli-
> tics, soon nothing would remain of the conquered-nation status
> which France had appeared to stoop to.[150]

The Yalta decision by the Allies greatly helped him implant the myth of
victorious France.

This myth was preserved by the Fourth Republic:

> The Fourth Republic did not want General de Gaulle's authority,
> but it could not dispense with his myth. It is only in his person that
> France never laid down her arms, never stopped to wage the war,
> and finally won it. Frenchmen substituted, for the period of four
> years charged with history, the name of General de Gaulle for that
> of France. This was done to enable them to forget the past and to
> begin their life again as though nothing had happened. One wonders
> whether this myth was not more harmful than beneficial for France,
> and whether it was not at the origin of the unreality and the lie which
> presided over the start of her new life.[151]

In any event, the myth has not helped Frenchmen find their place in
international life. Do they believe a fervent Gaullist who wrote recently:
"Gaullism shared with the great Allies the responsibility and the initiative
[*sic*] of victory?"[152]

The artisan of the myth has never abandoned his efforts to persuade his countrymen of its truth. In his first speech in liberated Paris, in August 1944, he exclaimed: "Why should we conceal the emotion which grips us all, men and women, who are assembled here, on our soil, in Paris, the city that rose up to liberate itself and did so by its own effort?"[153] On November 23, 1961, he addressed two thousand French officers assembled in Strasbourg; referring to the liberation of that city by a French division, he said: "This resounding success won by one of our armored units made up, to a certain extent, for the disaster which we had suffered before."[154] It is doubtful whether the Parisians in 1944 could really believe that they liberated themselves only by their own efforts, or that the French officers in 1961 were so credulous as to accept the legend of the liberation of Strasbourg as a compensation for the rout in 1940. Probably they recalled that the British-American troops were, after all, defeating the Germans around both Paris and Strasbourg.

Nineteen hundred and sixty-four was the twentieth anniversary of the Allied landings in France. De Gaulle refused to take part in the celebrations in commemoration of the Normandy landing; he could hardly say there that Normandy was liberated by Frenchmen alone. Instead he went to Toulon to celebrate the landing on August 15, 1944, on the southern coast of France, where an entire French corps was supporting the American forces. That landing was only of a supplementary nature, intended to distract German attention from the main Allied attack in the North. The Germans did not oppose a very stiff resistance, fearing to be caught in a pincer movement. Addressing his countrymen on that anniversary, de Gaulle said: "The fifteenth of August marked a decisive [sic] date in the vast military enterprise which the coalition had undertaken since June 6, 1944, in order to break down the power of the German Third Reich in Europe."[155] In his interpretation, that landing seemed to eclipse the battle of Stalingrad, the invasion of North Africa, the conquest of Italy, and the Normandy landing. The reason was simple: French armed forces played a different role there than in other Allied operations. The legend acquired gigantic dimensions.

Whom did Frenchmen have to believe? The Gaullist myth was denied any validity a long time ago by a patriotic Frenchman who wrote: "But, in spite of our braggadocio, we know perfectly well that we did not liberate ourselves by our own effort."[156] Recently a French historian also had the courage to speak the truth:

> France came out of the Second World War as she had done after the First World War, i.e., in the company of victors, but bled at a time when she was going through a demographic crisis, her resources

looted as never before, morally divided by the Vichy experience, her leading personnel decimated by the purge. General de Gaulle's obstinacy had triumphed, because France was again associated with the "Big." . . . Frenchmen quickly recovered the habit of considering their country a great world power. Had they the required means for that rank?[157]

Let us terminate this story of the French war record from 1939 to 1945, a story which must be recalled if one wants to understand both de Gaulle's prestige among his countrymen and their own confusion regarding the place due France, by this quotation from a book written by a Swiss:

Came the liberation by the Allies. A small minority had fought for it, a gradually growing minority had expected it, but, when it came, it was a gift from heaven for the great majority. The liberation exceeded all former hopes, brought the prestige of national victory, and renewed all the possibilities for self-flattery and for glorious delusions. The nightmare had disappeared. There was no 1940, no defeat, no collapse. But the shadow . . . has remained.[158]

III The Nuclear Deterrent Against Whom?

A word of caution

De Gaulle's military upbringing left a mark on his philosophy of international politics. In 1932, while still a professional officer, he wrote in his *Le Fil de l'Epée*: "Cradle of cities, scepter of empires, gravedigger of decadence, force makes law to peoples and determines their destinies."[1] No one could deny the great role that force has played in political history, but did de Gaulle not underestimate the importance of ideas? Was it force alone that determined the success of Christianity, of Islam, or, in our own time, of Communist ideology? Was the ultimate victory of the principles of the French Revolution ensured by force? These principles finally conquered Europe only after Waterloo. Even de Gaulle's own power in France does not rest on force.

Twenty-seven years later, a much older and wiser de Gaulle evoked, in a less exalting manner, the importance of military power in his address to the French officers on November 3, 1959: "The glory of a statesman has never been great if it was not gilded by the splendor of national defense."[2] This is his own ambition. A man who was never commander in chief of the French armies and who won his military laurels in the capacity of a young officer during the First World War and of a brigadier general during the French campaign in 1940, de Gaulle now seeks to be remembered for having modernized the French armed forces and having provided them with the most lethal weapons.

He might modify his other objectives, if circumstances were to compel him to do so, but one may be sure that he will never abandon his program of nuclear armament. Implementation of this program is so advanced that it is doubtful that his political opponents, who are tireless in criticizing his nuclear policy and clamor for its cancellation, would carry out their promises and threats if they came to power.[3] The British example is very instructive in this respect. The Labour party, as an opposition party, called for termination of British nuclear armament; but the Labour government is now in power and demonstrates no eagerness to implement this electoral promise.

The debate over a French nuclear force, which has been going on for the past few years, has been obscured by several factors. An American or a British critic might be influenced by his own national interests; his views might be vitiated by lack of objectivity. In France herself de Gaulle's opponents seized upon the nuclear issue as one of the main weapons in their struggle against his personal power. Yet those domestic opponents (vocal in all political parties) were responsible for the policies of the Fourth Republic, which took the first steps toward nuclear armanent. Only the Communists have consistently opposed nuclear armament under both Republics. As far as the other parties are concerned, the sincerity of their opposition to de Gaulle's nuclear policy is open to question. Some politicians are truly against the national nuclear force, while they favor French participation in a European (seldom in Atlantic) force. The others are fighting de Gaulle more than his nuclear program.

The debate is also vitiated by unknown factors. Will the French nuclear force always be obsolete because of rapid scientific progress in both the United States and the Soviet Union? Will the cost of nuclear armaments eventually prevent France from remaining in the race? Will it ruin the French economy? Probably no one can answer these questions with certainty. The nature of future scientific and technological progress cannot be predicted; hence the nature of weapons of mass destruction might change radically or might not change at all. The future cost of these weapons might grow at an alarming pace, or scientific-technological progress might reduce it. Will several other nations acquire nuclear weapons, and, if so, will these weapons become a "standard" part of modern armaments? There are too many unknowns involved to be sure whether de Gaulle is right or wrong.

His views should not be dismissed lightly for another reason. During his military career he was never inclined toward routine, doctrinaire military strategy. Both before and after the Second World War he paid due attention to the impact of scientific-technological progress on strategy and tactics. He has never proposed fighting the next war according to the patterns of the last. On November 3, 1959 he told French officers: "Military action is always contingent, i.e., it is always confronted with unexpected developments, is liable to an infinite number of variations, and never has any precedents."[4]

The cautious approach to this problem consists in listening calmly to all the arguments and in suspending judgment as to the wisdom or folly of de Gaulle's nuclear policy.

Independent French defense

De Gaulle's national pride cannot tolerate a situation in which the security of France depends on protection by a foreign power. He is also skeptical about the total reliability of such protection. France must, therefore, have her own credible nuclear deterrent in order to be both independent of the United States and capable of dissuading a potential aggressor. As soon as he got rid of the burden of Algerian war, he declared on May 15, 1962, that it was necessary

> to coordinate the creation of a modern national force with our scientific, technical, economic, and social progress in order that— within the framework of a necessary alliance and in the hope of an international relaxation of tension—we should be able, whatever happens, to play our own part in our destiny.[5]

At that and other times he insisted, however, on the necessity of maintaining the Atlantic Alliance, as another guaranty of French security. But his guiding axiom is: "The defense of France must be French."[6]

The same concept of French security ensured by a national nuclear force and by alliance with the United States is reflected in a statement he made on January 14, 1963:

> In any case I repeat, after having said it often, that France intends to have her own national defense. It is obvious that no country, in particular a country such as ours, can in the present day and age wage a modern world war by itself. To have allies goes without saying for us in the historic period we live in. But also for a great people the free determination of its destiny and the possession of means to preserve this self-determination are an absolute imperative, because alliances have no absolute virtues, whatever may be the sentiments on which they rest.[7]

France must have her own nuclear deterrent, because the American guaranty, necessary as it is, is not foolproof. De Gaulle has deduced this from the history of alliances, which, it is true, have never been eternal. Moreover, he is afraid that the nuclear stalemate might deter the United States from using its strategic nuclear weapons against the Soviet Union, even if the defense of European allies could not be assured otherwise. In the same statement of January 14, 1963, he referred, as he had several times before, to the uncertainty of the American guaranty:

> And then, above and beyond everything, the deterrence is now a fact for the Russians as for the Americans, which means that, in the event of a general atomic war, there would inevitably be frightful and perhaps fatal destruction in both countries. In this situation, no one in the world, particularly no one in America, can say whether, where, when, how and to what extent the American

nuclear weapons would be used to defend Europe. This does not in the least prevent the American nuclear weapons, which are the most powerful of all existing, from remaining the essential guaranty of world peace. . . . This [French nuclear policy] does not preclude by any means the coordination between the action by that [French] force with the actions by similar forces of our allies. But, for us, the integration is unimaginable in this particular case.[8]

He thus pointed out another important aspect of his policy. The strategy of the French armed forces, including nuclear, can be coordinated with that of other allied states, but integration, which implies American overall command, is rejected categorically.

There is no doubt that his opposition to integration under a joint allied command applies not only to NATO but also to a hypothetical European force. The Minister of Foreign Affairs, Couve de Murville, made it completely clear in his statement of April 4, 1966, in the National Assembly: "No one, obviously, can predict the form that a world war between the major powers would take if, by misfortune, one were to break out. What is known, however, is that its essential element would be the atomic weapon, and that this weapon is not and *can never be integrated* [italics mine]. It is and will remain national."[9]

De Gaulle firmly rejected all proposals and suggestions for integrating the French nuclear force with those of other countries, while he commented on January 14, 1963, on the Anglo-American Nassau agreement:

To turn over our weapons to a multilateral force, under a foreign command, would be to act contrary to that principle of our defense and our policy [he referred to the principle of an independent national defense] . . . this multilateral force necessarily entails a web of liaisons, transmissions and interference within itself, and on the outside a ring of obligations such that, if an integral part were suddenly snatched from it, there would be a strong risk of paralyzing it just at the moment, perhaps, when it should act. In sum, we will adhere to the decision we have made: to construct and, if necessary, to employ our atomic force ourselves.[10]

If the American-Soviet nuclear stalemate has cast some doubt on the reliability of American nuclear guaranty, the allies of the United States have recovered in exchange a greater independence of the American colossus and can afford to steer their policies as they like. This link between the stalemate and the independent course of French foreign policy is pointed out in his statement of July 23, 1964:

Since America and Russia have both equipped themselves with such an atomic arsenal, there exists between them a kind of automatic deterrent balance. But this balance really covers only them but not most of the other countries of the world, even when they are linked to one or the other of the two colossal powers. For the cause and the integrity of each of the others might not seem to their ally to be worth the trouble of being crushed itself in crushing its rival. And, nevertheless, those threatened by the ambition of one of the two giants are led to accommodate themselves, in relation to the other, with strategic, and therefore political, dependence in which, they think, they see the only chance for their security.[11]

Theory of nuclear saturation and anti-city strategy

The others might persist in their error and pay for the doubtful American guaranty of their security with political dependence on the United States; France will not do it. However, her nuclear deterrent must be credible to represent a true substitute for the American guaranty in case the alliance should be terminated or the United States should refuse to use its nuclear weapons in defense of France. De Gaulle's concept of a credible deterrent is founded on the belief that no prospective aggressor would be foolish enough to attack France, if he knew that France would be able to retaliate to such an extent that conquest of France would not compensate for destruction suffered by the aggressor. This concept he concisely described in a statement on July 23, 1964:

> Our first atomic air unit becomes operational this year. In 1966 we will have enough Mirage IV's and refuelling planes to be able to carry at one time, over a distance of thousands of miles, bombs with a total power exceeding that of 150 Hiroshima bombs. Furthermore, we are working on moving on from series A fission bombs to series H fusion bombs, the latter launched from either submarines, surface vessels or land. . . . We are in a position to think that six years from now our deterrent means will reach a total instantaneous power of 2,000 Hiroshima bombs. . . . The field of deterrence is thus henceforth open to us. For to attack France would be equivalent, for whomever it might be, to undergoing frightful destruction itself. . . . Indeed, since a man and a people can die only once, the deterrent exists provided that one has the means to wound the possible aggressor mortally, that one is very determined to do it, and that the aggressor is convinced of it.[12]

There is a contradiction in his argument. On the one hand, he says that any aggressor, as powerful as he might be, would not risk attacking France, because the French retaliatory strike would inflict too heavy damages. On the other hand, he is not sure that this is absolutely true, because he wants to have the additional guaranty by the United States, as uncertain as he considers this guaranty. Perhaps, in the 1970's, when the French nuclear force is composed of naval launching means and is much less vulnerable than the Mirage planes, he will feel that France no longer needs the American alliance. However, he has never made any allusion to this distant possibility.

His views are founded on the concept of nuclear saturation. According to this concept, two countries become equal in terms of defense if one of them, although inferior in economic strength and global armaments, possesses a nuclear deterrent of sufficient size to inflict unbearable damages on the aggressor.[13] One of the French theoreticians of nuclear war, General Pierre M. Gallois, describes nuclear saturation in these words:

> The atom neutralizes the armed multitudes, equalizes the size of populations, shrivels geographical distances, levels mountains, reduces the advantage which the "Giants" derived only yesterday from the vast dimension of their territories (retreat in space), and disregards atmospheric conditions ("General Winter").[14]

This is true if the belligerent, otherwise weaker than his enemy, possesses enough nuclear power to inflict mortal wounds on the aggressor.

French nuclear planning is of necessity based on anti-city strategy. The French deterrent is and will remain too small for anti-force strategy, i.e., to be used only against enemy nuclear forces. The unbearable damages de Gaulle has in mind could be inflicted only on enemy cities. His thesis is probably more realistic than the one which has enjoyed popularity in the United States. If one imagines an American-Soviet nuclear war, anti-force strategy does not seem plausible for important reasons. Firstly, it is rejected in the official Soviet thinking which envisages such a war as an attack not only on the enemy's nuclear forces but also on its cities. An anti-force strategy is impossible without the agreement of both belligerents to spare the cities. Secondly, the cities are close enough to the airfields and land-based launching pads to be affected by the explosions of megaton bombs. Thirdly, since the increasing invulnerability of nuclear forces (submarines, surface vessels, and even well-protected launching pads) makes them virtually indestructible, cities become attractive targets. In any event, the French Minister of

Information, Alain Peyrefitte, openly confirmed that French strategy would be "the strategy of anti-cities."[15]

This strategy encompasses only defensive use of nuclear weapons. Of course, if the French struck first against the Soviet Union in response to threatened Soviet invasion, they would be committing suicide because Soviet retaliation would obliterate France. The same Minister of Information said:

> We are satisfied with the building of a force much smaller [than the American or the Soviet] . . . but a force sufficiently formidable to dissuade an adversary from attacking us, because the risk which he would run would be much greater than the stake which we might represent for him. This force is not, therefore, a striking force but a deterrent force.[16]

This much could be said of a nuclear force of any size; the first strike would be too risky even for the United States or for the Soviet Union because of the unbearable damages it would bring in retaliation.

Need for, and criticism of, the Atlantic Alliance

General Gallois, who is not an authorized official spokesman, usually sustains theses which are almost identical with the governmental point of view and hence deserve attention. In one respect, however, he goes further when he affirms that "nuclear strategy has destroyed the concept of military alliance."[17] This radical opinion obviously overlooks a major aspect of the question. While it is not certain that a nuclear power would use its strategic weapons in defense of an ally, there is no certainty that it would not. This uncertainty in itself is a deterrent to a potential aggressor since he can never be completely sure that he can attack a weak nation with impunity because the latter's stronger ally might retaliate with its nuclear weapons. General Gallois also dismisses too quickly the possible effectiveness of defending a weaker ally by conventional or tactical nuclear weapons as though this were entirely impractical.

General de Gaulle perceives this essential value of alliance with the United States. This explains the contradiction in his public statements: on the one hand, insistence on the uncertainty of the American guaranty, and, on the other, the repeated affirmations that this guaranty is necessary for France.

Prime Minister Pompidou was the first French official to provide a clear answer to the questions which the former French statements raised: Why did the French government insist on the usefulness of

American alliance while it doubted its complete reliability? Why did it firmly oppose the American concept of graduated response and of a limited war in Europe and favor the strategy of an all-out nuclear war? He explained this in the two statements made on April 13 and 20, 1966, during a debate on NATO in the French National Assembly.

Replying to the parliamentary critics of the decision to withdraw from NATO, he said:

> With the United States of America . . . whose strength is today still essential to the security of the Western world, we wish to maintain the alliance concluded in 1949 that makes us united in the face of possible unprovoked aggression. . . . Within NATO itself, we have seen the replacement, gradual and without our agreement, of the initial strategy that was based on deterrence, and, consequently, on the immediate use of atomic reprisals, by a strategy called "flexible" which, under the pretext of lessening the risk of total war, actually consists in enabling the United States to limit the field of the initial operations by sparing the territory of the main potential aggressor. . . . The conventional forces of the alliance, alone integrated, even equipped with tactical atomic weapons whose use remains under American command alone, could not be sure of halting an attack from the East; this is the least that can be said. Such a strategy risks dooming us to atomic bombardment first, to invasion next. . . . Once, it is true, the NATO Council unanimously took [*sic*] a major decision. . . . The strategy approved by the Council was that of massive and immediate atomic retaliation. Officially, it remains the NATO doctrine . . . , but, in actual fact, this strategic concept approved by the NATO Council, unanimously, . . . has been abandoned by the Supreme Command in favor of the flexible response. It sufficed for Mr. McNamara to renounce Mr. Dulles's concept, and a strategy that the NATO Council had never approved became, in fact, that of the Command. Certainly, we protested. . . . What we criticize about that doctrine [of graduated response] is its being specifically conceived on the basis of America's geographical location, its . . . limiting the atomic battlefield by sparing the territory of the Soviet Union, and therefore the territory of the United States, and thereby creating a psychological risk, that of making it believed that the war could remain localized between the Atlantic and the Eastern Polish frontier, that is to say, in Europe, but a Europe doomed to destruction. You [the French par-

liamentary critics] think in terms of trench warfare . . . but in an era of missiles coming from the East and reaching France in one, two or three minutes, America in fifteen, all this is as outdated as the Hundred Years' War. If there were to be a third great war in Europe, it would be nuclear and Europe would be destroyed . . . , but the nuclear weapon is not made to win the war; it is made to prevent it. The aggressor's certainty that he would sustain intolerable losses is the only guaranty that we can have against aggression. . . . That is what leads us to remain in the Atlantic alliance. You think in terms of war, and of yesterday's war. We think in terms of deterrence, that is to say, of peace. Deterrence alone can guarantee peace, and for the West . . . the only deterrence is nuclear. You tell us: NATO has guaranteed peace in Europe for fifteen years. What an error, if you are referring to the integrated organization! What has guaranteed peace is the alliance, insofar as it brought to bear the threat of the American Strategic Air Command. . . . It is atomic power, primarily American, also British and French, that is preserving it [the West]. You believe solely in integration, and that an alliance without integration is of no use, while only the nuclear weapons that are not integrated really count. You believe that the war can be won, while we can only hope to avert it by atomic deterrence.[18]

The points made by the French Prime Minister at last disclosed the real thought of General de Gaulle. He believes that a limited war fought for Europe would be lost, and that the use of tactical nuclear weapons would completely devastate the European countries. He rejects the American concept of limited war as impractical. This does not mean that he really wants to fight an all-out nuclear war. He intends only to suspend the sword of Damocles over Soviet heads: the possibility of an American strategic nuclear retaliation for an attack on Western Europe. This is for him the only true guaranty of peace. This is why he wants to remain an American ally. However, NATO with its integrated conventional forces does not make sense within his frame of reference.

Pompidou's statements made it clear that the never-ending debate between France and her fourteen allies is what Frenchmen call a dialogue between the deaf. The two parties to that debate have been talking about different matters. The United States and its thirteen allies view the Alliance not only as a deterrent and a guaranty of peace but also as an actual weapon in case the Soviets commit an act of aggression.

Believing that the USSR is deterred from any military action in Europe by uncertainty regarding American response, the French government regrets that the United States publicly abandoned the former concept of massive retaliation. While the French Republic thinks about the best manner of maintaining peace in Europe, its counterparts in the Alliance, although also earnestly wishing for peace, debate the question of how the allies should effectively resist a Soviet attack, improbable as it is.

The French Prime Minister went so far in his sincerity to admit that French security rested on the American guaranty rather than on the French nuclear force; he declared: "To say that we would be unable alone to face up to aggression by one of the two big atomic powers is an obvious fact. . . . We do not blush at attaching some value to the alliance of our American friends or our European neighbors." He also admitted the absurdity of France's initiation of a nuclear war by saying: "In a nuclear war conducted with missiles, . . . the alert will be given by the bombs if they happen to explode on our soil."

One of the aspects of the Atlantic Alliance which irritates Frenchmen was mentioned by Prime Minister Pompidou on another occasion. It is that "the decision concerning the use of atomic weapons by the Alliance has been entrusted to the Government of the United States."[19] The French argument involves a contradiction. They refuse to abandon exclusive control over the French force and to integrate it with any collective force, be it Atlantic or European, but resent the United States' refusal to include European allies in the ultimate decision regarding the use of the American nuclear force. This is, however, what de Gaulle proposed to the United States in his memorandum of September 1958 where he suggested that this decision be shared with Britain and France.

The dependence of France on the American guaranty irks both Gaullist and anti-Gaullist Frenchmen. One of de Gaulle's adversaries who is himself a confirmed believer in a federated Europe, former Minister Maurice Faure (one of those Radicals who supported Lecanuet in the 1965 presidential campaign), says:

> For reasons of dignity and political prestige, Europe will not be able to entrust forever and entirely to the United States the task of ensuring its own security. The present situation, where a general appointed in fact by the President of the United States commands the NATO forces, and where the working out of strategic plans and the decision concerning the use of nuclear weapons are com-

pletely outside European jurisdiction, cannot be considered satisfactory. A better equilibrium must be found. Gaullism is right in this respect.[20]

His solution is a European nuclear force, which "should result in terminating the protectorate but not the alliance." This word "protectorate," which is used not only by Gaullists but also by their political opponents, is characteristic of French feelings about present relations with the United States.

The moderate rightist, Antoine Pinay, one of the Prime Ministers of the Fourth Republic, agrees with the Radical Maurice Faure that a European force would be the best solution:

> If it is necessary to create a nuclear force besides the one which the Americans have placed at the disposal of the Atlantic Alliance, we should begin by attempting to establish a European nuclear force prior to the decision to undertake a strictly national effort.[21]

Another Prime Minister of the Fourth Republic, Socialist Guy Mollet, also resents French dependence on American protection:

> Western Europe, as a whole, can hardly accept the status of a nuclear zone protected from the outside. One continent cannot indefinitely leave the task of its own defense to another continent. But the national force is too costly, lacks efficiency and impairs unity. The solution that remains consists in a European nuclear cooperation, in particular between Great Britain and France, within the framework of a close alliance with the United States.[22]

De Gaulle could reply that cooperation with Britain, a nuclear power, necessitates in the first place that France too be a nuclear power.

The publisher of the popular illustrated magazine *Match,* Raymond Cartier, comments:

> It is unnatural that the security of one continent be ensured by another continent for an unlimited and indefinite period of time. The gradual disengagement of America is an unavoidable phenomenon which would take place even if no atomic bomb were ever exploded. The terrifying risks of a nuclear war accelerate this process. They also make more urgent Europeans' need to possess their own guaranty of survival; this guaranty may be created only by a collective effort.[23]

An important group of studies of current French problems, the Jean Moulin Club, also insists on the undesirability of Europe's exclusive dependence on the American guaranty:

> One can imagine that Europe renounces nuclear armaments of any kind, while nevertheless remaining a part of NATO. The European members of NATO would produce neither bombs nor missiles and would entirely trust in nuclear defense by the United States. . . . This solution makes no sense, because first Britain and later France have undertaken the building of their nuclear forces. If one attempted to adopt this solution today, this would produce unfortunate consequences; it would consecrate a sort of political exit by Europe who could not then claim to become an equal partner of the United States.[24]

The anti-Gaullists claim, sincerely or not, that the only practical alternative to American nuclear monopoly within NATO and to political dependence on the United States consists in formation of a European nuclear force. As we shall see later, they too easily overlook the difficulties which make the European force hardly possible. If one were to follow Guy Mollet and in fact restrict the concept of European force to British-French cooperation, one would have to admit that de Gaulle was ready to envisage such cooperation at least prior to the Anglo-American Nassau agreement. French dissatisfaction with exclusive dependence on the United States suggests what the future French nuclear policy will be. If a collective European nuclear force cannot be created, what choice will de Gaulle's successors have, even if they are his present opponents, but to continue his policy of a national force?

A frequent French commentator on NATO, André Fontaine, also shares in the dissatisfaction with the American nuclear monopoly within NATO:

> What is called "the sword" of the alliance, in contrast to its shield made up of the conventional or tactical forces stationed in Europe, essentially escapes the jurisdiction of the allies who are consulted neither on the determination of objectives nor on the hypotheses of its use; a fortiori, they would not be consulted on the decision to use it. . . . The President of the United States may make any use he wants of some 98 per cent of the nuclear potential of the Western world. . . . This was the framework within which the decision to manufacture the French bomb was made long before General de Gaulle's return to power.[25]

As the Communists oppose the Atlantic Alliance itself, one can say that practically all Frenchmen, both advocates and opponents of a national force, would subscribe to this view of Maurice Faure: "We cannot accept the thesis of the United States according to which they should have the atomic monopoly within NATO."[26] De Gaulle has not been satisfied with the verbal lamentations over the American nuclear monopoly and French dependence; thus he has decided to build a French national force.

De Gaulle is also far from being an isolated voice in France when he points out the uncertainty of American alliance. General Gallois is one of the rare French commentators who admits that a similar problem exists for the United States. He writes:

> What becomes less probable in the atomic age is that the allied nations will jointly accept to run the risks, which have become exorbitant, for the sake of interests which are not vital for the majority of them.[27]

In other words, one cannot be sure because of the risks of nuclear escalation that the United States would expose its own national territory to devastations for the sake of a European ally, but it is no more certain that the European allies would fight for the United States. The latter aspect of the question is linked to a fear expressed in France that the European allies might be dragged into a general war, which the United States would start in a non-European area for the sake of its own interests, but which would eventually extend to Europe. Let us imagine, for example, that American action in Asia involved the United States in a war with China, and that the Soviet Union honored her alliance with China and joined the battle. Frenchmen ask the question whether they and the other European allies would have to face the prospect of an Asian war becoming a European war. They say that "our country would be directly exposed to danger, if an unfortunate American initiative started a conflict."[28] This fear is felt strongly not only because of American involvement in Asian affairs, but also because of the American-Soviet confrontation in October 1962. Cuba represented a vital problem for the United States, but not for the European allies. Frenchmen say that, if the confrontation had resulted in an American-Soviet war, they might have been dragged into hostilities for a reason of no concern to them. One may note, however, that in October 1962 General de Gaulle assured the American government of his complete solidarity with the United States.

This fear of being involved in a war initiated by American policy has been used by the French government as one of the arguments against French participation in NATO. For instance, Prime Minister Pompidou told the National Assembly in April 1966:

> If one day there should really occur, for interests that would be alien to France and to her obligations in the alliance, a conflict between the United States and the USSR . . . , who can maintain that the fact of having on our soil the American general head-quarters in Europe, with its communication network and its entire command apparatus, not to mention air bases and supply depots, would not constitute an obvious and serious risk for us? . . . All that could make us a target for atomic bombs.[29]

The French sentiments may be expressed in one sentence: they fear that the United States would refuse to use strategic nuclear weapons in defense of Western Europe if all other means were to prove insufficient, but they also think the United States might plunge them into a general nuclear war by its policy in non-European areas. They realize that the American quasi-monopoly of nuclear weapons in the Western camp leaves to the government of the United States full freedom of decision regarding the use of those weapons in Europe or elsewhere and also regarding the choice of policies which might end in nuclear escalation.

The fear that the United States would not risk devastation of its own territory for the sake of its European allies was expressed by the former Socialist Minister, Jules Moch, toward the end of the Fourth Republic, while he addressed the National Assembly on January 21, 1958; he claimed then that the Soviet possession of intercontinental ballistic missiles "has strategically devaluated the Atlantic Organization."[30] This opponent of de Gaulle agreed with General Gallois, who had come to the same conclusion:

> Military alliances have become greatly precarious. If it is hardly credible that a government would run the risk of annihilation in protecting its own most vital interests, it is certainly even less probable that it would run the same risk for the benefit of another country even though the latter country is an ally. . . . The present crisis of NATO is due to no other reason.[31]

He draws a reasonable conclusion from his statement:

> It is highly probable that the USSR, like the United States, will succeed in making its forces of nuclear reprisals invulnerable. Hence, in the event of armed confrontation between the two coun-

tries the only objectives available for destruction would be American and Soviet urban centers. This amounts to saying that they have no alternative but suicide or peaceful coexistence.[32]

Both the United States and the Soviet Union have accepted the necessity of peaceful coexistence. By the same token, both so far have done their best to avoid open confrontations which would involve them in an incalculable nuclear escalation. The Cuban incident of October 1962 could only strengthen their determination. The relative peace in Berlin proves that determination but also proves that Soviet-American peaceful coexistence confers the benefit of peace on American and Soviet allies in Europe as well.

Even Raymond Aron, who is one of the rare French writers with distinct American sympathies, concedes that the fears of his countrymen are not without reason. He recalls the statement Christian Herter, then Secretary of State, made:

> I cannot conceive of any President involving us in an all-out nuclear war unless the facts showed clearly we are in danger of all-out devastation ourselves, or that actual moves have been made toward devastating ourselves.[33]

Aron concludes:

> When both deterrent forces are relatively invulnerable, the territories of the duelists are, in effect, as well protected against a direct attack as possible, but other territories, included in the threat of thermonuclear reprisals, are not protected to the same extent.[34]

However, he is one of the few Frenchmen who also sees the reverse side of the coin:

> The Europeans suddenly have discovered that their security no longer rests on the certainty of the atomic answer by the United States if military demarcation lines were transgressed, but on the uncertainty of Soviet leaders as to American reaction in such a situation.[35]

André Fontaine is another Frenchman who does not overlook this important aspect of the American-Soviet stalemate and its implications for the security of Western Europe. He writes:

> The problem is not limited to the question of armaments. It does not suffice to have them. It is also necessary for the nation that

has them to create in the mind of a potential aggressor, in order to dissuade him from acting, certainly not the conviction that nuclear weapons would be used if necessary but at least the feeling that there is no assurance that these weapons would not be used. This is the doctrine called that of "reasonable doubt."[36]

This doctrine of reasonable doubt is weakened by statements like those of Christian Herter and the French officials; both tend to dispel Soviet uncertainty about possible American reactions to Soviet military moves calculated to change the European *status quo*. For instance, the French Minister of Information, Alain Peyrefitte, was not well advised, even from the point of view of French interests, when he said on May 28, 1963:

> One may wonder whether the Russians really believe that the American people would accept their own destruction for the sake of Europe. It does not matter much if we have doubts on this score, but it does matter to know whether the Russians would have doubts of this kind on the eve of a conflict.[37]

Fortunately, the Russians do not seem to be as skeptical as the French government regarding the value of American commitment to Western Europe. The Minister of Information went on:

> We believe that the French national force represents for us and perhaps for our European allies an appreciable additional guaranty of security, in spite of the fact that that force is small in comparison with the American; we so believe, because the use of American force may be considered doubtful, at least in Russian minds.[38]

If the Europeans should be skeptical, as the French government advises them to be, regarding the validity of American guaranty because the United States would not expose its cities to the Soviet second strike, why should they place their trust in the small French nuclear force? Is it conceivable that any French President, including de Gaulle, would expose Paris to destruction for the sake, let us say, of West Berlin? The very recent history of France would not encourage Europeans to entertain such hopes. The Munich agreement in 1938 and the French refusal to continue the war in 1940 occurred when France was not facing annihilation with nuclear weapons for the sake of her allies of the time, Czechoslovakia, Britain, and Poland.

The French apprehensions find another argument in the text of the North Atlantic Treaty. Its Article 5 defines the *casus belli* in the following words:

The Parties agree that an armed attack against one or more of them in Europe or North America shall be considered an attack against them all; and consequently they agree that, if such an armed attack occurs, each of them, in exercise of the right of individual or collective self-defense recognized by Article 51 of the Charter of the United Nations, will assist the Party or Parties so attacked by taking forthwith, individually and in concert with the other Parties, such action as it deems necessary, including the use of armed force, to restore and maintain the security of the North Atlantic area.

"Such action as it deems necessary" leaves to allies, including the United States, the choice of means to be used. While the North Atlantic Treaty leaves the choice of means to the signatories, it clearly states that an armed attack on one would oblige the others to help. General de Gaulle placed a restrictive interpretation on Article 5 in his letter to the President of the United States dated March 7, 1966. He said that France "was resolved to fight alongside her allies in case one of them were the object of an unprovoked aggression." The word "unprovoked" implied that France reserved for herself the freedom to examine each case and to refuse to join the other allies if the victim of Soviet attack seemed guilty of provocative policy. This freedom of evaluation was not provided for in the North Atlantic Treaty.[39]

The American doctrine of graduated deterrent does not encourage Frenchmen in the belief that the United States would immediately use its strategic nuclear weapons in case of an armed Soviet action. This doctrine does not appeal to them for the obvious reason that Western Europe is thickly populated and that a limited war, waged with conventional or tactical nuclear weapons, would end amidst the ruins of European cities. Their feeling of insecurity is also increased by the fact that the range of Soviet intermediate ballistic missiles covers Western Europe, while the intercontinental missiles are aimed at the United States. In case of an all-out nuclear war, if the Soviet Union risked its own destruction, it could probably inflict unbearable damages on both the United States and its European allies.

However, the Socialist leader, Guy Mollet, used a very pertinent argument in favor of the credibility of American deterrent guaranty. He said on May 5, 1963:

We may be sure today that the USSR will not start the war in Europe as long as 350,000 American soldiers, women, and children remain in Europe. This is the guaranty of our security, and is worth more than all our small atomic bombs.[40]

As long as any American troops are stationed on European soil, especially in West Berlin and West Germany, it is certain that the United States would not be passive if its troops were attacked by the Soviet Union. The USSR cannot advance beyond the present demarcation lines without engaging in battle with American soldiers. The uncertain prospect is the question of the kind of weapons the United States would use. After all, the Atlantic Alliance is in itself a factor of dissuasion, whatever French critics may say.

The nuclear stalemate between the two powers is a guaranty of European security; the first strike by either would inevitably bring the terrible punishment of retaliatory strike. As noted by General Gallois:

> Since the nuclear forces of the belligerents cannot be destroyed because of their submarine and air mobility, and since their land is exposed to destruction, the recourse to war has lost all sense. This recourse would be profitless, and in all probability would result in mutual suicide.[41]

Limited war

De Gaulle's concept of war in Europe rests on the assumption that it would be nuclear, either because the attackers would begin it with nuclear weapons or because the defenders would have to use such weapons to protect themselves. The French reject the American view that a war in Europe could be limited to the use of conventional or tactical nuclear weapons. The concept of a limited war in Europe might be attractive for the two Super-Powers, because it offers immunity to their national territories. It is certainly not attractive for any of the European allies, whose territories would be devastated even if only modern conventional or tactical nuclear weapons were used. On the other hand, the concept of an all-out nuclear war for Europe has nothing to offer to the United States, or to Russia; they would be exposed to immense destruction.

General Ailleret, the chairman of the French chiefs of staff, made clear the French strategic concept in his lecture for a group of officers on June 26, 1964:

> The French government does not believe, regarding Europe, in the efficacy of the strategy of graduated response championed by Mr. McNamara, the American Secretary of Defense. This strategy may be followed only in the settlement of secondary or minor problems. If Europe were the victim of an aggression in which only "conventional" means were used, the aggressor probably

would succeed in breaking through the "conventional" formations. These formations would be destroyed or compelled quickly to retreat. West Germany and probably a part of France would be invaded and would have to be reconquered. If the battle were fought from the beginning with tactical nuclear weapons, the destructive range of these weapons, taking into account the depth of formations, would extend to 1,500 kilometers on each side of the line of contact with the enemy. The exchange of nuclear fire, even of tactical fire, would completely devastate the European territory of 3,000 kilometers' width, from the Atlantic to the Soviet frontier. The only strategy capable efficaciously to defend [Europe] against invasion is that of the immediate counter-strike against . . . enemy territory by the most powerful weapons. . . . This French position is to some extent supported by the fact that NATO has never approved the strategy of graduated response in Europe.[42]

What General Ailleret seemed to overlook was that massive retaliation would involve vast devastation not only of the United States and the Soviet Union but also of Europe. Against Europe the Russians would be able to use their intermediate ballistic missiles without reducing their longer-range nuclear capacity.

An Australian writer has attracted attention to German interests; these could not be easily reconciled with the concept of limited war:

In Germany, which lives with the memory of the "saturation bombing" of 1944–1945 and also with the memory or legend of the Russian occupation, "conventional warfare" need not necessarily seem a more inviting prospect than the atomic kind.[43]

The French opposition to limited war might correspond to the interests of other continental allies. Neither an all-out nor a limited war has much to commend itself to the European peoples. The only reasonable way out of this strategic dilemma is the maintenance of peace in Europe. This requires moderation in international politics on the part of both the Super-Powers and their European allies.

Is the French deterrent credible?

As we have seen, the French concept of nuclear deterrence is founded on the belief that the prospective enemy would be foolish to attack France and expose himself to damages greater than the worth of France for his political designs. General Gallois illustrates this point with the British example:

Doubtless, if Great Britain could destroy with her limited nuclear means only 25 per cent of the Soviet population or economy, she would herself run the risk of being 100 per cent destroyed. But, for the [Soviet] aggressor . . . , what a stupid miscalculation! While he was rebuilding the ruins in his own country, reduced to three-fourths of its former power, the United States would not only bar the road to world hegemony but would continue in peace on its course toward prosperity.[44]

This theory has several shortcomings. Firstly, the British or French first strike, in response to a Soviet non-nuclear attack, would destroy a large part of the Russian territory but probably not its nuclear deterrent; this is nearly invulnerable, as General Gallois admits. The USSR would retaliate against Britain or France with intermediate missiles, while intercontinental missiles and missile-launching submarines would continue to keep watch on the United States. Secondly, there is no visible reason why the Soviet Union should attack Britain or France without intending to attack the United States at the same time. If the Soviet Union truly wanted to conquer Western Europe, it would strike simultaneously in Europe and against the United States, the only true obstacle on the road to Soviet dominion over Europe. Thirdly, in the less hypothetical example of West Germany, the main international preoccupation of the Soviet Union, Soviet troops would encounter American troops in the first battle, thus entangling the United States in the war. A conventional attack on France is impossible for geographic reasons without first conquering Western Germany. Fourthly, if France were threatened with Soviet invasion, carried out without strategic nuclear weapons, is it really probable that the French government would respond to a Soviet ultimatum with its own nuclear first strike rather than submit to Soviet occupation? The alternatives would be a Soviet second strike, which would annihilate the French nation, or Soviet occupation, under which this nation would, at least biologically, survive. French opponents to de Gaulle's nuclear policy raise the same points.

Another hypothesis, never officially enunciated, is that French nuclear bombs would act as a detonator for American strategic weapons. In other words, France would strike, in case of danger, with her nuclear weapons against the Soviet Union; the United States would then have no choice but immediate recourse to its strategic nuclear weapons to protect France and the rest of Western Europe. France would thus compel the President of the United States to engage in an all-out nuclear war by her own decision to be the first to strike against the Soviet Union if the latter attempted to conquer Europe. This detonator theory must have been discussed in Paris, because it is being refuted by those French authors who point out its naiveté: "But it is far from certain that the United States would accept in such an event the risk of even partial destruction because of unilateral action by one of its allies."[45] Paul Reynaud's criticism is even more explicit:

> But, they say, our atomic force, as feeble as it might be, would give us the capacity to compel the Americans to unleash an atomic war. . . . Firstly, there is nothing to prove that we should thereby compel the Americans to start that war. But what is absolutely certain is that, if we were to start the atomic war by an attack on Russia, we should be instantaneously destroyed. If the Americans engaged afterwards in an atomic war in response to our desperate appeal, they would come to the rescue of a corpse.[46]

The components of French deterrent force

The French nuclear program calls for the building of national force in two stages. In the first stage, i.e., in the 1960's, this force is composed of 50 light bombers of the type Mirage IV, armed with atomic bombs having three times the explosive power of the Hiroshima bomb. These planes can fly at very low altitudes and so are expected to escape detection by radar. The French air force commanders claim that the Mirages can penetrate the Soviet defensive system and carry out their mission.[47] If this is true, fifty bombs, each having an explosive capacity of sixty kilotons, could inflict extensive damage on several Soviet cities. Assuming that all 50 Mirages (each carrying one bomb) were able to penetrate Soviet defenses, Soviet retaliation capacity may be measured by the French Air Force commanders' admission that "five 100-megaton bombs would suffice to erase France from the map of the world."[48]

Moreover, the Soviet defensive system is not at a standstill. The Soviet Sam 3 ground-air missiles, capable of destroying low-flying planes, are being installed and will be a match for the Mirages. The speed of the supersonic Mirages is just over twice the speed of sound and is inferior to that of the best American planes. The Mirages can cover a distance of 2,500 kilometers and could not return to French airfields. However, the United States sold to France twelve KC-135 refueling planes, which enabled the Mirages to carry out their mission and return. (The distance they can cover is increased to 4,800 kilometers.) The destructive capacity of French planes could be further improved by arming them with air-ground nuclear missiles which could hit a target at a distance of a few hundred miles. Frenchmen differ in their estimates of the percentages of Mirages which would be able to deliver the bombs prior to their destruction by Soviet defenses; the most pessimistic estimate is that only three out of the fifty Mirages would attain their targets.[49] What is certain is that only a part of the total load of French bombs would inflict damage on Soviet cities.

The French government finally admitted in 1964 that it did not believe in the efficiency of its Mirages. The Minister of Armed Forces, Pierre Messmer, in November, 1964, told the finance committee of the National Assembly that the Mirages would not be able to pass through Soviet defenses after 1967. By 1968, they will be useful only for tactical missions. He expressed the hope that they would be replaced in 1968 by ground-to-ground ballistic missiles hidden in underground silos. These missiles would fill in the void between the first and second stages, i.e., until the time when the new nuclear force exists.[50]

The Mirages are vulnerable to destruction on the airfields either by Soviet intermediate range missiles or even by conventional air bombing. The short warning time for France—two to three minutes for enemy missiles and fifteen minutes for enemy planes—would not give the Mirages much chance if the Soviet Union suspected that the French government intended to use its deterrent. It seems that France could hardly afford the cost of keeping a large part of its Mirages constantly airborne to protect them against sudden destruction on the airfields. In any event, the Mirages do not represent a deterrent which would dissuade the Soviet Union from invading Western Europe. The true dissuasion lies elsewhere; it consists in the Soviet uncertainty concerning American reaction.

The second-stage French nuclear force will be a different proposition, assuming that France solves all problems involved in building nuclear-propelled submarines armed with nuclear missiles. The present program calls for the construction of three such submarines, each equipped with 16 missiles armed with thermonuclear warheads. These three submarines should be ready in 1972 or 1973. The force represented by these submarines would be supplemented by intermediate range missiles which could be launched from their subterranean launching pads located on French soil.

This program presupposes the solution of several problems: mastering the technique of atomic fusion and the production of thermonuclear warheads, the design and production of missiles—both intermediate ground-to-ground and those launched underwater from submarines—the construction of nuclear-powered submarines themselves, and, finally, the ability to face the cost.

Assuming that neither the United States nor the Soviet Union solves in the 1970's the problem of anti-submarine defense, the French nuclear force will be by that time technically a serious threat to an enemy, because it would be practically invulnerable. Small by comparison to the American or Soviet submarine fleets, it would not be negligible.[51] One may mention an argument in favor of its existence. If the Soviet Union were to contemplate an attack on Western Europe in the 1970's, it would have to take into account the existence of three nuclear deterrents: the American, the British, and the French. Both the British and the French will be minuscule by comparison to the American, but the point lies elsewhere. The Soviet leaders would have to answer three questions instead of one: which of the three Atlantic allies might reply to the Soviet attack with the strategic nuclear weapons, all three, only two or only one? This will certainly not facilitate their calculations.

The weaknesses of the second-stage French force are four: the absence of effective arrangements for passive defense (it is true that the United States and the Soviet Union are in no better position); the lack of active defense against enemy missiles; the great lag behind the United States and the Soviet Union in this respect; and the absence of an independent French system of early warning.

The French government has access to the uranium deposits in France (Vendée, Limousin, Forez, Massif Central, and Brittany) and also in the two friendly African countries (Madagascar and Gabon).[52] It used the testing grounds in the Algerian Sahara for its fission tests (part of the agreement with the Algerians at the time of their receiving independence in 1962), but is now preparing the fusion testing grounds in its own colonial possessions in the Pacific.

It is impossible to calculate the value of the French second-stage deterrent for one obvious reason. No one can predict the condition of the American and Soviet deterrents in the 1970's. Firstly, both countries make progress in active defense against enemy missiles launched from planes, from land-based launching pads, and from submarines, and may finally find the means of effective detection and destruction of submarines. Secondly, the armory of offensive means of mass destruction may be enlarged by new devices, including outer-space vehicles armed with thermonuclear weapons.

France took the first step in outer-space exploration by launching, on November 26, 1965, an 88-pound orbiting satellite. It was placed in orbit by a French-manufactured three-stage rocket. In spite of the light weight of the satellite, France proved that she had solved the problem of producing rockets, a great step forward toward the second-stage nuclear force armed with missiles.

The French debate concerning nuclear policy concentrates on the strategic nuclear weapons. General de Gaulle himself mentions only this aspect. It is rather strange that neither his supporters nor his opponents pay enough attention, at least in their public statements, to tactical nuclear weapons which gradually become a necessary part of armaments of American and Soviet armies, navies and air forces, and which are supplied to American allies under a system of two locks. Michel Debré makes only a passing allusion to this problem in the following passage:

> The atomic weapon and the tele-guided missile form the foundation of any military power. There is no conceivable defensive, i.e., no guaranty of security, without the possession of weapons to "dissuade" the potential aggressor. The use of "conventional" weapons may remain the rule of limited conflicts, but is it possible to imagine a decisive struggle for the freedom of France or of Europe without the use of modern weapons? Moreover, what will the distinction soon be between the "conventional" weapons and the new weapons? The air force, the navy, and the artillery will be influenced by an irreversible evolution. To be sure, the conventional military formations must continue to exist, but their capacity to guarantee national security will be very doubtful, if they are not integrated within a modern organization.[53]

No doubt each of the two major coalitions, facing each other across the demarcation line in Europe, must possess strategic nuclear weapons to ensure existence of the stalemate that is unfortunately the military foundation of European peace. But the question remains whether each major nation, as Debré claims, should possess the whole nuclear armory, including strategic weapons, or whether the massive deterrent possessed by the major ally in either coalition suffices for the security of other allies. Debré is on firmer ground, however, in the second half of his statement, when he indicates that tactical nuclear weapons are required for the arming of modern "conventional" forces. De Gaulle's policy will have this effect of eventually modernizing the French Army, Air Force and Navy and making them independent of American supplies. For instance the French forces stationed in Germany are provided with American tactical weapons which they may use, like the other allied troops, only with the permission of the U.S.A.

French criticism

Opponents of French nuclear arming have accumulated several arguments against it. They claim it is a waste of national money. The French socialist, Jules Moch, who is familiar with the problem because of his participation in the international conferences on disarmament, compressed all these arguments:

> A striking force may be used to attack, to reply to an attack, to threaten, or to influence. (a) Attack? Impossible. To inflict limited damages on a powerful adversary would condemn France to destruction during the following quarter of an hour. (b) Reply to an attack? Impossible. A nuclear attack would annihilate our small striking force together with our whole country even before our force could reply. (c) Threaten? No one would take seriously our threat, because those facing us would know that we know that France would not survive the implementation of the threat. A wooden sword is not a weapon of deterrence. (d) Influence our allies? If we tried to drag them into a conflict we provoke, they would not follow us and they would not even allow us to act in such a way.[54]

His criticism is well taken, except that the second-stage French force would be invulnerable to destruction under present technological conditions and could reply to an enemy attack. The question which could be raised in such an event is the same for all nuclear powers. Assuming that the enemy first strike were to devastate completely the national territory, would personnel of the retaliatory force still have enough determination to avenge their dead countrymen? In the case of France the question is more pertinent, because the enemy first strike would have the capability of erasing France from the surface of the earth.

The major difference between the United States and France is that France could be threatened by enemy invasion of her national territory, while the menace suspended over the United States is the possibility of nuclear aggression from the air. The United States does not need to contemplate, as does France, the choice between surrendering and being occupied following enemy invasion without the use of strategic nuclear weapons, or replying with thermonuclear attack against the enemy territory, with the certainty of paying the price of the obliteration of France herself. This is the major weakness of any French nuclear deterrent, even the most modern. The problem consists in the question whether any French government would prefer to commit national suicide rather than accept the enemy ultimatum. There lies the lack of psychological credibility of the French deterrent.

The supporters of de Gaulle's policy formulate well this particular problem:

> The political and psychological nature of deterrence consists in the determination of a whole nation not to surrender, in her fortitude in defying destruction and death rather than conceding defeat and subjugation. Deterrence depends as much on this will-power and this fortitude as on the might of weapons. It is otherwise a delusion whether one has or has not atomic weapons.[55]

The critics of the present policy agree that it is highly improbable that France, faced with this awful choice, would immolate herself in a heroic gesture rather than surrender. Raymond Aron writes:

> On that day when the Soviet Union addresses an ultimatum, the French government, left alone, will be compelled to capitulate, in the majority of cases, because the physical survival of French people will be at stake.[56]

Another serious writer agrees:

> There is nothing to vouch for the expectation that, if it [enemy attack] were to materialize, the possession of "modern" weapons would suffice to inspire in the French nation the resolution to defend itself at any price. The exiguity of national territory that could be devastated in a few minutes constitutes a terrible handicap and a serious incentive to defeatism.[57]

It is hard to imagine that even a heroic nation, menaced with enemy occupation, would prefer to commit suicide rather than surrender. This doubt is even stronger in the case of France after the sad experience of 1940 and in view of French relief in 1962 at being allowed to live in peace.

The other arguments against de Gaulle's policy relate to the early warning system, the lack of active and passive defense, the possible obsolescence of French nuclear force, and the cost of nuclear armaments. It is no secret that France has no early warning system of her own. Therefore, the "independent" French force has to rely on the American NATO system. "We are not independent regarding this major problem."[58] The French-NATO agreement on French participation in the American early warning system was concluded in 1960.[59] This is probably one of several reasons for the French Air Force commanders' statement: "The Atlantic Alliance has never been more necessary for French security than it is now."[60] Assuming that in time France will build her own early warning system, it will not offer much time for alerting the government, which would have to give orders to the military commanders, and for retaliatory action. As we have said, the alert against planes would amount to fifteen minutes, and against missiles only two or three minutes. This compares with the American early warning time of fifteen minutes in case of missiles, which is being extended to half an hour by the use of orbiting satellites as warning devices.

The French Air Force commanders readily concede that the nuclear deterrent "will have failed in its mission if it is used."[61] This is true of all nuclear deterrents, but in the case of the French deterrent the major doubt is the lack of psychological credibility that it would ever be used against a major nuclear power even for purely defensive purposes.

The French opponents are also worried by the scientific-technological lag behind the United States and the Soviet Union. They say that, while France is busy creating her own force, the two giants are constantly improving theirs: active defense, and new weaponry of mass destruction. Will she ever catch up with them? One of the critics says that the United States and the Soviet Union "will progress more quickly in proportion to their means which are infinitely greater than ours. We shall always lag behind, and this lag will constantly increase."[62] A group of studies by competent Frenchmen agrees with this opinion:

> Our lag, already considerable, added to the paucity of our material resources compared to the resources of other powers, might result in a situation where we got breathless for nothing in an effort constantly to modernize obsolete weapons. . . . The solution of the problem of deterrence is simply beyond our reach.[63]

The same group specifically applies this argument, in another publication, to the second-stage nuclear force: "In view of the pace of progress in the development of means of defense, it is not impossible that submarines might in ten years lose their invulnerability. France would again be in possession of a weapon as obsolete as the strategic air force is today."[64]

Deterrent against whom?

This discussion, in which the opponents have been proved right regarding the Mirages, which are becoming obsolete, and might prove right regarding the submarines, nevertheless overlooks two points. De Gaulle's policy will in any case give the French armed forces tactical nuclear weapons without which these forces would become obsolete. The other important point is mentioned only in veiled terms by the opponents and never by the French government. The number of nuclear powers has already increased from three to five, France and China joining the company. It is unfortunately probable that the proliferation will continue. Perhaps in the 1970's or later there will be several great nuclear powers. Assuming that the present international constellation is not eternal, and that France might face on the continent of Europe other enemies than the Soviet Union, Frenchmen might on that day be grateful to de Gaulle for his foresight. French deterrent might be of no use regarding the Soviet Union but might have a power of dissuasion against another future enemy.

Raymond Aron remarks with his usual perspicacity:

> I shall not conclude, however, that the French decision is indefensible, even insofar as national security is concerned, if one takes a long-term view of the matter. . . . The nature of modern armament is such that decisions taken today may find their justification fifteen or twenty years later. The French striking force . . . is the beginning of reassurance against the unforeseeable diplomatic future.[65]

A group of protagonists of national force join him in pointing out the uncertainties of the international constellation in the distant future: "[France] does not know what the attitude of her allies will be in ten or twenty years. This is why she wants to be ready for those remote developments, because the system of deterrence cannot be improvised."[66]

This problem of French security in the distant and unknown future, when new enemies might threaten France, is the most weighty argument in favor of French nuclear armament. Perhaps it is also the principal consideration in de Gaulle's mind. He is more familiar with military problems than most of his civilian opponents. It is hardly plausible to suppose that he is unaware of the convincing arguments which prove that the French deterrent lacks credibility regarding the Soviet Union. If he looks toward a distant future and wants to ensure France against potential enemies who are not yet nuclear powers, he can hardly say so, being the President of the Republic. A future enemy might be one or another of the present allies and friends. He has often said that no political constellation is ever eternal.

Nonmilitary reasons

Has he other motivations? The debates in France point out two other considerations: de Gaulle's alleged intention to conciliate the Army by offering it the most modern weapons, and his desire to win for

France a higher rank among nations. The former factor might have played a role at the time of the Algerian war, when de Gaulle felt acutely the hostile or only coldly loyal feelings of military officers. But even at that time, nuclear armaments could be considered by many officers a sort of Greek gift. Those who were used to the military routine, or were thinking only in terms of colonial wars, or were insufficiently trained in modern technology, might even have resented the prospect of a thorough modernization of French armed forces. The down-grading of conventional forces was facing them with an unavoidable retirement. Only officers with a truly modern outlook could be attracted by de Gaulle's plans. In any event, it does not seem that this motivation has played any major role in his thinking. He is not a demagogue who would buy his personal popularity at such a price to the national Treasury.[67]

The relation between nuclear armament and the status of a nation is highly debatable, but it is possible that preoccupation with French prestige might have been an additional argument in de Gaulle's thinking. Several French writers think that this relation exists.[68] It is not unexpected to find that Michel Debré is one of those who believe that the possession of nuclear weapons helps France "in not falling down to the level of those nations who would not be asked for their opinion regarding world problems or even regarding European problems."[69]

There is a grain of truth in these views. The present five nuclear powers are not nations of second rank. The acquisition of nuclear weapons reflects the possession of a scientific, technological, and industrial potential which a weak and poor nation does not have. However, it is not true that nuclear weapons, a powerful means of defense, represent a great asset in the diplomatic game. Raymond Aron is right in pointing out that:

> Great Britain has not gained any visible benefit from the possession of thermonuclear bombs and V bombers, whether in the Near East or the Common Market or the free-trade zone. General de Gaulle did not wait for the acquisition of a deterrent force to oppose the admission of Great Britain to the Common Market. . . . The French policy in Africa and Latin America is completely independent of American wishes, whether France has or has not a deterrent force.[70]

De Gaulle has been illustrating this point since 1958. The Mirages have not increased his independence in foreign policies, nor have they influenced foreign attitudes toward France. Whatever he has achieved has been achieved by diplomacy.

The same is true of other states. Neither the United States nor the Soviet Union can impose its will on France or China, but no one denies their power to destroy any country in the world. Even little Albania and Cuba have been able to challenge the two Super-Powers with impunity. But the United States and Russia would have been first-rank powers even if nuclear weapons had never been invented. Great Britain suffered the failure of her Suez Canal expedition for various reasons, but her nuclear weapons were of no use in the fall of 1956. West Germany certainly has as much as France to say about the future of Western Europe, but she is not a nuclear power. The influence and prestige of France among the peoples of the Third World is certainly due in no degree to her possession of fifty Mirages.

French protection of Western Europe?

Many Gaullists, and probably the General himself, believe that France, the only continental nation (except for Russia) armed with nuclear weapons, will eventually emerge in the eyes of Western Europe as its reliable protector vis-à-vis the Soviet Union, as a pillar of the European balance of power, and hence necessarily as the leader of Western European nations. Yet the Germans will not forget that in 1940 they routed the French armies and forced France to surrender, or that Western Germany alone is already economically the most important nation in Western Europe, ranking third in the world after the United States and the Soviet Union. Neither their national pride nor the sense of national dignity of other French partners in the Common Market would allow them to accept the status of satellites. This should be clear to Frenchmen who vociferously assert their national independence.

Prime Minister Pompidou declared on December 2, 1964, in the National Assembly, in the conclusion of debates on the military program, that: "Each of our soldiers, each of our atomic bombs serves Europe as much as France."[71] He forgot on that occasion his own government's frequent assertions regarding the uncertainty of the American nuclear guaranty. The editor of *Le Monde* offered a pertinent reply:

> Who in France would think that many million innocents should immediately be immolated if the Red Army were, for instance, to seize Berlin? This proposition would have to be considered in the light of the certainty that our whole exiguous hexagon would become the target of atomic destruction a few minutes later. Thus, whatever we do, the adversary will always have some good reasons for not feeling that he is truly dissuaded. Germans will have the same reasons for believing that, if the United States might one day be reluctant to expose their national "sanctuary" to devastation

for the sake of defending Western Europe, France would be even more inclined to refrain from action or to wait, in spite of her geographical proximity and partly because of this proximity.[72]

Raymond Aron, turning against the government its own argument writes: "They say that Americans would not be willing to sacrifice New York and Boston for the sake of London and Paris. So be it! But would Frenchmen be ready to sacrifice Paris for the sake of Hamburg or the whole of France for the sake of one [French] city or province?"[73] In the light of this pertinent critique the opinion of the former Prime Minister of the Fifth Republic sounds hollow: "The French force represents a guaranty for Europe as well as for France."[74]

The most pertinent reply is that of Western Europeans themselves. Paul-Henri Spaak, the Belgian Foreign Minister, firmly rejected the suggestion of exchanging the American nuclear shield for the French— which he evaluated as representing only 3 or 4 per cent of the American nuclear deterrent. He also alluded to the French Grand Design of becoming the sole protector of European security and thereby its leader, and firmly said that this French hegemony "would not be accepted by any European country."[75]

Cost and the conventional forces

The great question in the French debate is the eventual cost of nuclear armaments. Governmental optimism encounters the opposition's pessimism. An exact evaluation of that cost is impossible in view of the fact that France is a newcomer in the field, and that future expenses on the research, production, and maintenance cannot be figured out with precision. This question is compounded because no French government can predict the progress and innovations in the American and Soviet means of mass destruction. Will France always lag behind, with her nuclear force obsolescent, or will the French inventive genius allow France to become one day a peer of the Super-Powers regarding the weapons of mass destruction?

The impossibility of exactly predicting the size of future nuclear expenses is apparent, if one places side by side two statements by the French Prime Minister, both made in the same year. On November 5, 1962, he said:

The technological and scientific upheavals of our time . . . compel us to reexamine the nature of our military problem and to think of extraordinary, new methods and armaments both destructive and costly. These new methods and armaments represent for a country like ours a great and almost crushing burden. . . . We must make this effort of modernization whatever its cost. We must persevere till its completion, because we should otherwise become nothing but a protected country.[76]

On December 13, 1962, he sounded very optimistic:

The [military] effort, which we shall continue to make, does not exceed the French means. I want to affirm this once again. It is not bigger, in proportion to our whole national budget or to our national income, than the one which the United States, Great Britain, or Federal Germany consents to make.[77]

The official estimates of cost are too optimistic, because the expenses for the construction of the Pierrelatte plant, originally evaluated at 400 million dollars, already amount to one billion dollars and the final cost is yet uncertain.[78]

The military expenses represent approximately 20.5 per cent of the total French budget. The nuclear armaments have cost about 25 per cent of the military budget so far. The French military budget amounts to between 7 and 8 per cent of the gross national product, but the investments in the national economy represent 18 per cent as against 24 per cent of German gross national product reinvested in the German economy. The latter comparison raises the question whether the French economy will not be progressively outdistanced in its growth by the German economy, if the French nuclear armaments were to require an increasing percentage of national gross product. This would provide Germany with the opportunity to dominate the Common Market.

At the present time the French expenditure on nuclear armaments is not beyond the means, as is also true of Britain.[79] But the comparison, often made in France, between the French and the American expenses makes it clear that France will always remain a second-rate nuclear power in absolute terms. The French government would, of course, reply that France never intended to become a nuclear peer of the United States, but want only to acquire a credible deterrent for the French protection.

The total military expenses of Britain, France and Germany are almost of the same size, but each amounts to one-tenth of the American expenses. American nuclear expenses alone are equal to the total French budget; the American military budget amounts to twelve French general budgets and to five times the military budgets of all NATO allies. The American expense on military research only is equal to the whole French nuclear budget. These figures cause a French commentator to exclaim: "What is the miracle that makes us delude ourselves into believing that we should be able to acquire a [nuclear] force deserving this name, in spite of expenses fifteen times smaller and in spite of fifteen years' lag at the beginning of our effort?"[80]

As we have said, all the forecasts may be vitiated by the expenses which now are not taken into account because they are currently not needed. The present official estimates do not include the cost of building the French early warning and guidance systems without which France would continue to depend on the United States. The cost of submarines, missiles, and nuclear warheads might prove higher than expected, as the present stage is that of research, testing and the first steps of production. Other items, which will increase greatly the cost, are the expenses on maintenance of nuclear force and on the means of active and passive defense. Finally, France would have to make rapid strides in outer-space exploration to become a first-class military power. All this is never mentioned by the official spokesmen.[81]

The wisest conclusion is that of Raymond Aron:

> If we regard the sums spent by the United States on research and production of ballistic missiles and H bombs, our answer will be negative. But this sort of estimates is liable to objections. The period of time and the size of expenses required by the scientific and technological progress might be reduced by those who come later, who know what is the obtainable objective and who have collected much information regarding the road to follow. It is not impossible that the military problem of capability to inflict considerable damages on an enemy might be solved by different technological methods, some of them more and some of them less costly.[82]

The French government makes no secret of the fact that the nuclear armaments are being partly financed by the reduction of expenses on conventional armaments. The French Army is being reduced in numbers. This policy is the result of the French strategic concept, according to which a war in Europe can only be a nuclear war.

The French government is right in calculating that it could not afford to build the nuclear force and simultaneously maintain large conventional forces. On May 14, 1963, Prime Minister Pompidou defined the French option:

> If we were to abandon our atomic armaments, our own deterrent force, we should have been compelled to undertake, regarding the conventional divisions, an effort which would be, to say the least,

as costly and probably more costly then the building of deterrent force. I make this supposition, because our critics would not advise us to quit the Atlantic alliance or to resist the pressure by our Allies. I see the proof for what I am saying . . . in the military budget of the German Federal Republic, which is not atomic but which will be this year greater than the French military budget.[83]

His estimate of the future cost of nuclear armaments might prove to be too optimistic, but he was right in saying that France had to choose between the two kinds of armaments.

The French opponents stress the risks involved in the official view that the only war in Europe would have to be nuclear and support the American thesis that it would be safer to be able to respond to a Soviet conventional attack with conventional weapons. They are not attracted by the alternative: either effectively to deter any Soviet military move, even one of limited effect, by the threat of massive nuclear response, or, if the threat would not deter, to commit collective suicide.[84]

Paul Reynaud is one of those who adduce convincing arguments in favor of a flexible response:

> Americans tell us with common sense that the atomic war is so horrible and so fatal in its outcome that one should do everything to prevent the occurrence of a situation where suicidal war would be the only answer to a local engagement. We must be able to resist with conventional weapons an aggression by conventional weapons. If it were necessary, we might later have recourse to those tactical atomic weapons which play a role only on the battle-fields. And if the struggle continues, we might end by having re-course to the H (thermonuclear) bombs. It will then become a suicidal war, but we should first give the enemy time for reflec-tion; we hope that he would recoil before the prospect of destroy-ing his own nation. This is the concept of "escalation," of succes-sive stages.[85]

In any event, during the last several years France contributed only two divisions and approximately 450 military planes to the NATO forces; her military and air units placed under the NATO command were stationed in Germany. All other French armed forces had been withdrawn from NATO by President de Gaulle in the first years after his return to power. On July 1, 1966, even the French forces stationed in Germany were withdrawn from NATO. At the present time not a single French unit remains under the NATO command.

By way of comparison, one may mention that twelve German divisions (the whole German Army, the strongest in Europe, excluding, of course, the Soviet) are entirely integrated within NATO. The American forces stationed in Germany number about 220,000 men, and the British over 40,000. If the French forces, although no longer under the NATO command, were to remain on German soil, their strength would probably remain the same as now and would amount to approximately 70,000. (See Chapter IV)

From the American point of view, Western Germany is a much more valuable ally who neither revolts against the military integration nor objects to the American overall command, nor, finally, refuses to make a serious contribution to the collective defense. However, Frenchmen rather paradoxically resent the increasing weight of Germany in American military planning. The French nuclear force, which is not integrated, is too small to play any role in the American strategic thinking at any rate.

The policy of drastically contracting the size of land forces is reflected in the official program, which provides for a reduction in the number of young men called for military service. It is planned that in 1966 only 215,000 out of 400,000 young men who could have been compelled to serve will be taken. The land forces are conceived as composed of young men called for military service at the age of 18 and serving for 18 months and of professional personnel: officers, N.C.O.'s, and highly trained soldiers. This army would not be able to play any significant role in a major war and is intended to be a supplementary force in a nuclear war as well as a task force for local wars.[86]

France contracted military agreements with several African states, such as the Central African Republic, Congo-Brazzaville, the Ivory Coast, Dahomey, Madagascar, Mauritania, Niger, Senegal, Tchad, Togo and Gabon. These agreements, concluded from 1960 to 1963, oblige France to defend those countries against external aggression and to intervene in case the existing government in one of those countries should ask for assistance to suppress a domestic rebellion or coup. De Gaulle intervened only once, namely to support the government of Gabon against a domestic revolt. In Congo-Brazzaville he wisely refused to do so and allowed a leftist group to seize power. He was recompensed by the continuation of friendly relations with that country.

The French forces which would be called upon to implement the terms of agreements are divided into two groups: small garrisons located on the African soil with the assent of the governments concerned (these small forces are placed at a few strategic points and could rapidly intervene elsewhere), and three brigades stationed in France and ready to be dispatched in case of necessity. These three brigades number 35,000 men.

Nuclear armaments and scientific progress

Another controversial aspect of the nuclear policy is the question whether this policy will or will not help France in her scientific and industrial development. Prime Minister Pompidou declared on May 14, 1963: "To renounce our atomic effort would be tantamount to condemning France to be, in ten or fifteen years at the most, an underdeveloped country."[87] His predecessor is of the same opinion:

> Knowledge of that technology and the capacity for production are already the precondition of the industrial and scientific development of our country. . . . Our effort in building a national instrument of deterrence provides us with the human and material potential required for remaining an industrial and scientific power even of a second rank.[88]

Another supporter of Gaullist nuclear policy points out that the decision to build the Pierrelatte plant for the separation of isotopes was made in March 1957 by the then Prime Minister, Socialist Guy Mollet, who now strongly opposes the official policy. This plant will produce the enriched uranium 235 necessary for the nuclear-powered submarines and for nuclear warheads. He also notes that, owing to that plant, France will be able to offer the enriched uranium on the international market and compete in this respect with the United States. Furthermore, the plant will supply the enriched uranium to the French nuclear-power stations. Finally, he mentions that the construction and equipment of the plant will stimulate the technological progress of those industries which have been participating in its construction, such as non-ferrous, metallurgical, electrical, air-conditioning, and chemical.[89] Undoubtedly, the nuclear armament, like all military armaments, requires a formidable scientific research which has beneficial results for peaceful industrial purposes too. It ensures technological progress as well as the diversification and increase of the national industrial potential.

The opposition accepts the thesis that France should engage in a nuclear effort, but only for peaceful purposes. They would have preferred, they say, to build only that part of the Pierrelatte plant which is necessary for those purposes, while renouncing the completion of parts required for military purposes.[90]

The opposition also expresses the fear that governmental employment of a large number of scientists and technologists in nuclear research and production will result in the lack or delay of progress in the other scientific fields. "The French striking force paralyzes or limits progress in many fields instead of automatically stimulating progress of science and civilian technology, as it is claimed."[91]

In 1964 an important literary magazine, *Le Figaro Littéraire,* proceeded with an opinion poll among young French scientists who all opposed the official nuclear policy in varying degrees because they held that government-sponsored nuclear research absorbed 50 per cent of all research workers and 60 per cent of young scientists. They were worried that the scientific research in other fields would be adversely affected by the shortage of available scientists and insufficient state support, and that, eventually, French science as a whole would lag behind that of other advanced countries.[92] Only the distant future will pronounce the final verdict in this particular controversy, in which the anti-Gaullists overlook the fact that scientific research is also largely oriented by the government in the United States and exclusively planned by the government in the Soviet Union.

Referendum?

The liveliness of French debate demonstrates that the governmental policy is controversial. De Gaulle says that he is the partisan of referendum, because it is "the fairest, the most sincere and the most democratic procedure that could be devised. . . . Henceforth, on a subject that is vital for the country, all citizens may be directly called upon . . . to judge the matter for themselves and to assume their own responsibility."[93] Is there a more vital subject than the nuclear issue for Frenchmen and for all inhabitants of the earth? However, de Gaulle knows that all the political parties, except for his own U.N.R. and his supporters among the Republican Independents, oppose the nuclear policy. They might or might not be sincere in their opposition, but they all, including the Communists, would propagandize, prior to a referendum, for a nay vote. So far de Gaulle has not risked a referendum on this subject, which he considers so vital for France that he prefers not to leave the decision to "ephemeral" Frenchmen. Michel Habib-Deloncle, then Secretary of State for Foreign Affairs, told the Senate on October 15, 1963: "There is no need to hold a referendum."[94] He added: "We are sure to be supported by public opinion." He probably referred to public opinion polls to which his government attaches great importance.

These polls indicate, however, that the public opinion is sharply divided. Thirty-four per cent were in favor in August 1963 and 39 in April 1964, but in both cases those were only large minorities. The percentage of those opposed also increased between these two dates from 37 to 40. The only decrease was among those who had no opinion; their percentage fell from 29 to 21, an indication of the growing interest in the problem on the part of ordinary citizens.[95] The public support is not so great as the government claims.

Will his policy survive him?

The inconclusive public opinion polls and the vocal opposition of political parties do not authorize a hasty view that de Gaulle's nuclear policy will not survive him. Firstly, no one can be absolutely sure whether the Gaullists will not remain in power even after his demise. Secondly, the national nuclear force does exist. The difficulty of renouncing it has been illustrated by the Labour government in Britain. The possible proliferation of nuclear weapons would make it even more difficult. Finally, one can legitimately doubt whether the opposition, except for the Communists, is entirely sincere. Do they fight against de Gaulle only or against his nuclear policy? Even the fiercest opponents do not want France to be deprived of participation of one kind or another in the Western nuclear force. Moreover, it would be unwise to forget that the decision to forge a nuclear shield for France was initially made not by de Gaulle but by the governments of the Fourth Republic, by the same politicians who are now denouncing the futility of national force.

Prime Minister Pompidou was in a strong position when he reminded the opposition of the undeniable truth that:

> The French atomic accomplishments have been due to all of us. . . . All the governments have realized their importance. Parliaments have assented to the required financial effort. There is no other present venture of any kind that is more obviously the consequence of a long and perseverant effort.[96]

All the French commentators agree on this point. The government, led by de Gaulle but composed of Popular Republicans, Socialists and Communists, decided on October 18, 1945, that the Commissariat of Atomic Energy should make preparations for the use of atomic energy "in the various fields of science, industry and national defense."[97] Later on, while de Gaulle was living in retirement, the successive Prime Min-

isters of the Fourth Republic (Mendès-France, Edgar Faure, Guy
Mollet, Félix Gaillard and Bourgès-Maunoury) made the decisions
which allowed France to progress toward the acquisition of nuclear
weapons. Their cabinet colleagues agreed, and the parliaments voted
the necessary credits. In 1952 a statute was adopted for the development of atomic energy with the understanding that it might also help
in military defense. In 1954 the government of Mendès-France ordered
preliminary studies on the atomic bomb without yet making a decision
concerning its future production. In 1955 the parliament voted for the
supplementary credits required for these studies. Edgar Faure was at
that time the Prime Minister. His government also approved the plans
for the construction of a plant for the separation of isotopes. In 1956
the government of Guy Mollet adopted a five-year plan for the preparation of nuclear tests; in the same year a pilot-plant for the study of the
separation of isotopes was established at Saclay. In 1957 it was finally
decided that the plant for the separation of isotopes would be built;
without it de Gaulle would have been unable to start his nuclear program. At the beginning of 1958 the place was selected, and in April
of the same year the government decided in secret to plan the manufacture of the atomic bomb. This brief history indicates that de Gaulle
did not initiate the nuclear policy but only decided, after his return to
power, to continue it. The French commentator is right when he says,
in reference to the Moscow Treaty on the suspension of nuclear tests,
that: "I believe that no French Head of State or of government would
have signed the Treaty, because it would have been tantamount to saying that France would suddenly become the only country to halt its
military policy completely and to change it from top to bottom."[98]
This begs a rather rhetorical question: Will any future French government suddenly abandon de Gaulle's nuclear policy, which was also that
of the Fourth Republic? In 1963 China was in the same position as
France and, for the same reasons, refused to adhere to the Moscow
Treaty.

May one trust the sincerity of the opposition against this historical
background? It was Félix Gaillard, then Prime Minister, who said on
December 30, 1957, that:

> The French government does not intend to undertake the obliga-
> tion never to proceed with nuclear tests, i.e., never to produce
> atomic weapons, as long as an international agreement, which
> would provide for an effective control, would not ensure the ter-
> mination by all states of the production of nuclear and thermo-

nuclear weapons. Disarmament should not be limited to some states; it should be accepted by all states.[99]

This is exactly the position of the Fifth Republic. The governments of the Fourth Republic could afford to be more secretive concerning their nuclear policy, because this policy was not publicly revealed to the whole world until 1960 with the first atomic explosion in the Sahara.

Is the Socialist expert on the matter, Jules Moch, now completely sincere in his opposition, if he told the United Nations General Assembly in October 1958 that:

> The cessation of nuclear tests, if done by an isolated state, would not be a true progress but only an alibi. . . . France fervently wishes never to possess one single atomic or thermonuclear bomb. . . . But she formulates one condition for this renunciation, namely that the existing atomic powers stop, under an international supervision, increasing their stocks and begin reducing them. . . . Otherwise France shall not renounce the possession of weapons which other states have and which these other States constantly increase in quantity.[100]

He was at that time the official representative of the Fifth Republic at the international conferences on disarmament, where he vigorously defended the same thesis.[101]

Moscow Treaty and nuclear proliferation

If it is true that any non-Communist French government would have refused to adhere to the Moscow Treaty on the suspension of nuclear tests, is it surprising that de Gaulle had to take the same position as China? His distrust of the motivations which determine other states to pursue a given policy is very deep and founded on his axiom that all nations have in mind only their own national interests. He is far from being wrong in this respect, but his distrust deepens his belief that a French policy, strongly criticized abroad, must be correct because it is resented by foreign governments. His statement of October 23, 1958, made at his first official press conference, throws light on this particular aspect of his mentality:

> Everybody knows that we now have the means for providing ourselves with nuclear weapons, and the day is approaching when we, in our turn, will carry out tests. Perhaps this circumstance was taken into consideration when Moscow, Washington and London simultaneously concluded that the suspension of tests was suddenly desirable.[102]

The Chinese would have said the same, if they had so desired.

His refusal to adhere to the Moscow Treaty, signed on August 5, 1963, should not have surprised anyone. He said on July 29, 1963:

> We repeat also that a mere agreement on tests between Soviets and Anglo-Saxons, already invested with immeasurable power, and who do not cease to strengthen it and thereby to confirm day by day their respective hegemonies, a mere agreement will not prevent France also from equipping herself with the same kind of means, failing which, since others have these means, France's own security and her own independence would never again belong to her.[103]

His criticism of the Moscow Treaty was pertinent insofar as that Treaty did not halt the American-Soviet armament race but had only one important beneficial effect, the cessation of poisoning the atmosphere by the American and Russian tests. He said:

> Nothing prevents the two rivals, their tests having been halted, from continuing to manufacture missiles in increasing quantities and power and to equip themselves with increasingly advanced launch vehicles, rockets, airplanes, submarines and satellites. The savings they could perhaps make from halting tests will enable them to strengthen even further their means of destruction. That is why the Moscow agreement, I say this frankly, has only limited practical importance.[104]

He strongly suspected that the Asian-African outcry caused by the French plans for the first tests in the Sahara, was engineered by the existing nuclear powers:

> Of course, it is understandable that the powers which possess atomic weapons, that is the United States, the Soviet Union and England, do not wish France to acquire them. Of course, it is understandable that these three powers find, among the States which have more or less close ties with them, a response favorable to their thesis and unfavorable to the French plan.[105]

He was, not without reason, indignant that the Asian and African governments were suddenly alarmed by the French intention to carry out tests, at that time measured only in kilotons, while their reaction to the American and Soviet megaton tests was comparatively rather mild. He said on November 10, 1959: "Never has the United Nations invited the Anglo-Saxons and the Soviets to destroy the nuclear weapons which they possessed, nor even to stop manufacturing them. Never has it blamed some two hundred tests that have taken place in all sorts of areas of the world."[106] His bitterness was sincere when he witnessed, after the first French tests in 1960, the solemn protest of the African conference held in September 1961 in Casablanca and the no less severe criticism in the British press which forgot on that occasion the proverb that sauce good for the goose was also good for the gander.

It was only fair that the French government took the same position regarding the Chinese nuclear policy. The Minister of Foreign Affairs, Couve de Murville, told the National Assembly on November 3, 1964, that:

> Much is being said about China, as was formerly said about France, on the dangers of dissemination, on the need to do immediately everything in order to prevent it. The Government for its part has always believed that this was not the right way to face this problem. Indeed, we could only approve any action which would aim at preventing the accession of new States to the nuclear club, its being understood, however, that the latter would at the same time prepare for its own disappearance. How can one claim to deny others, unless they voluntarily renounce it for themselves, what one permits oneself? Experience proves, moreover, that this is never accomplished, except through force, which has never to my knowledge been considered.[107]

In spite of the Moscow Treaty, states other than France and China, might one day be tempted to follow suit, disregarding their own signatures of adhesion. Several have nuclear reactors and the required scientific-industrial potential. The list of possible candidates for membership in the nuclear club is long and includes most of the European countries; Canada, India, Australia, Japan; and the relatively developed Latin-American countries, such as Argentina, Brazil, or Mexico. In spite of international agreements and other considerations, Germany might also one day claim the right to have her own nuclear weapons.

Britain and France

Anyone who is inclined to criticize the French nuclear policy should remember that his criticism equally applies to the British policy. All the arguments advanced by the French government have been used by the British Conservative governments. (The Labour government is understandably more discreet.) This aspect of the question is too often forgotten in the United States which helped Britain to become and remain a nuclear power, while refusing (with the exceptions of sales of refueling planes and of enriched uranium) the same treatment to France.

The British opponents of national nuclear force call their adversaries "Gaullists," so much the arguments used by the Conservatives resemble those of de Gaulle and his supporters. This did not preclude the British government from trying to dissuade the French government from engaging in the same task. "Mr. Michel Debré heard on the occasion of his visit to London in April 1959 the same arguments strongly advanced as Mr. Félix Gaillard by the end of 1957 at the time of Mr. Macmillan's visit to Paris."[108] The only result achieved was to convince de Gaulle of the "Anglo-Saxon perfidy."

The Conservative Prime Ministers, Secretaries of State for Foreign Affairs and for Defense, and other members of government multiplied throughout the years all the arguments which the French government now advances. The British White Paper published in February 1964 sounds like a quotation from one of de Gaulle's statements: "If there were no power in Europe capable of inflicting unacceptable damages on a potential enemy, the enemy might be tempted to attack in the mistaken belief that the United States would not act unless America herself were attacked."[109] Lord Home, then Foreign Secretary, told the House of Lords on March 14, 1963, that one could not remain certain forever that the United States would always protect Britain with its own nuclear weapons. He and his cabinet colleagues had in mind the American fear of Soviet retaliatory strike.

Another British argument, familiar to the French government, consists in saying that there is no guaranty of the eternal similarity between the American and the British national interests. The Conservatives always wanted to reserve the British freedom of decision in case a conflict, not necessarily in Europe only, would call for the use of nuclear weapons, while the United States would not be vitally interested in the British quarrel. They did not forget the Suez affair of 1956. This consideration was accepted as legitimate by the United States in the Nassau agreement. An impartial observer, an Australian scholar, duly noted these points:

> Some of the decisions of British policy have carried a suppressed premise that there might develop a divergence of strategic interest between America and Britain. In fact, this might be called the suppressed premise behind the whole of the British nuclear weapons programme, from Mr. Attlee's first decision to build

atomic weapons when the McMahon Act cut Britain off from the American information in 1946. It has, however, seldom been put into words. One of the few occasions was Duncan Sandys' defence of the decision to build a hydrogen bomb in 1956. "So long as large American forces remain in Europe and American bombers are based in Britain it might conceivably be thought safe . . . to leave to the United States the sole responsibility for providing the nuclear deterrent. But, when they have developed the 5,000 mile intercontinental ballistic rocket, can we really be sure that every American administration will go on looking at things in quite the same way?"[110]

The statement was made on April 15, 1956, in the House of Commons. The United States and the Soviet Union now have intercontinental ballistic missiles.

The Conservative government also stressed several times that the cost of nuclear force was the necessary fee for retaining the rank of a world power. Prime Minister Macmillan was one of those who felt that Britain would otherwise lose her position as one of the three Big Powers; de Gaulle aspires to assure France the rank of the fourth.

Britain, like France, was compelled by financial considerations to sacrifice her conventional forces on the altar of nuclear armaments. Universal military service was abolished. The British contribution to NATO land forces is relatively small; and at time of simultaneous non-European crises Britain is hard put to face all her overseas commitments. This policy points out by implication that Britain also doubts whether a European war could be limited to conventional battles.

Britain so far has not ruined herself by the expenses on her nuclear armaments. This is encouraging for France, whose nuclear program is almost exactly the same as Britain's. At the present time, Britain relies on her bombers. In the seventies, they will be replaced by nuclear-powered submarines armed with Polaris missiles. According to the Nassau agreement, Britain will build her own submarines and the nuclear warheads, while she will buy the Polaris missiles from the United States. France will have to produce all three, but her nuclear force, unlike the British, will not be placed under American command. British force will be dependent on the good will of the United States not only for the early warning system, as the French is, but also for missile supplies. The sudden American decision in 1962 to abandon the production of Skybolt, in favor of which Britain in 1960 had stopped manufacturing her own Blue Steel, forced the British government to accept the Nassau agreement, but also taught Britain and France as well that dependence on a foreign Power might not always be advisable.

One may note that the British also accept, like France, the theory of nuclear saturation, i.e., that a first-class nuclear power would not attack a weaker one for fear of damages which the latter power's nuclear strike would inflict.

If the credibility of the French deterrent is questionable and if this deterrent is threatened with obsolescence because of the progress in the American and Soviet armaments, the argument is equally valid for Britain.

Finally, the British possession of nuclear weapons is neither more nor less dangerous for the other nations than the French is. Both countries are *status quo* powers, and neither may be suspected of intending to unleash a general war.

Unfortunately, the similarity of the two cases has often been overlooked in the United States where the main criticism has been directed against de Gaulle rather than against Britain. One cannot reject offhand as ill-founded this bitter comment by one of the Gaullist leaders, Christian de la Malène:

> Great Britain has always wanted to have her own independent strategic nuclear force. The United States not only has not been opposed to it but actually has helped in its realization. Nobody has felt exceedingly upset and nobody has declared that the Atlantic Alliance is in danger. It is rather difficult to understand why the French force would be more inconvenient than the British.[111]

This double standard provokes in de Gaulle and in many other Frenchmen the feeling that France cannot expect a fair hearing in Washington.

The United States and France

Michel Debré sees dark designs behind the American refusal to assist France in acquiring her own nuclear force. He writes:

> One can understand the interest represented, not only from the political but also from the economic point of view, by a privilege which would deprive European nations of any strong atomic and missile industries and would bar for them the road to any significant scientific and technological progress. The United States would then preserve its dominant position in economic and scientific development and the privilege of conquering outer space in the name of the free world.[112]

This accusation of harboring diabolically monopolistic intentions reveals the depth of bitter French resentment toward the United States. The true reasons of the American refusal to assist France may be summarized as follows:

1. The United States knows that its massive deterrent is amply sufficient to destroy the Soviet Union and believes that, if nothing else would help, the deterrent would be used to protect not only America but also its European allies. At least, it trusts that the Soviet Union is sufficiently deterred by the uncertainty as to whether the United States would or would not use strategic nuclear weapons in case of a European war. The American government has made it clear many times that the addition of European nuclear deterrents would be unnecessary, because it would be too insignificant in comparison to the American deterrent.

President Kennedy stated in 1962 his firm opposition to the proliferation of nuclear armaments and his refusal to assist France, but he also acknowledged the fact that France was becoming, by her own effort, a fourth nuclear power. The signature of the Moscow Treaty bound American hands; any assistance which would help a third state in carrying nuclear tests would amount to its violation. What is too easily forgotten in France is that, prior to that Treaty, the United States in 1962 sold the refueling planes which made the Mirage deterrent at least technically more credible. The French government, furthermore, did not disclose until 1966 the existence of a secret French-American agreement concluded in 1959 by virtue of which the United States undertook the obligation to supply enriched uranium fuel for the Cadarrache plant. The plant was working on a nuclear reactor which would become the prototype of reactors to be installed on future French submarines of the Polaris type. This agreement was unilaterally suspended by the United States in 1964. (See Chapter IV)

2. The logical conclusion from the position of the United States that its allies do not need their own nuclear forces is that they should help in preventing an all-out nuclear escalation. Their task should be to provide land armies for a conventional war in order to make that war possible and thus to avoid the nuclear holocaust. Neither Britain nor France has substantially contributed toward making the concept of graduated response a feasible strategy.

The United States accepts the necessity of arming its allies (including the French forces stationed in Germany) with tactical nuclear weapons, but also fears the consequences of an unauthorized use of these weapons. Hence it practices the policy of two keys; these weapons may not be fired without American cooperation. De Gaulle accepted this American veto which undermined his most cherished concept of the independence of French defense but certainly the two-key system spurred his resolve to provide French forces with their own tactical nuclear weapons.

3. The United States has acknowledged the existence of uneasiness among its major European allies concerning their lack of any influence on the NATO nuclear policy which is, in the last analysis, determined in Washington. It tried to find a solution satisfactory to all concerned in the concept of a Multilateral Force. This project failed for lack of response by the European allies; only Western Germany was really ready to participate. Neither Britain nor the others were enthusiastic. France flatly rejected it, because any military integration under the American command was repugnant to General de Gaulle.

Germany

There is hardly any compromise possible between the American and French nuclear policies. However, both governments are preoccupied with another problem, the German claims regarding nuclear weapons. Both of them and, in fact, also the other Atlantic allies may trust the German political wisdom, but they cannot help knowing that Germany is the only power in Europe highly dissatisfied with the existing political and territorial *status quo*. None of them would celebrate on the day Western Germany acquired an independent nuclear force. The Nazi period is not yet forgotten in Europe. This raises the question full of anxiety whether the Germans, entrusted with nuclear weapons, would be able to demonstrate the same self-restraint as the present nuclear powers. Finally, there is another fear, the fear that the Russians, if truly confronted with an immediate prospect of German nuclear armament, might respond with an action that would end in a general war. All those fears might be unfounded, but they do exist.

The argument used that de Gaulle gives a bad example to Western Germans is not convincing because, if the Germans wanted to acquire nuclear weapons, they could invoke other examples, for instance, the British. The real problem lies elsewhere: can the United States grant a privileged position to Britain and France and assist them in their nuclear policies, while refusing the same treatment to West Germany, which makes a very important contribution to the NATO forces and is one of the most reliable allies against the Soviet Union? This explains, at least partly, the American reluctance to assist France, although, it is true, the same attitude has never been taken toward Britain.

In any event, there is no risk of seeing de Gaulle help Germany to acquire her own nuclear weapons. He refuses to trust any foreign nation and knows that international friendships have a tendency to wither away. He has no interest in helping Germany to become once more the powerful neighbor on the other bank of the Rhine. His ambition to ensure for France the leadership of Western Europe is founded on the prospect of French nuclear monopoly in that part of the Continent. In January 1965 he used a very clever argument to dissuade the Germans from any nuclear ambition, including participation in the Multilateral Force. He told Chancellor Erhard that there was a self-evident incompatibility between the German reunification and the German attempts to participate in any manner in the nuclear forces.[113] He thereby alluded to the Soviet veto which precludes German reunification and which would become even more adamant if Western Germany were to acquire nuclear weapons in one guise or another.

Frenchmen mention several arguments to prove that Germany should not and will not have nuclear weapons. Some of them sound convincing, the others not. One of them refers to the exposed location of Germany and to the Soviet threats which Khrushchev, with his predilection for picturesque language, formulated in his letter of December 27, 1962, to Chancellor Adenauer. He said there that, if a third world war would break out, "federal Germany would burn down in flames like a candle in the first hours of the war." A Gaullist expressed a general French opinion in this statement:

> Only Western Germany has the intellectual capacity and the required technological means for becoming an atomic power like France and she also has the financial means to achieve this. However, she is bound by the provisions of the Treaty of Paris and is thereby forbidden to manufacture atomic weapons. If she disregarded that Treaty, it would probably be, in the present circumstances, the most probable "casus belli" for the Russians.[114]

The Paris agreements of 1954 forbid Germany to manufacture nuclear weapons. It is true that the history of international agreements on the limitation of armaments of a defeated nation is not very encouraging; these agreements were violated and finally denounced. In the present case, the Paris agreements of 1954 have a better chance of surviving because of the restraining influence of the German allies and the possibility of a violent Soviet reaction.

Another argument, which Frenchmen quote to reassure themselves, is the exiguity of West German territory, its proximity to the concentration of Soviet troops, and the lack of any suitable testing ground.

De Gaulle would gladly accept Western German financial assistance to build the French force in exchange for a French promise to use that force in Germany's defense. "The soundings of the German political leaders were unsuccessful."[115] The Germans would have been singularly naive to accept this sort of bargain.[116]

The Nassau Agreement

Being a convinced adversary of any joint allied military integration, de Gaulle was firmly opposed to both the Nassau agreement and to the American project of an Atlantic Multilateral Force. The Bahamas conference between President Kennedy and Prime Minister Macmillan marked an important date in de Gaulle's foreign policy. It persuaded him that nothing desirable regarding the French armaments was to be expected from the "Anglo-Saxons" and that France had to rely only on her own effort. In turn, it gave him a completely free hand regarding both the United States and Britain; expecting nothing from them in the nuclear currency, he was free to pursue his foreign objectives in utter disregard of their interests and desires. The discrepancy between his policy and the American has become, since the Nassau conference, even more visible, and de Gaulle's tone has sharpened. The same conference was the main reason, according to all French commentators, for his veto cast against the British admission to the Common Market.

He was offended in the first place by not being invited to Nassau where the two participants in the conference not only took decisions concerning their mutual relations but also jointly sent to him proposals which they had adopted without his being consulted. This tactical error of the President and the Prime Minister is retrospectively difficult to explain. Both should have known de Gaulle's personal pride and his touchiness regarding the rank of his "princess." The American and British archives were full of reports on both points, reports written during the last war. One of the sources of his animosity against President Roosevelt was precisely his conviction that he was not given the diplomatic treatment due him as the incarnation of France. Secondly, no government likes particularly to be told by two other governments that they offer it a bargain on which it had not been consulted and which affects its vital interests. The American-British proposals were to be accepted or rejected. De Gaulle rejected them. Thirdly, these proposals were in any event unacceptable in the light of his fundamental objectives.

His negative reaction can be understood only against the background of these objectives. One of them is, as we have seen, the independence of French defense and the rejection of foreign command and hence of any joint allied military integration. Another is that France has the right to be one of the three participants in the leadership of the Atlantic Alliance and should be conceded a rank equal to that of the Anglo-Saxon powers. He formulated this concept of the triumvirate in his memorandum of September 1958. This was his condition for any coordination of joint allied military and political strategies. Both objectives were disregarded in Nassau.

He seemed to expect (all French commentators agree on this point) prior to the conference that Britain, disappointed in the nuclear cooperation with the United States by the sudden decision concerning the Skybolt, would turn to France and offer a collaboration which would have been at that time very useful to France. Britain's accumulated knowledge and experience would be shared with France and thus help her to become more quickly a nuclear power. In particular, he thought that both countries would cooperate in the production of a missile that would replace the Skybolt. He was bitterly disappointed by the British decision to accept President Kennedy's proposals.

He overlooked, however, another aspect of the question. It was for the first time that the United States consented to place France on the same level as Britain regarding the nuclear collaboration. The French nuclear force of the future was to be composed, like the British, of nationally constructed submarines, but armed with American Polaris missiles. The nuclear warheads were to be produced by the European powers themselves. It is true that the British and French submarine fleets, armed with American Polaris missiles, were to be placed under the overall American NATO command, but each fleet could be used independently of the American wishes if "the supreme national interests" demanded. For the first time, the United States placed not only Britain but also France ahead of other allies, including Germany. It is true that the proposal was technically and financially less attractive to France than to Britain. France had not yet exploded a fusion bomb and would take a longer time to produce nuclear warheads for the Polaris missiles. She was only in the blueprint stage of nuclear-powered submarines. The pros of the Nassau proposals did not outweigh, in de Gaulle's mind, the cons.

De Gaulle rejected the proposals at his press conferences held on January 14, 1963. His arguments were as follows:

It is a question of constituting a so-called multilateral atomic force. . . . This multilateral force is assigned to the defense of Europe and is under the American NATO command. . . . As for the bulk of American nuclear weapons, it remains outside the multilateral force and under the direct orders of the President of the United States. . . . It truly would not be useful for us to buy Polaris missiles when we have neither the submarines to launch them nor the thermonuclear warheads to arm them. . . . When we will one day have these submarines and these warheads, what will the Polaris missiles then be worth? At that time we will probably have missiles of our own invention. . . . To build these submarines and warheads, the British receive privileged assistance from the Americans. You know—I say this in passing—that this assistance was never offered to us and you should know, despite what some report, that we have never asked for it.[117]

His criticism was well taken. France would have to rely only on her own effort for the production of the submarines and warheads, while it would have to pay for the Polaris missiles, which might become obsolete in the seventies, not only in cash but also in the acceptance of the American command. He added a characteristic observation:

It is completely understandable that this French [nuclear] undertaking does not appear to be highly satisfactory to certain American circles. In politics and in strategy, as in the economy, monopoly quite naturally appears to the person who holds it to be the best possible system.[118]

For him the Nassau proposal was calculated to deprive Britain and France of the independent national defense. If Britain accepted it, this was a flagrant proof of her resigned acceptance of American supremacy. She was an American Trojan horse and had to be barred access to the Common Market. He finally reaffirmed his most cherished principle: ". . . for us, in this specific case, integration is something that is unimaginable."

Michel Debré added his comment. The Nassau proposal allegedly was, among others, calculated to persuade Britain and France to spend their money on buying the American military material (the Polaris missiles), while financing themselves the construction of submarines and warheads. Finally, all this money would buy for the United States the perpetuation of its supremacy in the guise of American NATO command.[119]

MLF

After the rejection of the Nassau proposals it was obvious that France would no less firmly oppose the American concept of Multilateral Force. This concept, born in 1960 under the Eisenhower administration, took a definite shape under Kennedy's administration. It was conceived as a clever device for appeasing the dissatisfaction of European allies with the undivided American leadership in the Atlantic Alliance. The only credible Atlantic deterrent was American (98 per cent of the Western nuclear power) and could be used only on the orders of the President of the United States. The tactical nuclear weapons were locked by the two-key system and could not be used without American permission. Finally, the NATO supreme command was monopolized by American generals appointed by the President. The European allies felt reduced to a second-rate position. This feeling, vocally expressed by de Gaulle, was shared by others, including the Germans.

Among the major NATO powers only Germany was deprived of nuclear weapons. Not only the United States but also Britain and France had or were acquiring their national nuclear forces. It was felt in Washington that something had to be done to appease the European allies, notably Germany. The MLF was the answer.

The MLF looked less attractive in its final form than in the first suggestions which were sketched under the Eisenhower administration. The Democratic administration replaced the submarines, which initially were to form the NATO nuclear-armed fleet, with surface vessels also armed with Polaris missiles but obviously much more vulnerable to the enemy attack. The cost of the MLF was to be shared by the United States and those European allies who would consent to participate in the project. The crews of the MLF were to be supplied by the participating states, and the whole placed under the NATO, i.e., the American supreme command. The United States was to retain the veto power; the MLF would take no action unless so ordered by the American general who would be at the time commander-in-chief of NATO forces.

De Gaulle's first reaction was one of amusement rather than anger. He shared the British skepticism concerning the project. Could a fleet of surface vessels be operated by mixed crews of several nationalities? Would this enterprise be more lucky than the Tower of Babel? Would those vessels become a serious deterrent or would they be considered by the Soviet Union, in spite of their nuclear armament, as sitting ducks? De Gaulle expected that the lukewarm attitude of the British and the first tests of a pilot vessel would demonstrate impracticality of the American project to all allies.

Later he was alarmed by German enthusiasm for the MLF. For Germany it was an attractive way of having some access to the technique of nuclear weapons and also a sort of recognition of her equal status among the NATO allies. She was ready to contribute 40 per cent of the cost. It was not settled who else would participate in the MLF. Britain was skeptical and possibly ready to buy only a nominal membership for the sake of American friendship; she had to save her financial resources for her own national nuclear force. The others either refused to participate or offered lukewarm support. France, Portugal, Norway, Denmark, and Canada were not interested. Italy, Greece, and Turkey were ready to consider the membership, but Turkey later changed her mind, while one could not be too sure that a center-left government of Italy would be permitted by its Socialist ministers finally to make a positive decision. Holland, and even more, Belgium, hesitated and lacked great enthusiasm. It was possible that the MLF would become mainly an American-German affair.

De Gaulle was beginning to suspect that one of the reasons of American proposal was to detach Germany from her policy of close friendship with France and thereby to isolate France in Western Europe. His suspicion and his failure to dissuade the Germans contributed to his more skeptical reappraisal of the usefulness of a policy founded on Franco-German cooperation. For him Germany should not have two close friends, the United States and France, as the Germans wanted; they had to choose, and their acceptance of the MLF was one of the main proofs that they had chosen America. In July 1964 de Gaulle told the German government that their participation in the MLF would perpetuate the American hegemony in Europe and would run counter to his policy of winning Western Europe its independence. He failed to convince his German interlocutors.

On November 5, 1964, Prime Minister Pompidou publicly formulated de Gaulle's suspicion that the MLF had been conceived in order to detach Germany from France which would remain isolated in the midst of a Western Europe, grouped around the American-German alliance:

> Certain statements made us think initially that that Multilateral Force would become in essence a German-American bilateral agreement. Other statements could be interpreted in another sense, namely that the Multilateral Force would be a device for assembling the principal nations of NATO around it and for isolating France who had expressed, right at the beginning of conversations,

her preference for her own armaments. If the Multilateral Force should result in a sort of German-American military alliance, our first reaction would be that we could not consider this arrangement truly compatible with the present relations which we have with the Federal Republic and which are defined in the Franco-German Treaty. . . . In brief, we may ask ourselves whether this kind of project, this Multilateral Force would not destroy Europe, whether it would not be a challenge to some other countries, and, finally, whether it is not more or less directed against France.[120]

Pompidou accused the United States of harboring the design to isolate France, but his threats were addressed to Germany. He said in effect that the German participation in the MLF would put an end to the German-French cooperation. His reminder that not only France but also "other countries" (an unequivocal allusion to the Soviet Union and its Eastern European allies) would consider the German accession to the MLF as a provocation, was a hardly veiled menace that France, disappointed in Germany, could find a platform of understanding with the Soviet Union.

For de Gaulle everything was repugnant in the project: the American supreme command and veto, the integration of multinational fleet, and the costly membership fee which he could not afford, having to husband the French resources for the construction of her national nuclear force. Moreover, the use of American massive deterrent would continue to depend on the decision of the President of the United States.

The MLF provided an instructive illustration of the fact that de Gaulle is not an isolated voice in France. The project found hardly any support even among his opponents. One of them wrote:

To rest the Western alliance on two pillars (the United States and Germany) or on three pillars (England being added to the two others) is probably the best device for restoring the union of Frenchmen behind General de Gaulle. . . . Frenchmen are divided into three categories regarding the atomic policy of Gaullism, this policy being the essence of the regime. Some are opposed in any case to the national bomb. Others favor it in any case. Finally, the remaining, probably the most numerous, are torn by doubts; they are opposed to the national bomb as a matter of principle but they are also sensitive to the defects of the present nuclear strategy of NATO. The American project of MLF tends to align the third group with the second and even to draw closer a portion of the first group (Communists) toward the second group.[121]

The Communists are opposed to the national nuclear force but even more to any Atlantic multilateral force in which Germany would be associated. Their attitude reflects the Soviet position. The Soviet Union does not take as tragic the construction of the French force but is most firmly opposed to the German access in any form to the nuclear weapons.[122]

European force

The non-Communist opponents of de Gaulle's policy see or pretend to see an alternative not in the Atlantic multilateral force, but in a European force which would form one of the two pillars of the Atlantic Alliance. They resent the American dominant position within NATO, but want to safeguard the Alliance, while giving it a new form. Their preferences go all the way from a European participation in the elaboration of NATO strategy, including the determination of hypotheses where the United States would be obliged to use its strategic nuclear weapons, up to the creation of a European nuclear force separate but coordinated with the American force. Usually they see the first nucleus of that European force in a close French-British nuclear collaboration. In this latter respect they rejoin the Gaullist position which even now does not seem to be hostile to that collaboration with Britain on the condition, however, that Britain would assert her independence of the United States.

One of the most prominent "Europeans," Maurice Faure, would begin by the integration of the French and British nuclear forces, which would, however, be placed under the NATO supreme command. He would ask for the American assent to a joint definition by the United States and the European allies of the hypotheses for the use of nuclear weapons. Britain and France would each retain the right to use their respective nuclear force independently in case their supreme national interests required it. In brief, Maurice Faure would have been satisfied with the Nassau proposals somewhat modified.

However, he would like to proceed from this first stage to the second where a joint European force would be built around the French-British nucleus. He concedes that the European force would be impossible without the creation of a supranational European government, which he eagerly desires.

Without a political union there would be, in effect, seven "fingers on the trigger," the problems related to the particular situation of Germany would become insoluble, and the reconstruction of the Atlantic system around two equal partners would be impossible.[123]

The most interesting part of his observations is his attitude toward European-American relations: "The European force should . . . culminate in throwing off the protectorate but not in the evasion from the alliance." The Gaullists also want to throw off the American "protectorate" and also do not wish, at least under the present circumstances, to escape from the Atlantic Alliance, but their solution is more realistic.

The minimum agreement among the proponents and opponents of national nuclear force concerns one point, namely the desirability of joint American-European strategic planning and determination of hypotheses where the President of the United States would use the American massive deterrent in the defense of Europe.[124] This minimum requirement is not peculiar to France; it is the general wish of European allies. What is overlooked in this respect is the fact that the most precise definition of cases where American strategic nuclear weapons should be used would not provide complete certainty that the President of the United States would give the order to attack the USSR and expose the national territory to the Soviet retaliatory strike.

The concept of European force raises practically the same questions as that of an Atlantic force. Who would be empowered to give the fatal order: a collective body composed of representatives of various European governments, a supranational authority, or would that power be delegated to a few of the European nations? Assuming that the European force were composed of contributions made by the six Common Market partners and Britain, there is not the slightest chance for the other states to delegate the decision-making power to either Britain or France or to both only because they are already nuclear nations. The relatively small nuclear forces of Britain and France would justify the slogan "No annihilation without representation," which is raised concerning the much more credible and infinitely stronger American nuclear guaranty.

A collective body of six or seven governmental delegates would have to decide either unanimously or by a qualified majority (the major European states, such as Britain, France, Germany, and Italy, having more votes than the lesser states). One veto could paralyze the European force at the most dramatic moment of enemy attack. This veto would be probable regarding the decision which could condemn Western Europe to biological extinction or at least to a drastic reduction of the number of its inhabitants. The rapidity required for the issuing of orders to the nuclear force would not leave any time for consultations among the governments concerned, for instructing the representatives on the joint European body, or for any other deliberations. Several fingers on the nuclear trigger are inconceivable.

The third theoretical solution would be to progress toward a European federal state. Once this state existed, its government would be endowed with full European sovereignty, including power over the death or survival of federated nations. The least one could say is that a federated Western Europe is not for tomorrow. The recurring disputes between the Six over the various aspects of the Common Market and the visible intensification of national feelings in Western Europe do not allow the expectation that the Six would make progress in the near future toward a real federation, if even de Gaulle were not barring the road.

One of the Socialist leaders, René Schmitt, attracted attention to another aspect of a European force:

> European? It seems to me that this solution is difficult, because the Treaty of Paris excluded Germany from among the nations who might possess nuclear weapons. I realize that a European force would considerably increase the international tension and would make serious the risk of war.[125]

German participation in a European force would raise the same political questions as her participation in the MLF.

The Gaullist position would be completely clear but for the fact that the government must pay obeisance from time to time to the concept of a future European force in order to please the five partners in the Common Market. Prime Minister Pompidou used Sybylian language when he said in 1962:

> The day of the construction of a European political union is perhaps very near. This union will be extended to include defense. The contribution, represented by the French possession of nuclear weapons, will be an essential asset for that defense. It will be then possible to raise the question of a nuclear force within the European framework. But we cannot ignore the existence of special situations and of contracted obligations.[126]

Did he mean that France, the only nuclear power among the Six, would take over the role of the United States and would extend her guarantee to the Five? This seems probable, because the Gaullist expectation of French dominance in Western Europe is founded on the French nuclear monopoly. His last two sentences could have been interpreted as meaning that the other Five would eventually form a joint nuclear force with France, where all partners (except for Germany) would be equal in all respects, or, more probably, that the Five would be invited to make their scientific and financial contributions toward the development of the French force.

His Minister of Information was more generous in making promises to the Five. He said on May 28, 1963:

> France favors the creation of a European nuclear force. But this nuclear force presupposes the existence of Europe, its political existence, a Europe that would be provided with a political authority empowered to make the decision concerning the use of its nuclear forces. This political authority does not exist.[127]

Anyone could answer this public relations man that his own President would be the first to oppose the creation of a European political authority. His colleague, the Minister of Foreign Affairs, was more serious-minded when he told the National Assembly on October 29, 1963:

> If a European defense could be one day organized, this process could very well begin by an association between the English and the French nuclear forces. To say: "We must create a European nuclear force," amounts to supposing that this problem is already solved and overlooks the German question.[128]

It is characteristic that he used the word association, not integration. One may guess that de Gaulle would accept even today some form of association with Britain, for instance, regarding scientific research and production. As to any integration of the French nuclear force within a larger combination, he defined his firm opposition long ago. While raising his voice on June 5, 1952, against the European Defense Community Treaty, he called military integration of any sort "a stateless mixture."[129]

The true Gaullist thought regarding a European force is revealed by the former Prime Minister Debré: "The concept is chimerical."[130] It is difficult to disagree. The concept of a European force might be a convenient weapon in the domestic struggle of the opposition against de Gaulle, but is not a valid alternative to his nuclear policy.

One may close this chapter by quoting the opinion of former Prime Minister Edgar Faure who wrote in 1963: "It is certain that no government would abandon in any event a venture already carried so far."[131] It seems that he is right, and that no post-Gaullist government will abandon de Gaulle's nuclear policy, unless faced with a choice between the financial bankruptcy and the continuation of that policy.

Another final observation could be the following. There is no satisfactory solution to the nuclear problem. Neither the American deterrent nor the MLF or a European Force nor the separate national forces can save Western Europe from a holocaust in case of a major war. The only true alternative is peaceful coexistence. On this vital point there is no disagreement between the United States and France.

IV The Atlantic Alliance and the American "Protectorate"

De Gaulle's point of view

There are several reasons for de Gaulle's dissatisfaction with the present condition of the Atlantic Alliance. The nuclear problem is one of the main issues. Another is his inflexible opposition to the military integration of French forces within a joint allied system placed under a non-French supreme command. Third, he rejects the concept of an Atlantic community, which is for him only a disguise for the American "protectorate." His alternative is a politically united Western Europe of national states, united, i.e., aligned with France. This Europe would not denounce alliance with the United States as long as the potential Soviet threat exists, but would be an equal partner. Fourth, he contends that Western military and political strategies in Europe and elsewhere in the world should be determined and coordinated by the United States, France, and Britain; their title to that role is founded, according to de Gaulle, on their being the only Western nuclear powers and also on their worldwide vocation. As this proposal was rejected by the United States in 1958, he has placed an alternative before the United States: either to let France go it alone and complicate American foreign relations by her opposition, or to agree that it would be better to consult her.

Finally, there is a more profound reason for his disagreements with the United States. Sincerely convinced that he is always right, he has a lively aversion to political compromises. French membership in any international organization, be it the United Nations, the Atlantic Alliance, or the European Economic Community, restricts his freedom of maneuvering and is, therefore, a constant irritant. He likes to have free hands in politics. He would not have been happy in the Atlantic triumvirate if the United States and Britain did not accept his advice on every vital issue. This aspect of his character is one cause of misunderstandings between contemporary France and her partners, both the United States and European countries. De Gaulle cannot have his independent foreign policy and an Atlantic triumvirate or a politically united Western Europe at the same time.

152

The coordination of French and other foreign policies is difficult for another reason. General de Gaulle, as his admirers like to say, always has several irons in the fire. He simultaneously pursues several policies which are not necessarily compatible with each other in the hopes that, if one were to fail, the other would succeed. For instance, his objective of close cooperation with Germany does not preclude overtures to the Soviet Union. His desire to create a political union of the Six does not prevent him from trying to find a platform for a bilateral rapprochement with Britain. His friendly gestures toward Moscow go hand in hand with no less friendly gestures toward Peking, although these two Communist capitals are at loggerheads. Those watching his manipulation of the several irons in the fire may have legitimate doubts concerning a lasting coordination between his various and parallel policies and those of other states.

De Gaulle has frequently acknowledged French need of the Atlantic Alliance. He knows that the American nuclear umbrella is, in the final analysis, the main guarantee of peace and maintenance of the *status quo* in Europe. It is thereby the precondition of French independence. He would not disagree with Raymond Aron, who writes:

> France, Western Germany, Great Britain, individually or jointly, would be no counterweight to the Soviet Union. It is their cooperation with the United States that increases their capacity to say no to the Soviet Union and, if need be, to exert an influence on its policy. It is not the Atlantic Pact but their own weakness which has deprived them of their former independence.[1]

De Gaulle would disagree only with the last sentence because he himself has proven that an American ally may have an independent foreign policy and openly dissent from the United States, if international circumstances are favorable to this assertion.

While repeating that alliance with the United States is a necessity for France, he has at the same time done his best to loosen and eventually cut off the French bonds to NATO. His military policy has been conceived in utter disregard for the views of other Atlantic allies. His foreign moves often go counter to the policies of other members of the Alliance. An observer can ask himself the question: Is France still an ally or is she rather the most powerful among the unaligned states? The only fair answer would be that she is trying to be both. She neither repudiates the North Atlantic Treaty nor feels precluded by it from having a foreign policy which is close to uncommitment.

Uncommitment is the policy of independence, as the term itself indicates. For de Gaulle the main preoccupation is to ensure France tne greatest possible independence of other powers. His foreign policy is, like that of the more skillful unaligned statesmen, a policy of constant maneuvering between the mutually unfriendly Powers in an attempt to derive from their competition the greatest possible benefits.

De Gaulle thinks that France will realize gains for herself if she maneuvers between the United States and the Soviet Union, between the Soviet Union and China, between Germany and the Soviet Union, and also between the Western and Communist powers on the one hand and the unaligned countries of the Third World on the other. All those states are a pack of cards in his complicated game in which a jack might become an ace if changing circumstances devalue one card and enhance the value of another.

If one disregards the treaty commitments of France and the disparity in power, he would discover a certain similarity between the policies of the two Presidents: de Gaulle and Nasser. One aspires to Western European leadership independent of both the United States and the Soviet Union; the other wishes to build an Arab empire independent of the Communist and Western Powers. Both play the same game of balancing the United States against Russia and vice versa; both pay due attention to the profits they might derive from the Sino-Soviet rivalry; both want to be the spokesmen of the Third World. Without pushing this analogy too far, one may say that the similarity throws light on the difficulties which constantly arise in French-American relations. It is easier for Americans to understand openly uncommitted governments than to understand France, which wants simultaneously to be an ally and an unaligned nation.

This growing uncommitment of France is best described by its master artisan who thus depicted, on December 31, 1964, the variety of French policies:

> I have said: our independence. This means that our country, which does not seek to dominate anyone, intends to be its own master. The year which is going to expire has demonstrated and the year which is about to begin will confirm that, while becoming ourselves again in the political, economic, monetary and defense realms, or, to put it otherwise, while rejecting all the systems which would in fact place us under the hegemony known to us and disguised as "supra-nationality" or "integration" or "Atlantism," we are nevertheless ready for friendly cooperation with each of our allies, we contribute to the progress of Western European union, we remain very active

in giving aid to the developing peoples, we establish ever closer contacts with Latin America, that continent with great future and particularly near to us by its spirit and its heart, we resume our relations with China, and, finally, we multiply our contacts with the East European states in proportion to their domestic evolution which makes them look toward peace.[2]

Six months later he duly noted the American dissatisfaction with his policy of growing unalignment and once again unfurled his flag, dear to all uncommitted nations and attractive for several weaker committed peoples, the flag of revolt against the two "hegemonies":

The fact that we have resumed independence of judgment and action regarding all problems seems at times to displease a state which might believe that because of its power it is invested with a supreme and universal responsibility. . . . The reappearance of a nation whose hands are free, which we have again become, obviously modifies world politics which, since Yalta, seemed to be confined to two partners only. But since this division of the world between two hegemonies, and therefore into two camps, clearly does not benefit the liberty, equality and fraternity of peoples, a different order, a different equilibrium, are necessary for peace.[3]

He mentioned in the same broadcast speech "the common sense of remaining allies of our allies as long as the threat of domination arises in the East," and denied that he intended "to repudiate the American friendship." He frankly formulated the dilemma which faces France and her allies: how to be an American ally and at the same time pursue a policy of unalignment which from time to time necessitates open opposition to the United States. These two leitmotivs, somewhat contradictory, of the necessity of preserving the Atlantic Alliance and of the struggle against the American "hegemony," constantly dominate his public pronouncements.

The Foreign Minister, Couve de Murville, simplified the problem in a speech of October 29, 1963, when he said: "Since when in this world have we come to confuse conformism with solidarity? Systematic alignment is not a policy."[4] He knows better than anyone else that French foreign policy has been steadily evolving toward a systematic nonalignment. The French government publicly advertises its opposition to American policies within NATO, in Western Europe, in Latin America, in Africa, also in regard to such burning issues as Vietnam, China, or the Dominican Republic. It is its right to have any foreign policy it wants, and its views on various problems might sometimes be more realistic than the American. The point is that its public disagreements with the United States cannot be called "solidarity."

De Gaulle's consciousness of French ability to maneuver freely in the world and to formulate policies disregarding American wishes rests on his analysis of the present condition of international affairs. He proceeded with that analysis at his press conference held on July 23, 1964:

> It is clear that things have changed [since the aftermath of the Second World War]. The Western States of our old continent have rebuilt their economies. They are rebuilding their military forces. One of them, France, is becoming a nuclear power. . . . On the other hand, the monolithic nature of the totalitarian world is in the process of dislocation. China, separated from Moscow, enters on the world scene by its mass, its needs and its resources, avid for progress and consideration. The Soviet Empire, the last and the largest colonial power of this time, is seeing first the Chinese contest the domination it exercises over vast regions of Asia, and second is seeing the European satellites which it had subjugated by force moving further and further away. . . . Lastly, great aspirations and great difficulties are deeply agitating the developing countries. The result of all these new factors, complicated and interrelated, is that the division of the world into two camps led by Washington and Moscow respectively corresponds less and less to the real situation. With respect to the gradually splitting totalitarian world, or the problems posed by China, or the conduct to be adopted toward many countries of Asia, Africa and Latin America, or the remodelling of the United Nations Organization that necessarily ensues, or the adjustment of world exchanges of all kinds, etc., it appears that Europe, provided that it wishes, is henceforth called upon to play a role which is its own. Undoubtedly it should maintain an alliance with America in which, in the North Atlantic, both are interested so long as the Soviet threat remains. But the reasons which, for Europe, made this alliance a form of subordination are fading away day by day.[5]

It is impossible to disagree with him concerning the deep transformations in the international environment since 1949, the year of conclusion of the North Atlantic Treaty. The Western European allies have grown in stature; the distribution of power within the Alliance has been modified in favor of Europe, except for nuclear armaments. The rival camp is no longer monolithic. The growing assertion of independence by the

Third World is a self-evident fact. All these changes cannot help but have repercussions on the cohesion of the North Atlantic Alliance.

Peaceful coexistence

We have already noted two consequences of the American-Soviet nuclear stalemate: the lesser reliability of the guaranty offered by the major ally, be it the United States or the Soviet Union, and the increased feeling of general security, which is a consequence of the lesser probability of a major war in which the two nuclear giants would directly fight each other. In Europe, where the two giants face each other across the demarcation line dividing Germany, peace means the stability of the political and territorial *status quo*. This *status quo* is tolerable for France. She would, after all, be reduced to a relatively lower status in Europe if Germany were reunified and became once more the major continental nation.

The French government accepts peaceful coexistence as the necessity of our time. Michel Debré reflects the wishes of all Frenchmen, not only of Gaullists, when he writes: "Coexistence must be maintained, encouraged, and strengthened."[6] De Gaulle himself said that the only alternative is death: "If a world conflict were to break out, the modern technological progress would bring about death. If this is to be avoided, we must try to make peace."[7]

Realizing that the fear of major war is shared by the West and by the Soviet Union, de Gaulle thinks that the West has no reason to pay with concessions for peaceful coexistence. At his press conference, held on September 5, 1961, i.e., at a time of anxiety in the West caused by Soviet threats and pressing demands for a modification in the status of West Berlin, de Gaulle preserved a phlegmatic calm. He never took the Soviet threats seriously and gave a pertinent explanation of why the West could afford to remain firm in refusing to make unilateral concessions:

> Admittedly the Soviets possess terrible nuclear weapons, but the Western powers also have equally formidable ones. If a world conflict were to break out, the use of those forces of destruction would undoubtedly result, in particular, in the complete disruption of Russia and the countries which are a prey to Communism. . . . This, moreover, the Soviet leaders know very well in spite of all their boasting. Therefore, the Western powers have no reason not to consider the Soviet demonstrations with a clear eye and a firm heart.[8]

In 1965, for the same reasons, he called a vanished dream the slogans, once popular in the United States, of pushing the Russians back to their national frontiers and of liberating Eastern Europe (see Chapter VI). The emptiness of these slogans was proved in November 1956 on the occasion of the Hungarian revolt. For him, neither side may change the present European *status quo* by force.

His fear lies elsewhere. Would the two rivals one day deduce the ultimate conclusion from peaceful coexistence and reach a global agreement at the expense of their European allies? He has followed suspiciously all the American and Soviet efforts at *rapprochement*. During the heyday of relations between President Eisenhower and Prime Minister Khrushchev, de Gaulle asked, not without anxiety: "Who can say whether, in the future, if the political circumstances were completely to change, as it before occurred on the earth, the two powers with the monopoly of nuclear weapons would not make a deal to divide the world between them?"[9] What was he really afraid of? No American-French understanding could directly affect the French interests. The world of today may not be divided, as was the Roman Empire, into two empires. He knows very well that nuclear weapons would be of no political use in compelling the countries of the world to become either American or Soviet vassals. His own arguments regarding the growing importance of countries other than the United States and Russia militate against his hypothesis. What he probably had in mind was something else. A true American-Soviet understanding would reduce the field now open to other countries, including France, for freelance activities which often consist in exploiting the Soviet-American competition for one's own purposes. Moreover, his words were addressed, among others, to Bonn, where at that and other times people feared that the Soviet-American rapprochement could materialize only at the expense of the Germans. These fears are not altogether unfounded in the sense that any lasting understanding with the United States would appear worthwhile to Russia only on the condition of tacit American recognition of the existence of two German states. De Gaulle has no interest in appeasing these fears, because he offers the Germans an alternative to American friendship: a close cooperation with France which, as one of the four former occupying powers, retains a veto concerning any decision affecting Germany. His own reaction to the symptoms of an American-Soviet rapprochement consists of his overtures to Moscow. For instance, he followed President Eisenhower's invitation extended to Khrushchev by his own invitation to the Soviet Prime Minister to visit France. He is entangled in the same dilemma as the United States; the policy of friendship toward Germany is an obstacle in the rapprochement with Russia, while better relations with the Soviet Union cannot be easily reconciled with German friendship. Every time the

United States attempts to detach Germany from France it cannot expect any welcome in Moscow. Each time de Gaulle attempts to loosen the ties between Germany and America, his stock falls down in Russia.

Problems of the Atlantic Alliance and its reform

It would be ludicrous to reduce the internal crisis of NATO to the French problem. All alliances are subject to an iron law, which Field Marshal Montgomery formulated as follows: "No alliance founded only on fear has lasted or will last, because, as soon as fear decreases in intensity, the cement of the alliance begins to crumble."[10] This is true of all alliances, since all of them have always been founded on the fear of the same enemy. The Soviet menace loomed large on the Western horizon at the time of the conclusion of the North Atlantic Treaty. Its shadow seems now to have receded. The cement of the Western alliance has begun to disintegrate. Each time the Soviet Union uses threatening language or makes a menacing gesture at the most sensitive points, West Berlin and its access roads across East Germany, the cement is immediately reenforced and a united Western front is recreated.

The Atlantic Alliance was conceived as a regional undertaking limited in its scope to North America, Western and Southern Europe. Strictly speaking, the allies are free to formulate their individual extra-European policies as they like. In Europe their interests largely coincide, at least in the sense that each is opposed to the extension of Soviet influence, but no two allies have ever had identical national interests. This fact is manifest when one regards the divergent interests in the non-European areas. Several European allies maintain diplomatic relations with China and conduct lively trade with that country, which the United States considers its principal enemy in Asia. The political and economic relations between Cuba and the European allies are more or less normal, while Cuba is a thorn in American flesh. One could multiply these examples. The point is that the divergence between the American and French interests is not a unique or unprecedented case. What is rather unusual is the pleasure which de Gaulle takes in rubbing salt in American wounds and publicly displaying the divergencies of views. This is his manner of asserting French independence.

In any event, de Gaulle consistently claims that the Atlantic Alliance needs to be reformed. On November 5, 1964, his Prime Minister used a nutshell formula to express his master's concepts:

> The exit from the Atlantic Alliance is not our working hypothesis. There is no question of our abandoning the Alliance. . . . It is however true . . . that the functioning of the Alliance raises questions

and that its present organization does not satisfy us. . . . Our working hypothesis is that one must reexamine the Atlantic Alliance, remodel it and reorganize it. The rest depends on our partners.[11]

The master himself has reaffirmed the same two points:

The Atlantic Alliance is an elemented necessity. . . . Thus if, once again, there are divergencies between Washington and Paris regarding the functioning and organization of the Alliance, the Alliance itself . . . is not in question.[12]

He defined in 1960 the problem of reforming the Alliance in these words:

It is more than ten years since the Atlantic Alliance was organized in its present form. . . . But during the past ten years much has changed. First of all, it became evident that the possibilities of conflict, and consequently of military operations, were spreading far beyond Europe, were spreading all over the world. It became evident that the Middle East and Africa, in particular, were danger spots at least as much as Europe and that there existed, between the principal members of the Atlantic Alliance, political divergencies of views concerning these areas which, if the occasion arises, might turn into strategic disagreements. Then, too, the countries of continental Europe, France in particular, have regained their balance and their prosperity once more, and consequently, as this has been occurring, they regained the awareness of their personalities, especially regarding their own defense. . . . Under these circumstances, France considers that what was done ten years ago within this limited area and on the basis of integration must be brought up to date. . . . When the Treaty of North-Atlantic Alliance was drawn up, it specified in its text that it could be revised at the end of ten years. . . . What are the two essential points which we think should be revised? The first is the limitation of the Alliance to the single area of Europe. We believe that, at least among the Western world powers, there should be something organized, insofar as the Alliance is concerned, regarding their political conduct and, should the occasion arise, their strategic conduct outside Europe, especially in the Middle East and in Africa where these three powers are constantly involved. By the way, if there is no agreement among the principal members of the Atlantic Alliance on matters other than Europe, how can the Alliance be indefinitely maintained in Europe? . . . The second point regarding which France would like to see a change is the integration of the defense of Europe. It seems to us that the defense of each country, while being combined, of course, with that of other countries, must have a national character; this does not exclude in the least the principle itself of the Alliance.[13]

His demands throughout the years of his Presidency of the Fifth Republic have always been the same: termination of the NATO military integration, and coordination of extra-European policies between the Atlantic world powers, which are, in his opinion, three: the United States, France, and Britain. In 1960 he stressed the need for that coordination in Africa and the Near East, because he was preoccupied with the Algerian problem. Today he would ask for coordination in all parts of the world. As a matter of fact, a year later, when he was better able to foresee the end of French military liabilities in Algeria, he extended the field of proposed coordination to include Asia:

> Since the Atlantic Alliance was created, the threats of war have been no longer limited to Europe. They extend to the entire world, Africa and Asia in particular. Under these conditions, the Alliance, in order to last, must be extended to all these new areas.[14]

What are his assets in pressing for the acceptance of his requests? One of them is his own foreign policy which makes the carrying out of policies by the United States and Britain more difficult. Another is the geographically crucial location of France. The last is the text itself of the North Atlantic Treaty which makes his insistence on its revision legally legitimate.

An Australian author writes:

> The simple facts of geography give France an almost insuperable position of advantage vis-à-vis her NATO allies: the whole of NATO's conventional strategy in Europe depends on France as a fulcrum and its supply routes and "infrastructure" all lie in France.[15]

De Gaulle noted this French advantage at his press conference held on July 29, 1963. While stressing again "the elemental necessity" of the Atlantic Alliance, he pointed out in the same sentence that France, in spite of the present inferiority of her means, was "politically, geographically, morally, militarily essential to the coalition."[16]

He is on a firm legal ground when he invokes the text of the North Atlantic Treaty. Its Article 12 provides for a consultation among the allies in view of a possible revision. This consultation may take place any time ten years after the Treaty went into effect. Nineteen hundred and sixty was the first year in which the French government could have asked for a consultation. De Gaulle did not do it for reasons known only to himself. Probably he feared that the other allies would refuse to amend the Treaty according to his suggestions. In fact, he cannot expect support from any other ally. The other possibility open to him is to denounce the Treaty in 1969; Article 13 gives this right to every ally after the Treaty has existed for twenty years. Would he limit himself to threats of denunciation in order to wrest the desirable concessions, or would he go so far as to denounce it in case he fails to convince his main allies? It is impossible to predict the decisions he might make in 1969 or 1970. They will be dictated by French interests and by the world situation then. If by that time the Soviet threat disappears, and if he believes that the American alliance is no longer necessary, he would not hesitate for a moment to disengage France from the bonds which limit her freedom of action. In a contrary case he would remain in the Alliance as unhappy as he is today.

It is only fair to remark that the attitude in 1969 or 1970 of any of the signatories of the North Atlantic Treaty, including the United States, cannot be predicted now with any certainty. It suffices to imagine that a deterioration in the Sino-Soviet relations would compel the Soviet Union to pay equal attention to China and to Germany. Who could exclude as utterly impossible an American-Soviet understanding in the Far East and their acceptance of the *status quo* in Europe in order to make cooperation possible in Eastern Asia? Alain Peyrefitte, the Minister of Information, was entitled to ask the question:

> Insofar as the future is concerned, I may tell you that everyone can ask himself the question concerning the developments which will take place in America in ten or fifteen years. It is not an insult for our American friends to think that they might change their views in fifteen years. Who can know today with an absolute certainty what the American people will feel, think and decide fifteen years from now?[17]

In any event, on September 9, 1965, General de Gaulle forewarned all his Atlantic allies that he would end the military integration, i.e., the French membership in NATO, by 1969, the year when France would be legally entitled to terminate her North Atlantic Treaty commitments. He formulated this warning in an alternative manner: if the Soviet threat were to disappear completely by that time, France might withdraw from the Alliance itself; if not, she will certainly cease to be a member of NATO and would no longer accept the American supreme allied command. He said:

It is true that, in many areas, we have the best reasons for associating ourselves with others. But on condition of retaining our self-determination. Thus, so long as the solidarity of the Western peoples appears to us necessary for the eventual defense of Europe, our country will remain the ally of its allies but, upon the expiration of the commitments formerly taken, that is, in 1969 by the latest, the subordination known as "integration" which is provided for by NATO and which hands our fate over to foreign authority shall cease, as far as we are concerned.[18]

Anyone who would delude himself by thinking that this policy would disappear with de Gaulle would be well advised to read the statement by François Mitterand, the leftist candidate in the 1965 presidential election and the most outspoken adversary of de Gaulle. He told the journalists at his press conference held on September 21, 1965, that, if he were elected President of the Republic, he would not ask for the termination of the Atlantic Alliance but:

> I would examine separately, as the present Head of State is doing, each problem resulting from the Alliance. Thus, regarding NATO, General de Gaulle has done nothing but make his statement in advance of 1969, when the conditions for its revision will be fulfilled. De Gaulle is right to foresee this study and this reexamination, but he is wrong to do it in the words which he used and in the tone which is his own, in particular regarding the United States.[19]

Mitterand would have been more suave in tone, but his policy toward NATO might not have been very different. Mitterand was assured support in the presidential campaign by the Communist party. It is not surprising that the Communists welcomed his statement regarding NATO; they would do better and would denounce the Alliance itself. But what is more important is the Socialist attitude. They sincerely claim to be more "Atlantic" than de Gaulle, but supported a presidential candidate who largely agreed on this important matter with the present President of the Republic.

It is not impossible that de Gaulle's plan for the future organization of the Atlantic Alliance was explicitly formulated in an article which was published in the French *Politique Etrangère,* a quarterly review of the *Centre d'Etudes de Politique Etrangère,* a research institute with links to the French government. According to rumors noted by the Paris correspondent of the *New York Times* the manuscript of the article had been approved by the General prior to its publication.[20] This blueprint of a new allied organization was the product of discussions among French experts often consulted by the French government.

The authors of the blueprint proposed to replace NATO by superimposing two arrangements. The United States and its European allies would continue to be mutually bound by the treaty, but they would no longer jointly participate in an integrated military structure. The European allies alone would integrate their conventional military forces to some extent, but this integration would exclude nuclear weapons. Western Germany would have no access to these weapons but would have to rely, like the other continental European allies, on the French nuclear guaranty. This French monopoly of nuclear weapons would no doubt designate France as the probable candidate for the supreme command of that European organization. On this condition even General de Gaulle would accept a certain degree of integration of conventional forces. The Europeans would be granted the right to participate with France in elaborating plans for the use of French and presumably also British nuclear forces (if Britain were to accept the French plan and the exclusion of the United States, which is highly improbable) in the defense of Western Europe. This would be their "equality" on the nuclear plane.

The French plan would accomplish two of de Gaulle's aims at the same time: it would end the American "hegemony" in Europe and bar Germany from nuclear armament. Its authors claim that such a reorganization of the Atlantic Alliance would appease the fears of the Soviet Union and Eastern Europe and would prepare the ground for a reconciliation of the two parts of the Continent, i.e., for the emergence of that Europe from the Atlantic to the Urals, de Gaulle's ultimate Grand Design.

The weakness of the blueprint is self-evident. Why should the European allies prefer the French "hegemony" to the American, in spite of the fact that France is infinitely less powerful than the United States?

The triumvirate

Several months after his return to power, on September 24, 1958, de Gaulle addressed his famous memorandum to the President of the United States and the British Prime Minister. The text of that memorandum was never published, but its contents were not a State secret for long. All the sources agree with the summary of the memorandum given by *Le Monde* on October 28, 1960. According to that Parisian daily, General de Gaulle proposed

> The setting-up of an Anglo-French-American directorate of the Western alliance. This directorate would be empowered to elaborate

the political and military strategy of the whole free world as well as to make, in case of need, the decision to use the weapons of mass destruction. The memorandum also demanded the sharing of atomic secrets and of technological resources in general and the formation of combined commands in the various theaters of operations in the world. But, above all, the French government declared that it would make further French participation in the Atlantic organization conditional upon the acceptance of its claims.[21]

The General intended to kill several birds with one stone. First, he asked the United States to recognize France as a peer not only of Britain but also of itself. France, at that time still in the throes of the Algerian imbroglio, would suddenly be hoisted to the status of one of the principal world powers. She would be recognized as the dominant power in the Western part of the European Continent. Second, the United States would relinquish control of its nuclear weapons not only in Europe but anywhere else. It would have to accept two additional fingers on its nuclear trigger. Third, the two "Anglo-Saxon" powers were invited to abandon their own independence in the formulation of foreign policies, which would have to have the French blessing. This French control over the American and British policies would extend to the whole world, presumably including Latin America. Fourth, the United States was requested to assist France in becoming a nuclear power.

The enormity of these demands was such that one is entitled to wonder whether de Gaulle really expected that the United States and Britain would accept them. This question cannot be answered, but it is possible that the key to this puzzle is to be found in his final threat of subordinating further French cooperation within NATO to the acceptance of his proposals. Perhaps he wanted to excuse in advance the progressive withdrawal of French forces from the integrated NATO system.

Neither the United States nor Britain accepted the concept of triumvirate. The reasons were self-evident. De Gaulle, who cherishes the independence of French defense and foreign policy, should not have been unduly surprised that the United States was not prepared to share the control over its nuclear weapons with a nation which at that time did not have even a nucleus of nuclear armaments. In 1958, neither the United States nor Britain had any interest in a close coordination of foreign policies with France, who was entangled in the Algerian war. Public opinion in both countries would not have tolerated support of the French war effort in that colonial war. Finally, the United States could not single out France from its European allies for the role of a member of the triumvirate. The least Washington could reply was that Germany would have been entitled to be a fourth member of the directorate.

The reaction of other European allies demonstrated the impossibility of the United States' acceptance of de Gaulle's exorbitant demands. The first information regarding the memorandum was published on October 24, 1958, in the German newspaper *Der Mittag*. The European allied governments, who had probably learned the news also from other sources, began to protest. The Italian Prime Minister, Fanfani, declared on October 29, 1958, that Italy would not accept a position of inferiority within the Atlantic Alliance.[22] It is said that Chancellor Adenauer addressed a letter to de Gaulle in which he expressed his amazement on hearing of his initiative, which was contrary to the concept of strict French-German equality voiced by de Gaulle at their encounter at Bad-Kreuznach.[23] The Canadian government, which was also relegated by the French memorandum to second-class status, expressed its opposition to the concept of a triumvirate.[24] Norway and Holland joined the protesting chorus.

Two years later the protests were still continuing. The Belgian Foreign Minister Spaak, who was also at that time Secretary General of NATO, declared on September 21, 1960: "The three-power directorate and the termination of integration will not be accepted by the majority of countries in the Atlantic organization."[25] Chancellor Adenauer, a friend of France and of de Gaulle, nevertheless said on November 10, 1960, that it was normal for the United States, the dominant Western nuclear power, to be the leader of the Atlantic Alliance, but that no other nation could claim a privileged position.[26]

These negative reactions would have sufficed to justify the American refusal. They also pointed out another contradiction in de Gaulle's strategy. His policy of close cooperation with Germany could not be reconciled with the claim to a superior French role within the Atlantic Alliance. No German would pay this price for French friendship. His memorandum of September 1958 was also an unintentional warning to the five partners in the European Economic Community that his European union was not to be a union of equals but an association dominated by France. The least one may say is that the General is not the most skillful of diplomats.

It is rumored that he renewed his proposal for a triumvirate in a letter sent in January 1962 to President Kennedy.[27] On June 6, 1962, Prime Minister Pompidou made a veiled allusion to the same concept. While mentioning the necessity of a consultation on international problems among Western allies, he immediately added that such a consultation:

"meets its own limits quickly enough, due to the fact that the countries which belong to the Alliance are not interested to the same degree in all the problems in all the parts of the world."[28] This more flexible formula could have been either an indirect hint at the old proposal for a triumvirate, or a suggestion that the choice of governments consulted should depend on their vital interest in a given problem or a given part of the world.

After the American-British refusal to accept his proposals, de Gaulle immediately began the gradual withdrawal of French forces from the NATO Supreme Command.

Consultation, limited or unlimited liability?

Was there something in his proposals worth retaining for joint allied consideration? If anything, it was the concept of consultation among the allies concerned (not only the United States, Britain, and France) on European and non-European problems. It is obvious that all European allies should be invited to collaborate with the United States on a series of hypothetical situations in which American nuclear weapons would be used in the defense of Europe. This would reassure them of American intentions, while the final and fatal word would necessarily remain with the President of the United States. Probably no European ally would disagree with de Gaulle, who said on April 11, 1961: "The continental European States, which are by far the most exposed to danger, must know exactly with which weapons and under which circumstances their trans-Atlantic allies would join them in battle."[29]

The policies, including economic ones, toward the Soviet Union and its European allies would be more efficacious if synchronized. Finally, it seems that Western powers have an interest in coordinating their policies regarding the non-European areas. This coordination is now easier than in 1958, in view of the liquidation of most of the colonial liabilities of Britain, France, Belgium, and Holland.

Since the Atlantic Pact was signed on April 4, 1949, there have been two opposing concepts. One of them limits actions of the Alliance to a geographical area clearly defined, namely to Western Europe, and to one realm, the military defense against a threat by the Soviet Union. The other is founded on the consideration that this threat manifests itself in all parts of the world, that it is economic, political, and psychological at least as much as military, and that activities of the Atlantic organization should be adjusted to this situation.[30]

Halvard Lange, the Norwegian Foreign Minister, favored the narrower concept in November 1960, when he opposed any extension of the geographical realm of the Atlantic Alliance.[31] Probably most of the smaller Atlantic allies would take the same position.

This in itself indicates that the North Atlantic Council could not be the place where the policies of those allies who are really involved in the affairs of non-European parts of the world could be coordinated. To take an example, there would be no profit in trying to reach unanimity among the fifteen members of that Council on a coordinated policy in Southeast Asia, where such countries as Norway, Denmark, Belgium, Turkey, and Greece have no vital involvements.

Assuming that the Western nations, including France, have no interest in the expansion of Communist influence, be it Soviet or Chinese, in the non-European continents, one cannot disagree with de Gaulle's proposition that coordination of policies would benefit them all, especially those with vital interests or real influence there. The efforts of the West to retain its influence in Asia, Africa, and Latin America, and to reduce Communist influence, would be more efficient if the Western powers could avoid competition in these parts of the world. All of them need the raw materials and markets located in non-European underdeveloped countries. All of them would be in grave danger if the economic and human potential of Asia, Africa, and Latin America were to strengthen the power of the Communist group of states, even if this group were forever to be split into two rival camps.

De Gaulle was not wrong at all when he posed this problem on September 5, 1960:

> Confronted with this Soviet action and the parallel Communist-Chinese action, the Western powers could have greatly strengthened the cause of reason and progress if they had come to an agreement with each other and if they had given each other mutual support in the task of emancipation of peoples which were formerly their colonies, instead of appearing very often in a state of division and even of rivalry. . . . This has not yet been done. Is it too late to do it? I do not think so. I am convinced that the Western powers, once they accept the self-determination of peoples, as they actually do, should take council together continually (at least the Western world powers should do it) in order to encourage the peoples recently emancipated to find a reasonable path. . . . It is true that the pursuit of such a policy would have required an alliance which would not be confined within the limits of the present NATO.[32]

Actually, cooperation among the Western states truly involved in non-European areas would not require an extension of the geographical realm of the present North Atlantic Alliance, but only an agreement among those states on the margin of that Alliance. This agreement would not enlarge the responsibilities of the other allies who would be unwilling to accept commitments outside Europe. The first practical question would be which of the Atlantic allies would qualify for consultation on non-European affairs. De Gaulle's answer in his memorandum of September 1958 is obviously inadequate. Michel Debré, who might reflect de Gaulle's preferences in foreign affairs, formulates the problem in a more flexible manner:

> General de Gaulle has said that a Western policy can only be a synchronized policy. It is necessary to have mutual agreement. Conceptions cannot be elaborated in a sort of artificial multinational conference; they should be the result of discussions between the United States and those European states conscious of their responsibilities and with the will power as well as the capacity to face these responsibilities and their most far-reaching implications. . . . No doubt, all the European states cannot claim to participate, but the United States would find interest in a fundamental cooperation with some of them. This cooperation could be extended to other nations in function of the contribution which these other nations would make toward the world responsibilities of the West.[33]

This flexible formula allows for consultation among governments with true willingness to assume responsibilities in given areas of the world; it merits serious consideration. A French writer illustrates this choice of consultants with a few examples:

> Regarding Africa: France, Great Britain, Belgium, Portugal, and possibly Italy and the United States; regarding the Near East: Great Britain, the United States, and France, all three of them signatories of the 1950 agreements [on maintaining the balance of armaments of various States in the Near East], as well as Germany and Italy, who play a growing economic and diplomatic role in that area.[34]

Whichever states would in each case be invited to participate in consultation, most Frenchmen have no doubt that France should sit on all deliberations. De Gaulle himself has often claimed this worldwide role for France. For example, he told French officers on November 23, 1961: "As the relative distance between the continents is being constantly reduced, there is no danger or no conflict, whatever its site, which does not interest a world power such as France."[35]

Raymond Aron, who certainly is not a Gaullist, also favors consultation on non-European problems; he invokes very pertinent arguments:

> The progress of decolonization holds forth the promise of easier cooperation between members of the [Western] bloc in Asia and Africa. The economic rehabilitation of Western Europe and the deficits in the American balance of payments compel the Big Power to ask for the support of its partners in order to conduct a successful foreign-aid policy toward the Third World. It is even possible that Europeans might dissociate themselves from Yankee imperialism in South America, as the United States did regarding European imperialism in Asia.[36]

A concerted Western policy would preclude the cheap propaganda successes of one Western nation against another, like the verbal competition in Latin America; more important, it would ensure that Western aid to underdeveloped countries would be more efficient and less wasteful than it is now.

As useful and desirable as consultation would be among the Western powers concerned, one should not entertain too many illusions on this score. Consultation may produce, at most, a true coordination of policies, and, at least, an exchange of information and opinions. However, the Commonwealth is a living example of the usefulness of consultation even if the only result regarding controversial problems is to agree to disagree. In relations with de Gaulle it would be even more probable that consultation would produce, in most cases, no more than an exchange of views and an agreed disagreement. Even this would be useful, because it would help to dispel the mutual distrust which now reigns in American-French relations.

At present de Gaulle feels that he is under no obligation to consult the United States or Britain on his policies in non-European areas. He is convinced that he repays them in their own coin. Michel Debré explicitly levels this particular accusation against the United States:

> The United States wholeheartedly agrees with the Europeans that there should be a concerted policy toward Russia, but it also wishes to talk alone with Russia, without witnesses and without obstacles, and, if possible, to conclude agreements with her. The United States wholeheartedly agrees with Europeans that it is necessary to defend Western civilization, but it also wishes to assert the autonomy of its attitudes and policies in Asia, in Africa, and in

the Near East. It willingly believes, as any power which aspires to be supreme is inclined to do, that its attitudes and policies are identical with what the attitudes and policies of the whole West should be.[37]

It would undoubtedly help the American government improve its relations with France, and perhaps not only with France, if it would ask itself whether this reproach does not contain a grain of truth. Debré, of course, is convinced that French, and European advice in general, would be salutary for the United States:

> We believe that difficulties and conflicts in certain areas of the world, in particular in the Far East and Near East, which could face mankind with dramatic events, would be reduced in extent, and perhaps even in frequency, if the political actions of Western nations were coordinated.[38]

What is de Gaulle's present preference: an organized procedure of consultation, as he suggested in 1958, or the present situation, where he is free to formulate foreign policy, disregarding the wishes of the United States and being repaid in the same way? In any event, at a press conference held on July 29, 1963, he suggested a bilateral consultation between his country and the United States:

> In sum, for France, and I believe, for the United States, the friendship that unites them and the alliance that links them are above and beyond all jeopardy, but it is true that there are differences between the two countries in the face of certain international problems. The evolution of both countries has created this state of things which, once again, is not at all surprising, however disturbing it may perhaps appear to the Americans. In any case, in the relations between the two peoples, we believe that each must accept this new situation. That being done, it will doubtless be advisable to harmonize, in each case and to the greatest extent possible, the respective policies. France for her part is cordially, very cordially disposed to this.[39]

Whenever people on this side of the ocean feel indignant at seeing French policies going against American wishes, whenever they feel bitter on reading de Gaulle's critical statements regarding American moves in Vietnam or in the Dominican Republic, they should recall that he had not been consulted, for instance, in July 1958, at the time of the concerted Anglo-American action in the Near East following the Iraqi revolution. The United States and Britain debarked troops in Lebanon and Jordan, but neither felt it desirable to ask for French advice. However,

France had a legal reason for expecting consultation, being one of the three powers signing the 1950 declaration on the maintenance of *status quo* in the Near East. A French commentator says: "General de Gaulle's resentment was bitter, especially since Lebanon is a country of traditional French influence."[40] In international relations, as in all human relations, one should never forget the Roman proverb: *Do ut des*.

De Gaulle's views concerning the need for coordination of Western policies in non-European areas are nothing new. The same views were expressed under the Fourth Republic, even more urgently at that time because of the colonial involvements of France. Félix Gaillard, then Prime Minister, told the NATO Council in December 1957:

> An Alliance like ours is an experiment in cooperation without any historical precedent. It is true that this cooperation regarding defense is confined to a clearly defined geographical area. However, our mutual interests regarding political problems are intertwined far beyond this area. It is necessary that, where these interests quite naturally do not coincide, we should find the means for bringing our points of view closer to each other, and asserting thereby a greater solidarity in the face of dangers which are not confined to one place or one area.[41]

The Socialist opponent of de Gaulle, Guy Mollet, said in 1959 (these words were reprinted in 1962 in his own book):

> Serious objections are being made regarding the functioning of the Atlantic Alliance. . . . First objection: the Atlantic Alliance is limited in its geographical extent. It covers only Europe, which is only an Atlantic rimland, together with Italy, Greece, and Turkey, these three Mediterranean peninsulas separated from each other by gaps. Who does not see, however, that since 1954 and 1955, the Soviet Union has been persistently bypassing that area by a vast encircling maneuver? It is looking toward a breakthrough in the Near East, toward Asia and Africa. The Atlantic Alliance, reduced to the defense of only a part of the Continent, runs the risk of becoming a European Maginot line. . . . Second objection: the Atlantic Alliance is restricted in its jurisdiction. . . . It has remained so far principally a military instrument. . . . However, who does not see that the Soviet Union has been increasingly using for the last several years (with a flexibility which could be a model for us) nonmilitary means of action? Under the cover of "peaceful coexistence," it has had recourse to new "weapons," i.e., economic and commercial infiltration, support offered to the most fanatical nationalists, the

supply of war material, psychological warfare, propaganda, etc. . . . The third objection: the Atlantic Alliance is restricted in the jurisdiction of its directing bodies. An illogical situation undermines allied cohesion: the NATO Council, which should be the directing body of the Organization, has no way of knowing precisely which of the most powerful means of defense, in particular which of the secret weapons, are truly at the disposal of the Alliance. . . . Instead of integrating the bulk of its military forces and its institutions, the Organization confines itself to the integration of conventional troops and armaments of military weaker countries, while the Big Powers consider their most perfect means of defense as a sort of national preserve. The interdependence of the partners is not, therefore, founded on equality. One example suffices: the United States and England have nuclear weapons not placed under the NATO command. Although the adversary possesses the same weapons, these two countries refuse to help their allies in the acquisition of these weapons. This reservation in regard to strategic responsibilities weighs heavily on the Alliance and divides the allies into second-class partners, whose freedom of action is restricted, and principal partners, who claim to be the leaders of the free world. . . . The United States . . . has never made a secret of its intention to have a free hand in areas of the world beyond NATO jurisdiction.[42]

Those inclined to think that de Gaulle's griefs are personal should listen with attention to these two former Prime Ministers of the Fourth Republic. If one did not know who was speaking, he could very well believe that the authors of these quotations were Ministers of the Fifth Republic. In this respect, as in several others, de Gaulle expresses ideas shared by most Frenchmen. Only his style is his own, and only his distrust of the intentions of French allies is deeper than that of his non-Gaullist countrymen.

Distrust of the American ally

"Our allies are also our adversaries," de Gaulle is alleged to have said.[43] His distrust of French allies was manifest during the last war; a French writer thus depicts de Gaulle's state of mind at that time: "Free France fights on three fronts: against the German and Japanese enemies; against Vichy, whose spirit of capitulation it denounces; and against Anglo-Americans. There are moments when it is no longer clear who is the principal adversary."[44] The reader of de Gaulle's contemporary pronouncements may also wonder who is the principal adversary: the Soviet Union or the United States. His own countrymen could have asked this question while listening, for instance, to his speech of June 16, 1965. He told them:

> Thus, two great states were brought to the summit of power, because other states were temporarily weakened and also because these two states had the quasi-monopoly of atomic weapons and the means of outer-space exploration. Hence the one and the other seek (this is human) to extend their hegemony far beyond their frontiers. One of them does it by imposing a totalitarian regime on its satellites. The other uses different means which certainly are less reprehensible and less harsh; its means consist in the offer of protection and assistance and, if need be, in military intervention as witnessed in Vietnam, in Laos, and in the Dominican Republic.[45]

His diatribes against American "hegemony" are due largely to his conviction that the Fourth Republic was an American protectorate. His first Prime Minister, Michel Debré, openly admitted on August 16, 1959:

> The national renewal of our policy does not aim at isolation, but is a reaction, certainly in accord with the realities of our world, against those forms of alliance which, due to our weakness, brought about our enslavement to foreign powers. As we know, these foreign powers do not hesitate to thwart our vital interests, especially in Africa.[46]

A suspicious and critical attitude toward the United States is not limited to de Gaulle. Anti-American sentiment exists under the Fifth Republic as it existed under the Fourth. "From one end to the other, i.e., between 1947–49 and 1958, the phenomenon of anti-Americanism, of resentment of dependence, appears to have existed beyond the possibility of any denial," writes a French political scientist, who notes also the persistence of this feeling in today's France.[47] Public opinion polls from 1954 to 1957 allowed the following conclusions regarding the French feeling prior to de Gaulle's return to power:

> The United States has too much influence in France and does not treat her as an equal. Its fundamental interests are often different from ours. A European union would reduce this American influence; this prospect is welcomed. The United States often takes an attitude toward overseas territories which is also unfriendly to France. . . . Its policy toward Communist China does not always find support in public opinion. In particular, it fiercely opposes Chinese admission to the United Nations, while the dominant trend in France would consider it normal.[48]

One of the reasons for these sentiments was the discrepancy between French colonial policies in Indochina and Algeria and the lack of American sympathy for the colonial empires. Frenchmen felt at that time that Americans were on the other side of the fence in their feelings and perhaps even in their actions. American opinion that the Algerian war should be terminated by a negotiated compromise was resented as an encouragement given to the Algerian rebels.[49] Even now, after decolonization, Frenchmen recall, not without bitterness, the American lack of sympathy and support for the French colonial wars. One must know this background to understand that de Gaulle's policy toward the United States does not go against national feelings, which are flattered by termination of the "American protectorate."

To realize to what extent the French President's strictures against American "hegemony" reflect a widespread feeling among Frenchmen, it suffices to listen to this one among many voices:

> The decision to ensure independence is positive to the extent that it hinders the tendency of great powers to establish their hegemony. . . . Nothing justifies the claim by one people, only because it is for the time being the richest and militarily the most powerful, to decide without appeal what is good or what is not good for the rest of mankind. We think that a great number of opposition leaders do not repeat it enough in their conversations with our American friends.[50]

The author, who is not a Gaullist, mentions the French reproach to Americans: "*faits accomplis,* brutal pressure, and intransigence."

When President Johnson rather unfortunately called de Gaulle's nationalism "narrow," *Le Monde,* a consistently anti-Gaullist newspaper for the educated public, defended the French President:

> M. Johnson criticized the General, without naming him, in the speech of May 7; he accused him of being a narrow nationalist. The use of the word "narrow" shows that he hardly knows the man. It is possible to criticize the General on many scores, but certainly not for the alleged narrowness of his political views. . . . But the worst nationalism, is it not that of the powerful ones who do not allow others to discuss the use they make of their power? This nationalism is perhaps "wide," but it nevertheless feeds those "narrow nationalisms" which the President of the United States deplores.[51]

De Gaulle's efforts to enlarge French influence in underdeveloped countries, including Latin America, his recognition of the Communist government of China, his warmer attitude toward the Soviet Union and

Eastern Europe, his criticism of American policies in Vietnam, Cuba, and the Dominican Republic, and his aspiration to balance American influence by a Western European union are some examples of policies which find favor in France, not excluding the opposition. His domestic opponents criticize his tactics rather than his policies, which often run counter to American foreign policy.

Opposition to NATO

Was the policy of pulling out French forces from NATO inaugurated in revenge for the American refusal to consider the memorandum of September 1958, or would it have taken place anyway? The latter hypothesis is more probable in view of de Gaulle's attachment to the independence of French defense. He said on November 3, 1959: "This system of integration has outlived itself."[52] Indeed, it has come to an end; the two French divisions and 400 to 450 combat places stationed in Germany were withdrawn from NATO on July 1, 1966.

In the same year, 1959, he refused to store on French soil the nuclear warheads for missiles with which the American bombers stationed in France were to be armed. The bombers had to be transferred to Britain and Germany. His explanation was as follows: "France considers that, if atomic weapons are to be stored on her territory, they should be in her hands, in view of the nature of these weapons and of the consequences which their use might have."[53] It is only fair to add that similar reasons motivated Norway and Denmark in refusing to store American nuclear missiles on their soil.

In the same year, de Gaulle withdrew the French Mediterranean Fleet from NATO. In 1963 he did the same with the French Atlantic Fleet. All these measures were pinpricks; they did not seriously hurt the military posture of NATO. The French warships assigned to NATO remained under French command in peacetime; they would come under NATO command only in case of war. The American bombers could be transferred to airfields in Britain and Germany.

The serious aspect of his policy lies elsewhere. He rejects the concept of a joint allied supreme command in peacetime but, by implication of his moves, also in wartime. This is a strange attitude for a former professional officer who knows that the allies of the First World War, after a bitter experience of separate national commands, had come to the conclusion that the only practical method was to create an inter-allied supreme command. This lesson was remembered during the Second World War, and the allied supreme command was accepted. The ally making the greatest contribution had one of its generals appointed the supreme commander of allied forces. In the First World War it was

Marshal Foch; in the Second, General Eisenhower. It is now rather natural that an American general holds this post. De Gaulle seems to forget that the nature of war has changed so much with nuclear weapons that the allies, if their forces were not integrated in peacetime and placed under a unified command, would have no time for improvisation after the outbreak of hostilities. His answer is that the American nuclear forces are not integrated, and that they represent the main Western means of defense.

British tactics, French tactics

France asserts her influence in the world by a foreign policy unco-ordinated with Washington. Britain uses a different method. She does not oppose the United States (the only flagrant exception was the Suez Canal affair in 1956, when she, characteristically, had a cause in common with France). Instead, Britain tries to influence the formulation of American policies with her discreetly given advice. Raymond Aron and Australian specialists on foreign affairs fully agree on this point. Aron writes:

> Since December 1941 British governments have been convinced that the American alliance has been indispensable, first to win the war and later to guarantee the security of Great Britain. They accept "American leadership" as unavoidable. In consequence of this decision, or in resignation, British tactics always consist of the same moves: to begin with, the British try to convince American leaders that they should adopt a policy which London believes to be the best, and to influence, if necessary, American public opinion and the mass media. After American leaders have made a decision, even a decision contrary to London's preferences, the British loyally follow the American leader without losing hope that events or criticism will open his eyes. . . . Frenchmen have neither the same means nor the same methods. Governments of the Fourth and the Fifth Republics maneuver in a different manner. The Governments of both Republics rarely discuss [with the Americans] and frequently use the method of obstruction.[54]

The Australians have come to the same view:

> Where the British Government has in effect settled for influence with Washington, General de Gaulle has remained preoccupied with independence. Again, this contrast in attitudes is not surprising. Over the past twenty-one years, British policy-makers have won enough of their arguments with Washington to make reasonable the conviction that the cultivating of this relationship is their

most useful line of diplomatic action. France, and de Gaulle personally, have had a much lower percentage of successes. In fact, looking back, one is struck by the number of grudges which any French nationalist might feel against "the Anglo-Saxons."[55]

These British tactics are possible for a reason peculiar to Britain. The two countries are bound together by many ties. The same language, the same cultural traditions, the same uninterrupted attachment to democratic ideals, the stamina of the British people demonstrated in the dark hours of 1940 and 1941 give Britain a unique place in American affections. No other nation has or could hope to have the same privileged position or the same sympathy and trust. Although Americans are not predominantly Anglo-Saxons in the ethnic sense, they are close cousins of the British people in spirit. If the French government wanted to imitate British diplomacy in Washington, they would win fewer successes. This fact cannot be helped and partly explains de Gaulle's frontal assaults. It explains as well his conviction that Britain is an American Trojan horse. Doubtless, Britain, a member of the Common Market or of a European political union, would not support any anti-American moves.

French withdrawal from NATO

As we have seen, the French President frequently forewarned that he would not tolerate the French military integration under the NATO supreme command for long. The ultimate deadline he mentioned in his statements was 1969. He would be legally entitled in that year to denounce unilaterally even the North Atlantic Treaty itself. However, he stated at his press conference held on February 21, 1966, that he intended for France to remain bound by that Treaty after 1969, the date fixed in it for the unilateral right of every signatory state to terminate its obligations.[56] He reaffirmed once again that the Atlantic Alliance continued to be *useful* for France, but he used this new word instead of his former more emphatic words: "an elemental necessity." He cautiously qualified his intention by saying that it might disappear if international circumstances were to change so radically that the Atlantic Alliance would no longer be necessary for his country.

At the same press conference he announced that France would soon take the required steps for complete disengagement from NATO obligations, which in his mind are distinct from the North Atlantic Treaty itself. This decision should not have surprised anyone familiar with his earlier declarations. The only new element was the note of urgency. The allied capitals understood that this time he meant business, and that he would soon terminate French association with NATO.

In February 1966 the General repeated his well-known arguments to justify French disengagement from NATO: the change which had occurred in the international situation since 1949 (the date of signature of the North Atlantic Treaty), the diminished threat of Soviet military aggression against Western Europe, and the uncertainty of American guaranty due to the American-Soviet nuclear stalemate. He added a new argument, namely that NATO military integration under American supreme command might drag the European allies, against their intentions and interests, into an American war fought initially in a non-European area. He illustrated this argument with the Korean war and the Cuban missile crisis. While France had fully supported American policy during the Korean war, de Gaulle's mention of the Cuban crisis in October 1962 may have appeared convincing to many of his countrymen. The United States made the decision to confront the Soviet Union with the alternative of direct military conflict or withdrawal of Soviet nuclear weapons from Cuba, without prior consultation with its European allies. General de Gaulle further warned the Europeans that an escalation of the war in Vietnam might eventually involve them in a worldwide conflagration. He thus made an allusion to the possibility of such a course of events in Southeast Asia that would end in direct military confrontation between the United States and the Soviet Union, which was already supplying North Vietnam with military matériel at the time of his press conference.   According to his argument later elaborated by Prime Minister Pompidou, NATO military integration would have this result, because American and allied European forces would not be able to disengage themselves in case of a Soviet-American conflict originating outside of Europe; the Soviet Union would regard the American allies in Europe as enemies in view of their being placed under the American supreme command and the presence of American troops and military bases on allied European territories. In brief, the President and the Prime Minister maintained that the United States might become involved through its extra-European policy in a war with the Soviet Union, and European NATO allies would have no option.

The French President announced at the same press conference that his government would soon begin a gradual withdrawal from NATO, to be completed at the latest by April 4, 1969. Later he reduced the period of time allocated for French withdrawal to April, 1967. He added that French-Allied military cooperation in case of war in Europe would be ensured by the newly negotiated agreements, which could also provide for a very limited peacetime coordination. He specifically mentioned the need of such agreements regarding French forces stationed in Western Germany. It was obvious that these forces could not remain on German soil once their subordination to the NATO supreme command had been cancelled, except by virtue of a German assent. Later, the French government cleverly offered the Federal Republic a choice between total withdrawal of French forces by July 1, 1966, or the conclusion of an agreement regarding their future status. Politically the Federal Republic has a true interest in the presence of French troops, even independent of NATO, because they represent a visible French pledge to participate in the guaranty of Western German security. Any Soviet aggression against the Federal Republic would immediately involve not only the NATO allies but also France, if her troops continued to be stationed on the German territory, and she would have to bear the brunt of hostilities together with the other allied and German troops.

If no Franco-German agreement were concluded and France pulled her forces out of Germany, she would not lose her right to have a voice in any negotiation concerning the German problem because she would still be entitled to maintain her garrison in West Berlin. While the Federal Republic considers West Berlin an integral part of West Germany, the three Western allies do not officially recognize this view. If they did, the Soviet Union would immediately contest their right as former occupying powers to protect West Berlin against encroachment by Soviet or East German authorities. Hence France could pull her forces out of West Germany and still exert an influence on the evolution of the German problem as a whole. Any of the three Western Powers with garrisons in West Berlin may advocate a change in the status of West Berlin to the prejudice of German interests by accepting the substitution of East German agents for the Soviet on the roads of access across East Germany to West Berlin. The latter move would carry with it an implied recognition of the Democratic Republic of Germany and the acceptance of the Soviet thesis that there are two equally sovereign German states. The self-evident German interest requires, therefore, the cultivation of good relations with all three Western Powers present in West Berlin. This trump card would remain in French hands despite evacuation of French forces from Western German territory. However, geography itself provides the Federal Republic with a negotiating asset regarding the French garrison in West Berlin; the road of access for its supplies crosses both the West and East German territory. The Federal Republic and France, who are in addition partners in the EEC, have a mutual interest in arriving at an acceptable compromise solution which would allow France to maintain her forces in Western Germany.

Looking at the same problem from a purely military point of view, one cannot overlook the fact that the two French divisions and about 450 combat planes, now stationed in Germany, would have to surrender their tactical nuclear weapons lent by the United States. If the United States should ask for the return of those weapons, supplied under the system of two locks and only to the NATO allies, the military value of French forces would be significantly lowered until such time as France produced her own tactical nuclear armaments.

General de Gaulle notified his allies at the same press conference that all foreign forces and bases on French soil must be withdrawn or else placed under French control. The latter alternative offered the possibility of some mutual accommodation, at least regarding certain facilities which the NATO allies, especially the United States, had hitherto enjoyed in France. This alternative to a liquidation of those facilities was somewhat overlooked in the allied reactions to his policy of disengagement.

Undoubtedly this policy opened a grave crisis in the Atlantic Alliance. One can measure its seriousness only against the background of the present situation. The NATO Supreme Command is located at Rocquencourt, the important Central European command at Fontainebleau, and the U. S. Headquarters at Saint-Germain-en-Laye. American military personnel stationed in France numbers 26,000. The United States has nine (four of them important) air bases, while Canada uses two small airfields. Above all, the allied logistic problem is closely related to the geographical place of France in Western Europe. The French territory is the site of a center of NATO telecommunications; the fuel pipeline for the NATO forces in West Germany begins at the French Atlantic harbor of Donges and crosses the French territory; fifteen NATO munition, fuel, other military supplies and spare parts depots are located in France; France cooperates in her own interest in the NATO early-warning and other air-defense systems; the American Navy uses the facilities of one of French Mediterranean ports; France represents the only direct geographical link between NATO forces in Western and Southern Europe.[57] Finally, this crucial geographical position of France is enhanced by the importance of her air space. If the use of that space were denied, the mobility of allied military planes would be considerably reduced. The French government gave a significant warning to its allies in the summer of 1966 by requiring its permission for allied flights over the French territory each month in advance instead of the former general permission granted for the whole year.

If France quit the Atlantic Alliance, a solid neutral belt, made up of France and of permanently neutral Switzerland and Austria, would form a barrier between the two sectors of the Alliance. A look at the map of Europe suffices to show how unwise are statements which claim that the Atlantic Alliance would not be greatly affected by French withdrawal from the Alliance itself, a move which de Gaulle fortunately does not contemplate. These statements would make sense only if the United States returned to its former strategic concept of massive nuclear retaliation in response to any aggressive Soviet move; but this concept was abandoned long ago.

The transfer of various NATO commands to another country would be the easiest task. The relocation of air bases, of the center of tele-communications, and of various depots would involve the risk of their being concentrated within a smaller area. Modern nuclear weapons require the greatest possible dispersal. These facilities could be moved to Western Germany, Belgium, and Holland, but they would then be exposed to the danger of being overrun by a swift Soviet advance. The same holds true for the transfer of the fuel pipeline to the harbor of one of the same three NATO members. Could oil tankers replace the fuel pipeline for the supply of the allied forces fighting in Germany?

No arguments will alter the simple fact that France's geographical location represents a pivotal significance for the Alliance, if one adopts the American strategic concept of a limited war fought for Europe. France is an indispensable hinterland for the allied troops stationed in Germany. A German newspaper remarked that a limited war with the Soviet Union would be inconceivable if its strategy were confined to West German territory. It has the size, as the paper put it, of a handker-chief.[58] This would be true even if one added the small Dutch and Belgian territories to the West German. The allied forces need more room for maneuvering in a limited war, in which tactical nuclear weapons would probably be used by both belligerent armies, forbidding any prolonged concentration of troops. The French withdrawal from NATO poses a problem of direct interest to all allies, but preeminently to West Germany.

The French President cannot be threatened with the withdrawal of American guaranty of French security. France, allied to the United States or not, lies west of the Rhine and would always be protected by the American alliance with the Federal Republic. If Soviet attack were met by a graduated military response, the American forces fighting east of the Rhine would be *ipso facto* engaged in a combat also for the safety of France. If the President of the United States were to decide that the only way of defending West Germany would be the use of strategic nuclear weapons against the Soviet territory, his decision would serve France as well.

However, there are also weak spots in the negotiating position of the French government. First, President de Gaulle himself admitted that the Atlantic Alliance continued to be useful for France. His Prime Minister made this admission crystal clear in a later debate in the French National Assembly. (See Chapter III) Hence the French government has no interest in reducing the military efficiency of the Alliance to the point of its becoming useless for France and other European countries.

Second, France needs to participate in the allied early-warning system. A Frenchman could reply that this system offers such a short warning time that it is almost without value. However, if France had no warning system of her own at the time when her nuclear submarine fleet was completed, the NATO early-warning system would give her government those very few minutes needed for ordering the submarines to inflict the second strike on the enemy. This in itself would have a deterrent significance.

Third, France can hardly afford an open rupture with her five partners in the Common Market, all of whom are members of the Alliance. They all remain faithful to NATO and would expect France to be accommodating in finding a workable substitute for the former French participation in the allied military integration. Negotiations with the Federal Republic might be somewhat eased by the French offer to extend the present facilities on the French soil for the German armed forces in exchange for German assent to the continued stationing of French troops in Germany.

On the whole, there seems to exist enough room for a businesslike negotiation between France and her fourteen allies. Both parties to the present dispute have a vital interest in safeguarding the Atlantic Alliance and its ties to France. It is possible that de Gaulle's challenge came at a time when the Alliance needed not military disengagement, as General de Gaulle thinks, but adjustment to new conditions and a streamlining of NATO itself.

The French point of view was officially communicated to each of the remaining fourteen allies in almost identical memoranda transmitted on March 10 and 11, 1966. These memoranda were in effect an invitation to mutual negotiations. The recipient governments agreed to act jointly. In fact, several matters will require bilateral conversations, especially on questions of direct concern to the United States or the German Federal Republic.[59]

While the French memoranda of March 10 and 11 did not add anything new to what General de Gaulle said at his February press conference, the French government clarified its views in the following set of memoranda submitted on March 31 to the same allied governments.[60] For the first time the deadlines were specifically stated. The French government announced that its forces in Western Germany would no longer be subject to the NATO command beginning July 1, 1966, and would be withdrawn from Germany on the same date if their status were not by that time newly defined. It added that, if these forces were to remain in Germany, presumably by agreement with the other allies and, in the first place, with the Federal Republic, it was ready to establish a military liaison mission at the NATO command. Both the United States and Britain are interested in negotiations concerning the future status of French forces in Germany, as these powers have their own forces in that country.

France requested in the same memoranda the removal of all NATO commands from French soil by April 1, 1967, at the latest. If fixed the same deadline for the evacuation of NATO military depots, but conceded that longer periods might be necessary for the transfer of the most important. It asked for the liquidation of American and Canadian military and air bases by April 1967. Other problems related to the French withdrawal from NATO were left to future negotiations. In particular, the French government expressed its readiness to envisage a new agreement regarding the conditions under which the fuel pipeline could continue to be operated in France. The French memoranda did not mention several problems: the American tactical nuclear weapons now in the possession of French forces in Germany; the NATO early-warning system in which France surely has an interest; the telecommunication network; the future use of French air space by allied planes; and the site in Paris of the North Atlantic Secretariat and Council. (The French government probably feels that the Secretariat might remain in Paris and the Council hold its sessions there; both are not necessarily related to NATO but rather to political aspects of the Alliance.)

Prime Minister Pompidou justified, in a television interview in early April, 1966, the French withdrawal from NATO. He invoked the old argument that allied military integration did not make sense if the nuclear forces of the United States and Britain were not integrated. His government disclosed, also in April, the unilateral American suspension of a secret agreement concluded in 1959 by the United States and France.[61] This disclosure probably was calculated to prove that the French unilateral denunciation of several agreements with NATO and the United States was a sort of delayed answer to the equally unilateral American action. The agreement of 1959 provided for American supply of 968 pounds of enriched uranium to be used by a French land-based reactor. This reactor was to be a prototype for the reactors of nuclear-powered French submarines. The United States delivered 374 pounds and refused in 1964 to supply the remainder possibly in reprisal for the withdrawal of French naval units from NATO. France had to rely henceforth on her own Pierrelatte plant, which will eventually produce enriched uranium. Anyone who knows the importance de Gaulle attaches to his nuclear program may easily imagine his state of mind on learning that the United States had decided to withhold its help.

The French government not only unilaterally denounced several allied agreements, but also did not respect the Franco-German Treaty of 1963.

It failed to consult the German government prior to its action; yet this treaty obligated both governments to consult each other on matters of common concern. NATO was undoubtedly a problem of highest concern for the Federal Republic. This French lack of respect for the treaty, hailed in 1963 as a historical achievement, demonstrated that politically the treaty was a failure.

The French government remained silent on an important aspect of its action. The evacuation of NATO and American headquarters, airfields, depots, and possibly of the fuel pipeline, and their transfer to other countries will entail a very heavy expenditure. As all these facilities had been installed on French soil with full French agreement, the other allies had a legitimate claim in asking France to pay a share of the cost of removal. This was another matter for future negotiations.

One of the difficulties in these negotiations will be the maintenance of a common front by all the fourteen allies who will face France across the table. However, this will not be easy, as they already show divergent views concerning the best manner of handling this awkward issue. The first stiff reactions by the United States and Britain did not meet with general approval. Among major allies, the Federal Republic hesitates to endorse an adamant American-British attitude, because she wants to maintain friendly relations with France. The two have not only a common interest in the existence of the EEC, but Bonn also fears that its strong opposition on the NATO issue might push General de Gaulle into rapprochement with the Soviet Union at the expense of Germany. Moreover, the Germans realize that their common stand with the United States and Britain in the quarrel with France might arouse dormant suspicions among other European nations. These would not welcome any NATO directorate of "big brothers"—and even less one with German participation. The last war is not forgotten, and Germany has not yet acquired the full trust of lesser European countries which suffered under Nazi occupation.

It is not even completely certain that Britain will maintain her present stiff attitude. Everything indicates that the Labour government contemplates a cautious approach to the Common Market. Every member state of the EEC has the veto regarding the admission of new members; France cannot be bypassed, as she could not be in 1963. This is probably not the time to irritate General de Gaulle with an uncompromising British view on NATO, if Britain wants to remove the French veto. (See Chapter V)

It would be erroneous to think that there exists any analogy between the Common Market issue and the NATO problem in French domestic politics. The survival of the Common Market was a problem of direct interest to many French voters. (See Chapter I) The ability of Lecanuet in exploiting this issue during the presidential electoral campaign cost de Gaulle the loss of majority on the first ballot. The withdrawal of France from NATO might result in the loss of a portion of moderate votes for the Gaullist candidates in the spring parliamentary elections, but might also result in their gaining a portion of leftist votes. Most Frenchmen feel that there is no real threat of Soviet military aggression and hence they do not attach great importance to the French disengagement from the allied military integration. Possibly the majority of Frenchmen welcome de Gaulle's move as a challenge to the "American protectorate," whatever they mean by this term. Finally, the Communist voters will not disregard their party's approval of de Gaulle's decision. One may also be sure that the General will appeal to French national pride and present his move as calculated to enhance French independence of foreign powers.

In the latter part of April the French National Assembly held a debate on the NATO issue.[62] The opposition parties were divided by this issue but also by their own political squabbles. The debate turned around the Socialist motion of censure. The Communist deputies refused to support the motion. The Popular Front, established only for the purpose of the presidential electoral campaign, foundered on the Atlantic issue, which divided the Communists from their electoral allies, Socialists and Radicals. It was clear more than ever that, if the three parties, which had supported Mitterand for President, were to gain a parliamentary majority in the spring elections, they would be unable to form a Popular Front government. They had no common platform regarding foreign policy.

This could have been remedied in case of an electoral victory of the opposition parties, if the Socialists were prepared to return to Gaston Defferre's concept of close cooperation of all non-Communist opposition groups. These hopes were ruled out, at least for the time being, by the uncompromising attitude of the Socialist party and those Radicals who followed Mitterand's lead.

As was noted in Chapter I, the presidential election was followed by the formation of two groups by the defeated candidates. Mitterand founded the Left-Democratic-Socialist Federation, composed of Socialists, leftist Radicals and clubs. Lecanuet built up a rival federation called the Democratic Center and including the Popular Republicans and the Independents. (Those Independents who were Gaullist and followed the lead of the former Minister Giscard d'Estaing formed a separate group called Independent Republicans.)

All the non-Communist traditional parties were ready to sponsor the

Socialist motion of censure. The bone of contention was the question of whom the Socialist deputies would allow to sign it. This question of signatures split up the Radical group. Eighteen of the Radical and affiliated deputies shared the view of Maurice Faure and the former Prime Minister Félix Gaillard; they wanted to exert pressure on the Socialists in order to obtain their assent to open the motion for Popular Republican and Independent signatures. They intended by this bias to revive Defferre's concept. They hoped that a united front of all non-Communist opposition parties would pave the way to a merger of the Left-Democratic-Socialist Federation and the Democratic Center. If they had been able to convince the Socialists, the prospect of a viable parliamentary majority to succeed the present Gaullist one would become a realistic alternative offered to French voters in 1967. But even the Radical deputies were far from unanimous. Twelve of them, led by Mitterand, who had a personal interest in the survival of his federation, opposed their colleagues and defended the Socialist stand.

The Socialist parliamentary group decided to maintain their refusal to admit the Popular Republicans and the Independents to the signature of the motion of censure. Finally, the motion was submitted with only the Socialist and Mitterand's Radicals' signatures. The traditional parties offered a sorry spectacle to French voters. Not only were they unable to coalesce into one grouping, but the majority of Radical deputies deserted Mitterand and demonstrated their preference for cooperation with the Democratic Center rather than with the Left-Democratic-Socialist Federation. The latter Federation, without a good portion of Radicals, remained a shaky organization; it amounted to not much more than its backbone, the Socialist party and its sympathizers.

This squabble among the opposition parties was more like a musical comedy rather than serious politics. Frenchmen could see that the opposition was divided into three groups: the Communist party hostile to any Western alliance, the Socialists supported by leftist Radicals and equally leftist clubs, and the Popular Republicans allied to the Independents. This spectacle proved that no viable anti-Gaullist majority was in sight. Maurice Faure deduced the conclusion: "This procedural question [of signatures on the motion of censure] conceals a problem of substance. This is the problem of an alternative to the present majority. . . . We think that no such alternative majority is possible in this country except by a union of the left and the center. The others [the Socialists and Mitterand's Radicals] seem to believe that it is possible to govern together with the Communists, but the country does not want this to happen."[63] He was unjust in accusing the Socialists and his fellow Radicals of intending to form a Popular Front government; the very motion of censure proved that the Communists and the others could never agree on a joint foreign policy. But he was right in saying that no stable alternative government was in sight to replace General de Gaulle's regime either after the parliamentary elections in 1967 or, if the inter-party quarrels continued, after his death.

The motion of censure accused the President of the Republic of having decided to denounce French participation in NATO without previously consulting his own government and parliament and without trying to find a solution in negotiations with the French allies, and expressed apprehension that this policy would culminate in the isolation of France and in an intensification of the French nuclear effort at a growing cost to the national budget and at the expense of the welfare of French poorer social classes.

The motion of censure was defeated; only 137 deputies voted for it out of the total of 465. In spite of the pro-Gaullist majority in the National Assembly, the motion should have gathered over 200 votes. However, the Communist deputies did not vote for it. Only the Socialist and almost all Radical deputies supported it, while the other opposition groups were split. Twenty out of fifty-four Popular Republicans and Independents, who took part in this parliamentary division, refused to cast their votes for the motion. The NATO issue not only separated the Communists from their 1965 electoral allies, the Socialists and the Radicals, but also divided the two right-center groups which were the pillars of the Democratic Center. This parliamentary vote proved that the whole opposition could not be united on this issue in the parliamentary elections in 1967.[64]

The doubts in France regarding NATO and its present structure are not confined to General de Gaulle's supporters; they are reflected in the following comment by *Le Monde,* which cannot be accused of sympathy for the General: "It is necessary to concede that NATO, as it has existed for the last several years, does not correspond any longer, on the military plane, to what its founders had wanted and had proclaimed."[65]

V Western European Union Versus French Independence

Is he a "European"?

Is de Gaulle a "European"? The answer is yes and no. Yes, he has favored since the end of the last war a European unity founded on the reconciliation of all European peoples. This is his distant vision of Big Europe. At the same time he has also been a convinced partisan of a close union of Western Europe as a counterbalance to Soviet Russia. The realization of Western Little Europe is in his mind the precondition of Big Europe, which would necessitate the balance of power being restored between the two parts of the Continent.

Little Europe would become, in his vision of the future, a third Super-Power which would act, at first, as an arbiter between the United States and Russia, and later on, when it had acquired strength and no longer needed American alliance, would be by itself a sufficient counterweight to Russia. On that distant day the two parts of Europe would discover that they form one fraternal family. Big Europe from the Atlantic to the Urals would become a living reality. It would then recapture its former decisive voice in world affairs.

To understand de Gaulle's European policies one should never forget the key word: France. The union of any Europe, Big or Little, is justified in his eyes only because it would serve the vital interests of France.[1]

But France must not be "dissolved" in a cosmopolitan European "hodgepodge." She must under any conditions retain exclusive control over her state. His Little Europe should be made up of six sovereign states, each holding to its ultimate right of veto. He calls it "Europe of the states."[2] Michel Debré coined the term "Europe of the Fatherlands."

De Gaulle's European outlook is jealous of any outside interference. Little Europe should be economically protectionist and politically and militarily independent. So long as the American alliance is necessary, Western Europe should act at least as an equal partner, free to disagree with its American ally. If he had his own way, Little Europe of the Six would become, like France, an uncommitted ally.

As a matter of fact, Prime Minister Pompidou placed "European" Europe at an equal distance from the United States and the Soviet Union: "Europe must be European, that is, independent, and must have an inde-

189

pendent policy. There is no question of opposing Europe to the United States. But neither should one oppose it to Soviet Russia."[3]

De Gaulle's record since 1958 is complex. After he had returned to power, he was confronted with the Treaties of Rome, signed in 1957, on the European Economic Community and on Euratom. They were signed but not yet applied. He decided to honor the signature of the Fourth Republic. His government put order in the French financial and monetary situation, which was in a deplorable condition, and thus enabled France to face the responsibilities of a member of the Common Market. He has assented to the acceleration of transitory periods during which the tariffs between the member states have been gradually lowered. His insistence on the extension of the Common Market to agriculture has been dictated by French interests, but a fully integrated economy of the Six could not exist without the integration of their agriculture. His policy in this respect characteristically coincided with that of the European Commission.

His critics say that he is a bad European, because he has adamantly refused to take even the most timid steps toward a supranational structure of Little Europe. On this point he disagrees with the other member states of the EEC. They do not mind the power of initiative vested in the European Commission and are less afraid of the Council of Ministers adopting binding decisions by a majority vote. They favor control over European policies by a European parliament elected directly by the citizens of the six nations. He would rather have no Europe than a supranational Europe.

His tactics regarding his five partners are liable to criticism. If he wants to gain his points, be it the agricultural Common Market or the opposition to supranational institutions, and his ministers fail to convince their European colleagues, he has recourse to ultimatums and refusals to participate in the common work. He fixes a date on which the five must accept his point of view or else . . . ! He recalls the French representatives from Brussels and thus prevents any further progress. This is the diplomacy of Napoleon at the Congress of Erfurt. But France today is not Napoleonic France, and she has not subdued her partners by the victories of Wagram, Jena, and Austerlitz. They consider themselves equals of France and do not like dictates. Whenever they have yielded, agricultural integration has progressed, but the concept of supranationality has suffered a new defeat. His abrupt methods might be risky for the future of Little Europe of the Six.

The big question is whether the interests of the Six are already economically so entangled that a divorce is almost impossible, or whether the Five may still oppose their will power to his and refuse to yield. If he threatens to take home the French marbles and terminate the Common Market game, they might withdraw their marbles and place them in another game. Their weapon of reprisal would be to propose to Britain and the other associates in the European Free Trade Association to terminate the present economic division of Western Europe and to form one big free-exchange zone from which only France would be excluded. This sort of association of twelve states would not need a common agricultural policy; that is vital only for France. Germany would be happy, for instance, with the limitation of free trade to industrial goods. This European economic zone would certainly be welcome to Britain, barred from the Common Market by the French veto, and perhaps to the United States, which is interested in easy access to the European market for its agricultural products and in the low tariffs for its industrial goods. A liberal Europe of the twelve would be more attractive for the outsiders than de Gaulle's protectionist Common Market.

If the test of wills between France and the Five were to end in this way, this would be de Gaulle's Waterloo. France would be economically isolated and confronted with coordinated commercial policies of the twelve European states. This is what even the Gaullists feared in 1965 after another of de Gaulle's Napoleonic gestures of anger.

Little and Big Europe

As we have said, de Gaulle has two visions of Europe: Big and Little Europe. The latter Europe should be organized in the first place, and the former Europe would follow in due course. This sequence of events emerged in his mind only after his disappointments with both Britain and the Soviet Union. In 1944 he was optimistic; he visualized a European association embracing the whole geographic extent of Europe: "After the terrible lacerations she had undergone in the last thirty years, and the vast changes which had occurred the world over, Europe could find equilibrium and peace only by an association among Slavs, Germans, Gauls, and Latins."[4] In 1944 no one was excluded from the European unity: "The unity of Europe could be established in the form of an association including its peoples from Iceland to Istanbul, from Gibraltar to the Urals."[5] The British reluctance to join their destinies to those of continental Europe and the Soviet menacing ambitions compelled him to shelve this Grand Design, but not to forget it.

Soon after the Allied victory he decided that the more practical plan was to unite only Western Europe, as a necessary and preliminary condition for the ultimate emergence of Big Europe from which no European people would be excluded. He himself depicted his more modest vision in the following words:

to persuade the States along the Rhine, the Alps, and the Pyrenees to form a political, economic and strategic bloc; to establish this organization as one of the three planetary powers and, should it become necessary, as the arbiter between the Soviet and Anglo-American camps.[6]

This Little Europe would become a third force capable of acting as a referee between the Russians and the Anglo-Saxons.

His statements have not varied throughout the years. In 1947 he talked of Western Europe "organized as a bloc capable to contain any possible claim to hegemony and to become a factor of equilibrium between the two rival masses. The maintenance of peace will need this stabilizing factor."[7] In 1951 his Western Europe was to be a complex "which will have the capacity to establish an equilibrium between the two great powers."[8] In 1962 he had the same ambition:

> Who in good faith can dispute the fact that France . . . must help to build Western Europe into an organized union of states, so that gradually there may be established on both sides of the Rhine, of the Alps, and perhaps of the Channel, the most powerful, prosperous and influential political, economic, cultural, and military complex in the world?[9]

This time the united Western Europe was expected to become not only one of the planetary powers but the first among the three. Two years earlier he had already depicted Little Europe as "the greatest political, economic, military, and cultural power that has ever existed."[10]

In 1960 he voiced the ambition dear to most Western Europeans, to recover through common action the former "grandeur" lost in the two World Wars:

> Neither the Rhine, nor the Low Countries, nor the Alps, nor the Pyrenees, nor the Channel, nor the Mediterranean, for all of which they fought so long and so bitterly, any longer set them one against the other. . . . On the contrary, the nostalgia inspired in each of these nations by her relative decline in relation to the great new empires has drawn them closer in the feeling that together they could regain this grandeur for which past centuries had given them the talent and the habit. . . . To contribute to building Western Europe into a political, economic, cultural, and human group, organized for action, progress and defense—that is what France wants to work toward.[11]

He did not hide his ambition for France at the time when he was occupying no official position and could be frank. Her grandeur would be not only her share in the recovered grandeur of united Western Europe. She was to be the destined leader of that Europe. In 1948 he proudly proclaimed: "France must assume the duty and dignity of being the center and keystone of a group, whose arteries are the North Sea, the Rhine, and the Mediterranean."[12] He repeated it in the same year: "It is necessary to build Western Europe. . . . But it is France who is the physical and moral center of this group."[13] At that time his calculation was quite realistic. Western Europe, without Britain and with Western Germany only rising from the ruins of her defeat, could have had only one leader: France, recognized by the other victorious powers as one of them. Today his ambition has not changed but rests on the French nuclear monopoly.

The American alliance should assist Western Europe in eventually declaring itself independent of the United States; he said it frankly in 1960: "But if the Atlantic Alliance is necessary at *present* for the security of France and of the other free peoples of our old continent, they must, behind this shield, organize to achieve their joint power and development."[14] (Italics mine.) And after? The answer will depend on the policy of the Soviet Union. If the potential Soviet threat continues, the alliance must be maintained, but Western Europe will act as an ally equal of the United States. He said on December 31, 1963, that his government would continue to work in the following year for

> the union of Europe, including as soon as possible the regular and organized cooperation of Germany, Italy, the Netherlands, Belgium, Luxemburg, and France in the domains of politics, defense, and culture, as will be the case in that of economics. . . . Next, we must assist our Western Europe, once it is united, in practicing with America a truly concerted political, economic, and strategic entente.[15]

Foreign Minister Couve de Murville, in his speech of November 3, 1964, in the National Assembly, was no less clear concerning future relations with the United States:

> It is often said of Europe that it should find its place in the Atlantic world, whose other pillar would be the United States of America. A dialogue would be instituted between the two, the dialogue of the continents. I do not say no, but if there is to be dialogue, that means that there are two policies, one of which would be defined in Europe and the other in Washington. The two policies would not be hostile, contradictory, or irreconcilable by definition. But there would have to be two. If not, the dialogue would be replaced by a monologue.[16]

This Western Europe—independent of, if allied with, the United States
—de Gaulle calls European Europe:

> Europe must assume its share of the responsibilities. . . . But which
> Europe? That is the question. . . . According to us French, it is a
> question of Europe's being made in order for it to be European. A
> European Europe means that it exists by itself for itself, in other
> words, in the midst of the world it has its own policy.[17]

All-European equilibrium and bilateral relations

His other vision of Big Europe has never been forgotten. He said on
May 15, 1962, that it was indispensable "to contribute to the construction of Europe . . . so that the expansion and action of this complex aid
French prosperity and security and, at the same time, reestablish the
possibility of a European equilibrium vis-à-vis the countries of the
East."[18] This balance of power between the Western and Eastern parts
of Europe will be the foundation of European unity:

> On our old continent, the organization of a Western group, at the
> very least equivalent to that which exists in the East, will one day
> make possible, without risk to the independence and freedom of
> any nation and taking into account the probable evolution of polit-
> ical regimes, to establish a European entente from the Atlantic to
> the Urals.[19]

On November 22, 1959, he recaptured his vision of 1944:

> Yes, it is Europe from the Atlantic to the Urals, it is Europe, all
> those old lands where modern civilization was born and flourished,
> it is Europe entire that will decide the destiny of the world. If the
> European peoples, on whichever side of the Iron Curtain they may
> be situated, are able one day to establish concord among them-
> selves, peace will be ensured for the world. If, on the contrary, they
> remain divided into two blocs opposed to each other, war will
> sooner or later destroy the human race. The world responsibility
> of Europe is now greater than it ever was.[20]

This vision of the distant future leaves no place in Europe for the United
States.

He is proud of that Big Europe: "Our Europe is the main home of
modern civilization. It would be absurd if today, when so many men, in
particular the starving two billions, aspire to be admitted to the fold of
that civilization, the Europeans themselves were to scatter and thus let
its home fall down."[21] There is here no mention of another center of

modern civilization, the United States, toward whom the underdeveloped countries also look for inspiration. Four years later he was in a more generous mood and conceded to the United States ("the eldest daughter of Europe," as he calls it) a place within our civilization: "There is a modern civilization. Europe invented it and later transported it to America. Today the West is, on both sides of the Atlantic, its source and its master artisan."[22]

If de Gaulle encounters disappointments in his Western European policy, for instance, if cooperation with Germany does not progress smoothly, he seeks bilateral and limited contacts with any European nation willing to enter into a dialogue with France. These bilateral contacts are not limited to Little Europe but extend from the Atlantic to the Urals. Toward the end of April 1965 clouds began to gather on the horizon of Little Europe; the storm was to break out in the summer. At that time de Gaulle made a speech on radio and television in which his two visions of Europe encroached on each other:

> In the political sphere, we must, without renouncing our American friendship, behave like the Europeans we are and, in that capacity, work hard in order to re-establish, from one end of our continent to the other, an equilibrium founded on the mutual understanding and cooperation of all the peoples who live on it as we do. This is exactly what we are doing by reconciling ourselves with Germany, by proposing a real solidarity of the Six to our neighbors on both sides of the Rhine and the Alps, by re-establishing with the Eastern countries, as they emerge from their oppressing constraint, the relations of active understanding which formerly linked us to them. . . .
>
> Finally, when it is opportune to combine in a given field our inventions, our capabilities, and our resources with those of another country, we must often choose one of those countries which are closest to us and whose weight, we think, will not crush us. This is why . . . we are setting up a common industrial and agricultural market with Germany, Italy, Belgium, the Netherlands, and Luxemburg; we are tunneling through Mont Blanc in cooperation with the Italians; we are improving the navigability of the River Moselle in association with Germany and Luxemburg; we are joining with England in building the world's first supersonic passenger aircraft; we are ready to extend this Franco-British collaboration to other types of civil and military aircrafts; we have just concluded an agreement with Soviet Russia concerning the perfection and exploitation of our color television techniques.[23]

No supranationality

The only possible answer to our initial question is that de Gaulle is a European, but a conditional one. He has never made a secret of his two conditions: his Little Europe must be economically, politically, and militarily an independent union and should never become a unit of an Atlantic community dominated by the United States; and it should rest on the coordination of policies of its member states without any trace of supranational institutions. His whole European record testifies to this concept. He has never opposed the idea of a united Western Europe, but neither did he ever yield in his adamant opposition to supranational institutions. For reasons known only to himself, his two conditions merge into one. He has said and repeated that a supranational Western Europe would be dominated by the United States. He apparently assumes that the five partners of France would not have the will power to resist American pressure; the French veto is the only guaranty of European independence.

It would be a gross error to conclude from de Gaulle's former opposition to all European treaties, concluded between 1951 and 1957, that he did not want a Western European union. He was opposed to those treaties, because all of them contained an element of supranationality. The first major step toward that union was the treaty on the Coal and Steel Community, signed on April 18, 1951. It bore the mark of supranationality. It created a High Authority composed of members appointed by their respective governments but expected to act independently of national instructions. The High Authority's decisions are directly applicable to producers of coal or steel without the need of an *exequatur* by the six governments. These governments are represented on the Council of Ministers. Depending on the nature of problems, the High Authority may act on its own after only consulting the Council or it must seek the Council's approval, which is given either unanimously or by a majority vote. In other cases the Council may issue binding instructions to the High Authority. What repelled de Gaulle was the power granted to the High Authority to act independently of the member states and the right of the Council of Ministers to make certain decisions by a majority vote. This supranational aspect of the Coal and Steel Community provoked him so much that he contemptuously baptized it "a coal and steel hodgepodge." The Treaty was ratified by the French houses of parliament over the negative votes of Communists, Gaullists, and the extreme right.

The treaty on the European Defense Community, signed on May 27, 1952, roused de Gaulle's ire because it touched his most sensitive nerve, national control over the French armed forces. Its integrated European army, which would include French units, was completely unacceptable to him. But at that time almost all French parties were split on this issue, except for Popular Republicans, who were favorable, and the Communists, who were unanimously opposed. The treaty was rejected by the majority of the French National Assembly; all the Gaullist deputies voted against it.

Finally the two treaties, signed in Rome on March 25, 1957, came up for public discussion. The treaty on the European Economic Community was drafted with an eye on the failure of the European Defense Community and hence contained a lesser ingredient of supranationality than the Coal and Steel Community. However, the EEC Commission, composed of nine members appointed by their respective governments but independent after their appointment, was given the power of initiative. The power of decision was reserved for the Council of Ministers, where each Minister was to implement the instructions of his government. This Council could reject or approve the proposals of the Commission, but these proposals could be modified only by unanimous vote of the Council. If the Commission submitted no proposals of its own, the Council could make decisions only by unanimity.

There are three aspects of the Treaty of Rome de Gaulle did not like in 1957 and does not like now. First, the right of the Commission to submit its own proposals to the Council of Ministers seemed exorbitant. Second, beginning with January 1, 1966, the Council of Ministers is empowered to make decisions on important matters by a majority vote. Important matters include common agricultural policy and the tariffs applicable to the third states. However, each of the Six retains its veto regarding the admission of new members and the grant of status of associated states to such nations as do not seek full membership. France, Germany, and Italy are given four votes each, Belgium and Holland two each, and Luxembourg one vote. The required majority for the acceptance of the Commission's proposals being twelve votes, it is clear to de Gaulle that France may be outvoted. Third, the treaty created, like the Coal and Steel Community Treaty, a European Parliamentary Assembly composed of delegates of national parliaments. The treaty foresaw the possibility of election by the direct and universal suffrage of citizens of the six countries. Having no excessive love for the French parliament, he could like only less the prospect of a supranational parliament.

His representative in the French Council of the Republic, Michel Debré, pronounced a violent diatribe against the Treaties of Rome. De Gaulle told him that it was not necessary: "What for? After we shall have returned to power, we will tear up those Treaties."[24] The two Treaties of Rome were approved by the French parliament over the combined Communist, Gaullist, and extreme-right opposition.

It is interesting to note that one of the most intelligent among de Gaulle's adversaries, Pierre Mendès-France, was also opposed both to the European Defense Community (his tactics as Prime Minister at the time contributed to its defeat in the French parliament) and to the Treaty of Rome on the Common Market. During the preliminary debate on the Treaties of Rome, in January 1957, he protested against the supranational aspects of these treaties and exclaimed: "France must not be the victim of a treaty. A democracy abdicates by delegating its powers not only to a domestic dictatorship but also to an external authority."[25] His followers among the Radicals voted against the ratification of the Treaties of Rome.

De Gaulle promised Debré that he would tear up the Treaties of Rome after his return to power. However, when he came to power in 1958, he implemented their provisions honestly. He probably hoped that he would patiently nibble away the supranational elements of the Common Market and that the five other governments would eventually yield to his pressure to save the substance of economic cooperation.

De Gaulle's views have never varied on this subject. What he said on October 8, 1952, continues to be his firm opinion: "The problem consists in building Europe, which would be a major blessing for the whole world. But it should not be an imbroglio of 'pools.' It should be a confederation of states."[26] His ideal of European organization appeared as early as November 12, 1953:

> I have considered that the best institutions are those which are the simplest, namely a periodical and organized Council of Heads of Government which would have at its disposal joint services for the preparation of its decisions in the political, economic, cultural, and military domains; and a deliberative assembly.[27]

In other words: "To organize European solidarity without infringing upon national sovereignty—this seems to be the conception of Europe President de Gaulle has chosen."[28]

Only an indefatigable optimist could believe that an association of sovereign states, each endowed with a veto, would be able to present a united front in international affairs. But de Gaulle might be right in thinking that the six nations are not ready for merger into a federal state. National consciousness is too sharp to allow for a delegation of powers over their welfare and, above all, over their security, to a federal government which would be composed, from each one's point of view, of a foreign majority. The contemporary example of Belgium is discouraging. The Walloons and the Flemings, who have lived under the same roof for centuries and who have been citizens of independent Belgium since 1830, are engaged in a sharp conflict; the growing trend among them is toward a looser state structure and the transformation of Belgium into a federal state, the Walloons and the Flemings becoming autonomous masters in their respective parts of the country. The least one may say is that it would take the Six a very long time to become another multilingual Switzerland. For the time being, de Gaulle is not wrong when he holds that national states are the only reality. The real issue is to what extent these states could safely delegate some of their powers to supranational institutions. This is the major issue between de Gaulle, on the one hand, and the French opposition and the five other governments, on the other hand.

He depicted most clearly his own concept on September 5, 1960. This statement is the key for anyone who wants to understand his European policy:

> To build Europe, that is to say, to unite it is evidently something essential. . . . Only one must proceed in this venture not by following one's dreams but according to realities. Now, what are the realities of Europe? . . . Indeed, the States are those realities, States which certainly are very different from each other. Each of them has its own spirit, its own history, its own language, its own misfortunes, glories, and ambitions; but States are the only entities which have the right to issue orders and the power of coercion. To imagine that something can be built that would be effective for action and that would be approved by the peoples outside and above the States —this is a dream. Of course, it is true that, while waiting to come to grips with the European problem as a whole and face to face, it has been possible to institute certain organs which are more or less supra-national. These organs have their technical value, but they do not have and may not have either authority or political efficacy. So long as nothing serious happens, they function without causing much trouble, but as soon as a dramatic situation appears, as soon as a major problem is to be solved, one discovers that a "High Authority" has no authority over the various national entities, and that the States have it. . . . Once again, it is quite natural that the European States should have at their disposal organs specialized in the problems which they have in common, but the right to take decisions belongs to them alone. This right must remain theirs. They may take decisions only by common consent.[29]

His concept relegates European bodies such as the Coal and Steel High Authority or the EEC Commission to the rank of international experts whose only task is to prepare the decisions of governments and to help in the implementation of these decisions. This concept is much narrower than the texts of the European treaties and could work, without protest on the part of other signatories, only after the revision of these treaties. De Gaulle does not conceal his view that this concept should be observed in particular in the organization and functioning of the Common Market. Referring on May 15, 1962, to the different opinions of his opponents, he said:

> I want to point out the arbitrary nature of a certain idea that was voiced during the recent discussions in Paris and that claimed to exclude economic problems from the agenda of meetings of Heads of State or Government, whereas these problems are the daily and most important issues for each of them in their respective countries.[30]

His argument deserves close attention. The European Economic Community, once it is fully constructed, will be much more than a simple customs union. It will have one policy regarding such vital matters as commercial relations with other countries, the admission of new member states, monetary and general financial problems, social legislation, free circulation of capital, equal right to work irrespective of nationality (businessmen, workers, and farmers in particular), taxation, transports, energy, agriculture, and other questions which directly or indirectly relate to economic life. The welfare of citizens of the six countries will depend on that joint policy. These are highly political problems, because neither businessmen nor workers nor farmers—in fact, no citizen—could remain indifferent to the repercussions of the common European policy on their individual well-being. Are those citizens ready to delegate the decisions relating to these vital matters to a supranational body or to a majority of governments represented in the EEC? This is the question raised by de Gaulle when he remarks:

> One takes political decisions, when tariffs are modified by joint action, when coal mines are being closed, when wages and social welfare contributions are equalized in the six States, when each of these six States allows workers from the other five States to settle on its territory, when decrees are issued for the implementation of these decisions, or when Parliaments are requested to vote the necessary laws, credits and sanctions. One takes a political decision when agriculture is being included within the Common Market. . . .

The same is true when one examines the applications submitted by the third States for their membership or their association. It is still a political decision when one comes to consider the requests already announced by the United States concerning its economic relations with the Community.[31]

His conclusion is: "I have already said, and I repeat, that at the present time there cannot be any other Europe than a Europe of States, apart, of course, from myths, stories, and parades."[32]

His point of view may not be dismissed lightly by invoking the alluring image of a United States of Europe. Raymond Aron, frequently critical of his foreign policy, writes:

> The High Authority of the Coal and Steel Community has made practically no use of its supranational powers which it has on paper, and has not made majority, nonunanimous decisions binding for the national governments. The Brussels Commission possesses on paper less of these so-called supranational powers, but this is not the crux of the problem. Let us assume that the Common Market has been realized according to the Treaty of Rome. Germany, France, Italy would each continue to have her own foreign policy, her own distinct political history, her own police, and her own army. To claim that the Common Market must lead necessarily to a European federation (or to a European federal state) amounts to assuming that the economic factor determines at the present time and, so to speak, includes the political factor, or that the abolition of customs barriers would automatically abolish the political and military barriers. These two assumptions are false.[33]

This is a view not very different from that of de Gaulle. A French specialist of the Common Market agrees with Raymond Aron when he remarks that the High Authority of Coal and Steel Community has not used its supranational powers regarding important matters without seeking preliminary approval by the Council of Ministers, i.e., by the six governments.[34] He considers that the actual role of the European bodies is: "not to act as authorities which impose their decisions on national governments but rather to reveal the existence of common denominators among these governments."[35] A European body composed of members who do not receive instructions from their governments is, indeed, well situated to rise above national horizons and advise the governments on the best road to follow in their cooperation; it cannot compel the governments to accept its advice.

A distinguished French economist warns that the six nations have not lost sight of their particular interests, which they expect to be fully taken into consideration in the formulation of a joint Common Market policy. He is also opposed to a federal system, which

> would have to be founded on a federated Europe, i.e., a group of peoples which would be ready, if necessary, to sacrifice their national interests for the sake of interests of the European federation. If this were true, it would be indifferent to a Frenchman whether a new industry were implanted in France, or, for instance, in the Netherlands. . . . He would have to accept a situation where the rate of growth of the French economy might be lower in a unified Europe than it would have been in a divided Europe. But the federal spirit is absent or is yet absent. The national egoisms have, certainly, not been abolished by the Treaty of Rome. . . . It is not enough to demonstrate that the union brings the production of the Community to its maximum; one must also prove that it brings each national production to its respective maximum.[36]

Even the famous initiator of the Coal and Steel Community and an ardent "European," the late Robert Schuman, advised in a book published in 1959 to proceed cautiously:

> Would it be possible at the present time to conclude an agreement by virtue of which governments and parliaments would accept any decision made not by a unanimous vote but by the majority of states or by the majority of a common Assembly? We talk about serious decisions relating to the issue of peace or war, i.e., which concern the lives of citizens, the independence of nations and the integrity of their territories. I do not believe that we are ready for such a transfer of responsibilities whereby a majority of international wills could impose itself on the national will in a realm where the very existence of the country might be involved. One would have to dread an explosion of passions and suspicions. The very idea of a federal government or of a federal parliament would imply, I think, such a power of majority decisions binding for the federated states. I consider that this would amount to overlooking the need for progressing by stages and to taking jointly but unwisely the road which would lead to the abandonment of national sovereignty regarding matters of vital importance.[37]

Robert Schuman had in mind a political federation; de Gaulle has the same views regarding the economic federation. It is impossible to say in advance of actual experience whether the full implementation of supranational provisions of the Treaty of Rome would encounter such resistance by the states concerned that it would endanger the survival of the European Economic Community. Only the test of experience could decide the issue as to whether de Gaulle or the other five governments are right. He does not want to try.

The "technocrats," the majority vote, and the European Parliament

De Gaulle's first objection is directed against the present powers of the Brussels Commission, namely the right to submit its own proposals and thus face the six governments with the necessity of accepting or rejecting them *in toto*. He would confine the Commission to the role of a group of experts who prepare proposals, but only on the express instructions of the governments. However, he admitted several times that the Commission was doing a good job. In fact, the Commission usually supported the French claim for fully including agriculture in the Common Market.

Whenever he patted the Commission on the shoulder, he never failed to remark that the true progress of the Common Market depended on the governments. Referring to the help which the Commission gave to the French negotiators concerning the integration of agriculture within the Common Market, he said on January 31, 1964:

> The Brussels Commission having objectively accomplished work of great value and having offered the negotiators, as they discussed, carefully studied suggestions, the governments nonetheless were obliged to assume their responsibilities and to take decisions. . . . We should note that, from that point, it is incumbent on them alone to see to the implementation by their respective countries of the commitments they have jointly undertaken. However important the work and counsels of the Brussels Commission have been and should continue to be, we have seen clearly that executive power and duty belong to governments alone.[38]

He sometimes baited the Commission by his contemptuous allusions to the "technocrats." Yet the Commission stood on his side not only regarding agriculture, but also in 1958 when the French government opposed the British attempt to dilute the EEC in a larger free-trade zone, later on when France refused to loosen the Treaty of Rome's bonds to facilitate British accession, and also when France insisted on the conclusion of an agreement on aid and a preferential tariff between the EEC and the former African colonies. Since 1958 the Commission has been "a natural French ally in negotiations with the French partners or with the third countries."[39] This alliance between the Commission and de

Gaulle lasted as long as France insisted on strict observance of the Treaty of Rome. But it could not last forever. After the Commission had suggested in 1965 that further progress regarding agriculture should be combined with a dose of supranationality, the alliance broke down. The conflict long delayed came into the open.

De Gaulle seems to believe that members of European bodies should not claim independence from their respective national governments but rather act as spokesmen of those governments. The concept of an independent international agent escapes his understanding, as he proved in 1961. The term of office of Etienne Hirsch, then President of the Euratom Commission, was to expire, but everyone expected that the French government would agree to its extension. The French government refused to do so and insisted on the appointment of another French citizen. The reason was well-known: Mr. Hirsch defended the prerogatives of Euratom and had poor relations with the French Ministers.[40]

De Gaulle's second objection is to the majority vote in the Council of Ministers; this majority vote is provided for in the Treaty of Rome beginning with January 1, 1966. It is not improbable that in 1965 he welcomed the opportunity which the Commission unintentionally offered by its proposals on the implementation of supranational provisions of the Treaty of Rome, and was glad to precipitate an open conflict. He might have wished to have a full explanation on the future shape of the EEC prior to the approaching date when his views could be outvoted by a majority in the Council. He alluded to this problem at his press conference on May 15, 1962, when he defined supranationality: "a sort of hybrid in which the six states would undertake to comply with what would be decided by a certain majority."[41] His Minister of Information, Alain Peyrefitte, indirectly expressed the French government's opposition by defending the principle of unanimity: "International cooperation and the principle of unanimity do not result in a deadlock or inefficiency, as certain people have joyously predicted."[42] This second objection is the most important for de Gaulle.

His third objection concerns the European Parliament, which would be elected directly by universal suffrage and would have real powers of legislation and control over the European budget. He accepts the existence of the present European Parliament, composed of delegates designated respectively and separately by the six national parliaments and having only consultative powers. Any other European Parliament would conflict with his concept of national sovereignty. Alluding to the views of "Europeans," he ironically observed on May 15, 1962:

> At the same time, although there are already six national Parliaments, plus the European Assembly, plus the Consultative Assem-

bly of the Council of Europe . . . , we should, it seems, elect yet
another parliament, a so-called European one, which would lay
down the law for the states. These are ideas that may, perhaps,
beguile certain minds, but I certainly do not see how they could be
carried out in practice, even if there were six signatures on a piece
of paper. Is there a France, a Germany, an Italy, a Holland, a Belgium, a Luxemburg, that would be ready, regarding any question
which is important for them from the national and international
points of view, to do something that they would consider harmful
only because this would be recommended by the other countries?
Would the French people, the German people, the Italian people,
the Belgian people, the Dutch people, or the Luxemburg people
dream of submitting to laws adopted by foreign deputies if these
laws were to run contrary to their own deep-seated will? This is not
true. There is no way, at the present time, for a foreign majority to
compel recalcitrant nations.[43]

The last sentence is very important, because it has the same validity
regarding a majority in the European Parliament as it has regarding a
majority rule in the EEC Council of Ministers.

De Gaulle fears, perhaps, that a European Parliament, elected by universal suffrage, would side with the advocates of supranationality and
would support the EEC Commission rather than the national governments.[44] However, such a parliament would be the best instrument for
expressing opinions prevailing within the European electorate. These
opinions might be distorted by national delegates to the present European
Parliament, because these delegates are elected to their respective national parliaments mainly on domestic issues. The general European
problems would be faced by the citizens of the six countries only in direct
elections of the European Parliament. Is de Gaulle really afraid that his
own countrymen would then demonstrate a lesser aversion for supranationality than he attributes to them? In any event, he never submitted the
issue of supranationality to a popular referendum in France. He does
not want to run the risk of being repudiated by the French people on
these two major problems: the nuclear question, and the best form of
European union.

Supporters of the European Parliament elected by universal suffrage
overlook, however, certain preliminary difficulties. The delegates to the
present European Parliament are designated by the national parliaments
in such a manner that the Communist parties are never represented.
However, the Communist groups in the French and Italian Parliaments
are large, and their electors usually make up 20 to 25 per cent of the
total electoral bodies. The Communist party is outlawed in Western Ger-

many. If the European Parliament were to reflect all the views held by the six populations, the Communist party would have to be allowed in Western Germany, and the directly elected European Parliament would include a large group of French and Italian Communist deputies who might very well obstruct Western European cooperation—supranational or between the national governments.

De Gaulle can never get rid of his American nightmare. He sees the shadow of American hegemony in every corner of Europe. It is not too surprising that he accuses the supporters of a supranational Europe of being, intentionally or not, American Trojan horses, because such a Europe would allegedly become a satellite of the United States. In 1962 he alluded mysteriously to a "federator who would not be European."[45] In 1964 he pointed out who this non-European federator would be:

> We have seen many people . . . advocate for Europe not an independent policy, which in reality they do not visualize, but an organization unsuited to have one, linked in this field [political field], as in that of defense and the economy, to an Atlantic system, in other words, American, and consequently subordinate to what the United States calls its leadership. This organization, entitled federal, would have had as its bases, on the one hand, a council of experts withdrawn from the affiliation to the States, and which would have been dubbed "executive"; and, on the other hand, a Parliament without national qualifications, and which would be called "legislative."[46]

Merger of the Communities

All these problems, on which de Gaulle's France holds strong opinions, would come into the open on the occasion of the projected merger of the three existing European Communities: the Coal and Steel, the Economic, and Euratom. This merger is necessary because the present division of jurisdiction does not make much sense. The Economic Community must have one coordinated policy on energy, and its competence should include coal and atomic energy. Steel industries are crucial in any economy. The merger of the three Councils of Ministers and of the three executive bodies was the logical outcome. The six governments agreed in 1964, and the final decision was embodied in the treaty signed on April 8, 1965. The Coal and Steel High Authority, the Euratom and the EEC Commissions, will give place in 1966 to one European Commission. It will be composed of fourteen members. After the future merger, which should take place prior to July 1, 1968, the date recently fixed by the six governments for the final completion of the Common Market, the composition of the single European Commission will be reduced to nine persons, the number of members of the EEC Commission. There will also be one Council of Ministers for the three Communities.

The controversy regarding the powers of that single Commission was avoided at that time by a clever compromise; it will enjoy different powers, larger or narrower, in each of the three Communities. It inherits all the rights of the former executives, including the supranational powers of the Coal and Steel High Authority, but these powers will remain as they were defined by the respective treaty for each of the three Communities. The same jurisdictional arrangement was adopted for the single Council of Ministers.

It is obvious that this is a provisional solution, and that the merger of the Communities themselves may not be deferred indefinitely. This merger will involve a revision of the Treaty of Paris and the two Treaties of Rome; the whole problem of supranationality will then be reviewed. If the agricultural crisis, at least partly due to the French attitude, had not broken out in 1965, it would have faced the Six not much later on.

Prior to that crisis the main lines of the common agricultural policy had been agreed upon. It was expected that the process of building up one Common Market would be terminated on July 1, 1967, instead of 1970, as fixed in the Treaty of Rome. By that time the customs union for industrial products would be completed, while the Six would have the same fixed prices for agricultural products, would pay levies to the Community fund on imports of farm products from third countries, and would jointly subsidize exports of the surpluses unsold within the Common Market. At the beginning of 1965 a feeling of great optimism prevailed, although the Five were not too happy at the prospect of financing the exports of French surpluses to the third countries. France seemed to have won a major victory in the agricultural sector. Then a thunderbolt came down from the blue sky.

The crisis

On March 31, 1965, the EEC Commission submitted to the six governments, without previously consulting them, its proposals concerning methods of financing the joint agricultural policy. Rightly or wrongly, it estimated that the time had come for a clarification of the future shape of the European Community. It attacked France on its most vulnerable sector, agriculture, but the real purpose of the battle was to force France to make concessions on supranationality in order to obtain the assistance of the EEC in alleviating the French farm problem. The challenge was bold. The Commission must have expected that the Five would not capitulate this time and would support its stand. The various "belligerents" in this war of nerves had different objectives in view. The Commission would have liked the full integration of agriculture within the Common Market, which would be completed almost three years prior to the date of 1970, as fixed by the Treaty of Rome. Its wish was, in this respect, that of France. But it also wanted to steer the evolution of the Community toward supranationality. France was absolutely opposed. As for the Five, they were willing to go along with the Commission, but would have perhaps been quite satisfied to abandon supranationality for the sake of being freed of their former assent to a common agricultural policy.

The Commission's proposals were conceived within the framework of former agreements of the Six on agriculture. The European agricultural fund was to face heavy expenses beginning July 1, 1967: subsidies for exports of farm surpluses unsold on the Common Market; support to farmers if affected by the lowering of prices on agricultural products or by the cancellation of former state subsidies; and contributions to the national rural investments. It was calculated that the annual expense would be near 1,300 million dollars. The levies on farm imports from third countries (a sort of penalty paid by the members of the EEC for buying farm products elsewhere), which were to be paid to the EEC fund, were expected to produce 600 million dollars. The deficit could be met either by additional contributions of member states or by transferring to the Community budget the money derived from custom duties levied on imports of industrial goods from the third states. The former solution would not have raised major constitutional problems. The Commission proposed the latter solution. It was expected that the annual revenue of the EEC would amount to 2,400 million dollars. The Common Market budget would have a great surplus.

This created a problem: Who would decide how to use this excess in the budget? The Commission proposed that this power be given to the European Parliament (formerly called the European Assembly). The draft budget would be prepared by the Commission, and, if approved by the European Parliament, it could be modified by the Council of Ministers only by a majority of five. The political challenge to France was obvious. The powers of the Commission would be greatly increased, because it hoped to have the support of the European Parliament, which had no sympathy for de Gaulle's anti-supranational stand. The Parliament would acquire control over the purse; de Gaulle knew that this was the beginning of the evolution of the English parliament toward its becoming a powerful body. Moreover, the Belgian Foreign Minister, Spaak —the only one among the five Foreign Ministers to give a half-hearted support to France—formulated an objection to the proposals, which could only increase de Gaulle's apprehension. He said that a European

Parliament, composed, as it now is, of delegates designated by the national parliaments (these delegates do not proportionately represent the respective populations of the Six), would hardly have the moral stature required for control over the Community budget. The logical solution would be to elect it by universal and direct suffrage.

The Commission put another proposal in the bag which could only displease the French government. It said that financing sales of surpluses should be conditioned on the strict observance by the exporting state of a jointly agreed commercial policy regarding third states. France sells a part of her surpluses to Russia, East Europe, and China. The Five would acquire control over her economic policy toward the Communist states; Germany especially could exert pressure regarding French-Soviet relations.

The challenge was deliberate. De Gaulle was given an opportunity to open the battle for a revision of the Treaties of Paris and Rome prior to the date when the majority rule in the EEC would become law. The French government reacted sharply. Its Foreign Minister, who happened at that time to be chairman of the Council of Ministers of the EEC, unexpectedly closed the session on July 1, 1965, by declaring that further discussions were useless because of the fundamental disagreement among the Six. He did not even give the other Ministers an opportunity for a thorough debate on the Commission's proposals. The crisis, which he called grave, was opened.

One must add that Minister Couve de Murville made an important concession to the Five at the beginning of the short session of the Council of Ministers. He declared that France was ready to pay a price for the rejection of the EEC Commission's proposals, namely to delay the imposition of levies on agricultural imports from the third states from July 1, 1967 (the date formerly accepted by common agreement) to 1970, the year fixed by the Treaty of Rome for the full integration of the Common Market. This concession, which was not discussed because of the brusque ending of the session, allowed one to measure fully the importance of the question of supranationality for de Gaulle; he was prepared to buy the rejection of the Commission's proposals at the expense of French agriculture.

The next French move was to recall all its representatives from Brussels and to refuse to participate in the sessions of the Council of Ministers. This amounted to a sort of rupture of diplomatic relations with the Commission, and also to the suspension of cooperation with the Five in the bodies of the EEC. France continued to observe the already binding decisions, such as the lower tariffs, in trade with the Five. Its noncooperation was calculated only to block any further progress. The Common

Market was faced with the prospect of completion in 1970 at best, as provided for in the Treaty of Rome, rather than in 1967, as had been generally expected before the crisis broke out.

The Five could, if they wanted, accuse France of committing a breach of Article 5 of the Treaty of Rome which stipulates that "member states shall refrain from any measure which could imperil the achievement of the goals defined in the present Treaty." They did not do it in order not to aggravate the crisis.

The price France was apparently willing to pay was the suspension of the former agreements with the Five on the financing of joint agricultural policy. These agreements of January 14, 1962, December 23, 1963, and December 15, 1964, needed completion, which was scheduled for June 1965. The official communiqué of the French government accused its five partners of bad faith. In effect, it reproached them with seizing the opportunity, which the Commission's proposals had provided, to renege on the former agricultural agreements. It threatened to deduce all "political, economic and legal consequences" from this situation.

The capitals of the Five were far from jubilant, sensing that the Common Market was facing its most serious crisis. But the French industrialists and farmers were not happy either. The French industries, already oriented toward the Common Market, would have been confronted with a major problem if the crisis were to end in a dissolution of the EEC. The farmers, loaded with surpluses, had pinned all their hopes on EEC assistance: free access to the Five, fixed prices for farm products which would be higher than the present ones in France, and subsidies for export of surpluses. The opposition parties exploited the crisis for a severe criticism of de Gaulle's foreign policy. It was apparent that he did not have the general support of his people for his policy of adamant opposition to supranationality. The French government was compelled to give assurances to the farmers that they would not pay the cost of the quarrel. Its subsidies to wheat growers were to be raised from 700 million francs to 1,100 million, to fill the void created by the lack of EEC subsidies. This would have left less in resources for national education or for the badly needed financing of low-rent apartment houses.

Economically France was not in the best shape for facing the alternative of disintegration of the Common Market. If isolated and perhaps confronted with an understanding between the Five and the EFTA, she could hardly engage in successful competition on the international market. Since 1958 her industrial production has increased by 39 per cent, like the British, while the rate of growth during that period was 46 per cent for Belgium, 52 per cent for Germany, 58 per cent for Holland, and 75 per cent for Italy. Her biggest increase of exports was gained by trade with the Five. Her industries were being renovated at a fairly slow pace. Her prices were steadily rising. Finally, she was saddled with agricultural surpluses.[47]

France occupied next-to-last place among the Six regarding the proportion of gross national product reinvested in the national economy. The percentages for 1963 were as follows:

Proportion of GNP Reinvested in the National Economy (1963)[48]

Country	Per cent
Luxembourg	27.6
Germany	25.2
Holland	24.0
Italy	23.2
France	19.8
Belgium	19.6

The slower rate of modernization of French industries is reflected in lower concentration of production. The following table illustrates this particular problem:[49]

Number of employees at one factory	Percentage of the total of factories		
	France	Italy	Germany
10–50 employees	25	21	12
50–100 employees	12	11	10
100–500 employees	30	24	30
500–1,000 employees	12	8	12
Over 1,000 employees	21	36	36

A French specialist on the Common Market tried to calculate in 1964 what price France would pay for carrying out de Gaulle's threats, such as the one he proffered on January 31, 1964: "For France, it was necessary that the Community include agriculture, failing which we would have been compelled to resume our freedom in all respects and there would have been no Common Market."[50] His answer was as follows:

1. Thanks to the Treaty of Rome, French industrialists have had to free themselves of the long protectionist tradition. This consequence . . . is the most important among all the consequences for which we may credit the Common Market. . . . Numerous French enterprises have outlined their investment programs and have organized their commercial networks in accordance with the existence of the EEC. The share of the EEC in the total trade of our country increased from 22 per cent in 1958 to approximately 38 per cent in 1964. . . .

2. With what weapons have we to fight against the American

competition if we do not build up industrial complexes on the scale of the Six? . . .

3. If it is difficult to say generally who profits the most from the Common Market, it is certain that we would suffer more than the others because of the disappearance of collective financial funds created by virtue of the Treaty of Rome. Our country alone has almost a half of all the arable land of the Community; hence it will be the principal beneficiary of the European Fund for Agricultural Orientation and Guaranty which, as we know, ensures that the Community will assume the financial burden of surpluses. The overseas countries and territories of the former French Union have received almost the total amount of financial assistance granted by the European Fund for Overseas Development. Finally, we and Italy have been the principal recipients of money from the European Bank of Investments and from the Social Fund.[51]

During the first five years of the Common Market's existence the former French colonies in Africa received 511 million dollars out of a total of 581.25 million which the European Fund for Overseas Development had at its disposal. They are expected to receive in the following five years approximately 80 per cent of the present available fund of 800 million dollars.[52]

The benefits derived by France from the Common Market may also be measured by the expansion of her foreign trade. Since 1958 French industrial exports to the Five have increased by 195 per cent, and agricultural exports by 253 per cent. During the same period of time industrial exports to other states rose only 40 per cent, and the agricultural exports only 52 per cent. French trade with the five partners represents almost half of the commercial exchanges with other countries which, like the Five, do not belong to the French monetary zone.[53]

The weakness of the Five in this or any other battle with the French President consisted of their being five whose attitudes had to be coordinated, and of their own interest in the survival of the Common Market. The battle was a test of wills.

The other combatant, General de Gaulle, laid his cards on the table at a press conference held on September 9, 1965. He fully defined the French position by asking for a revision of the Treaties relating to the European Community. Actually, he only confirmed in plain language what he had been hinting at since his return to power.

He justified his position by invoking the doubtful theory of *clausula rebus sic stantibus,* as other statesmen had done before him whenever they wanted to get rid of an embarrassing international obligation. According to this theory, a state may unilaterally denounce any treaty if it claims that a radical change has taken place in international circumstances since the signature of that treaty. This is what the French President claimed on September 9, 1965. According to him, the Treaties of Paris (on the Coal and Steel Community) and of Rome (on the EEC and Euratom) were negotiated at a time when France was still weak. They were calculated to bring benefits only to the French partners. The main effect of the Treaty of Paris was to restore German sovereignty over her coal and steel resources and to ensure Italy a cheap supply of coal and steel for her industries. The Treaty of Rome on Euratom intended to make France share her nuclear know-how with her partners but also to hinder her in the military use of her nuclear resources. The Treaty on EEC was calculated to open the French market to industrial imports by her associates without any compensation for French agriculture.

It is hard to imagine that de Gaulle really believed in his version of history. Not only did he overlook the benefits France had reaped from the EEC, but he seemed to forget that in the 1950's Germany and Italy were just emerging from the abyss of their defeat, and that France was not then a defenseless country compelled to accept foreign dictates.

De Gaulle concluded from his interpretation of history that the Treaties of Paris and Rome had to be revised if France were to continue her co-operation within the EEC. He raised three issues:

1. Agriculture must be fully integrated within the Common Market. In other words, the former agreements of the Six, suspended by the crisis, should be implemented and completed by additional agreements. This would not require any revision of the Treaty of Rome.

2. The Brussels Commission must be stripped of its "supranational" powers, i.e., the right of initiative in formulating proposals which the six governments may either accept or reject *in toto* or may amend only by a unanimous vote.

3. The rule of unanimity in the EEC Council of Ministers must be maintained beyond January 1, 1966, and remain the binding principle forever.

The latter two demands could be met only by revision of the Treaty of Rome. General de Gaulle said:

> I must add that in the light of this event [the 1965 crisis], we have more clearly measured the situation in which our country would risk finding itself tomorrow if one or another provision initially provided for by the Treaty of Rome were actually applied. Thus, according to that text, the decisions of the Council of Ministers of the Six would, beginning on January 1, 1966, be taken by a majority

vote; in other words, France would run the risk of seeing her hand forced in any economic matter, therefore social and often even political, and, in particular, what would have seemed gained in the agricultural area could be, despite her, placed at stake again at any moment. In addition, from that time on, the proposals made by the Brussels Commission would have to be adopted or not, as they are, by the Council of Ministers, without the states being able to change anything, unless, by a stroke of good fortune, they were unanimous in drafting an amendment.[54]

He placed before the other five governments the alternative of either accepting his suggestions for a radical elimination of supranational provisions in the existing Treaties, or facing French withdrawal from the Common Market. He told them that they had to choose between "the abusive and fanciful myths" and "common sense and reality." This was another ultimatum, the strongest he addressed to the French partners.

Incidentally, he had probably deliberately committed a mistake. The Brussels Commission had, since the entry into force of the Rome Treaty, the right to formulate its proposals, which the Council of Ministers could amend only by a unanimous vote. This it did, among other things, at the beginning of the 1965 crisis. De Gaulle might have wanted to dramatize the issue of urgent revision of the Treaty of Rome by claiming that the Commission would acquire that right only on January 1, 1966. This was the same time the Council of Ministers would be empowered to make decisions by majority vote, which would suffice for approval of the Commission's proposals.

It is interesting that, while the fate of the Common Market was thus hanging in the balance, the French Communist party was revising its own former position. Its Secretary General, Waldeck Rochet, declared in September that: "We take into account the existence of the Common Market."[55] This might have meant that the French Communists, as the Italian had done before, were abandoning their former fruitless opposition to the Common Market.

The bitterness in the reactions of the Five was due largely to de Gaulle's dictatorial manner. His Foreign Minister was suddenly instructed to close the session of the Council of Ministers without giving an opportunity for the other Ministers to seek a compromise solution. His government began to boycott the meetings in Brussels. All this reminded the Five of his former threats to withdraw from the Common Market if they did not accept his views on the joint agricultural policy. For instance, he told his press conference, held on July 29, 1963:

It is a waste of time to talk about the European Economic Community if it were to be understood that Europe would not get the bulk of its food supplies from its own agricultural production which is amply sufficient. One wonders what France would do within a system where there would soon no longer be any customs duties except for her wheat, meat, milk, wine, and fruit?

Then he delivered his ultimatum concerning the adoption by the Five of the French demands regarding agriculture: "This must be accomplished before the end of this year. . . . The year 1963 is decisive for the future of a united Europe."[56]

He had similarly fixed the end of 1961 for an earlier agreement on agriculture. In January, 1963, he unilaterally vetoed British admission to the EEC, without any prior consultation with the other five governments and while negotiations were still going on in Brussels. Each time he won, and the Five yielded, but each time he poured another drop into the cup of resentment which the French partners felt. Unlike Bismarck or Richelieu, de Gaulle is not a diplomat as well as a statesman.

The bitter feelings among the Five could only have been increased by an insolent article written during the 1965 crisis by the editor-in-chief of the newspaper of the Gaullist Union for the New Republic, *La Nation*. His thesis was that only France, "the thousand years' old nation," whose "soul and vocation are indestructible," had a historical mission recognized in the world. She could not forfeit her vocation and assent to be downgraded in a supranational community, unlike the other five nations "so recent or so contested." Then he characterized each of the four associated nations, caring not even to mention little Luxembourg. He had this to say about Germany: "Her unity was accomplished by Bismarck only recently owing to the Prussianization of various regions of her territory; she has demonstrated to the world her highly proclaimed will to dominate as well as her uncertainty regarding her true destiny." For Italy: "She owes the first beginnings of her unity to the unifying genius of Napoleon III and to a few men influenced by the ideas of the French Revolution. But this unity remains perhaps more formal than real." For Belgium: "created only in 1830, bilingual and visibly increasingly binational." And for Holland: "The low horizon of her laborious people has been rather constantly limited by their obstinate preoccupation with the acquisition of wealth."[57] One can imagine the feelings of German, Italian, Belgian, and Dutch people on hearing this sort of "compliment" addressed to them by a spokesman of the Gaullist party.

Significance of the Common Market

The stake in the battle was big indeed for all the six countries. Together they form a first-class economic unit, one of the three giants in the world. Their total population of 180 million stands in comparison with 190 million for the United States and 230 million for the Soviet Union. Their production of steel is almost equal to the Soviet output and only lower than the American production. They are jointly the biggest importer in the world and the second exporter, coming after the United States. Their gold reserves are equal to the American ones. Their rate of growth has been faster since 1958 than that of the United States: industrial production increased between 1958 and 1963 by 44.7 per cent, the American by 33.5 per cent; their gross national product grew by 26.4 per cent, the American by 22.5 per cent. The rate of increase in production of the Six was 5 per cent for 1964 as compared with the 1963 level of production. This is a very satisfactory rate.

It is impossible to say to what extent the booming economies of the Six are due to the existence of the Common Market, but it is an important factor. This is certainly true of France, as it is of the other Five. Exports among the Six increased greatly from 1958 to 1965:[58]

Belgium	287
Netherlands	268
France	361
Italy	473
Germany	263
(1858 = 100)	

Exports from one member to another, in percentage of its total exports, followed a sharply ascending curve from 1958 to 1965:[59]

	1958	*1965*
Belgium	45.1	61.9
Netherlands	41.6	55.7
France	22.2	40.9
Italy	23.6	40.2
Germany	27.3	35.2

These two tables illustrate clearly the economic importance of the Common Market to its members. The proportion of their mutual exchanges in their total foreign trade is bound to increase further, in particular after the elimination of all customs duties, which is to take place on July 1, 1968. The same tables demonstrate that Italy and France have been the principal beneficiaries; they almost doubled the proportion of exports to their partners in their total foreign trade.

All the Six would be the losers if the Common Market were to disintegrate. This is the ace in de Gaulle's game, as it is equally an ace in the hands of the five French partners. However, the French President's resilience is usually greater than that of his partners, and the interest of the Five in the survival of the Common Market might prove stronger than their attachment to the text of the Treaty of Rome.

The progress of the construction of the Common Market, in spite of recurring crises related to the agricultural problem, was, until the summer of 1965, very satisfactory. Actually, the pace was accelerated beyond the expectations formulated in the text of the Treaty of Rome. The end of the transition period, which the Treaty fixed for 1970, was expected to come in July, 1967, because of the complete agreement on the agricultural policy which seemed to be in sight. The tariffs between the Six were reduced on January 1, 1965, by 70 per cent in comparison to the 1958 level. The external tariff applicable to trade with third countries was being erected by the gradual raising or lowering of national tariffs of the Six to a median common denominator. Everything had seemed to be for the best in the best of Common Markets until the tempest of the summer of 1965.

This great quarrel was due, as we have said, to two problems dividing France from her associates: supranationality and agriculture.

Agriculture

De Gaulle's thesis that the Common Market should embrace agriculture is an all-French thesis. What he said at his press conference of January 31, 1964, expressed a quasi-unanimous French opinion:

> For us, it was necessary that the Community include agriculture. . . .
> Let us agree, therefore, that, of the Six states, we are the most interested in this important agricultural problem, for, of the Six, we are the ones who can supply the most grain, meat, milk, butter, cheese, wine and, with Italy, the most fruit and vegetables; this has led us to be the most pressing in Brussels.[60]

Any other French government would have pressed with the same obstinacy for the acceptance of French demands. The only big difference would have been that it would have used persuasion instead of threats and would not have threatened to quit the Common Market, if the Five would not agree.

The French thesis results from the French situation. The problem may be summarized in a few words: the modernization of agriculture brings in its wake the surpluses for which the domestic market is too small. Agriculture continues to occupy an important place in the domestic economy. Almost half of the total arable land of the Six belongs to France. The French farmer works on the average of 33 acres of land, while the average for the EEC is 20 acres. Consequently, France is by far the most important agricultural producer among the Six.

While the proportion of farmers in the total French active population has been steadily declining (the result of modernization), and while the rural exodus to the cities continues, farmers are electors and their aspirations cannot be neglected. They, like farmers in all the well developed countries, want to have their fair share in the national prosperity, i.e., to be sure of a decent income, and this depends on selling their produce at a reasonably remunerative price. The government is compelled to maintain remunerative prices one way or another. De Gaulle was more than once reminded of farmers' expectations by their public demonstrations, including holding up traffic on the highways by placing tractors in the middle of the road.

The surpluses are going to increase with modernization of techniques. There is possibly another reason for the expectation of an increase of surpluses. France has over 10,000,000 acres of uncultivated land, of which almost 2,000,000 could be cultivated if irrigation were introduced. This land, situated mainly in the Southwest, the central parts of the country, and in Corsica, might attract Italian peasants who would have the right, under the Treaty of Rome, to settle in France.

The French Minister of Agriculture declared in 1961: "No solution to French agricultural problems may be found within the French frontiers."[61] The author of one of the best books on the social aspects of the problem writes:

> France . . . definitely seems to have joined a small group of countries for which the exportation of foodstuffs is an unavoidable necessity. Moreover, she runs the risk, regarding some of the categories of foodstuffs, of having to cope with permanent surpluses.[62]

She faces many competitors on the international market: the United States, Canada, Australia, Argentina, and a few others. As their competition lowers the international prices, they all have to maintain high domestic prices in order to keep their farmers satisfied and at the same time must subsidize their exports. They have to sell abroad at a loss, at a price below the cost of production. The domestic consumer and taxpayer foots the bill. The other developed countries, which import agricultural products, are the beneficiaries of this competition among the producers. They buy at a low price and hence are able to keep the cost of living down; this enables them in turn to export their industrial goods at a lower price. Germany and Britain are in this enviable position. The paradox of the situation consists in the fact that the developed countries, which are industrialized but also big agricultural producers, like the United States and France, subsidize their own industrial competitors. The way out of this situation was suggested in 1962 by the French government. It proposed to the main producers of agricultural products to put an end to their war of prices on the international market by an agreement on the minimum international price for wheat. The United States seemed to be inclined to consider the French proposal but on the condition of fixing a maximum quota of output for each producing country. The French government refused, arguing that its agriculture had not attained its full productivity, being only in the process of modernization. The idea of an international agreement was dropped.[63] Another French idea was to make a concerted international effort for the use of surpluses in feeding the undernourished in the underdeveloped countries.[64]

In the meantime, the only practical policy was to turn for help to the five associates in the Common Market. The interests of the Five did not coincide at all with the French. All the Five import agricultural products and pay lower prices to the third countries than those demanded by the French producers. Germany imports farm products to the tune of half her consumption; moreover, a part of imported cereals is transformed into meat products. She is inclined to buy in the countries which purchase her industrial goods in exchange. Her own agriculture is heavily subsidized to maintain reasonably high incomes for German farmers. Holland is an importer of cereals to feed her livestock; she exports animal products such as butter, cheese and meat articles. Italy must import for her own consumption.

The main importers to the Five are the United States, Canada, Argentina, and the agricultural producers among the EFTA countries such as Denmark. Germany alone takes almost a half of these imports. This is the reason why France could not have her way without arriving at an understanding with Germany.

It seemed at the beginning of 1965 that the Six had surmounted all the hurdles and fixed the outline of their common agricultural policy. Their understanding was arrived at mainly at the sessions of the EEC Council of Ministers in January 1962, December 1963, and December 1964. The principal points of the agreement were as follows:

1. The price of wheat was fixed beginning with July 1, 1967, at 425 German marks. This is a price higher than the French but lower than the German. This price is fixed in its equivalent in gold and would not be affected by the devaluation of currencies. The Six agreed also on unified prices for cereals other than wheat, as well as poultry, eggs, beef, and pork. The prices for other farm products (milk, etc.) were to be fixed prior to July 1, 1967. By that time the free circulation of farm products throughout the territory of the six countries would have been stimulated by the parity of prices. In other words, the markets of the Five would be wide open to French exports.

2. Germany, Italy, and Luxembourg, which expected that their farmers would be to some extent the losers because of the French imports, and also because their agricultural prices were to be lowered, were

to receive subsidies from the EEC to help them pay adequate compensations to their producers.

3. The Five agreed to pay a penalty if they continued to import farm products from the third countries. They would have to take levies on those imports. The levy would represent the difference between the price paid to the third country and the fixed Common Market price. These levies would go to the European Fund for Agricultural Orientation and Guaranty, created in 1962.

4. This Fund would be spent each year to finance surplus exports to the third countries, the payment of compensations to the three countries obliged to lower their farm prices, and for the reorientation and diversification of national production. Italy and Luxembourg would have been the main beneficiaries of the Fund for the latter purpose. But the Fund would be used mainly to subsidize the exports to the third countries; France alone would benefit by this arrangement. It was expected that the Common Market could absorb about one-fourth of French surpluses; three-fourths would have to be sold to the third countries at the international market price, i.e., at a loss. This system has been in force since 1962, but the Fund financially assisted France only for a part of her sales below cost. (In 1965 this part was 50 per cent of the French loss.) It was agreed that beginning with July 1, 1967, the total difference between the actual price received by France and the fixed Common Market price would be paid by the Fund. The grave problem of French surpluses would have become the problem of all the Six.

5. The resources of the Fund derived from the import levies would not be sufficient for all those purposes. The balance could come from the contributions made by the national treasuries. If this system were adopted, France, Germany, and Italy would each contribute the equivalent of 28 per cent of the sum needed annually, Belgium and Holland 7.9 per cent each, and Luxembourg 0.2 per cent. This solution would not have encountered French opposition. We have seen that the EEC Commission proposed a different solution, namely to earmark the whole revenue from custom duties received on all industrial imports from the third countries as another source of money for the Fund.

The unfinished business in 1965 was the fixation of prices for those farm products which had not yet been equalized, and the problem of financing the common agricultural policy between July 1, 1965, and July 1, 1967. This latter problem was not solved at the session of the Council of Ministers held in June 1965, because the EEC Commission related it to the question of the future Community budget and its supranational aspects. France preferred to face the suspension of the whole agricultural agreement, arrived at with great difficulties in 1962, 1963, and 1964, rather than to make any concession on the ticklish problem of supranationality.

The agricultural agreement, imperiled in the summer of 1965, would have played a decisive role in further development of the Common Market. First, it was agreed to advance the date of completion of the Market from 1970 to July 1, 1967. On that day all internal tariff walls would have been finally abolished and one common tariff would be introduced for the imports from the third countries. Second, the fixation of equal prices for farm products would have tended to equalize the cost of industrial production. Third, none of the Six would have any interest in devaluating its currency. The prices of farm products being fixed in computation units, the devaluation would force the government to raise its domestic farm prices. In consequence, salaries and wages would go up, and the benefits in foreign trade expected from the devaluation of currency would be frustrated. Fourth, it was hoped that the monetary stability would induce the Six to inaugurate a joint monetary policy. Perhaps the Six would eventually assent to have one currency.

France seemed to be gaining on all cards. However, she would also have to pay for the agricultural agreement. As her farm prices would have gone up on July 1, 1967, this would not only further stimulate greater production and bring about larger surpluses, but also raise her salaries and wages. In consequence, the production cost of her industrial goods would increase. To that extent she would have faced greater difficulties in international competition, including within the Common Market. (These comments are equally pertinent regarding the agreement on agriculture reached by the Six in May 1966.)

Such countries as the United States, which heavily exports agricultural products to the Common Market, would be to some extent penalized by the enforcement of the agricultural agreement of the Six. Their exports would have been taxed by the levies, and they would encounter a stiffer French competition not only within but also outside the Common Market; France, financially backed by the Five, could offer her farm products at a low price on the international market.[65]

Revival of the Common Market

De Gaulle intended, prior to the presidential election, to fight a decisive battle with the Five over the problem of supranationality. He wanted nothing less than a formal revision of the Treaty of Rome in order to reduce the powers of the Brussels Commission and to eliminate the majority rule in the Council of Ministers.

If the age of a man were measured not by the date on his birth certificate, but by his ability to adjust to new circumstances, de Gaulle proved once again that he was not a decrepit old man. Soon after the elections, he deduced his own conclusion from Lecanuet's success and put an end to the French boycott of the Common Market agencies. His government hinted that it was ready to enter into conversations with the Five, who were no less eager to patch up the quarrel. They made a conciliatory gesture by accepting Luxembourg as the place of negotiations instead of Brussels. This restricted the negotiations to the six governments without the participation of the EEC Commission. The French President demonstrated his capacity for retreating from the initial position which proved to be a dead-end street. He poured water in his wine. Both sides to the dispute were ready to seek a compromise, because both wanted to save the Common Market from disintegration.

On January 17 and 18, 1966, the French government sent to the Five two memoranda in which it did not ask for a revision of the Treaty of Rome, but made other suggestions.[66] The main points of these memoranda were as follows:

1. The EEC Commission would be requested to coordinate its actions with the six governments closely. It would continue to exercise its treaty right of initiating proposals for common action, but would be obliged to consult the six governments prior to its own adoption of these proposals, and would be forbidden to disclose their contents either to the European Parliament or to the public prior to their submission to the Council of Ministers. In other words, the French government capitalized on the tactical errors committed in March 1965 by the Commission, which had made public its sweeping proposals regarding the financing of the common agricultural policy without first consulting the six governments.

France also asked for a lowering of the Commission's prestige. The letters of credence of diplomatic representatives, accredited to the EEC by the third states, would have to be handed over not only to the President of the Commission but also to the President in exercise of the Council of Ministers. Future requests by the third states for closer cooperation with the EEC should be immediately communicated by the Commission to the Council of Ministers. Relations with other international organizations would be withdrawn from the Commission's exclusive jurisdiction and would become a joint responsibility of the Commission and the Council. Members of the Commission were to be requested to observe strict neutrality in their public statements in case of disagreements between the six governments. The information policy of the EEC would no longer be formulated by the Commission alone, but jointly with the Council. Finally, the Council was requested to exercise strict control over the Commission's implementation of the EEC budgetary policy.

2. In addition, France proposed the adoption of a timetable for the

settlement of the following outstanding problems: the majority vote in the Council of Ministers; the future cooperation between the Council and the Commission; the ratification by all national parliaments of the treaty of April 8, 1965, concerning the merger of the present three Councils of Ministers, and the three executive bodies of European Communities (Coal and Steel, Euratom, and the EEC). The French parliament ratified this treaty in the summer of 1965, but other parliaments delayed their action because of the crisis within the Common Market. The French government had two objectives in view: first, to change the composition of the new single Commission, in particular to eliminate the President of the EEC Commission, Walter Hallstein, and the Dutch member, Sicco Manholt, both convinced supranationalists; second, to prepare the ground for the ultimate merger of the three Communities themselves. This merger would necessitate a revision of the Treaties of Paris and Rome and could possibly offer another opportunity to raise the question of unanimity or majority rule.

3. As was to be expected, the French government insisted on a rapid adoption of final arrangements concerning the agricultural Common Market, and on a joint agreement regarding trade with the third states.

The two consecutive sessions of the Council of Ministers, held in January, 1966, in Luxembourg, resulted in a compromise rather advantageous to France. A comparison of the initial French proposals with the adopted arrangement discloses that many points suggested in the French memoranda were accepted by the Five with some modifications.[67]

The main items of the Luxembourg compromise were as follows:

1. The Commission retained its right to initiate proposals, but was instructed to consult the six governments prior to submitting these proposals to the Council of Ministers and was forbidden to disclose their contents publicly until after the completion of procedure of consultation. Letters of credence of heads of missions, accredited by the third states, must henceforth be handed over to both the President of the Council and the President of the Commission. The two bodies must consult each other regarding any requests by the third states for closer cooperation with the EEC as well as on the contacts to be maintained with other international organizations. The information policy was to be entrusted to an *ad hoc* created body whose task would consist of coordinating the related activities of the Council and the Commission. The Council was finally instructed to increase its control over the drafting and implementation of the EEC budget.

If anyone suffered a defeat in January 1966, it was the Commission, whose independence of action was greatly reduced by common agreement of the Six. France scored a success in her fight against supranationality.

2. She fared much less well regarding the other aspect of supranationality. The Six were unable to find a suitable compromise regarding the majority vote in the Council of Ministers. However, the Five made a concession to France. They agreed that, whenever the proposals of the Commission would affect very important interests of one or several member states, they would make the utmost effort to find a solution acceptable to all six governments. At this point France made a reservation, namely that consultation among the Six should continue until unanimity was assured. The Five and France disagreed on this important matter. The Five retained their treaty right to take decisions by a majority vote after the failure of attempts to reach a unanimous agreement. This could be interpreted as the forewarning of future conflicts between France and the Five. In fact, all the Six probably do not relish the prospect of being outvoted on such matters as would affect their vital economic interests. The disagreement seems to have a rather academic significance.

3. The Six agreed to settle, as a priority matter, the pending problem of financing the joint agricultural policy, but France had to concede in exchange a simultaneous discussion of the joint policy to be adopted in the GATT negotiations (the so-called Kennedy Round). The Five, Germany in particular, intended to make the final agreement on the agricultural policy conditional on French readiness to pay for it by a more liberal approach to the question of trade with third states, notably the United States and the EFTA members.

The Six also consented to discuss the other pending questions related to agriculture, such as the determination of common prices for those products for which there was no agreement as yet (rice, sugar, olive oil, oil-yielding seeds and milk), and the creation of a common market for fruits and vegetables.

4. They also promised that the documents of ratification of the treaty for the merger of the three Councils and the three executive bodies would be deposited during the first quarter of 1966, provided that the required parliamentary assents were obtained, and that they would reach an agreement by that time concerning the composition of the future single European Commission. They expressed an intention to begin discussions regarding the latter matter soon. The deadline was selected too optimistically, as neither March nor the following months brought the expected agreement on the composition of the future Commission.

The long-continued battle between de Gaulle and the Five ended in a compromise, without victors or vanquished. But the reduction in the prerogatives of the Brussels Commission, as well as the flexible interpretation of the majority rule, relegated supranationality, de Gaulle's nightmare, to the remote future at best.

The Six proved in May 1966 once again that their interests were so deeply involved in the Common Market that they had to find compromise solutions to further their economic integration. On May 11, 1966, they reached a new agreement at a conference held in Brussels. This was done despite their divergent political views on such important issues as NATO and the British membership in the EEC. The cool relations between France and Germany, the main protagonists in the May negotiations, were not judged an impediment for agreeing on economic issues.

The May agreement, greatly beneficial for French agriculture, will be another obstacle for Britain in trying to join the Common Market. On the one hand, it is improbable that France would consent to modify this agreement, vital to her interests, or that the Five would renege on their signatures. On the other hand, Britain would have to change her domestic agricultural policy entirely and agree to levy an entry tax on agricultural imports from the Commonwealth members in order to be admitted to the EEC.

The main points of the agreement signed on May 11 are as follows:[68]

1. On July 1, 1967, the territories of the six partners will be open to free circulation of all agricultural products (except for wine, for the time being) imported from one of them to another. These products will be sold everywhere within the Common Market at prices fixed in the various agreements concluded by the Six (the prices for olive oil, fruit, vegetables, sugarbeets, milk, and beef were determined by the agreement reached on July 24, 1966).

2. Imports of agricultural products from the third countries will be subject to levies which will amount to the difference between the Common Market prices and those actually paid by the importing member state.

3. Ninety per cent of the revenue from these levies will go to the European Fund for Agricultural Orientation and Guaranty. This will amount to one half of the expected resources of the Fund. The other half will be derived from the annual contributions paid by the Six according to the following scale: France, 32 per cent; Germany, 31.2 per cent; Italy, 20.3 per cent; Holland, 8.2 per cent; Belgium, 8.1 per cent; and Luxembourg, 0.2 per cent.

This Fund, whose annual revenue will probably amount to 1.7 billion dollars, will be used for subsidies to be paid to the countries (principally France), which export their surpluses to states other than the Common Market members; for the aid to member states who must improve their agriculture, for instance, through irrigation (Italy and Luxembourg will be the main beneficiaries); and for the compensation to farmers who will have to sell their products at the Common Market prices, if these prices are lower than now practiced in their respective countries (those will be mainly German farmers).

The French share will proportionately be the largest. It is being calculated that France will receive annually about 45 per cent of sums spent by the European Fund. This will be used mainly to subsidize French sales of surpluses to the third states. Germany will probably not derive more than 18 per cent of the Fund's annual expenses. In other words, she is expected to be the principal financial guarantor for the successful export of French surpluses to the third countries.

4. In 1965–66, the Fund will reimburse 60 per cent of the French losses incurred in the sales of surpluses to the third states. This ratio will increase in 1966–67 to 70 per cent. Finally, beginning with 1967–68 the total French loss will be repaid by the Fund; the Five will in effect finance French exports of surpluses.

5. These provisions will not apply to sales to the Democratic Republic of Germany, because the Federal Republic does not recognize Eastern Germany as a separate state and usually calls it the Soviet Zone. France sells large amounts of agricultural products to the DRG. However, it did not cost her much to make this political concession to the Federal Republic. She still may sell any quantity she wants to other Communist states which may in turn resell it to East Germany.

6. All custom duties on manufactured goods will be totally eliminated on July 1, 1968. On the same day the Common Market will have a uniform tariff applicable to imports from all third states. Thus the customs union will be finally achieved eighteen months ahead of January 1, 1970, the date fixed in the Treaty of Rome. The duties, which had existed between the Six in 1958, had already been lowered by 80 per cent prior to the May agreement. The further reductions will take place in two stages: 5 per cent on July 1, 1967, and 15 per cent on July 1, 1968.

The May agreement was a great success for France. Despite the crisis of the summer of 1965, mainly caused by de Gaulle, she was able to erase all harmful consequences of that crisis by ensuring the restoration of the agreements on agriculture as they had been prior to 1965. Her main goal, the integration of agriculture within the Common Market, is now guaranteed by her partners' signatures. Her problem of having 46.5 per cent of the Six's cultivated land but only 27 per cent of the total population of the Common Market has become the joint problem of all the Six. President de Gaulle had good reason to congratulate the French negotiators on their return from Brussels. This does not mean, however, that the other five nations are losers. For instance, Germany is now certain that her industrial exports to the Five will not be hindered after July 1, 1968, by any customs duties.

At least, the economic Little Europe has become a living reality in which all the Six have vital stakes. The Common Market will now have another "European" lobby: ten million farmers have acquired a stake in the economic integration of their six countries.

Political union

De Gaulle does not underestimate the benefits which the French economy derives from the EEC. However, his principal objective is to progress toward political union under the same unalterable condition that this union would not deprive the participants of their individual veto and that no supranational institutions would be established.

The battle between him and his partners over supranationality in a political union is, in a sense, shadow-boxing, because the Six have never seriously examined the question of whether they could agree at all on one foreign and military policy. This is, however, the crux of the problem. A common front of the Six in international affairs would presuppose the existence of an agreement on the main objectives of their concerted foreign policy. This agreement is highly improbable. First, de Gaulle's France wants to have a politically united Western Europe in order to loosen the bonds to the United States; the other Five are Atlantic-oriented. Second, they would like Britain to participate in the Western European union which France opposed in 1963. In particular, Belgium and Holland would feel reassured by the British membership because of their latent fear of the domination of Western Europe by a French-German duumvirate. Third, the common defense policy is inconceivable, while France is an enemy of NATO integration and the Five are all for it. Fourth, only Germany would insist that its reunification become the main objective of the union; neither France nor the other countries are vitally interested in the matter.

The French Foreign Minister was realistic when he frankly conceded in a debate in the National Assembly that: "It will unfortunately require quite a lot of time to define even the initial elements of a European policy."[69] He was just as realistic in observing that the defense and foreign policies of a politically united Europe could not be determined by a majority vote.

These political difficulties would arise anyway. The political union could be founded on the coordination of six national policies, as de Gaulle wants, or on some kind of supranational institution, as the Five say that they prefer. The difficulties would not disappear with any arrangement. No magic formula would do the trick. Robert Schuman was profoundly right when he warned that no nation would delegate the power of decision over her destinies, including death or survival in a nuclear age, to a supranational body. This holds true for the Six, especially since their foreign policy objectives are far from identical. Neither de Gaulle nor his French "European" opponents are willing to admit it. The five other governments have not faced this crucial problem either. This is why the heroic battle between de Gaulle and the Five over the mechanics of political union is shadow-boxing.

While listening to the noisy verbiage of the French Gaullists and "Europeans," who quarrel over the question of *how* to organize the political union of the Six and seem to forget the other question of *why* this should be done, it is refreshing to hear the rare voices of common sense. These voices point out the almost insuperable difficulty of defining the objectives for a joint foreign policy. One of those sober-minded Frenchmen writes:

> The political union today is a dream not only because of the strength of national sentiments but also because one state, Germany, considers the restoration of its integrity (it is difficult to measure today the effects of this restoration on the union) as more important than all the other objectives.[70]

Another distinguished Frenchman shares the same point of view: "The majority of citizens of the Federal Republic cannot as yet renounce revisionism. The majority of French citizens cannot accept revisionism. A viable political Europe shall not be constructed as long as its frontiers are not agreed upon."[71] He adds that a full and public confrontation of views of the Six on the German problem would have the following effect: "The scaffolding of illusions and lies, which the chanceries have been erecting for the last twenty years, would crumble down like a castle built with cards." De Gaulle bears his part of responsibility for this castle of cards; for twenty years he has advocated the concept of Western European union, but has never seriously examined the preliminary question of whether the Six would be able to agree at all on the foreign-policy objectives of that union. As is to be expected, he always refers to one political objective of that union dear to his heart, a "European" Europe, but passes silently over the others.

If one compares his statement regarding the institutions of political union made on September 5, 1960, with that which he made on May 15, 1962, he finds out that de Gaulle's position remained the same both at the beginning of the battle for a political union and after its termination in a complete disagreement between France and the Five. This is what he said on September 5, 1960:

> To ensure regular cooperation between the states of Western Europe is what France considers as desirable, possible and practical

in the political, economic, cultural and defense domains. This requires an organized and regular cooperation between responsible governments, and then the work of organs specialized in each of the common domains; these organs must be subordinated to the governments. This requires periodic deliberations by an assembly formed by delegates of national parliaments and, in my opinion, this will also require, as soon as possible, the holding of a solemn European referendum so as to give this launching of Europe the character of popular support that is indispensable.[72]

The idea of a European popular referendum could not be accepted by the Five unless they amended their constitutions. Nevertheless, it was interesting. It immediately raised the whole problem of what sort of questions the six peoples would have to answer: a vague concept of political cooperation, as de Gaulle would have wished? Or answers to these precise questions: a cooperation of governments or a supranational Europe? An Atlantic Europe or a European Europe? A common defense integrated within NATO or coordinated European forces independent of the American supreme command? One policy on the German problem, including German unification and the German eastern frontiers? Generally, a foreign policy coordinated with that of the United States or an independent one, apt to contradict the American foreign policy? In any event, de Gaulle did not insist on his proposed referendum and subsequently dropped it.

On May 15, 1962, he defined the same French position:

> Western Europe—whether it be the matter of its action vis-à-vis other peoples, of its own defense, of its contribution to the development of areas that are in need of it, or of its duty regarding the international equilibrium and relaxation of tension—Western Europe must organize itself politically. . . . What is it that France is proposing to her five partners? I shall repeat it once again: in order to organize ourselves politically, let us begin by the beginning. Let us organize our cooperation, let our Heads of State or Government meet periodically to examine together our common problems and make decisions with regard to these problems. Their decisions will be the decisions of Europe. Let us set up a political commission, a defense commission and a cultural commission, just as we have already an economic commission in Brussels which studies common problems and prepares the decisions of the six governments. . . . Moreover, the Ministers in charge of these various fields will meet whenever necessary to implement jointly the decisions that will be taken by the Council. Finally, we have a European Parliamentary

Assembly that meets in Strasbourg and is composed of delegations from our six national Parliaments. Let us enable this Assembly to discuss common political questions as it already discusses economic questions. We shall see in the light of actual experience, after the lapse of three years, what we shall be able to do to strengthen our ties.[73]

This program had no trace of supranationality. One of the French critics pointed out its fundamental weakness:

His Europe should be a simple association of peoples. But then, how could a joint aspiration to assert total independence of the United States arise within this association? It will not suffice that France wants this autonomy and follows a strictly independent policy . . . in order that her associates be irresistibly led in the same direction.[74]

It seemed from 1959 to 1961 that the Five were ready to consider the French plan. They agreed to have regular meetings of their representatives and to consult on common political problems. Finally, they decided on July 19, 1961, in agreement with France, to appoint a committee of diplomatic experts to examine methods of collaboration. This committee was known under the name of its chairman, Christian Fouchet, a French diplomat. The committee took a French proposal for its discussion basis.

The main points of that proposal were as follows:

1. The existing European institutions (the Coal and Steel Community, the EEC and the Euratom) would not be affected by the political organization. In other words, the element of supranationality in them would not be questioned on the occasion of discussion of a political union.

2. The fields of cooperation should include foreign affairs, defense and cultural exchanges, the economic problems being reserved for the existing Communities.

3. A Council of Heads of State or Government would be formed. It would meet three times a year. These sessions would be supplemented by three sessions of the Ministers of Foreign Affairs.

4. The European Parliamentary Assembly would be authorized to debate foreign policies, defense problems and cultural relations.

5. A political commission would be established. It would be composed of high officials of the respective Ministries of Foreign Affairs. It would have no power of initiative, but would be expected to prepare the discussions of the Council of Heads of State or Government and to watch over the implementation of Council's decisions.

6. The decisions of the Council would require unanimity for their validity. However, if any five governments were in agreement, they could

implement their joint decision. The sixth government would remain free to disregard a decision adopted over its opposition.

7. After the lapse of three years the Treaty on the political union would be open for revision. At that time the Six could agree to strengthen the organization in the light of past experience and even proceed with the merger of the political Community and the three existing Communities.

None of the Six was required by the French proposal to relinquish its veto. The supranationality was excluded. However, the Five seemed to be ready to accept the proposal. Then de Gaulle changed his mind. On January 19, 1962, he instructed his representative in the committee to amend the French proposal. The amendments were sure to meet with the hostility of the Five. De Gaulle must have realized it or he overestimated the French influence in Western Europe.

His amendments were as follows:

1. The powers of the Council would be extended to include economic problems. This was equivalent to saying that majority rule provided for in the Treaties of Paris and Rome for the decisions of the Coal and Steel, Euratom and Common Market Councils of Ministers would be abolished. De Gaulle implicitly demanded a revision of these Treaties.

2. The European Parliamentary Assembly would have the right only to adopt recommendations, while the initial French proposal had given it the power to submit proposals to the Council, which would have been obliged at least to examine them.

3. The future revision of the political community arrangement was no longer limited in scope by the reservation that the institutions of the existing Communities would not be altered.

4. The admission of new members (read: Britain) to the political union would require the unanimous assent of all members. The Five's suspicion that de Gaulle had no sympathy for the British candidature was thus reenforced by his claim for veto power over the matter.

De Gaulle could blame only himself for the consequences of this drastic modification of the original French proposal. The Five's reaction was negative. On February 15, 1962, he tried to repair the damage in his conversations with Chancellor Adenauer. He agreed to include a reference to the Atlantic Alliance in the preamble of the treaty on political union and to omit economic problems from the jurisdiction of the political Council. In effect, he abandoned his former intention to smuggle his opinions on curtailing the powers of the existing Communities.

However, his step backward came too late. In the meantime, negotiations with Britain for her admission to the EEC were progressing. Belgium and Holland made the European political union conditional upon the British membership. Logically, their position was vulnerable. On the one hand, they insisted on a supranational Europe, but even more vigorously they claimed that Britain, opposed to any supranationality as firmly as de Gaulle, should be a member. Their point of view was expressed by, among others, the Belgian Foreign Minister, Spaak, in an interview granted on May 9, 1962, to *Opera Mundi Europe:*

> I have been, I am, and I remain a convinced partisan of what is called "supranational Europe," that is to say, of a Europe organized in a way that would allow, in the last analysis, after a debate as complete as possible, to make the decisions by a majority vote, without veto; this is necessary to avoid deadlocks and impotence. . . . However, if I cannot have the Europe I desire, I can envisage the possibility of having a different Europe: "Europe of the Fatherlands," that is to say, a Europe that is not organized and, according to my judgment, inefficacious. But I find at this point that British presence in this sort of Europe is very important, not to say essential, because England would contribute her stability, her experience and, insofar as small countries are concerned, the promise of equilibrium.[75]

Probably what Belgium and Holland really wanted was not a supranational Europe but British membership as a factor of equilibrium regarding France and Germany. The British participation would have also been a guaranty that the European union would not be used as an instrument against the United States and as a means of weakening the Atlantic Alliance.

The British view on how a united Europe should be organized was practically identical with that of de Gaulle. At the time of negotiations between Britain and the Six on British accession to the Common Market, Prime Minister Macmillan thus formulated the British position:

> I myself believe that the bulk of public opinion in this country, and certainly any conservative Government, is firmly against the extinction of separate national identities and would choose a Europe which preserved and harmonized all that is best in our different national traditions. We would, I think, favour a more gradual approach worked out by experience, instead of a leap in the dark, and this is a view shared by many leaders of opinion in Europe.[76]

At least one leader would have fully agreed; that was de Gaulle. The Conservative stand on the matter had full support of the Labour party; Harold Wilson said on February 11, 1963, in the House of Commons: "We shall make more progress, whether in economic or political cooperation, the less we aim at federal or supranational solutions, the more we work within an inter-governmental framework."[77] Harold Wilson has not modified his stand after becoming Prime Minister. He declared in Bristol on March 18, 1966: "We reject any idea of supranational control over Britain's foreign and defense policies."[78]

De Gaulle was opposed to British membership but shared the British predilection for a Europe of States. The French comment was: "What he wanted was a Europe 'à l'anglaise,' but without Englishmen."[79] The Five did not agree to let him have his English cake baked in France.

The negotiations on political union stalled in April 1962. De Gaulle's veto against the British admission halted them altogether. De Gaulle then adopted the attitude of wait-and-see. He did not submit new proposals and remained cool to the various initiatives of the Five in 1964–65. After the Italian Foreign Minister, Fanfani, had proposed to hold a meeting of Foreign Ministers in Venice to reexamine the question of political union, the French government replied that the time was not propitious for the meeting. De Gaulle himself said on December 31, 1964: "France has submitted her proposals. They remain valid. The problem consists in adopting them."[80] The tone was again that of Napoleon at the Congress of Erfurt. The Five were offered only "the right" to adopt the French proposals which they formerly had rejected.

On April 14, 1966, the French Foreign Minister finally admitted in a statement made in the National Assembly that there was no hope at present for an agreement between the Six on their political union. He said:

> I am obliged to note that none of our partners shares our views. Shall I give corroboration of this? Every time, for the past six years, that we have together discussed measures to take toward what is generally called political Europe, everyone has always taken the stand that defense was a taboo subject: that is NATO business. As for international policy, doubtless one could be bold enough to discuss it a little bit, but the really appropriate forum was, nevertheless, that of NATO. If there are really two contradictory concepts . . . , they are those of European integration and of Atlantic integration.[81]

He indicated only one of the main obstacles: the attitude toward the United States. If he were completely sincere, he would have mentioned the two other obstacles: the agreement of the Six on any joint nuclear policy, and their attitudes toward the Soviet Union, in particular regarding the German question.

Maurice Faure, the most ardent French "European," conceded that de Gaulle was not the only one to be held responsible for the failure. He said:

> Today not all of the difficulties are of his making. Certain recent speeches by Mr. Luns and Mr. Spaak, obviously inspired by London, are moving away from the initial European orientation and are bad omens for any future attempts at integration.[82]

Although the negotiations in the early sixties and later divergencies of views among the Six on fundamental external matters such as NATO might have proved that a Western European political union was a dream rather than a realistic concept, the French President declared at his press conference of February 21, 1966, that he would welcome the initiative of any of the Five for a reopening of negotiations.[83] However, he reiterated his well-known condition that the political union of the Six should consist in periodical contacts between the governments of otherwise sovereign states. He did not retreat an inch from his former stand as reflected in the Fouchet plan.

Asked at the same press conference whether the political union would include Britain, de Gaulle replied that the Six should first build their own union and perhaps examine the question of future accessions later. However, none of the Five changed its former view that Britain should be one of the original members of a political union of Western Europe.

The existence of the Common Market somewhat restricts the freedom of formulation of foreign policy by the Six. At least, none of them may conduct a policy frankly hostile to any of the others. This is possibly the furthest extent of political collaboration they may realize. De Gaulle's third planetary power is beyond his reach.

Britain

De Gaulle is frankly suspicious of the American "hegemony" in Europe and does not like the United States which he does not know, having never lived there. The same is true of almost all other anti-American Frenchmen. He and they fight against an adversary of whom they have a hazy image of their own construction. This is not true of Britain, which de Gaulle knows well. This is one of the reasons why his attitude toward Britain is more flexible. He is suspicious of the British "perfidy," but it would be a gross exaggeration to say that he dislikes the British. He took his place in history owing to Britain. He was the eyewitness of the British heroic stand in 1940–1941. The least one may say is that he has a deep respect for Britain.

He knows that Britain is a tough partner. He wrote in his *Memoirs:*

> To resist the British machine, when it set itself in motion to impose

something, was a severe test. Without having experienced it oneself, it is impossible to imagine what a concentration of effort, what a variety of procedures, what insistence, by turns gracious, pressing or threatening, the English were capable of deploying in order to obtain satisfaction.[84]

Being a tough politician himself, his respect for the British could only increase during his wartime political quarrels with them. The battles were between the two adversaries of equal moral stamina. At his press conference of January 14, 1963, when he vetoed British admission to the EEC, he nevertheless paid a tribute to Britain which was, no doubt, sincere:

> The consideration and the respect due that great state and that great people will not be altered in the least. What Britain has done over the centuries and throughout the world is recognized as gigantic, even though there have often been conflicts with France. The glorious participation of Great Britain in the victory that crowned the First World War, we French will always admire. As for the role played by Britain at the most dramatic and decisive moment of the Second World War, no one has the right to forget it. . . . This very day no one can dispute the fitness and the valor of the British.[85]

His views on the relations between Britain and Western Europe are therefore more sophisticated than on the subject of the American-European relations. He does not preclude the possibility that it might be in the future interest of France to have Britain, freed of her ties to the United States, associated with Western Europe. His negative attitude is not irrevocable. Moreover, he favors a bilateral collaboration between France and Britain.

However, it is his veto that barred Britain from membership in the Common Market. He was probably suspicious of British sincerity, recalling that Britain did her best to prevent or dilute cooperation between the six continental nations.

Traditionally Britain was opposed to any unification of the European Continent. She fought major wars to prevent it. In the past her struggles against unification evoked sympathies on the Continent, because unification was attempted by a great power wishing to impose her hegemony on the other European nations. In her wars against Spain, France, and Germany she could rely on many continental allies. But the EEC confronted her with the altogether new problem of a voluntary association of Western European nations. As there was no hegemon, Britain could not expect to find continental allies who would fight her political battles.

At first the British did not believe that the continental nations would be capable to cooperate, that France and Germany in particular would forget their former enmity. They did not take too seriously the first steps taken by the Six. They declined the invitation to join the Coal and Steel Community and refused to participate in the negotiations for the Common Market. After the signature of the Treaties of Rome they expected that the experiment would fail because of the disagreements among the Six, the fear of Germany and the Benelux countries of losing the other European markets, and the reluctance of French industrialists to face an open competition with the Five.

The British government proposed in 1958 that the Six include the Common Market within a large free-trade zone, which would become the platform of commercial cooperation between the Six and the other European countries. The Five would perhaps have accepted this proposal, but de Gaulle demurred. In November 1958 he abruptly put an end to the negotiations already underway between Britain and the Six. He thus saved the Common Market, which otherwise would have been smothered in the cradle.

The next British step was to form in November 1959 a rival association composed of Britain, Sweden, Norway, Denmark, Switzerland, Austria, and Portugal, i.e., of those European countries which, for various reasons, could not or did not want to enter the Common Market. This European Free Trade Association was built on principles agreeable to Britain: the progressive lowering of mutual tariffs on industrial goods, no reference to agricultural products, no agreement concerning the tariffs applicable to trading with the third countries, and the rule of unanimity. The weaknesses of the EFTA were several: Denmark, exporter of farm products, could not be too happy that no preferential tariff would exist for the trade in those products (it was to face as before the competition on the British market by Canada, Australia, and New Zealand); the market of the Seven for industrial goods was not protected by a tariff wall against the external competition; finally, there was an internal disequilibrium within the EFTA: Britain represented half of the economic power of the Seven as measured in the gross national product and the size of external trade. This disequilibrium was tangibly demonstrated in the fall of 1964 when the Labour government, unilaterally and without consulting the other six partners, decided to raise the tariff on imports by 15 per cent.

The principal reason for this British creation was to have a tool of pressure on the Six and eventually to obtain concessions for the British access to the Common Market. This move entirely failed. The EFTA proved to be a weak reed. The true problem appeared in all its nakedness: either to remain outside the Common Market and pay the price in the form of a slower rate of economic growth and lesser political influence on the Continent, or to take a plunge and apply for full membership in the Common Market. The former policy of missing the bus but trying to puncture the tires, as a British newspaper put it, failed.

The Conservative government took the plunge, hoping, however, that it would obtain from the Six various concessions and would not be asked to adhere to the Treaty of Rome without reservations. Prime Minister Macmillan declared on May 16, 1961, that his government was ready to open negotiations for British accession. A summit meeting of the Six, held on July 18, 1961, welcomed the British readiness to join them but on the condition that Britain would be willing to accept all the obligations of a member state of the Common Market. On July 31 Prime Minister Macmillan confirmed the British intention to become a Member of the Common Market while reserving for the negotiations the problems of British agriculture, of the Commonwealth, and of the interests of the other members of the EFTA. He remarked that Britain would welcome a Western European political union according to de Gaulle's formula (which he cited) of Europe of the Fatherlands.

The British-EEC negotiations began on November 8, 1961. Britain was deeply split up. The Labour party was opposed. Its M. P.'s as well as 21 conservative M. P.'s refused to vote for a motion in the House of Commons which proposed to approve the opening of negotiations. The Gallup polls showed a third of the country favorable to the entry into the Common Market, a third undecided, and a third opposed.[86] The pressure of the Commonwealth countries for the preservation of their preferential access to the British market was heavy. The British government was placed by this pressure and by divided national opinion in a position where it could not but insist strongly on acceptance by the Six of its conditions for access to the Common Market. Its leeway in the Brussels negotiations was not very great.

The reasons for the decision made by the Conservative government were serious. An Australian specialist on foreign affairs writes:

> As the EEC internal tariffs drop further . . . the likelihood of further replacement of British imports by German in other members of the Six will increase. . . . It was to avoid this, above all, that Britain agreed to apply for entry in the first place. Exports to the EEC countries are not a major aspect of British external trade (having varied from 14 per cent to 19 per cent of the total British exports between 1953 and 1962), but they show the biggest growth for all British exports, and could be expected to have grown further if Britain had entered EEC. . . . Finding markets elsewhere is a diffi-

cult business. The Commonwealth of Nations is gradually declining as a British export market, although it took 35.7 per cent of British exports in 1962; the growth of local manufactures and the attractiveness of goods from Britain's competitors are the reasons, neither of which (especially the former) is likely to diminish in the future. The other EFTA countries have proved disappointing as a growth market; Britain has held her own there, but not increased her exports. . . . Another important consideration involved in possible British entry has been the likelihood that, in this event, London would fairly soon establish itself as the financial and investment center of the Common Market. . . . Capital market leadership would obviously confer upon the member-country involved not only direct advantages in the form of the invisible earnings to be gained through the provision of these financial services, but also indirect advantages through the facilitation of one's own trade which the ready access to these services would permit.[87]

Another reason was the growing trend among the American corporations to invest in the booming Common Market rather than in Britain, whose economic pace was much slower. Even British firms were opening their plants in the territories of the EEC member states. In 1961 the British share in the American investments in Europe fell from the former 50 per cent to 41 per cent.

The French reaction to the announced British decision was less than enthusiastic. The French industrialists, who were bracing themselves not without apprehension for the competition with the German industries, did not like the prospect of having to face the British competitors as well. The French farmers were afraid that the German reluctance to including agriculture in the Common Market would be strengthened by a similar British attitude. The official reactions were reserved but not hostile. De Gaulle himself was not discouraging on September 5, 1961, when he said:

> We know very well how complex the problem is, but it appears that everything now points to tackle it, and, as far as I am concerned, I can only express my gratification not only from my own country's point of view but also from the point of view of Europe and, consequently, of the world.[88]

The French domestic opposition was favorable to British accession on the condition, which was also the official condition, that the British accept all the implications of the Treaty of Rome. Guy Mollet said:

> If England adheres to the Treaty of Rome as this Treaty has been

drafted by the Six, that is to say, if she accepts its political implications, we shall say yes. If, on the contrary, the agreement with Great
Britain should in effect transform the Common Market into a free-
trade zone, we should say no and say it resolutely.[89]

Maurice Faure, the leader of French "Europeans," welcomed the British
candidature retrospectively in 1964, but added the same reservation:

> But there should be no question of reserving a privileged status for
> Great Britain or of allowing her to combine the advantages of
> belonging to several different systems. Accession to Europe implies
> for her and for us . . . choices which are not only economic but also
> political and military.[90]

These statements sounded not very different from de Gaulle's; the hint
was clear that Britain would have to accept a "European" Europe. After
de Gaulle's veto a newspaper with moderate right leanings passed the
following judgment: "Great Britain has expressed her wish to enter the
Common Market, but she has not demonstrated her real intention to
accept the imperatives and sacrifices of a common policy."[91] The Socialist
Populaire stated at the same time that Britain would have had to accept
"all the principles, all the rules, and all the obligations" of the Treaty of
Rome.[92] If a coalition government of opposition parties had negotiated
with Britain, its position probably would not have been very different
from that of de Gaulle. The only difference was spelled out in the National Assembly by the Socialist deputy, André Chandernagor, who said:
"When I say that we should have demanded the observance of the Treaty
of Rome, this does not mean that we should have used the same methods
as you have done, and, certainly, our motivation would have been different."[93] A former Prime Minister of the Fourth Republic, René Pleven,
while criticizing the abruptness of official veto, added: "We do not
at all reproach the government for its firm stand."[94] What the opposition
unanimously condemned was the impolite Gaullist diplomatic method in
casting a veto without consulting the other five partners.

The EEC Commission also insisted on full British acceptance of all
the implications of the Treaty of Rome. In September 1962 Mr. Hallstein, its chairman, declared on behalf of the Commission that the Six
could not grant to the countries intending to join the Common Market
any concessions which would modify the fundamental principles of the
Treaty of Rome.[95] Earlier, in June 1961, he told the European Parliamentary Assembly that Britain would have to accept the main provisions
of the Treaty or become only an associated state but not a full member.[96]
After de Gaulle's veto the European Parliament adopted a resolution in

which it welcomed the accession of Britain and other European states but on the condition that these accessions would not endanger the process of integration, and that the Treaties of Paris and Rome would not be modified or the structure of European institutions altered.[97]

So long as the French government participated in the laborious negotiations with Britain and defended the Treaty of Rome, it was not isolated at home and could count on the sympathy of the EEC Commission. France had, however, more diverse interests with Britain than the other Five who were more accommodating. These differences may be summarized as follows:

1. *Agriculture*. France, quite legitimately, was apprehensive that Britain would make a common front with Germany and Holland, being also a big importer of agricultural products. She would have done it not only in order to maintain the cost of living at the present level, but also to satisfy the claims of those members of the Commonwealth, such as Canada, Australia and New Zealand, for whom privileged access to the British market was a vital matter. It was to be expected that Britain would fight against the system of levies on farm products imported from the outside of the Common Market or would insist that the levies be as low as possible. She would probably have opposed the whole concept of subsidizing French sales of surpluses to the third countries, because it would have helped France to compete on the international market with those members of the Commonwealth who were producers of farm products of temperate climate. The French commentator is right when he says:

> The British could not have, of course, an overflowing sympathy for this sort of operation, because they have so far been the main beneficiaries of the anarchy in the world's agricultural market; big buyers, they practically are making law and are profiting from the low prices they pay for their food supplies.[98]

Great Britain absorbs one-fifth of the agricultural exports of the world, taking second place after the Common Market importers, who purchase one-third of those exports.

Another aspect of European agricultural imports placed Britain and France at opposite poles. Not without great difficulty, France obtained preferential treatment from her partners for the imports of tropical products from her former colonies in Africa. This was a way of supporting French influence in French-speaking Africa. The British quite rightly asked for the same preferential system for their own former and present African and Caribbean possessions, competitors of French-speaking Africa.

2. *General commercial policy.* The British orientation coincided in this respect with the views of the Five but clashed with the French. France wanted a protectionist Common Market, while Britain would have promoted a liberal policy toward the third countries, including the United States.

3. *"European" or Atlantic Europe.* This political consideration was foremost in de Gaulle's mind. He wanted a Europe independent of the United States, while Britain was certain to oppose it. His anxiety was strengthened by President Kennedy's speech made on July 4, 1962, in Philadelphia. The President proposed a vast Atlantic zone of free trade. The mutual drastic reduction of tariffs between the Common Market and the United States would have, from the French point of view, completely opened Western Europe to American agricultural and industrial products. Competition on that vast scale was not attractive for French industries, and French farmers were sure not to welcome it.

The French President suspiciously observed the American pressure to persuade the British that it was in their interest to join the Common Market. On April 24, 1961 the Secretary of the Treasury, Mr. Douglas Dillon, welcomed the widening of the Common Market by the accession of Britain and the six other members of EFTA, but he added that the United States hoped that the outside tariff wall of the Market would be reasonably low. Britain looked to de Gaulle as a prospective American agent, both economic and political, within the European Community.[99]

4. *Who was to be the leader of Little Europe?* De Gaulle could have no doubts that Britain, once a member of the EEC, would compete with France for that leadership. Moreover, she had better chances than France because her pro-Atlantic orientation was attractive to the Five. The Australian commentator is correct in saying:

> England within Europe would certainly have done its best to block any drift from the Atlantic concept of Europe, and would probably have had enough support from Italy and the minor powers to do so. [One may add that Germany would have also supported this British stand.] It is therefore hardly surprising that de Gaulle has been less than enthusiastic about British membership, especially since Britain would also have been, in effect, a competitor for the general leadership of Europe, and a more formidable one than the only other contender, Germany, not only because of its developed nuclear forces and its tradition of being in the diplomatic "major league" but because it is not embarrassed like Germany with a past that the minor powers still remember with a *frisson*.[100]

On April 10, 1962 Mr. Edward Heath, Lord Privy Seal and the head of the British delegation in Brussels, made a statement, which could be understood as a veiled bid for the leadership of Little Europe. He said that to be effective the European union would have to have a common defense policy and a European point of view. He viewed the future as a cooperation of two great units: Western Europe and the United States.[101]

All these prospective problems involved in the British candidature did not incline the French negotiators to be accommodating. The negotiations dragged on because even the other Five did not feel that Britain was making sufficient concessions to the opinions of the others. Retrospectively, it is impossible to say whether the negotiations could eventually have been crowned with success. Perhaps Britain and the Five were right in claiming that only de Gaulle's veto prevented success. But it is also possible that the French government did not underestimate the chances of success when it said that the negotiations would have failed even if France had allowed their continuation.

It is equally impossible to be sure that de Gaulle would have made substantial sacrifices at the expense of the economic interests of France if the British were ready to offer to him, as their part of the bargain, nuclear cooperation with France. In any event, the Nassau agreement overflowed the already full French cup. This was the ultimate reason for his veto.

Prime Minister Pompidou still left Britain's door to the Common Market open on the eve of Prime Minister Macmillan's visit to France. He said on December 13, 1962:

> In a few hours the British Prime Minister will be the guest of the President of the Republic. We shall receive him in the most friendly and most constructive spirit, ready to rejoice in all the efforts Great Britain is making in order to get closer to Europe, to which she is bound by so many interests and recollections. We are ready to make her transition easier, while, of course, upholding the view that Great Britain's entry should not destroy the structures, slow down the achievements, or compromise the results which we have gained, in particular regarding the defense, vital in our eyes, of our agricultural interests.[102]

The meeting of Macmillan and de Gaulle at Rambouillet ended in a misunderstanding. The British Prime Minister departed sure of French acquiescence to British membership in the Common Market. The French President was no less sure that Britain was ready, after her disappointment with the Skybolt, to replace nuclear cooperation with the United States with cooperation with France. The following comment is generally accepted as true:

In the event, it was the agreement on defense between Britain and the United States, reached at Nassau, which decided President de Gaulle. This agreement, strictly speaking, had nothing to do with the EEC. But it was an indication that Britain wished to retain the so-called "special relationship" with the United States which had caused President de Gaulle so much trouble during the war and had more recently enabled Britain to escape American strictures (persistently leveled at France) on the maintenance of a separate nuclear force.[103]

De Gaulle himself placed his own authority behind this interpretation. He confided to his friends:

M. Macmillan had come to tell me that we were right in building our striking force. "We also have ours," he told me. "We should combine them within a European framework independent of the United States." Then he takes leave and departs for the Bahamas. Of course, what took place there changed the tone of my press conference of January 14th.[104]

At about the same time, also at the beginning of 1963, he made a similar observation:

It makes me feel melancholic to see England going toward the United States, because she might act as an American salesman. . . . In the Bahamas she turned over her poor atomic force to the Americans. She could have turned it over to Europe. She made, therefore, her choice.[105]

He was angered by what appeared to him to be British duplicity. His belief that Britain would be an American Trojan horse within his Little Europe was strengthened. Not waiting for any consultation with the Five, he cast his unilateral veto. This veto settled the matter, because Article 237 of the Treaty of Rome required the unanimous assent of all member states for the admission of a new member.

At his dramatic press conference of January 14, 1963, he emphatically rejected both the British candidature and the Nassau agreement. Once again he demonstrated his weakness, his lack of diplomatic skill. The Brussels negotiations revealed that Britain was willing to join the Common Market but only if she were given privileged status regarding her agriculture, trade with the Commonwealth and the colonial possessions, and liberal commerce with the third countries. The French negotiators were very adroit in exploiting this British position. Their tactics were simply to insist on full British acceptance of the Treaty of Rome. They enjoyed the sympathy of the EEC Commission and had in this respect full backing at home. It was possible that they would eventually compel the Five and Britain to acknowledge the impossibility of reaching an agreement in full respect of the Treaty of Rome. The odium of rupture would not have been borne by France. But de Gaulle lacks patience. Angered by the Nassau agreement, he brusquely put an end to the negotiations, which could not be continued without French assent.

These are the crucial passages of his statement of January 14, 1963:

> Then Great Britain applied for membership in the Common Market. She did so after refusing earlier to participate in the Community that was being built, and after then having created a free trade area with six other States, and finally . . . after having put some pressure on the Six in order to prevent the application of the Common Market from really getting started. Britain thus in her turn requested membership, but on her own conditions. This undoubtedly raises for each of the six States and for England problems of a very great dimension. England is, in effect, insular, maritime, linked through her trade, markets and food supply to very diverse and often very distant countries. Her activities are essentially industrial and commercial, and only slightly agricultural. . . . In short, the nature, structure and economic context of England differ profoundly from those of the other States of the Continent. . . . The question is to know if Great Britain can at present place herself, with the Continent and like it, within a tariff that is truly common, give up all preferences with regard to the Commonwealth, cease to claim that her agriculture be privileged, and, even more, consider as null and void the commitments she has made with the countries that are part of her free trade area. . . . It must be agreed that the entry first of Great Britain and then of those other States will completely change the series of adjustments, agreements, compensations and regulations already established between the Six, because all these States, like Britain, have very important traits of their own. We would then have to envisage the construction of another Common Market. But the 11-member, then 13-member and then perhaps 18-member Common Market that would be built would, without any doubt, hardly resemble the one the Six have built. . . . It is foreseeable that the cohesion of all its members, who would be very numerous and very diverse, would not hold for long and that in the end there would appear a colossal Atlantic Community under American dependence and leadership which would soon completely swallow up the European Community. This is an assumption that can be perfectly justified in the eyes of some, but it is not at all what France

wanted to do and what France is doing, which is a strictly European construction.[106]

Did he slam the door forever? He said at the same press conference:

> Then, it is possible that Britain would one day come round to transforming herself enough to belong to the European Community without restrictions and without reservations, and placing it ahead of anything else, and in that case the Six would open the door to her and France would place no obstacles in her path, although obviously the mere membership of Britain in the Community would completely change its nature and its volume.[107]

Was he sincere and if so, what had he in mind? Certainly a British evolution which would loosen her ties to the United States and to the Commonwealth. Britain would become a European, no longer an Atlantic, island.

But perhaps he thought farther ahead. It is possible that he remembered his own statement made on November 17, 1948:

> Do not imagine that, if the Reich were to reappear with its former power and ambitions, France, any France, could participate, without reservations, in a European union which would then unavoidably find its center in that Reich.[108]

He might not dramatize this prospect now, but he probably shares the general French uneasiness whenever they evoke the possibility of a reunified Germany which would take first place within Little Europe. In that event, admittedly distant, he or his successors would welcome Britain as the third big partner in the European Community. France alone could not balance a unified Germany, but Britain and France could. Michel Debré makes a very discreet allusion to that remote future: "If we had a tripartite agreement—Great Britain, Germany, and France —peace would be established on the Continent. . . . But this task is so difficult."[109]

Neither de Gaulle nor most of his compatriots would disagree with this view:

> It would be hypocritical to believe that seven-eighths of the Europeans, from the Atlantic to the Urals, would refuse even today to underwrite with both hands this opinion expressed by François Mauriac: "Insofar as I am concerned, I continue to think that everything can be reduced to this proposition: so long as there were several Germanies, we could walk there as we pleased. After one Germany had been finally born, we did not laugh any longer.

Today, as there are two Germanies, we may again sleep at least with only one eye open. If these two pieces are again pasted together, we shall be again a rabbit who sleeps with both eyes open." The day might come when federal Germany would ask her allies and European associates to take an unequivocal attitude; this will be the day when she would decide to assume her national responsibilities fully . . . which the European Community risks diluting. What would the leaders of that Community then say, if the following alternative were placed before them: either to absorb a Germany suddenly increased by eighteen million inhabitants or to reject her? . . . How to avoid the situation where the new political power of a unified Germany would make her succumb to the temptation to turn her allies into satellites? . . . The only possible counterweight for a unified Germany within Europe of the Fatherlands would be Great Britain.[110]

The author of this opinion adduces figures in favor of his thesis. The population of West Germany is 57 million, that of East Germany 17 million; together a unified Germany would have a population of 72 million as against 112 million for the remaining Five. If Britain were a member of the European Community, the total for the Five and Britain would increase to 165 million. Taking the steel output as an indication of the economic potential, he cites the following figures: for Western Germany, 33.6 million tons; for Eastern Germany, 3.6 million; for a unified Germany, 37.2; for the Five, 40 million, and for the Five and Britain, 61 million.

De Gaulle's veto deeply irritated the other five governments. They thought, not without good reason, that it was a strange way of practicing cooperation to place a *fait accompli* before the partners. Their national pride was hurt. For a time the atmosphere between France and the Five was icy cold. Their displeasure was manifested, among other ways, by their delay in signing the treaty between the EEC and the African states on mutual commercial and financial cooperation which France considered very important. Finally, they yielded, and the forward march of the Common Market was resumed.

The question of British membership has been suddenly reopened after the 1966 British elections. During that electoral campaign only the Conservative and the Liberal parties strongly advocated the integration of British economy within the Common Market. Their arguments were convincing.[111] For several years British economic growth has been much slower than that of the members of the EEC. The following table is the best illustration.

Growth of Gross National Product from 1954 to 1965[112]
(in billions of dollars)

	1954	1965
USA	400	650
The EEC countries	135	240
Britain	60	85

It is obvious that the British economy needs the stimulus of foreign competition on its own domestic market. The protectionist tariff on imports other than agricultural has been more harmful than useful. Its average level is only slightly higher than the American but much higher than that of the Six.[113]

Trade with the Commonwealth countries has been steadily declining in proportion to the total British foreign trade, while exchanges with the Western European nations (both the British partners in the EFTA and the Common Market) have been following the opposite curve. The economic future of Britain seems definitely to lie in Europe rather than overseas. If she were allowed to join the Common Market, she and the Six would together form an imposing economic community. The gross national product of Britain, France, and Western Germany alone amounted jointly in 1964 to no less than 57 per cent of the American product.[114]

It is even possible that the long-term political future of Britain will be more closely tied to Europe than to the Commonwealth. Since the independence of non-white members the political ties of the Commonwealth have been becoming looser than they were prior to the Second World War. To take two examples, the Indian-Pakistani hostilities were ended by an agreement reached in Soviet Tashkent, not in London, and the problem of white supremacy in Rhodesia proved that the British view was hardly acceptable to English-speaking Africa.

In any event, the Labour party, which had openly displayed during the electoral campaign its reserved attitude toward the British membership in the Common Market, suddenly changed its mind after the electoral victory. The Labour government has moved closer to the Conservative and Liberal stand. The Speech from the Throne, which outlined the program of the Labour government for the new Parliament, indicated that Britain was ready to join the Common Market if her own and the Commonwealth's essential interests were safeguarded. This approach was very much like the one adopted by the Conservative government in the early sixties. If the Labour government hoped to succeed where the Conservative government had failed, it was unduly optimistic. The same impression of unrealistic optimism was produced by a speech which Mr. George Thomson, the Minister in charge of European affairs, made in

April 1966 at the Lord Mayor's banquet. He said that the Common Market laws and regulations were not engraved on stone tablets and were not brought down by some European Moses. However, it might be that the British government would adopt a more flexible attitude on the day when a true opportunity for beginning negotiations with the Six would appear.

In any event, Britain learned one important lesson from the failure of former negotiations, namely that it would be unwise to start formal conversations with the Six unless one were sure that no impassable obstacles would face her. Her government has limited itself so far to informal soundings in the six capitals. Five of these capitals responded warmly; Paris has not been discouraging. However, no one can be sure of French intentions until the French government apposes its signature on an agreement for the British accession.

The most formidable hurdle is the problem of French agriculture. We have seen that France wrested vital concessions from her partners. The latest agreement of May 1966 sealed the full integration of agriculture within the Common Market. Neither de Gaulle nor any other French government would relinquish the fruits of that victory for the sake of Great Britain.

British farmers would probably accept the replacement of the present state subsidies by higher prices (the Common Market prices) for their products. Their farms are fully modernized and could sustain continental competition. The true problem of British acceptance of the Common Market rules lies elsewhere. If the prices for agricultural products were to be raised to the Common Market level, the cost of living would go up. Wages would have to be raised. British export prices for manufactured goods would consequently be higher, and these goods would compete less successfully on the international market, at least during the initial stage. Later on, the streamlining of British plants would make up for that initial handicap.

The problem of preferential tariffs for Commonwealth agricultural products appears less vital now than in the early sixties. It is mainly limited to New Zealand who exports wool, lamb, butter, and cheese to Britain. The British market is by far the largest market for dairy products in the world. New Zealand provides 40 per cent of British butter imports. In 1964 she exported 49 per cent of her total exports to Britain and only 18 per cent to the Common Market. These stark facts would compel Britain to protect the interests of New Zealand and to ask for appropriate concessions from the Six. There would be no difficulty regarding wool and lamb since there is no continental competition; the problem consists in granting Britain the right to preserve preferential tariff for imports of butter and cheese from New Zealand.

The British accession would raise very difficult but not insoluble economic difficulties. Politically, the obstacles might now be lesser than before. De Gaulle might have lost his former hopes for a speedy formation of the Western European political and defense union. If so, the question of British competition for leadership in that union might have become irrelevant.

The two countries remain deeply divided by their respective attitudes toward the United States. The Labour government's recent decision to maintain the British presence east of Suez increased Britain's dependence on the United States. She is not strong enough to play any significant role in the areas east of Suez alone. However, the attitude toward the United States divides France from the Five as much as from Britain. They adopted more or less the same stand as Britain on the current NATO issue. This has not prevented France from closely cooperating with the Five in the Common Market. If the European Community were to remain economic, there would be no reason for de Gaulle to fear British accession unless Britain attempted to upset the existing agricultural regulations.

The views of France and Britain on European affairs are closer to each other than it seems at first. Neither is enthusiastic about German reunification. Both are unwilling to help Germany get access to nuclear weapons. France recognized the Oder-Neisse frontier as final; judging by the British press, England accepts it tacitly as something that cannot be modified. Both countries desire a steady improvement in relations with the Soviet Union and Eastern Europe. In fact, the divergence of interests between the German Federal Republic on the one hand and Britain and France on the other hand is deeper than the difference of views between Britain and France.

Only the Sphinx in the Elysée Palace could say whether all these arguments have changed de Gaulle's attitude toward British membership in the Common Market. If he were to waive his veto, the problem of British associates in EFTA would not be difficult to solve. Austria is already negotiating with the Common Market for the status of an associated state. Portugal could receive the same status of an associated but still underdeveloped country as Greece and Turkey have. Denmark and Norway would certainly join at the same time Britain did. Sweden might follow suit. Only Switzerland might be prevented by her permanent neutrality from acceding as a full member. She might follow the Austrian example though; Austria is also a permanently neutral country and is willing nevertheless to become an associated state.

American Goliath

Whatever external battle de Gaulle fights, he always attacks two adversaries: the one who is facing him and the other whom he sees hiding behind the enemy's front lines. The other is the real adversary, the American Goliath whom the French David is obstinately chasing away from Europe. De Gaulle pictures himself as a Saint George fighting the dragon who, like Hydra, has many heads. Britain was denied access to the European Community mainly because she was a traveling salesman for the United States. De Gaulle's scenes of jealousy staged in Germany are motivated by the fear that she is too deeply committed to the American giant. The flirtation with the underdeveloped countries is colored by the same American complex.

At his press conference of July 29, 1963, he unburdened himself:

> Some of you will remember that it [the misunderstanding with the United States] was the case, for instance, in the heroic times when I was led to occupy the islands of Saint Pierre and Miquelon, or at the time of the formation of the liberation government in North Africa, or when I happened to disapprove of Yalta and to decline to go to Algiers for a meeting with Roosevelt who was returning from that deplorable conference or, after victory, when it was a question of maintaining our troops in Stuttgart until France was given an occupation zone in Germany. This was the case later with regard to the project of a European Defense Community, which consisted in depriving our country not, of course, of its military expenses but indeed of its army, and which, from my retirement, I categorically opposed. And it is also the case today on very important issues, such as the organization of Europe, the creation of a French atomic force, the Franco-German Treaty, etc.[115]

He has never forgotten or forgiven either the treatment he received at the hands of the United States during the last war or the diplomatic relations America maintained with the Vichy regime. It does not matter that the United States wanted to be present in Vichy to fight the intrigues of the Vichy politicians who exerted a pressure on Marshal Pétain to join Germany as a belligerent. At that time the reenforcement of Germany by the French fleet would have influenced the course of events. It is true that President Roosevelt did not like de Gaulle and did not believe in his prestige among Frenchmen at the time of the American-British occupation of North Africa. De Gaulle won that battle with his political skill. He has easily forgotten the diplomatic recognition at Yalta of France as one of the victorious four powers, or that this recognition met with the Soviet, not only American, reluctance. His memory has not retained several other facts, such as the liberation of France by the American forces and the Marshall Plan. He does not want to remember that the project of the European Defense Community was born in the minds of the contemporary French government, which considered that this was the least dangerous form of German rearmament. His resentments do not bear qualifications.[116]

His "etc., etc." stand for the following events, which also have had an influence on his and, more generally, the French state of mind:

> In the whole sphere of colonial policy the French have a long list of grievances against "the Anglo-Saxons," from the memory of Roosevelt's encouragement to the Sultan of Morocco during the Casablanca conference, and his famous remark about the French having milked the Indo-Chinese cow long enough, to the Anglo-American resistance to any restoration of French influence in Syria and Lebanon during the war and just after, their less than sympathetic attitude in the French conflicts with the Moroccan and Tunisian nationalists, and in the French struggle in Algeria, as demonstrated, for instance, by their continuing to supply arms to Tunisia despite a high probability that they would end up in the hands of the Algerian nationalists. Even on the one occasion in which France found Britain an apparently useful ally in its dealing with the Arabs, Suez, Britain turned out, from the French view, to be a broken reed, collapsing under the pressure of American disapproval.[117]

These "etc., etc." could not have been publicly spelled out by the French President, because he has repudiated the French colonial past and wants his image as colonial liberator to remain untarnished. But they are present in French minds and partly explain the lack of friendly feeling for the United States. One could quote many politicians who voiced these grievances at the time of the Fourth Republic. De Gaulle would say that the colonial retreat was unavoidable, but that it should have been a free French decision; the Americans should not have poked their nose in those affairs.

When the French President sees American intrigues behind the difficulties he encounters in Little Europe, he has in mind, among other things, the American wish for the Common Market's liberal commercial policy, or what he calls the dilution of the EEC within a vast Atlantic free-trade zone. This is why he did not welcome President Kennedy's proposal to cut drastically the tariffs between the United States and the Six or Seven (at that time the American administration hoped for British accession).

Frenchmen suspect that the former enthusiastic American support for the concept of the European Community has undergone changes. At the time when the Soviet threat seemed to be imminent, the United States felt that it was in the general Western interest to build a strong Western Europe which would represent a bulwark against the Soviet ambitions. However, the enterprise succeeded beyond all hopes. A prosperous and dynamic Europe of the Six emerged from the ruins. This is how a French writer sees the change:

> The Six are becoming dangerous competitors on the international market. They drain the dollars, compel the American industrialists to install their factories in Europe in order to be able to sell, etc. . . . [The American administration] does not tire of recalling that one out of seven American farmers works for foreign countries, that one out of three workers is employed by the exporting firms, and that new jobs could be created owing to a bold policy in foreign trade.[118]

He adds the following comment on President Kennedy's proposal: "It did not escape European attention that, in the present condition of monetary exchanges, Americans would be the main beneficiaries of a total customs disarmament in relations with the EEC."[119] In other words, American farmers would continue to invade the Common Market with their products to the disadvantage of French agriculture, while the American industries would freely compete with the Six within their own countries.

A French scholarly publication thus depicts the change in the American attitude:

> For a long time the United States has looked at the success of the European Economic Community with the mixed feelings of amazement, admiration and distrust. . . . Doubtless, America has feared that the "fabulous success" of the Common Market (Mr. Dillon's expression on April 24) may harm her own interests during the long crisis in her balance of payments. Perhaps American leaders have the impression that the strengthening of a close European Community, combined with the French claims regarding nuclear armaments, would result in a positive weakening of American political influence in Western Europe. Whatever it might be, Americans have conceived the project for the widening of the Community (some people would say: to drown it) by transforming it into a vast agreement on the reduction of tariffs and on an Atlantic free-trade zone. . . . The Community, as a living organism, with its internal economic relations harmonized, would see its existence limited to the radiant morning of its "fabulous success," *a dead young girl loved by the gods.*[120]

It would be a dangerous delusion to think that de Gaulle's distrust of American influence in Europe is nothing but his personal feeling. The principal French "European," Maurice Faure, says: "The legitimate interests of Europe . . . cannot be always identical with those of the United States. . . . The United States must understand that there is no Community without preferential tariffs."[121] The President of the French branch of European Movement, who is not de Gaulle's admirer, voices a similar "Gaullist" view:

> One of the reasons for a united Europe was, on the morrow of the last world war, to avoid the American hegemony. . . . If, by a stroke of misfortune, there were a serious failure, a paralyzing crisis within the Common Market or the dispersal of its members, this "hegemony" would be immediately ensured by an agreement easily reached between London, Washington and Bonn.[122]

De Gaulle's suspicions are shared by most Frenchmen. His strident diatribes also find an echo among many Europeans who would like to sing the same tune, but *sotto voce*. A Belgian scholar and fervent partisan of the European Community writes:

> President de Gaulle's attitude toward the United States was not unpopular. It had favorable repercussions in a large section of public opinion outside France, in the very countries which were officially hostile to Gaullist policy. . . . It is impossible to contest that a feeling of humiliation regarding the trans-Atlantic protector and hegemon is lively in the numerous layers of European population. General de Gaulle has touched a string perhaps dangerous but certainly sensitive. Hence the non-French "Gaullists" are numerous even in the countries which, like Holland, are traditionally distrustful of France, and where the government regularly adopts attitudes opposite everything that may resemble the Gaullist doctrine. It is equally true that even the European opinion favorable to NATO is irritated by the American talk about "interdependence," while the United States itself acts independently whenever its vital interests are involved in Cuba or elsewhere.[123]

This sympathy for de Gaulle's declaration of European independence might be due to what the same writer notes: "We live in the era of a renaissance of nationalism."[124] The economic rehabilitation and development of Western Europe and the accompanying feeling of recovered strength has stimulated sentiments of national pride in the six countries and corresponding impatience with a military and political status inferior to that of the United States. De Gaulle is the Pied Piper of that new feeling of recovered self-confidence.

The President of the EEC Commission, Mr. Hallstein, expressed this feeling of confidence when he observed that the third states must reconcile themselves to tariff discrimination by the Six. He sarcastically joked: "If two human beings contract marriage, this is also a discrimination against all the others. The only way to avoid this discrimination is to suppress the institution of marriage."[125] If de Gaulle borrowed this figure of speech, he would say that marriage is a sacred institution and no extramarital relations should be tolerated. The American Don Juans should be chased away.

He fears that they persist in their illegitimate endeavor. One of his nightmares was, for quite a time, the problem of American investments in France. Again his fears were only not his own. His Socialist opponent and for a time a would-be counter-candidate for the Presidency of the Republic, Gaston Defferre, denounced the American "colonization" of France. A great many other anti-Gaullists also warned against the infiltration of American capital, which would end with domination of French economic life.[126]

The anti-American slogan of Gaston Defferre deserves attention. He proposed his candidature in order to rally the whole left-center opposition, excluding the Communists, around his name. A professional politician, he must have sensed that a dose of anti-Americanism was necessary for a man who aspired to lead anti-Gaullists. He probably wanted to prove thereby that his patriotism was no less warm than de Gaulle's. After a visit to the United States, he reassured his prospective followers that his France would be no less independent than de Gaulle's:

> As I am the candidate opposed to General de Gaulle, it is quite natural that the Americans, who observe events from afar, believe that our foreign policy, if I become the President, will be the opposite of his policy. As he practices a constantly hostile policy toward America, the Americans may conclude that I should be their docile ally in every respect. I went, therefore, to tell them that they should have no illusions on this score. I felt that I must tell them in a clear, friendly and sincere way that, once the bad temper and whims of General de Gaulle are eliminated by events, serious problems and sometimes conflicts of interests would remain in our mutual relations. . . . I am a decided and firm partisan of the protection of our factories and our production; this protection should prevent American competition from installing itself in Europe without any control or brakes.[127]

He also espoused de Gaulle's thesis of 1958 that no American decision on the use of nuclear arms anywhere in the world might be made without

French consent.[128] A candidate who opposes de Gaulle on domestic issues visibly cannot count on large support unless he demonstrates his "Gaullism" in foreign affairs, especially regarding the United States.

However, French specialists were far from unanimous regarding the "dangers" represented by American investments or the possibility of an effective defense. It was pointed out that the rapid accretion of dollar reserves was partly due to these investments, and that the strength of the French franc would be undermined if the flow of dollars was suddenly stopped and the investments were liquidated.[129] A distinguished economist pertinently observed that:

> The American capital . . . which is invested in an industry producing for the Common Market may indifferently be invested in any of the six countries and stimulate the growth of the one which offers the most attractive conditions.[130]

His argument was that France could not prevent imports from American plants installed in any other of the five countries, but would lose, by discriminatory treatment of the American investments in France, the advantages related to these investments—such as the stimulation of industrial growth, the implantation of the most modern techniques of production, and the inflow of dollars. The disadvantages usually pointed out are the fear of American control over important branches of industrial production, the purchase of existing French factories, the elimination in competition on the domestic market of the nationally owned plants, the possibility of instructions given by the maternal corporation in America to its subsidiary in France to avoid competition on certain international markets with products offered there directly by the maternal corporation, and the exploitation of American rather than French patents.[131]

It is interesting to note that the EEC Commission to some extent shared the French preoccupation. Its Vice President, Mr. Robert Marjolin, declared in March 1965 in the European Parliament that it would be useful to have "a detailed statistical survey of direct investments which come from the third countries. This should be completed by a mechanism of consultations between the governments and the Commission regarding the pertinent national policies."[132]

A non-French voice expressed the same uneasiness:

> It is undeniable that French preoccupations correspond to the worries of many Europeans. The American oligopolies occupy all the first places in the vanguard of great corporations with the world's capacity. . . . The American implantation continues to increase either by the creation of sub-corporations or by the purchase

of the stock of formerly European corporations by the trans-
Atlantic companies which thus "annex" the [European] corporations.[133]

The official campaign against further American investments or for
close governmental control over them suddenly subsided after the publication in July 1965 of a study by the French Ministry of Industries.
This study appeased the former fears by concluding that: "Taken as a
whole, the foreign investments, including the American, remain on a not
excessive level either in relation to the gross national product or in comparison to the situation in the other European countries."[134] The total of
foreign investments, according to this official study, was five billion dollars, the U.S. investments being one-half of this sum. By contrast, the
French investments abroad were as high as eight billion dollars. The
Minister of Industries concluded that he did not recommend a policy
discouraging foreign investments.[135]

In 1964 de Gaulle, still alarmed by American investments in France
and fearing that American capital would take a controlling position in
important branches of French industrial production, linked that question
with the international monetary system. He did it at one of his most
important press conferences, held on February 4, 1965. He assaulted the
present monetary system founded on the so-called gold exchange standard (i.e., a system which allows the states to hold dollars and sterlings
in addition to gold as the guaranty of their currencies) as unrealistic and
unfair. He said that since the gold reserves of the Six were now equal to
those of the United States and gold was constantly flowing from America
to Western Europe, the dollar was no longer as good as gold. The gold
exchange standard permitted the United States to settle its deficits in the
annual balance of payments by exporting paper dollars and thus to enjoy
"a unilateral facility" denied to other states. He pointed out the American
vulnerability in words which sounded like a threat: "Circumstances are
such today that it is possible to wonder how far the difficulties would go
if the states which hold dollars sooner or later reached the point where
they wanted to convert them into gold."[136] He did not spell out the
obvious conclusion that the mass conversion of dollars into gold by the
European states would result in the devaluation of the dollar, but it is
this that he had in mind. As a matter of fact, France later began selling
the dollars, which certainly did not help the United States in its difficulties
with the balance of payments.

The French President proposed to replace the present monetary system with a return to the gold system, i.e., the regulation of deficits in the

international balance of payments by transfers of gold from the debtor to the creditor state. His suggestion was received with mixed feelings in the United States and Britain but was greeted with great satisfaction in the Soviet Union, which was certainly glad to discover another controversial issue dividing the "capitalist" states.

Smaller European states

De Gaulle put forward, among others, one argument to justify his opposition to British membership in the Common Market, namely that the increase in membership would weaken the cohesion of the European Community. Nevertheless, he accepted the status of associated states for Turkey and Greece, and seems openminded regarding the association of minor members of the EFTA, such as Austria. He favors the extension of the Common Market, if only it does not involve the prospect of the new member's being a "salesman" for the United States. He would have admitted Spain, if he could overcome the political resistance of the other Five. For him Spain is Spain, Russia is Russia, China is China, no matter what regime might temporarily preside over the destinies of "eternal" nations. He probably sees in Spain another Latin nation which, with France and perhaps Italy, could counterbalance the non-Latin elements in Little Europe. Michel Debré, one may presume, does not betray his chief's thought, when he writes:

> Europe . . . is not limited to the states which signed the Treaties that established the Communities. Thus, the presence of Spain is desirable as soon as her political situation allows. This is not only in the interest of France but also in the interest of Europe. The European nations should have an active policy in the Mediterranean. . . . Greece, Italy, France, and Spain have an interest in coordinating their views and actions in the name of, and for, Europe.[137]

One may add that France is militarily cooperating with Spain; the troops of both countries, for instance, were engaged in July 1965 in joint maneuvers in the Pyrenees.[138]

French opposition

What does the non-Communist French opposition offer as an alternative European policy? The answer was given on June 13, 1962, in the National Assembly. Two hundred ninety-two deputies of the parties, ranging from the moderate right to the Socialists, voted for the following resolution:

> We propose the strengthening and merger of the organization of the

Communities which should be realized in one or several stages, the election of the European Assembly by universal suffrage, and the institution, progressively extended, of majority vote within the Council of Ministers. We reaffirm our conviction that only a united Europe, an equal partner of the United States, within the Atlantic Organization, will preserve the future of our liberties and future peace.[139]

The traditional parties were sincere in favoring the election of the European Parliament by direct and universal suffrage and in their fidelity to the American alliance. However, they also affirmed their desire to see a united Europe becoming a peer of the United States. Their assent to the majority vote in the European Council of Ministers should be qualified by a few observations. If the same parties were in power, it is doubtful that they would disregard Robert Schuman's warning against the majority vote on political questions which involve the most vital interests of France. The majority vote in the Common Market is another matter, although even there the present opposition could not be expected to bow meekly to a vote which would favor the Five and would be prejudicial to the French economic life, for instance, to her agriculture.

Probably all opposition leaders would subscribe to the following statement by Guy Mollet regarding the justification and main objective of the European Community: "It is only by uniting Europe that we shall create in the world a force that will make the Americans understand that we are allies but not satellites."[140]

A French political scientist voices a criticism which perfectly fits the French domestic opposition:

As to the substance of the issue I am unable to find Europeans today who clearly define what they understand by Europe, in particular regarding defense, the atomic force, the policy to be followed toward the United States, the supranationality or geographical frontiers of that Europe.[141]

The resolutions and speeches on the mechanics of the European Community do not supply an answer as to what the joint European policy should be. The same author notes that there is a common ground where de Gaulle and the opposition meet: "The opposition, like General de Gaulle, has a tendency to believe that the policy of a united Europe should necessarily be the policy which Frenchmen prefer."[142]

There is much more in common regarding foreign affairs between the President of the French Republic and his domestic opponents than is visible to a casual observer.

Popular support

Public opinion polls indicate that the orientation of de Gaulle's European policy either has popular support or does not encounter strong criticism, except when he seems to threaten the very existence of the Common Market.

> The general tendency is very favorable to the unification of Western Europe. . . . Sixty-four per cent of the French are its partisans, i.e., 90 per cent of those who express any opinion. Opinion is divided regarding the principle of supranational authority: 58 per cent of those who express an opinion are favorable, and 42 per cent are opposed. But if everything is taken into consideration and insofar as they have any opinion and also insofar as a choice is possible, Frenchmen clearly prefer close ties between member states of the Community to the establishment of a supranational authority. Political unification within the Common Market corresponds to the wishes of six out of ten Frenchmen, i.e., of the three-fourths of those who express an opinion. . . . On the level of international relations, the European sentiments of the majority of Frenchmen seem to be linked to the belief in a third world force and to the aspiration for a certain political independence from the United States. . . . The sections of public opinion, who are the most "European," are those that wish the most to have that autonomous Europe.[143]

These French feelings resemble the sentiments largely shared in the five other countries of the European Community:

> Europeans no longer feel threatened by the USSR, as they did fifteen years ago. . . . The time when Europeans let their principal ally act without their having anything to say will never come back. . . . The incontestable popularity of Gaullist policy derives from these considerations.[144]

> In conclusion, if it is incontestable that the French Fifth Republic rendered considerable services to Europe, it did not, however, accelerate the process of political cohesion. It cancelled the Algerian mortgage which was, in the past, paralyzing all European actions; it found itself very frequently beside the EEC Commission in many controversies; it reminded Europe of its vocation of grandeur and inspired it with the ideal of a greater freedom of initiative in its relations with the United States; finally, it aided the six countries in realizing that they had a world stature. Whoever seeks to unite Europe practices a world policy; nobody has been

more convinced of it than President de Gaulle. However, at the same time, the emphasis, too unilaterally French, and the brutal, even contemptuous tone of the successive press conferences, repelled rather than carried along the French partners.[145]

This qualified compliment coming from a Belgian scholar is fair to the French President. It is a fitting conclusion for the present chapter.

VI Several Irons in the Fire: Germany, Russia, and China

Ups and downs in French-German relations

The French President has several irons in the fire. This is true now more than ever. He watches them all, ready to discard, at least for a time, the one which is bending in his hand and take hold of another which is warming up to the desired temperature. None of the foreign irons is discarded forever, because who knows whether the bent one would not be straightened out by a new turn in international circumstances. An iron which lets itself be manipulated by the American hand is left in the fire until such time when, de Gaulle hopes, it would scald the hand.

These complicated tactics are best evidenced by his policies toward Germany, Russia, and China. Germany is for him, as she is for the Soviet Union, the primary international problem. His attitude toward that country has been evolving rapidly during his lifetime and has had a decisive influence on his policies toward the other great powers. In turn Germany to him has been *the* enemy, a cherished friend, or a useful partner who nevertheless cannot be trusted. Emotions have played little if any role in the formation of these successive images. The determining factors have been the German ratio of power as compared with the French and that of other European nations, and, of course, German policies toward France and other important countries. His images of the Germans whether shared or not by the majority of his countrymen, cannot be understood apart from the views which have prevailed in France in each particular historical period.

Between 1871 and 1918 Germany was France's "hereditary enemy." The shock of being singlehandedly defeated by the German forces and the loss of Alsace-Lorraine deeply affected French mentality. The Germans, on whose territory the French kings and Napoleon had for the most part walked as they pleased, whom Frenchmen had liked as long as Germany was divided into many quarreling states, these same Germans, united by Bismarck, inflicted a total defeat and took away a French province. This seemed unbearable. The French yearned for revenge. They turned for help to Russia and the former "hereditary enemy,"

261

England. The revenge sought from 1914 to 1918 proved too costly. Alsace-Lorraine was recuperated, but France was bled white.

The First World War convinced Frenchmen that Germany was the stronger of the two, and that the time of singlehanded victories over the eastern neighbor had passed forever. The American return to isolationism, the uncertainties of Soviet policies, the sympathetic attitude of the British toward the former enemy, and the lack of support from the major allies of the First World War for the *status quo* created by the Treaty of Versailles instilled fear. Would France have to fight next time alone against a powerful Germany? Was the victory in 1918 a Pyrrhic victory? Could France afford once again another purposeless holocaust? French reaction was not uniform; but many, including those who had faced the Germans in the trenches, asked the question whether it would not be more reasonable to come to terms with Germany, which was visibly rising up again to the status of the dominant continental power. After the abandonment of strict enforcement of the Treaty of Versailles, including French occupation of the Ruhr, the new trend began to receive an increasing number of supporters. Reconciliation with Germany became a fashionable idea. It never was carried to its logical end: the termination of alliances with the Eastern European countries, and the acceptance of a thorough revision of the Treaty of Versailles. The Third Republic and the Weimar Republic were both seeking a rapprochement, but it was an equivocal effort. Germany expected that Frenchmen would be logical, while Frenchmen refused to be so. The result of those French-German efforts was nil when Hitler came to power. Yet it was not quite nil, because the grain planted in the French soil by the Third Republic did not die, and the flowering plant made its appearance, to the surprise of many, soon after the Second World War.

The policy of reconciliation with Germany was initiated by Edouard Herriot, Prime Minister in 1924, and indefatigably carried on by Foreign Minister Aristides Briand. It was inspired by what was called the spirit of Locarno, which symbolized the final acceptance of the German-French frontiers by both parties. For both Herriot and Briand the reconciliation was to be the cornerstone of what Herriot called in January 1925 "the United States of Europe"; in 1929 Briand launched, without success, the same idea of a European federation, which at that time was a stillborn concept.

Lieutenant Colonel de Gaulle sympathized with those who distrusted Germany and were opposed to the policy of rapprochement. Although he probably realized better than most of his countrymen that France was overshadowed by a more powerful Germany, it was and is inconceivable for him that his "princess in the fairy tales" could possibly play second fiddle. Her grandeur demands that she occupy first place or, if forced from that position, sit in her corner and play the fiddle alone. Judged retrospectively by his refusal to play second fiddle to Britain in the American orchestra, one may be sure that he rejected in the late twenties the prospect of association with Germany superior in every aspect of power. Yet even he permitted himself a dream. He speculated for a moment in his *Vers l'Armée de Métier,* published in 1934:

> The alternate victories have decided nothing and have satisfied no desire in the relations between the Gauls and the Germans. . . . It is not true that either people ignores the value of the other and is not inclined sometimes to muse about the great feats which they could accomplish together.[1]

The dream remained a dream; de Gaulle foresaw that the First World War was not the last to be fought between the two adversaries and advocated modernization of the French armed forces to prevent a débâcle.

Hitler's Germany found many Frenchmen ready to continue the policy of reconciliation. This time it was called appeasement by its adversaries. After the defeat of 1940, Vichy France frankly accepted the role of second fiddler in the Nazi European order. In this sense, Laval was one of the precursors of the postwar reconciliation. He said on April 27, 1942:

> My policy is founded on reconciliation with Germany. Barring this reconciliation, I do not see any possibility of peace either for Europe or for France or even for the world. I am convinced that Germany will be victorious, but, if even she were defeated, my policy toward her would remain the same, because it is the only one possible in the interest of final peace.[2]

Collaborating Frenchmen (their number at that time was much greater than what would be admitted today) later welcomed the policy of reconciliation under the Fourth Republic because they interpreted it as a sort of vindication of their own collaboration with Nazi Germany, conveniently forgetting that the situation had fundamentally changed in the meantime.

De Gaulle's early views

At that time de Gaulle was the leader of other Frenchmen who refused to accept the defeat as an irrevocable fact. For them Germany was the enemy. De Gaulle wanted to end the German threat once and for all. It is not superfluous to recall his thoughts of the time, first, because he would revive them if Germany ever again looked more powerful than France, and, secondly, to appreciate the flexibility of his mental processes. His changing attitudes toward Germany illustrate most clearly his ability to adjust to changing international circumstances. He depicted in the *Memoirs* his state of mind toward the end of the war:

> In one man's lifetime, France was the victim of three wars caused by her neighbor across the Rhine. . . . In the dangerous world already looming before us, our life exposed again to the threat of war by a neighbor who had so often demonstrated its taste and its talent for war would be incompatible with our country's economic development, political stability and moral equilibrium without which all efforts would remain futile. . . . What will the evolution be of the German people after their imminent defeat? . . . Obviously, the condition of our security would vary according to the answer that the future would bring. But as long as we did not know the answer, we had to proceed as if Germany might remain a threat. What pledges should we seek? . . . The abolition of a centralized Reich! This, in my opinion, was the first requirement necessary to prevent Germany from returning to her bad propensities. . . . If each of the States within the German federation could exist by itself . . . , there would be every likelihood that the federation as a whole would not be inclined to subjugate its neighbors. This would be even more likely if the Ruhr, that arsenal of strategic matériel, were given a special status under international control. . . . Lastly, there was every reason to make a separate State of the Saar which would maintain its German character but would be united to France by economic ties.[3]

He went further in the interview with the London *Times* in 1945:

> The Rhineland . . . is . . . a borderland. . . . The military and political security of these four nations [France, England, Belgium, and Holland] requires that that territory be placed under their strategic and political control (each would exercise this control in the zone of particular interest to her), and that it be politically detached from the rest of Germany.[4]

A glance at the map would reveal the image de Gaulle had in mind. Germany, already stripped (by Stalin's fiat) of large eastern territories, would lose the most industrialized provinces in the west; the remainder would be a powerless and truncated country composed of several quasi-independent states only loosely confederated.

In 1947, although he already included Western Germany within his

Little Europe, his former distrust did not desert him, as evidenced by his statement on November 12 of that year:

> The future of Germany, which we envisage, is not the Reich but a Germany reconstructed on the foundation of individual German states. We do not see anything inconvenient in a federation of those states, if each of them has again all the rights which the Reich abolished.[5]

What he desired was a return to the *status quo* that existed prior to 1871. France's security would be guaranteed by the multiplicity of German states. He, a realist, forgot that Germany of the forties was no longer Germany of the Treaty of Westphalia. Germany was united in the hearts of Germans, and this could not be undone.

Most Frenchmen shared his feelings:

> At the time of liberation, the French public desired, above all, that Germany be made harmless. Parties were completely agreed on this matter. (In May 1946 three-fourths of electors of all parties were partisans of the detachment of the Ruhr from Germany and of its being placed under an international political and economic control.)[6]

De Gaulle thought also about another guaranty:

> Perhaps it would be possible to renew in some way the Franco-Russian solidarity which, though frequently ignored and betrayed, remained no less a part of the natural order of things, as much in relation to the German menace as to the endeavors of Anglo-Saxon hegemony.[7]

In 1944 he went to Moscow and signed a new treaty. But Stalin and the "Anglo-Saxons" were to disappoint him. None of the three great powers accepted his plan to dismember Germany.

French-German partnership

At no time, did his mind refuse to toy with other possibilities. Himmler provided him with an unexpected opportunity for musing. During the last days of the war he sent de Gaulle a message which suggested close German-French alliance against both the Anglo-Saxons and the Russians. Of course, de Gaulle did not reply to this voice of a dying world, but he noted in his *Mémoirs* that: "Apart from the flattery in my behalf that decorated this message from the brink of the grave, there was certainly an element of truth in the picture it sketched."[8]

In 1945, after he went to see defeated Germany, he realized that she could not be dangerous in the immediate future:

> It would be a long time before that conquering Reich, which thrice during one man's lifetime had rushed to domination, could rise up again. . . . Moreover, I hardly had any doubts that Germany would remain divided into two parts, and that Soviet Russia would insist on keeping at her disposal those very German territories from which had sprung up the impulses toward *"Lebensraum."* Thus, amidst the ruins, mourning, and humiliation which had submerged Germany in her turn, I felt my distrust and severity fade in my mind. I even thought to glimpse possibilities of understanding which the past had never offered.[9]

The Soviet Union rejected his plan for dismembering Germany, but partitioned her in the Russian way. Germany was divided into two parts which later were to become two German states. In this new situation he was willing to envisage a French-German cooperation, the cornerstone of his Little Europe. Western Germany alone was not strong enough to leave France the role of second fiddler; nay, she herself might even accept that unenviable position.

His new view was reflected in the speech made on September 25, 1949:

> The man of common sense sees the Germans where they are, in the very middle of our Continent; he sees it in spite of all the sadness and all the anger aroused by the name of Germany in the hearts of millions and, most of all, of Frenchmen. . . . He also sees Europe, whose very large and very precious part has been cut off by Soviet domination. He also sees England drifting away and attracted by the trans-Atlantic mass. He concludes that European unity must, if only possible and in spite of everything, include the Germans. But common sense demands that to accomplish such a task the German and the French peoples one day reach a direct and practical understanding; this understanding should reflect the fact that these two peoples complement each other. . . . There will or will not be a Europe—depending on whether an agreement between the Germans and the Gauls, concluded without any intermediaries, is possible.[10]

In a few sentences he formulated his program for the French-German reconciliation, the foundation of Little Europe, which should be constructed without "intermediaries," i.e., without "Anglo-Saxon" interference. Once his decision had been made, he resolutely moved forward.

On March 16, 1950, he spoke of the reconciliation with a warmth which one would not have expected from the man of June 18, 1940:

> After all, why should the Rhine not one day become a street where Europeans would meet instead of being a ditch over which they always fight each other? After all, I do not find in the history of any people, of any coalition, a victory which would equal the victory of Catalaunian plains where Francs, Gauls, Germans and even Romans together routed Attila. . . . If one did not compel oneself to look coldly at things, one would be impressed by the prospect of what could be achieved by German and the French valor combined, the latter extended to include Africa. There would arise, no doubt, the possibility of common development that could transform free Europe and even give hope to that Europe which is no longer free. In short, it would amount to assuming Charlemagne's venture but, this time, making it rest on modern, that is to say, economic, social, strategic, and cultural foundations.[11]

With his remarkable gift for literary phrase and historical evocation, he committed himself to the "Carolingian" program. This was becoming the commitment of the majority of his countrymen. A historian of the Fourth Republic says: "Since the end of the war, there are Frenchmen who believe that it is impossible to build the future on dislike and fear. Most of them participated in the Resistance."[12] The attitude of Frenchmen, who had fought Nazi Germany and had suffered at the Germans hands, was as surprising as the conversion of the Free French leader to the apostolate of cooperation with Germany. The reconciliation owes much to them and to de Gaulle, because they and he could have retarded the process if they persisted in their former anti-German feelings. The protests of patriots of the last war could not have been silenced.

Popular acceptance of the marriage of convenience

The new concept could easily rally those who had collaborated with Nazi Germans, and that mass of Frenchmen who had lived more or less quietly under the enemy occupation. Robert Schuman's proposal in 1951 for a Western European Coal and Steel Community, the first concrete step on the road to reconciliation with Germany, did not encounter any outcry in France. De Gaulle criticized, not its German aspect, but the supranational elements in the Treaty of Paris.

The merit of laying the foundations belonged entirely to the Fourth Republic. At that time de Gaulle, living in self-imposed retirement, was denouncing the treaties which the governing parties were concluding. The cap was turned in 1951. The next step, the treaty for the European

Defense Community, almost wrecked the vessel of European construction, if not its sistership of German-French amity. A bitter controversy divided the parties. The specter of German rearmament, appearing so soon after the war, revived the old fears. Those who opposed the ratification were animated by this fear, or were inspired by de Gaulle's protests against the dilution of the French Army in a cosmopolitan European Army, or were moved by both sentiments. The atmosphere was so heated that Paul Reynaud, a former Prime Minister later converted to the idea of cooperation with Germany, exclaimed:

> When the military leaders dominate the German government . . . are you sure that they will resist those offers (economic and political) which will come from the East and that they will not join the other camp? . . . Those men of the fresh and joyous war, those militarists, those former Nazis will again be at the helm of an independent Wehrmacht.[13]

His lively imagination evoked the nightmarish prospect of the German armies allied to the Soviet forces and again marching on Paris.

The treaty for the European Defense Community was rejected by the majority in the French National Assembly. But three years later the march toward organized Little Europe and cooperation with Germany was resumed with the Treaties of Rome. The new French attitude was also indicated by the approval of the reunification of the Saar with West Germany.

The conversion of France to this new creed has been well described by a French political scientist:

> The old tradition of the "hereditary enemy" collapsed with a suddenness which astonished the French themselves. . . . France and Germany certainly do not feel affection for each other, but I believe that there exists a profound awareness of mutual advantages in close collaboration. . . . One can therefore say that France and Germany are joined in a marriage of convenience which has turned out to be happy, in spite of the fact that it is not a marriage based on romantic love.[14]

This business-like nature of the marriage was confirmed by the public opinion polls in the last years of the Fourth Republic.

> A favorable evolution seems to have begun toward the end of 1956. The dominant trend in public opinion reversed itself beginning with that date; the tendency toward a limited trust grew stronger than the opposite tendency. . . . The favorable trend

increases very markedly in relation to the higher social-cultural level; this implies that the trend is buttressed by arguments which are logical rather than by emotional reactions.[15]

Later polls, including the most recent, indicate that the trend has been steadily gathering force. In 1963 (the year the French-German Treaty was signed) 54 per cent of those questioned approved their President's policy of cooperation with Germany, only 15 per cent disapproved it, and 31 per cent expressed no opinion. Sixty-one per cent were glad that the French-German Treaty had been concluded, only 14 per cent found it undesirable, and 25 per cent declined to answer the question.[16]

Why is it that Frenchmen have so rapidly approved of the close cooperation with the former "hereditary enemy"? There were several reasons. First, this idea was not new, as we have seen. Second, the German occupation of France was mild compared with the atrocities committed in Eastern Europe and Russia and even with the repression in Norway or Holland. The Nazi period did not plant seeds of implacable hatred or resentment. Third, Germany took over from England the role of the "hereditary enemy" only in 1871. England had played that ungrateful role for centuries, beginning with the Hundred Years' War. It was not an impossible proposition for Frenchmen to forget the resentment accumulated during a historical period of only 75 years. It was no more difficult for the Germans, though their anti-French feelings went back to the Napoleonic invasion. But since that time they were defeated only once and conquered France twice. One may better understand this aspect of reconciliation if one will refer to the history of German-Western Slavic relations. In the East of Europe the resentments of the Poles and Czechs had a history of a thousand years and could not be forgotten as easily as in France. Fourth, France owed her national beginnings to the Germanic period of her history; it is not without cause that her very name was derived from that of the Franks, although de Gaulle prefers to call Frenchmen Gauls to stress the ancient background of his people. For good reasons Charlemagne is considered a French and a German hero. During the long history of French-German relations the Germans never had opposed France with a united front until 1871, if one excepts the short episode of 1813–14. The German Protestant cause was supported by Catholic France during the Thirty Years' War. In the eighteenth century French was the language of cultivated Germans, including Frederick the Great. Throughout centuries France was able to increase her national territory by the amputations of lands of the former Roman Empire of the German nation. There are no French-speaking areas in Germany, but Alsatians speak a German dialect. On the whole, the long history of relations with Germany left Frenchmen with pleasant rather than unpleasant recollections. Finally, the two World Wars ended in the débâcle for both nations. France's victory in 1918 was Pyrrhic, and she was crushed in 1940; Germany was vanquished in 1918 and 1945. Both could ask themselves the pertinent question whether there was any sense in their repetitious struggles begun in 1870. The answer of both parties was the marriage of convenience.

The honeymoon

De Gaulle's return to power was greeted in Germany with serious misgivings. However, the fears that he would break the ties between the two nations were soon dissipated on the occasion of the first meeting of the two elderly statesmen, de Gaulle and Adenauer. The meeting on September 14, 1958 of the Frenchman from the Northeast and the Rhineland German was the beginning of their mutual and deep friendship. De Gaulle's concepts were not unwelcome to the German Chancellor, whose sympathies for France had originated in the aftermath of the First World War, who did not like the British, and who was far from sure of the constancy of American support for Germany. So long as Adenauer remained at the helm, the French-German honeymoon lasted almost without quarrels. De Gaulle committed an error of judgment, because he took Adenauer for Germany and built his hopes on the old Chancellor. The eventual retirement of Adenauer could bring only disappointments.

What could France offer to Germany? First, the French market for the German industries within the EEC framework. Second, refusal to engage in a flirtation with the Soviet Union and a firm stand regarding the *status quo* in West Berlin and nonrecognition of the German Democratic Republic. De Gaulle promised on March 25, 1959, that "we would not allow West Berlin to be given up to the regime of Pankow. Furthermore, we are not prepared to recognize this regime as a sovereign and independent State."[17] France, one of the four former occupying powers, had a veto regarding both problems. The Germans knew that as long as de Gaulle was their friend, they could count on his will to resist any Soviet pressure and to stiffen, if necessary, the American and British attitudes regarding West Berlin and Eastern Germany.

The biographer of de Gaulle thus depicts his hero's expectation of the time:

> De Gaulle believed Federal Germany was the best possible interlocutor. She remained, in spite of everything, vulnerable to the evolution in the relations between the East and the West. She did

not want Eastern Germany to be recognized, under any circumstances whatsoever, as a sovereign state. She did not want the status of Berlin to be modified. . . . In other words, Western Germany would be, among all the French partners, obviously most sensitive and most responsive to the French offers and overtures.[18]

This calculation later proved to be erroneous.

The honeymoon of the Adenauer era was full of equivocations. They abounded in the joint communiqué issued on September 14, 1958, at the end of the first Adenauer-de Gaulle meeting:

> We believe that the former hostility should be ended once and for ever and that Frenchmen and Germans are called upon to live in mutual understanding and to work side by side. We are convinced that the close cooperation between the Federal Republic of Germany and the French Republic is the foundation of any constructive venture in Europe. This cooperation will strengthen the Atlantic Alliance and is indispensable for the whole world. We think that this cooperation should be organized and should, at the same time, include other nations of Western Europe with which our two countries have close ties.[19]

The reference to the Atlantic Alliance certainly meant for the German Chancellor the continuation of the military integration under the American supreme command. De Gaulle understood it as the placing of that alliance under the American-British-French triumvirate from which Germany was to be excluded. Both were in agreement that their cooperation was to include the four other nations already members of the European Community; but, if not Adenauer, at least the other Germans interpreted that sentence of the joint communiqué as an invitation to Britain.

In any event, Adenauer could feel happy. "Not only the French government but also the French people have given Chancellor Adenauer the warmest welcome. This proves that the era of bad feelings between the two countries belongs to the revolved past."[20]

De Gaulle repaid the visit in November 1958 by going to Bad-Kreuznach, where he pledged his support for the maintenance of free West Berlin. The mutual visits by the two leaders continued throughout the following years. The zenith was reached in September 1962. The French President made a truly triumphal tour of West Germany, greeted everywhere with an enthusiasm rarely equalled in France. He told the Germans his program for the mutual cooperation:

> If we have consigned our quarrels and furies to oblivion, it is not in order to get asleep. On the contrary, we must make of this

reconciliation the common source of strength, influence and action. Union, why should there be a union? First, because we both are directly threatened. In the face of the Soviet ambition to become the dominant power, France realizes that an immediate peril would threaten her body and her soul if Germany, the outpost, were to yield; and Germany does not ignore the fact that her destiny would be sealed, if, behind her, France did not support her. Furthermore, union is necessary, because the Alliance of the free world, that is to say, the mutual obligations between Europe and America, could not long retain its reciprocal trust and solidity if there were not on the ancient Continent a massive center of power and prosperity of the same order as the one which the United States represents in the New World. This massive center may have no other foundation but the solidarity of our two peoples. Finally, union is necessary in the perspective of a relaxation of tension and, later on, of an international comprehension which would allow the whole of Europe, once the ambition to dominate by an obsolete ideology would no longer exist in the East, to establish its equilibrium, its peace and its development from the Atlantic to the Urals. This will be possible on the imperative condition that the West follow the policy of a living and strong community, that is to say, in essence one and the same Franco-German policy.[21]

He asked the Germans to work with him for the realization of his two visions of Little and Big Europe. Only a few of them could retain a cool mind in the atmosphere of enthusiastic French-German effusions and were able to read between the lines. If they refused to follow his policy fully, what would be their fate? France could cease to support Germany, and German destiny would be sealed. However, the time was not propitious for indiscreet interpretations. De Gaulle himself was carried away by the enthusiasm of German crowds assembled everywhere to greet the great Frenchman. He went as far as to appeal to the former German military glories in his speech in Hamburg at the German War College:

But what can and should be the importance of solidarity between our two armies in this Franco-German union which everything demands that we build up? It is in the French and in the German nature that we have never achieved anything great from the national or international point of view without an eminent share of our or your military in the achievement. The organized cooperation of our armies, in view of one and the same common defense, is essential for the union of our two countries because of that trait in our nature as well as because of the existence of the danger that threatens us both.[22]

This philosophy of history was surprising in a man of vast intellectual culture. If neither France nor Germany ever accomplished anything great except by arms, did the achievements of a Goethe, a Schiller, a Kant or of a Descartes, a Pascal, a Balzac, to mention a few who are not generals, count for little in the true greatness of both nations? For once, de Gaulle seemed to have lost control over his emotions. Flattered by the enthusiastic German reception, he spoke as though the German military laurels had not been won twice at French Sedan, in 1870 and 1940.

During this period of warm French-German relations, French-Soviet relations were at the freezing point. There is a sort of law of nature which operates in the relations between the Western powers, on the one hand, and Germany and Russia, on the other. Any improvement in the relations with Germany causes a cooling off in the relations with the Soviet Union, and vice versa. The United States and Britain know it as well as France.

Nikita Khrushchev could not hide his feelings during his official visit to France in March 1960. He tried in vain to revive the former French animosity against the Germans and to remind Frenchmen of the old Russian-French alliance. Finally, he could no longer control himself. At Verdun the French Minister, Louis Jacquinot, affirmed that France wanted to live in peace with all nations, including her former enemies. This friendly gesture to Germany was too much for the Soviet Prime Minister, who angrily replied:

> Your speech is so diplomatic that I do not know whether, in your opinion, the Germans came to you as aggressors or as guests. We cannot forget the German attack against the Soviet Union. We do not invite you to unite with us in order to make war on Germany, but to prevent the Germans from starting a new war.[23]

The French government remained deaf to this appeal. It preferred the German to the Soviet friendship.

The French-German Treaty

De Gaulle and Adenauer crowned their friendship with the conclusion of the bilateral treaty of mutual French-German cooperation in 1963. At that time plans for the political union of the Six had been stalled. The two elderly statesmen thought that they had a substitute in the treaty which could, in due time, be extended to the reluctant Four.

At the end of September 1962, after de Gaulle's visit to Germany, the French government sent a memorandum to Bonn which was later to become the substance of the treaty signed in January 1963. It may be true that neither de Gaulle nor Adenauer cared for the solemn form of a treaty, and that this was due to the insistence of the German Foreign Office,[24] but the ideas embodied in the treaty were suggested in the French memorandum. The latter document contained de Gaulle's cherished concept: a regular cooperation between governments without any trace of supranationality. It proposed to have frequent and periodical meetings between the Chiefs of State and between the Ministers for Foreign Affairs and National Defense as well as other Ministers whose jurisdiction would be concerned with French-German cooperation. Military cooperation, already inaugurated in 1960, was to continue. It would include not only France's offer of storage depots for German armaments, training grounds for the German Army, and two French airfields for German Air Force use, but also cooperation in the production of armaments and in military research. Characteristically, the French government did not say a word about nuclear collaboration; the French national nuclear force was to remain exclusively French.

Cooperation was to extend not only to foreign and military affairs but also to the cultural sphere, in particular by promoting the teaching of the language of one country in the schools of the other. Finally, the two governments were to work together within the framework of the Common Market.[25]

Negotiations for the treaty did not last long. On January 22, 1963, it was solemnly signed by the French President and the German Chancellor. Its main provisions were as follows:

1. Regular cooperation between the two governments was to be assured by periodic meetings between Heads of State (at least twice a year), the Ministers of Foreign Affairs (at least three times a year), and the high officials of the two Ministries for Foreign Affairs (at least once a month). Contacts between the diplomatic representatives of the two countries abroad, meetings between the Ministers of National Defense (at least every three months), between the chiefs of staff (at least every other month), and between the Ministers in charge of education would become regular events. A French-German institute would organize cultural exchanges.

2. The two governments were to consult each other prior to making decisions on any important external matter, in particular regarding all problems of mutual interest. This consultation should aim at assuming, if possible, similar positions. It should, among others things, relate to

problems of the European Communities; political and economic relations with the Communist East; all matters debated in international organizations such as NATO and the United Nations; and aid to the underdeveloped countries, which should include joint projects.

3. The two governments were to evolve common strategic and tactical military doctrines. Their armed forces were to cooperate, and their armaments industries to work and conduct research together.

4. Cultural exchanges were to be intensified by teaching German in French schools and vice versa, and by exchanges of young persons.

The treaty was concluded for an indefinite period of time without any clause allowing for unilateral denunciation. It embodied the French concept for the organization of Little Europe (no supranational institutions) but was reduced in scale to bilateral cooperation.[26]

Prior to the signing of the treaty de Gaulle was very optimistic about the future of French-German friendship. On January 14, 1963 (at the same press conference at which he barred British access to the Common Market and emphatically declined to join the United States and Britain in the Nassau Agreement) he declared:

> Among the new elements that are in the process of shaping the world at present, I believe that there is none more striking and more fruitful than the French-German pact. Two great peoples, which have for so long and so terribly opposed and fought each other, are now turning toward each other with the same impulse of sympathy and understanding. It is not only a question of a reconciliation demanded by circumstances. What is happening in reality is a kind of mutual discovery of two neighbors, each noticing the extent to which the other is valid, worthy and attractive. It is from this then that springs the desire for a rapprochement manifest everywhere in the two countries which conforms with reality and which commands politics, because, for the first time in many generations, the Germans and the Gauls realize their solidarity.[27]

His euphoria was not to last long. He mistook his confident relations with Adenauer for an identity of views between the two governments. The scholarly French publication *L'Année Politique* was more realistic in observing: "After all, it was a de Gaulle-Adenauer understanding rather than a French-German one that was taking shape. If the old Chancellor were to disappear, what would remain of this understanding?"[28] De Gaulle was to answer in the summer of 1963: a faded rose!

He must have been surprised by the reservations which the treaty evoked in the German parliament. The treaty was submitted in the first place to the German Federal Council, the upper chamber representing the states of West Germany. The members of that Council are designated by the state governments and express in the Council the views of those governments. The ratification was accompanied by the adoption of an interpretative resolution in which the Council welcomed the treaty as a symbol of the French-German reconciliation, but invited the federal government to carry it out in the spirit of the main objectives of German foreign policy: the reunification of Germany, common defense within the framework of the Atlantic Alliance, European union with British participation, and the reduction of tariffs through negotiations between the EEC, on the one hand, and Britain and the United States, on the other. Every point was contrary to the foreign policy objectives of the Fifth Republic. This resolution, adopted by 29 votes (12 members of the Council abstaining), tore off the veil of equivocations in the de Gaulle-Adenauer understanding. It pointed out the great contradiction between the goals of the two countries.

The lower chamber of the parliament went even further. Instead of a resolution, it attached a preamble to the treaty, an unheard of procedure of amending unilaterally an international agreement. The French government was not asked to agree. Owing to this preamble the treaty was finally unanimously approved by both chambers; all three parties, including the opposition party of Social Democrats, cast approving ballots. The vote for the ratification, accompanied by the no less unanimous approval of the preamble, signified that the German parliament was for the reconciliation of the two nations but also that it did not want to approve de Gaulle's foreign policy.

The preamble adopted on May 16, 1963, is worth citing integrally because it revealed the basic divergence between the two countries:

> Convinced that the treaty of January 22, 1963, concluded between the Federal Republic and the French Republic will strengthen and make effective the reconciliation and friendship between the German and French peoples,
>
> Taking note of the fact that the rights and obligations of the Federal Republic, which result from multilateral treaties to which it is a contracting party, will not be modified by this Treaty,
>
> Expressing the resolute wish that the implementation of this Treaty be oriented toward the principal objectives which have guided the Federal Republic of Germany throughout the years,

acting in cooperation with its allies, and which determine its policy, namely:

Maintenance and strengthening of the Alliance of free peoples, in particular of the close association between Europe and the United States of America;

The right of self-determination for the German people and the restoration of German unity;

Common defense within the framework of North Atlantic Alliance and the integration of armed forces of member states of that Pact;

The unification of Europe according to the patterns set up by the existing European Communities and by admitting Great Britain and other states which want to join, as well as the strengthening of the existing Communities;

Lowering of tariffs in the negotiations carried within the framework of GATT between the European Economic Community, on the one hand, and Great Britain and the United States of America as well as other states, on the other hand;

Aware of the fact that a Franco-German cooperation, carried according with the above objectives, will be beneficial for all the peoples, will help to maintain the world's peace and, at the same time, will contribute to the well-being of the French and German peoples,

The Bundestag hereby ratifies the following statute approving the Treaty.[29]

The German parliament thereby notified de Gaulle that Germany unanimously refused to serve as his foreign policy instrument.

The treaty was approved in the French National Assembly in June 1963 by a majority of 325 against 107 nays and 42 abstentions; all Communist and Socialist deputies voted against, together with a small number of Popular Republicans and Radicals. The opposition, except for the Communists, did not protest against the principle of cooperation with Germany, but had its own misgivings concerning various aspects of de Gaulle's foreign policy. The opposition's point of view was expressed in the following preliminary motion submitted by the Socialists, Radicals, and Popular Republicans:

The National Assembly declares that it is necessary to reassert France's aspiration to build a democratic Community of European peoples founded on the transfer, limited in scope and gradual, of sovereignty to the Community institutions, and to strengthen cooperation between Europe and the United States, especially through the integration of armed forces. It denies its authorization of the ratification of the Franco-German Treaty of January 22, 1963.[30]

The opposition chose NATO and the supranationality of European Community as the two issues for picking a quarrel with de Gaulle. The motion was defeated by 277 votes of the progovernmental majority against 183 opposition votes (41 Communists, 67 Socialists, 37 out of 39 Radicals, 32 out of 55 Popular Republicans, and 6 nonaffiliated deputies). The Communists voted not for the motion but against French-West German cooperation.[31]

Disappointment and its reasons

De Gaulle was compelled by the attitude of the German parliament to realize that the honeymoon was over. On July 2, 1963, he gave a dinner for a group of French parliamentarians. He told them in reference to the recently ratified treaty: "You see, treaties are like young girls and roses; they do not last long. If the Franco-German Treaty is not to be implemented, it will not be the first case in history." He cited from Victor Hugo's poem: "Alas, I have seen young girls dying."[32]

De Gaulle was unrealistic in expecting that the Germans would blindly follow his leadership. The greater his former hopes, the more he was disappointed. Since the latter half of 1963 his tone in speaking about Germany has become distinctly cooler.

On July 23, 1964, he stated the disappointing effects of the French-German Treaty or, rather, lack of effects:

> It must be noted that, if the French-German Treaty made possible limited results in some areas, also if it led the two governments and their services to establish contacts which, for our part, and altogether, we judge can be useful and which are, in any case, very pleasant, up to now a common line of conduct has not emerged. Assuredly there is not, and there could not be any opposition, strictly speaking, between Bonn and Paris. But, whether it is a matter of the effective solidarity of France and Germany concerning their defense, or even of the stand to take and the action to pursue toward the East, above all the Moscow satellites, or correlatively of the question of boundaries and nationalities in Central and Eastern Europe, or the recognition of China and of the diplomatic and economic mission which can be assumed by Europe in relation to that great people, or of peace in Asia and particularly Indochina and Indonesia, or of the aid to give to the developing countries in Africa, Asia and Latin America, or of

the organization of the agricultural common market and consequently the future of the Community of Six—one could not say that Germany and France have yet agreed to make together a policy and one does not dispute that this policy should be European and independent. If this state of affairs were to last, there would be the risk, in the long run, of doubts among the French people, of misgivings among the German people, and, among their four partners of the Rome Treaty, an increased tendency to leave things as they are, while waiting, perhaps, to be split up. . . . She [France] is now strong enough and sure enough of herself to be able to be patient, except for major external changes which would jeopardize everything and therefore lead her to change her direction. . . . In waiting for the sky to clear, France is pursuing, by her own means, that which a European and independent policy can and should be.[33]

His threat was not even couched in a smooth diplomatic phrase. He told the Germans that, if they persisted to cling to their Atlantic concepts and if they would not align their foreign policy with his own, he might change the course. It was clear that his new course might lead him to Moscow, where he was awaited with impatience. The warnings continued. In 1964 a French parliamentary delegation, which included Gaullist deputies, paid a visit to the East German parliament. One of the Soviet leaders, Nikolai Podgornyi, was received in the same year with all the marks of cordial respect and hospitality. Earlier, in his annual speech to the French people on New Year's Eve, 1964, de Gaulle mentioned Pankow among the several capitals of the totalitarian states. Eastern Germany was no longer a "regime" but a state; this was his way of telling the new German Chancellor, Erhard, that his cordial pro-American effusions during his official visit to the United States were not liked in Paris. De Gaulle might have been thinking of the Federal Republic when he told his guests at the garden party for the French deputies in June 1965 that "a priori, one may not and should not trust anyone."[34]

Obviously the French-German Treaty has not produced that close cooperation de Gaulle expected in 1962. The treaty stipulated that both governments would consult each other on all important international affairs. In 1964 France recognized the Communist government of China and decided in 1966 to withdraw from NATO, admittedly two very important steps, without taking the trouble of consulting Bonn. The Federal Republic adhered to the Treaty of Moscow on the suspension of nuclear tests in spite of the French refusal to do the same.

These three decisions revealed the profound divergence of views. Germany was aligned with the United States; France disregarded the American policy if it suited her own purpose.

One of the most interesting aspects of the Luxembourg and the subsequent Common Market negotiations in 1966 (see Chapter V) was the attitude of West Germany. This time the opposition to France was spearheaded not by Holland, as it had been the case in former years, but by the Federal Republic. The German government was no longer ready to make unilateral concessions regarding the agricultural problems for the sake of French friendship. It strongly insisted on the reciprocity of concessions, each new step in the direction of integration of European agriculture being conditioned on the French willingness to assent to a more liberal attitude of the Six in the GATT negotiations with the third states, especially the United States and members of EFTA.

It is unlikely that during the French-German honeymoon the federal government of Germany would have adopted the same rather stiff position toward the French withdrawal from NATO as it did in 1966. The German Minister of Defense went so far as to declare that it was better to have NATO without France than Europe without NATO. The French-German Treaty was so forgotten in both capitals that not only did Paris not consult Bonn on its intended move, but Bonn drafted its reply to the French note concerning the French forces in Germany after consulting not Paris but Washington and London.

Ironically, the most positive results of the treaty came from cultural exchanges. The French-German Office for the Youth has successfully promoted thousands of meetings between the youth associations of both countries, and the teaching of French in Germany and of German in France has been progressing. The deterioration in political relations has had no effect on those fruitful cultural exchanges which might have, in the long run, more lasting influence than the political quarrels between the two governments.[35] No one could disagree with de Gaulle when he said on September 9, 1965, that the French-German Treaty "remained in the stage of cordial potentiality."[36]

How could de Gaulle have not foreseen that the Germans would not align themselves behind the Fifth Republic, if only for the reason that they were Germans and not Frenchmen? The discrepancies between his objectives and those of the Federal Republic were visible to eyes even less experienced than his own. They were and remain several:

1. The first is related to the respective attitudes toward the United States and NATO. No doubt the Germans, formerly dominant in Europe, are not happier than Frenchmen regarding their dependence for

national security on the American guaranty.[37] But they fully realize that this guaranty is the only available shield against Soviet ambitions. They know better than anyone else that Soviet Russia has no love for them and would be glad to keep Germany divided forever. The Germans have no choice; neither the French nuclear force nor their own conventional divisions could become a substitute for the American alliance. They would be the last to ask the United States to evacuate American troops from their national territory. They might fear at times the possibility of an American-Soviet deal at their expense, but would offer no excuse for such an American move. If forced to choose, they would choose the United States rather than France. To use the matrimonial metaphor again, they would be the happiest if they could have two wives, American and French, who would not quarrel. De Gaulle asks them to enter into a monogamous marriage which they simply cannot afford.

Dr. Eugen Gerstenmaier, speaker of the German Bundestag and one of the Christian Democratic leaders, himself a confirmed partisan of cooperation with France, summed up the German problem in two sentences. In the lecture he gave at the Sorbonne on October 21, 1964, he recalled "the extraordinary reception Germany gave the French Chief of State" in 1962. He added to this evocation a significant sentence: "When President Kennedy visited our country a few months later, he was received with the same warmth."[38] This is what irritates the French President the most, this divided loyalty of the Germans.

Adenauer's successor—Chancellor Ludwig Erhard—said that one of the objectives of German foreign policy was "to strengthen the alliance of free nations on both sides of the Atlantic in such a way that it will be able to stand up to any future threats."[39] His Foreign Minister, Dr. Schroeder, was even more emphatic: "We should do all we can to preserve the ties linking us with the greatest power of the Free World."[40] In the same speech of May 3, 1965, Dr. Schroeder mentioned one of the reasons for German fidelity to NATO: "Like every other member of NATO Germany is entitled to be integrated effectively in the organization of the Western nuclear deterrent potential."[41] He knew that the way to this objective was the MLF or some such arrangement to which de Gaulle was strongly opposed. The leader of the Social Democratic party, Willy Brandt, gave his support to the official stand after his return from a visit to Paris in April 1963 where he had a talk with the French President. He declared: "I had the opportunity . . . to explain that we could not make a choice between Paris and Washington or between Paris and London, and why we could not do it."[42]

The interested parties to this French-German controversy, the United

States and Britain, did not remain passive, but did their best to reassure Germany of their friendship. President Johnson's warm reception of Chancellor Erhard in the fall of 1963 and Queen Elizabeth's visit to Germany in 1965 were calculated to detach Germany even further from France. Paul Reynaud is right in saying that: "If France were one day foolish enough to invite Germany to make a choice between herself and the United States, Germany would choose the United States."[43]

2. The second conflict concerns the external orientation of the European Community: Is it a closed club of the Six or an association readily open to contacts with the other European states and the United States? The German government never tires of stressing its desire to see Britain joining the European Community. It also refuses to cooperate in the French effort to use the Community as a device for stifling all American influence.

The French President retaliated by threatening Germany in his speech made on November 22, 1964, at Strasbourg. Referring to the French-German reconciliation, he said:

> But there must be a proportionate justification for such a complete and commendable transformation in our moral attitudes and actions by comparison to what they used to be for three centuries. What kind of justification, if not the achievement, together with Germany, of a very old and also very modern ambition: the construction of a Europe that would be European, in other words, an independent Europe, powerful and influential within the free world.[44]

He implied that if this justification were to disappear because Germany refused to participate in building that "European" Europe, i.e., wanted to maintain close ties with the United States, the whole French policy of friendship could be called into question.

3. France's opposition to the MLF and her unwillingness to associate Germany with the French nuclear effort evoke German suspicion that France takes in fact the same attitude as Russia and does not want Germany to have access to nuclear weapons in any form whatsoever.

4. The French position on the main German problem is, to say the least, equivocal. The French President declared on May 15, 1962:

> We think that, in the present international situation, the elements of which are tension, threat and cold war, it is vain to wish for a satisfactory settlement of the German problem. This appears to us to be the same as trying to square the circle. . . . I repeat, in light of the extremely precarious balance that exists between the East

and the West, our view on Germany is that it is not opportune at the present time to alter accomplished facts. We believe that these facts must be taken as they are and lived with.[45]

What he said was true because Germany could not be unified over the Soviets' absolute veto. But one does not rub salt in the deep wound of a friend by telling him a bitter truth that he knows as well as anyone else. His advice to live with the fact of a divided Germany must have sounded bitter to German ears.

On February 4, 1965 he proposed a program for German reunification which amounted in practice to postponement *ad calendas Graecas.* He began by sketching a somber background:

The German problem is, indeed, the European problem. . . . Is it necessary to say that the events which have occurred during the first half of this century made this problem more disturbing and burning than ever? Already, because of the German Empire, the First World War had caused a gigantic shock in the west, east, north and south of Europe. But then the Third Reich's immense effort to dominate; its armies' invasion on one side as far as the Channel, the Atlantic, the Pyrenees, the Adriatic and the shores of the Mediterranean, on the other as far as the Arctic, the approaches to Moscow, the heart of the Caucasus, the Black Sea, the Aegean; the action of its submarines on all the oceans of the globe; its tyranny established over twelve European States, its hegemony over four others; the violent death of forty million men, military and civilian, as a result of its acts, particularly the systematic extermination of ten million prisoners—all that inflicted terrible wounds on the body and soul of the peoples. . . . Doubtless, the subordination imposed on the vanquished, demolished and decimated, the accomplished facts in the territories which were once East Prussia, Posnania and Silesia, the end of the Austrian Anschluss and of the "protectorate" over Czechoslovakia, the country's organic partition through the creation of zones and the Berlin status, had first made the direct fears, which Germany had for so long inspired, recede. . . . But the tragedy nonetheless left very deep scars. In short, it was with circumspection, indeed, with some uneasiness, that public opinion in Western Europe sometimes viewed the economic expansion, military re-birth and political recovery of the Federal Republic, while the Sovietized regimes in Eastern Europe made use of the peoples' instinctive distrust of the Germans to justify the cold war against the free world, inveigled, so to speak, by the "German revengers." . . . Moreover, a large part of world opinion, while recognizing the precarious nature of what became of the old Reich and while disapproving of the brutal ruse of the wall and barbed wire, accommodated itself to a situation which, for whatever it was worth, was not preventing the co-existence. . . . Oh, doubtless one can imagine things continuing as they are for a long time without provoking tomorrow, any more than they aroused yesterday, a general conflagration, since the reciprocal nuclear deterrence is succeeding in preventing the worst.[46]

The de Gaulle who spoke this time was no longer the de Gaulle of September 1962 who warmly responded to the enthusiastic German reception. It was the wartime de Gaulle indicting the Germans for having twice caused world catastrophes. He even unearthed the old French thesis that the Germans were exclusively to blame for the outbreak of the First World War. The whole Nazi record was recalled. Finally, he disclosed his uneasiness at the political, military, and economic recovery of Germany—which only three years before was destined to be a bosom friend of France.

If Western Germany alone was causing this uneasiness, could he wish to see her becoming much stronger through union with Eastern Germany? He said calmly that things as they were could continue for a long time without causing a general war. Was it a wishful thought?

In any event, he proposed his own plan which would in effect shelve the problem of German reunification. A German "Gaullist" (they do exist) could come to his defense and say that no other statesman, including German politicians, has ever been able to propose a plan more effective and easier to carry out than de Gaulle did. This is true, because the question of German unification is, under the present circumstances, a problem of squaring the circle. De Gaulle's plan is interesting for another reason. It was so unrealistic that the French pragmatist seemed to say no while he took great pains to spell out his complex yes.

His plan was as follows:

> What must be done will not be done, one day, except by the under-standing and combined action of the peoples who have always been, who are and who will remain principally concerned by the fate of the German neighbor—in short, the European peoples. . . . Certainly, the success of such a vast and difficult undertaking implies many conditions. Russia must evolve in such a way that it sees its future, not through totalitarian constraint imposed on its land and on others, but through progress accomplished in common by free men and peoples. The nations which it has satellized must be able to play their role in a renewed Europe. It must be recog-

nized, first of all by Germany, that any settlement of which it would be the subject would necessarily imply a settlement of its frontiers and of its armaments in agreement with all its neighbors, those on the East and those on the West. The six nations which, let us hope, are in the process of establishing the economic community of Western Europe, must succeed in organizing themselves in the political domain as well as in that of defense, in order to make a new equilibrium possible on the continent. Europe, the mother of modern Civilization, must establish herself from the Atlantic to the Urals in harmony and cooperation with a view to the development of her vast resources and so as to play, in conjunction with America, her daughter, the role which falls to her in progress of two billion men, who desperately need it. . . . Doubtless, these conditions appear very complex and these delays seem quite long. But, after all, the solution to a problem as vast as that of Germany can only have large dimensions and consequences. France, for her part, believes that this problem cannot be resolved except by Europe herself, because it is on the scale of the whole of Europe.[47]

De Gaulle is not a man to waste his time on scribbling down dreams of a utopia. But he was utopian in his speech. He must have been talking with a hardly repressed smile, amused by the practical joke he played at the expense of his former friends who had disappointed him so bitterly. His plan was not better than a practical joke. The restriction of the German problem to its European dimensions excluded the United States, the only power in the West stronger than Russia. He relegated the solution of that problem to a utopian future. Russia would have to become democratic and release its dominion over Eastern Europe. The "European" Western Europe must probably be built up under the protective French nuclear umbrella. The Big Europe would become a recovered paradise of nations loving and trusting each other. But Germany would remain a black sheep in this paradise. She could not be trusted. Her neighbors would have to force her to accept the present frontiers and would have to limit her armaments, certainly forbidding nuclear weapons. Only then could the two parts of Germany be reunited. It is not surprising that he admitted freely that the realization of his plan would involve "quite long" delays. In effect, he told the Germans: never, never! These words, gloomy for the Germans, were received with joy in Moscow. The Russians only asked why he was not logical and did not recognize the existence of the German Democratic Republic as a fact of international life.

It is reported that he disclosed his true feelings on the subject at a meeting of the Council of Ministers in 1958. A former member of his government, the Popular Republican Pierre Pflimlin, remarked: "We have no interest in zealously exerting ourselves on behalf of German unity." De Gaulle is said to have replied: "I am happy to hear you utter these words. I have been saying the same for the last thousand years."[48]

One of his ardent supporters writes: "Everyone knows that Paris does not wish to see the reunification of the two Germanies, and that there is no equivocation concerning our diplomatic attitude regarding the Oder-Neisse frontier."[49]

The French President refused to answer two questions at his press conference held on February 21, 1966: what his attitude toward the West German access to nuclear weapons was, and whether German re-unification would be in the French national interest. The indiscreet journalist could have answered them himself, because the views of General de Gaulle were not a secret to anyone familiar with the implications of his public statements. However, the General gave a vague answer to the question relating to German reunification by referring to his well-known conditions spelled out a year before: the formation of a European Little Europe which would become an equal partner of the United States and would eventually ensure an equilibrium between the Western and Eastern parts of Europe, and the restoration of amity and peace in the whole of Europe between the Atlantic and the Urals. He again relegated the problem of German reunification to an uncertain and remote future.[50]

He met Chancellor Erhard in the same month and promised to plead the cause of German unification in Moscow on the occasion of his official visit there in June. The Germans could hardly expect, after his press conference in February 1965, that he would strongly insist on the termination of the country's division. In any event, the German government did not authorize General de Gaulle to offer any concessions on its behalf in exchange for the Soviet assent to reunification. He himself could not offer Moscow anything more than he had already conceded (recognition of the Oder-Neisse frontier and his opposition to German access to nuclear arms). He could not fulfill the Soviet wish by agree-ing to a modification of the status of West Berlin or recognizing the German Democratic Republic. As a matter of fact, in March 1966 France joined the United States and Britain in opposing East Germany's request for admission to the United Nations.

5. The question of East German frontiers is another issue which divides France from Germany. This is the second most important prob-

lem in German minds. The official German position, upheld until last year, is well-known: Germany had the right to return, after reunification, to her frontiers as they had existed in 1937, i.e., prior to the Nazi annexations. This meant that Poland would have to relinquish the territories she had annexed after the last war and that the Soviet Union would have to restore the northeastern part of East Prussia it had annexed at the same time. Chancellor Erhard reaffirmed this official view as late as June 14, 1965.

This official stand immediately brought forth certain questions. Would a reunified Germany be happy with the 1937 frontiers fixed by the Treaty of Versailles, while the democratic Weimar Republic had denounced the same frontiers as an injustice done to Germany? Would she be ready to tolerate the reestablishment of the Polish "Corridor" and of the Free City of Danzig? Another moot aspect of that official view was the question of the Sudetenland. In 1937 it belonged to Czechoslovakia. However, the Germans claim that the three million Sudeten Germans who had been expelled after the last war and their descendants have the right to return and to self-determination. Does it imply that those expellees would have the right, after their return, to vote for the transfer of the Sudetenland to Germany?

For the time being, these questions are academic because Germany is divided, and the Democratic Republic of Germany has recognized the new *status quo*. Unofficially Germans have various views on the matter. Some accept the present boundary lines as final; others would revise them without claiming a pure and simple return to the ante bellum situation; still others sincerely adhere to the former official formula. The great majority feel that the nonrecognition of postwar territorial changes will be a bargaining asset in future negotiations for reunification. The German government could then partly or wholly relinquish its territorial claims in exchange for Soviet consent to unification. This is the reason for the Germans' adamant refusal to talk now about any definite concessions and for their insistence that the Western powers should not weaken their future negotiating stand by recognizing the new frontiers.

The former official stand of the Federal Republic regarding the eastern frontiers of a unified Germany has been replaced in 1965–66 by a more flexible attitude. This change coincides with the end of Adenauer's era and the beginning of a new epoch in the German thinking about the future. The former era was that of German rebirth from the ashes of total defeat. By the end of the last war Germany was occupied, divided into four zones by the victorious powers, and became for a few years only a subject of international politics without a voice of her own. The cold war split up the former Allies and provided Adenauer, one of the greatest of German Chancellors, with an unexpected opportunity for the reintegration of Western Germany into the international community. Machiavelli said that great statesmen are made by the opportunity which history offers and their own ability to take hold of that opportunity. Adenauer seized the opportunity offered by the cold war and ably integrated Western Germany into the Atlantic Alliance and the European Community. The Federal Germany again found an important place in the international community as one of its sovereign members. Western Germany became a prosperous nation thanks both to the German capacity for hard work and American assistance. Her democratic system and her growing political, economic, and military stature relegated the Nazi defeat to the pages of history. This gigantic task was accomplished during the Adenauer era. But Germans, nevertheless, were daily reminded of the past by the division of their country into two states, one of them a mere Soviet protectorate. This painful problem was skillfully pushed to the background by Adenauer for the sake of the urgent and immediate task of economic rehabilitation and development, and of gaining acceptance in the West as a trusted and equal partner.

Adenauer relinquished his Chancellorship at a time when his own goals for the Federal Republic were successfully reached. The appointment of Erhard marked the beginning of a new era. Nothing remained to conceal the existence of a major national aspiration: the reunification. This problem came to the forefront of German preoccupations. The division of the country contrasted with the regained feeling of self-confidence and power. None of the West German parties could any longer pay only lip service to the German right to self-determination and reunification. The debates which have been going on in this new era have uncovered the fact that the most burning German problem was unsolvable in the face of Soviet veto and the existence of nuclear stalemate. The Federal Republic alone is not strong enough to impose her will on the Soviet Union. Her Western allies are also helpless and may only pay lip service, not always sincere, to the German right to be free and united in one state.

The Germans also notice another paradox. Since 1956 the Eastern European countries have been regaining a large amount of domestic autonomy and have ceased to be mere Soviet satellites. The Soviet Union leaves them alone on two conditions: they must be governed by their respective Communist parties, and they are not allowed to depart from their solidarity with the Soviet foreign policy. Only one true satellite remains: the German Democratic Republic whose present regime would not survive the departure of Soviet divisions which are the only obstacle for East Germans in joining their Western country-men.

The Federal Republic, confronted with its major national problem, is unable to square the circle, to use de Gaulle's expression. Hence its politicians, publicists, and churches are desperately seeking a way out. This caused the West German government to adopt a more flexible attitude toward the problem of frontiers, as a sort of invitation to the Soviet Union to come to the negotiating table. The new stand consists of saying that the Federal Republic would begin talks regarding reunification by restating the legal right of a unified Germany to the 1937 frontiers. If the bargaining proved to be promising, territorial sacrifices could be made; they would be not only the price for the reunification but also the consequence of defeat. The scope of these sacrifices would be determined by the course of negotiations.

So far this more flexible stand has not evoked any encouraging answer from Moscow.

Insofar as one may know, the Western powers do not have any hopes that the postwar frontiers could be modified, but they agree officially not to challenge the German position. Neither the United States nor Britain has recognized the validity of Polish and Soviet annexations. The only Western country to do so is France, a strange decision for a country which desires the closest cooperation with the Federal Republic. A government that wants to be allied to another state usually espouses its quarrels. Reciprocity is the heart of international relations. De Gaulle is not, as we have seen more than once, logical in his policies. The Federal Republic should support all his policies, but on March 25, 1959, he publicly discarded one of its fundamental claims:

> The reunification of the two parts now separated into one Germany which would be entirely free seems to us a normal goal and a no less normal destiny of the German people, provided the Germans do not re-open the question of their present frontiers in the North, the South, the East and the West, and that they accept to integrate themselves, on the day when it will be possible, within a contractual organization for the cooperation of the whole Europe in freedom.[51]

His reference to the Eastern frontiers was as clear as possible. His use of the term "frontiers," not "the Oder-Neisse demarcation line," implied French recognition. The Prime Minister then, Michel Debré, was even more precise on October 13, 1959: "The maintenance of the *status quo* is in our view the very condition of an understanding with Russia; we include in this *status quo* the status of Berlin, the present regime of federal Germany as well as . . . respect for the existing frontiers, of all frontiers, including the one which is usually called the Oder-Neisse line."[52]

The close and confident cooperation of the Federal Republic and France is in itself the problem of squaring the circle. The divergence in their views is profound and involves the most vital interests of both countries. This divergence relates to their policies regarding third states. Fortunately they have no direct quarrels. Both recognize their present frontiers as final, and neither has any ambition which could be realized only at the expense of the other party. What will remain, in any case, of the efforts of the Fourth and Fifth Republics is the burying for good of the old hatchet of mutual hostility. The two countries have every prospect of remaining good neighbors; but good neighbors do not necessarily agree on their policies toward other states.

The old distrust

Assuming for the sake of the argument that Germany would again become aggressive, one knows de Gaulle's view. He does not make a secret of what his policy would then be. He said on March 25, 1959: "If the present Germany seemed dangerous to us, then no doubt the memory of trials suffered because of her actions and the desire to prevent their recurrence would incline us to make our demands."[53] In April 1960, at the time of his official visit to the United States he told American journalists where he would look for friends if Germany again threatened France: "As long as there was the threat of domination in Europe, in the center of Europe, France and Russia quite naturally established closer mutual ties, and they were allied in the perilous times."[54] He added immediately: "At the present time there is no threat in the center of Europe. Germany, as she is now, does not threaten anyone."

There is no longer any hostility between the two peoples, but the old distrusts are slow in dying out. Michel Debré writes:

> Yes, memories of war and occupation are with us. They bring back the image of our dead friends, the echo of horrible tragedies, remembrance of the time when the dignity of citizens was measured by the intensity of their hatred of Germans. . . . Yes, the German conquering, racist and anti-French Grand Design might one day reappear. But political action is not determined exclusively by recollections and apprehensions.[55]

There are Frenchmen who even doubt whether the reconciliation is irreversible: "It would be premature to believe that the past has been buried. Governments ready to recall it might come to power. . . . Nationalist trends remain powerful in the world. Why should they bypass France and Germany?"[56] It is more probable, however, that the French-German reconciliation is final. François Mitterand expressed the view of a great majority of Frenchmen when he said that "French-German reconciliation is an obvious international necessity." Reconciliation does not, of course, imply identical views. To take one example, Mitterand, during his candidacy for the Presidency, offered his unreserved support for de Gaulle's stand on the German Eastern frontiers. In September 1965 he said:

> To raise this problem [of the Oder-Neisse line], regarding which General de Gaulle long ago defined his position, would amount to questioning the existing equilibrium of the world and creating a new cause for upheavals. Wisdom consists in upholding what exists. The reopening of this problem would preclude any chance of solving the German question by an agreement between the East and the West and of ensuring the peace Germany needs.[57]

German or French Rapallo?

A good number of Frenchmen, fond of historical analogies, are afraid that Western Germany, if disappointed in her cooperation with the Western nations, might turn toward the Soviet Union and conclude another Rapallo agreement. Their imagination depicts the somber image of a Russian-German alliance. Guy Mollet's statement made in 1959 (reproduced in his book published in 1962) is characteristic in this respect:

> If Western Germany were abandoned by us and if she saw that the efforts of German democrats, of all German democrats without exception, to be associated with the West and to be European, have produced no results, why should she not renew tomorrow the tragic German-Soviet alliance?[58]

An Australian author gives him a common-sense answer: "The oft-paraded spectre of the 'new Rapallo' is really no more than a spectre in this period: it is not a feasible alternative policy."[59]

This historical analogy is, indeed, a specter and, like most historical analogies, it only misleads, if taken for guidance in current international politics. The relations between West Germany and the Soviet Union do not in any way resemble the former relations between the two countries. If one glances at the pages of the history of cooperation between Russia and Germany (in the seventeenth century it was Brandenburg, in the eighteenth and several decades of the nineteenth century it was Prussia), one discovers that both countries were of comparable strength and both could easily find a platform of understanding in dividing the spoils in Central and Eastern Europe or in jointly protecting their acquisitions in that part of the Continent. The partitions of Poland provide one illustration, the Russian-Prussian understanding after the Congress of Vienna another. After the First World War, Germany was defeated and Russia greatly weakened both by that war and the consequences of the October Revolution. The Rapallo agreement, followed by the German-Soviet military cooperation, was an agreement between the two powers seeking to regain their former status. The Nazi-Soviet pact of August 23, 1939, was founded on the division of spoils in Eastern Europe.

Today the Soviet Union is one of the two Super-Powers. Its nuclear might stands guard on the frontiers of the Soviet zone of influence which reaches out into the center of Germany. Germany is divided into two states, one of them a Russian protectorate. Furthermore, there is no business to transact between the Federal Republic, which could ask only for unilateral concessions, and Russia, which would have to make them for the sake of a new Rapallo.

It suffices to look at the problem from the Soviet point of view. Let us assume that the West German government would propose to Moscow to exchange the reunification of Germany for the neutrality of a unified but democratic Germany. The Soviet Union would have to retreat from its foremost frontier on the Elbe and allow a powerful Germany to become its Western neighbor. This Germany, the first power on the Continent, could not be forever compelled to refrain from nuclear armaments or to follow Soviet wishes in her foreign policy. Her people, especially those who now live in Eastern Germany, would probably not tolerate the existence of the frontier on the Oder-Neisse for long. The German government would have to ask Russia for a second pledge of friendship: retreat from the Oder and possibly the restoration of all the lands Poland and Russia annexed after the last war. If the Russians retreated from their present second frontier on the Oder (this is as much the Soviet as the Polish boundary), could they be sure that Germany, now an equal power, would not remind them of the former situation in which the two states divided Eastern Europe into their respective zones of influence? The last Soviet retreat could well be to their national frontiers. One cannot see why the Soviet leaders would be unable to make this analysis and for no compelling reason accept a new Rapallo which this time would amount to the ruin of their influence in Europe. On top of everything, gratitude is an unknown virtue in international politics. A powerful Germany probably would, like the Weimar Republic, practice the game of balance between the West and Russia, without fully committing herself to either.

Anyone who reads the Soviet press cannot have the slightest doubt that the German question is the Soviet Union's number one problem. The Communist domestic propaganda does not allow the Russians to forget for a moment the enormous human and material losses which Nazi Germany inflicted on their country. It seems that the Soviet leaders, be they Khrushchev or his successors, have a genuine fear of another resurgence of a powerful Germany. They miss no opportunity for reaffirming their stand, which amounts to an adamant veto of the reunification of the Germanies and of any alteration of present frontiers in Central Europe. It suffices to read the pertinent part of report of the Central Committee, which its Secretary General, L. I. Brezhnev, submitted to the Twenty-third Congress of the Soviet Communist Party in March of 1966, and the speech of A. A. Gromyko, Soviet Foreign Minister, to grasp the importance of the German question in the thinking of the Soviet government.

The image which Brezhnev painted of the Federal Republic was that of an enemy. He said: "The politicians on the bank of the Rhine dream that they might take hold of atomic bombs, overthrow the frontier posts, and thus realize their cherished aspiration: to change the map of Europe and take revenge for the defeat in the Second World War."[60] He sounded very much like de Gaulle in February 1965 when he recalled that "German aggression, twice in half a century, was unleashed on many European nations." He hastened to welcome the new trend in French policy: "Our relations with France have been significantly improved. This is a positive phenomenon which corresponds to the coincidence of interests of both states regarding several important international problems and to the old tradition of friendship between our two nations. A further evolution in the Soviet-French relations may become a weighty factor in strengthening European security."

Minister Gromyko, who covered a whole gamut of external problems in his speech at the same Congress, insisted on the vital importance of Europe: "There, westward of the frontiers of the Soviet Union and of our friends and allies, only a narrow strip of land separates the armed forces of NATO from those of the Organization of Warsaw Pact. There, in Europe, a state is located which has adopted for the motto of its foreign policy revenge for the defeat in the last war. . . . The German question is one of the most important elements of European security; or, to speak more exactly, European security depends on the creation of such a situation in which the repetition of German aggression would be precluded for ever."[61] Then he went on to remind his audience of the Brest-Litovsk Peace Treaty which Germany and her allies had imposed on a weak and defeated Bolshevik Russia, and of the horrors of the last war. His conclusion was a reiteration of the usual Soviet stand:

> The Soviet Union and our allies will never resign ourselves to accepting plans for the access of the Federal Republic of Germany to nuclear weapons. . . . We do not like the advice that we should make minor concessions to the revengers in order to avoid a situation where they would end by making greater demands. The Soviet Union, our friends and allies, and, we believe, all other states that suffered from Hitlerite aggression will not base their security on the satisfaction or dissatisfaction with the existing situation on the part of those West-German forces which want to revise the results of the Second World War. . . . Not one of the frontier posts on European soil needs the blessing of those who do not like the results of the last war. . . . The state frontiers of our friends and allies are as solidly guaranteed as our own frontiers.

As the most advanced Soviet boundary lies in effect on the river Elbe, Gromyko proclaimed the Democratic Republic of Germany "a powerful bastion of peace."

This stand leaves no room for any useful Soviet-German negotiation regarding reunification but might represent a link between the USSR and de Gaulle's France. He is not eager to see the two German states reunited either and is equally opposed to the German access to nuclear weapons. The other link is the same animosity toward the preponderant American influence in Europe. De Gaulle's image of a "European" Europe perfectly fits the Soviet interests, but would de Gaulle feel satisfied if the United States withdrew and left that "European" Europe face to face with the whole might of Soviet Russia? He himself gave the answer in the talks he held in Moscow in June 1966. He bluntly told the Soviet leaders that their country's presence was useful in precluding the American hegemony in Europe, but that American presence was equally necessary to prevent the Soviet hegemony. This was his first admission that the United States played, after all, a role beneficial to Europe.

The Soviet interest in the preservation of the *status quo* in Central Europe, including the existence of two German states, may be even better understood by figuring out an improbable hypothesis of a Germany reunified but under a Communist regime. Would this serve Russian national interests? Germany would be the most powerful European state west of Soviet frontiers. She could not be held for long under the Soviet protectorate. The quick growth of polycentrism within the Communist movement and especially the Sino-Soviet split prove that every Communist country, if favored by international circumstances, places its national interests above the so-called "proletarian internationalism." Probably a Communist but unified and powerful Germany would display the same attitude and come to espouse the territorial claims now voiced by the Federal Republic. Eventually the Soviet Union would find herself surrounded by two inimical Communist powers, Germany and China, attracted to each other by their animosity toward Russia. This prospect may hardly appeal to the Soviet leaders who might feel happier with the present *status quo* rather than with the image of a unified though Communist Germany. This argument *ad absurdum* tends to demonstrate that Soviet Russia has become a *status quo* power in Europe, if by this qualification one means a power that would not be regretful if the *status quo* were to be frozen forever. But it does not mean that such a power has a flabby foreign policy or would not try to enlarge its zone of influence in other areas of the world on the contemporary condition that this extension of influence would not be fraught with the risk of nuclear conflagration. By contrast, a power is "revisionist" if it would be depressed by the prospect of petrification of the *status quo*. This is the case of Communist China and would probably be the case of a unified though Communist Germany.

The argument sometimes heard that Russia would have to retreat in Europe because of the Chinese threat is naive. China is not a nuclear peer of Russia despite her first steps in the atomic armaments. For a long time to come she could not envisage a nuclear duel with either Russia or the United States. An armed aggression against the Soviet Union would be an invitation to be not only vanquished but badly mutilated. If one were to look toward a hazy and remote future, he could see other aspects of the Russian-Chinese problem. Like the Japanese in the forties, the Chinese would have two alternative prospects of expansion: toward the Russian Asian territory or toward Southeast Asia with its rice, raw materials, the sixteen million Chinese settlers and weak national structures to oppose their imperialism. By that time, China, assuming that she would be a first-class nuclear power, would probably learn what is known to the United States and Russia— that strategic nuclear weapons afford protection but should not be used for fear of a disastrous retaliation.

China represents, for the time being, a political threat to the Soviet

Union, the threat of splitting up the Communist movement and thus partly blunting one of the tools of Soviet foreign policy. The West cannot help in any way in this competition with China; it can only make it more difficult for the Soviet Union by its own actions in the underdeveloped countries. Vietnam is an illustration. The United States has unintentionally compelled Russia to try to outbid China or to face loss of prestige among the Communists and radical nationalists in Asia, Africa, and Latin America.

If China were ever to become an adversary of stature for her two opponents, the maritime (the United States) and the continental (Russia), the two opponents could come to an agreement in the Far East. Neither would have to pay a price in Europe for that agreement, the coincidence of their interests in the Far East being in itself a sufficient justification for an understanding. If that agreement has not yet been reached, the reason is the ideological, not only national, motivation of Soviet foreign policy.

The German-Soviet Rapallo is a ghost which should not haunt the Western chancelleries. But a German in a pessimistic mood could very well imagine a French-Russian Rapallo at German expense. General de Gaulle said in 1960 in Washington: "It is true that at no time has there been any opposition between the French and Russian peoples. There is no conflict of political interests between France and Russia."[62] This would be completely true if the Soviet Union accepted the present *status quo* in Europe as final, which she possibly does.

Probably the French-Soviet Rapallo is also an academic hypothesis. De Gaulle has said many times that the Atlantic Alliance was a necessity for France; he does not yet trust the Soviet intentions. Moreover, his freedom of movement is restricted not only by the joint participation with West Germany in that Alliance but also by the French membership in the Common Market. France can hardly enter into an anti-German understanding with Russia. Moreover, she has no quarrels with Germany, except regarding the "European" or Atlantic Western Europe.

The threat made in the summer of 1965 by the extremist Gaullists that France, if faced with the prospect of failure of the Common Market and of an understanding between the Five and the EFTA, would withdraw from the Atlantic Alliance, should not be taken too seriously. The present French-Soviet flirtation is probably no more than a way of frightening the Germans and compelling them to be more amenable to French wishes.

In any event, the temperature in French-German relations has significantly fallen since 1962. When de Gaulle went to Germany in June

1965 there were no enthusiastic crowds to meet him. The German press, both Christian Democratic and Socialist, was cool. He was no longer a hero. He, who had appeared in 1962 as the most reliable ally regarding Russia, came back this time after having made several friendly gestures toward the Soviet Union. If the Germans had any hopes in 1962 that they would be associated with the French nuclear effort, they knew better in 1965. De Gaulle even opposed their participation in the MLF, joining in this respect the Soviet Union. The German press reminded him of his recognition of the Oder-Neisse frontier. One of the German newspapers told him: "Yes, for an independent Europe, but never a *Gross-Frankreich* with Western Germany as its province." Another newspaper said: "The Federal Republic neither wants nor may be a 'junior' partner of France. . . . France could be the first among the peers, but neither more nor less."

Chancellor Erhard honestly told the French President at the official dinner: "Our positions are somewhat different, and our conversation of today has shown that a number of differences exist between our conceptions."[63] At his press conference on May 15, 1965, he referred to one of these differences of views:

> Any formula for German reunification like the Europeanization plan, which could produce the impression abroad that one turns away from the United States, is bad. . . . The essential difference between Germany and France consists in their respective attitudes toward the integration of defense. We have always been for it.[64]

Speaking in 1965 on the radio on the anniversary of the German surrender, Adenauer's successor implicitly rejected for his country a role as second fiddler to France or anyone else:

> Germany cannot be relegated to a political no man's land and to the inferior rank of a country without history. She has not foregone the right to play her part in world politics and will continue to help actively in shaping world history.[65]

De Gaulle's national pride was met with German pride.

Warmer relations with Russia and Eastern Europe

Frustrated in Germany, the French President began to look toward Moscow. Was it phantasmagoria or a move to appease the German apprehensions, when de Gaulle tried to persuade Chancellor Erhard in February 1965 that the only realistic approach to the problem of German reunification was to inspire confidence in Moscow regarding the future intentions of a united Western Europe? He assured the

Chancellor that only France among all Western Powers was able to achieve an improvement in the relations with the Soviet Union, because no hatred divided Frenchmen from Russians and no fundamental difference of interests separated them from each other. He depicted France as the future honest broker between Germany and Russia, but added that his efforts in this direction would be frustrated if Germany participated in the MLF and thus increased the Soviet suspicions.[66] It is impossible to say whether he was really so optimistic or was reassuring the Chancellor in order to slow down his drifting toward the United States.

What was certainly true in his position was the fact that France was at that time the only Western power in favor with the Moscow press but this was precisely because of the deterioration in the French-German relations. The worsening in relations between the United States and the Soviet Union, due mainly to the situation in Vietnam and to the MLF project, postponed the prospect of mutual understanding to an unknown future. Moscow no longer considered Britain an honest broker between the two Super-Powers because of her support of American policy in Vietnam in exchange for the American support for the British stand in the conflict between Malaysia and Indonesia and for the American protection of British interests east of Suez. In contrast, the Soviet-French relations have been steadily improving for various reasons. One of them was the French disappointment in Germany. Another was de Gaulle's withdrawal from NATO; he was the only Western statesman willing to weaken the bonds of the Atlantic Alliance. Finally, the French and Soviet points of view coincided on several other matters: Vietnam, Cuba, the Dominican Republic, Congo, the MLF, and general criticism of American policies in the Third World. De Gaulle's strictures against the two hegemonies were liked rather than resented in Moscow. The fact that they made a good impression in Peking was of no importance, because France, not being a Communist power, could not affect the relations between Russia and China. The Russians singled out the anti-American aspect of those diatribes for the good reason that France was a member of the Atlantic Alliance but not of the Warsaw Pact.

General de Gaulle's concept of Big Europe had everything to commend to Russia. Unlike some Frenchmen, for whom Western civilization stops somewhere on the East German borders and on the Italian-Yugoslav frontiers, de Gaulle is too intelligent to negate the fact that there is only one civilization in the whole of Europe. He shares with most of his countrymen a vague nostalgia for the French-Russian friendship in spite of all former disappointments. If the German threat were ever to reappear, the return to the former alliance would be his remedy. He would then repeat what he said on May 7, 1944:

> Once the enemy is chased away, Frenchmen will want to become a center of practical and direct Western cooperation and a permanent ally of the East, that is to say, in the first place, of our dear and powerful Russia.[67]

The evolution of international events wanted otherwise. France became an ally of the United States, but de Gaulle is right in saying that no direct conflict of interests separates his country from "dear Russia." He told Stalin on December 8, 1944: "There are no conflicts in the direct relations between France and the Soviet Union. We have always had and will have them in our relations with Britain."[68] Today he would tell Stalin's successors exactly the same, except that he would substitute the United States for Britain. Sixteen years later, while officially visiting the United States in his capacity as the President of the French Republic, he reassured the Russians by saying: "No feeling of rivalry or animosity animates France in relation to the Russian people. On the contrary, she has a feeling of true and traditional friendship for them."[69] He spoke for all Frenchmen. However, a great portion of them would repeat his kind words with a reservation. They like Russia, but dislike her present regime. He has no sympathy for the Soviet ideology either, but considers that ideology a passing episode in the long Russian history. The only lasting reality for him is the Russian nation, whose interests have often coincided with the French and might coincide again.

Nevertheless, he was rather passive in his relations with Moscow during the first years of his Presidency. Those years, 1958 to 1963, were entirely devoted to the cultivation of good relations with West Germany. He was denounced in Moscow as an accomplice of the German "militarists and avengers." His firm position regarding the status of West Berlin and East Germany caused him to be out of Soviet favor more than most Western statesmen were. It was also the time when Khrushchev was making a valiant effort to come to an understanding with the United States in the hopes of mutual recognition of the finality of the *status quo* in Europe, including implicit American recognition of the existence of the Democrat Republic of Germany and of West Berlin as a free city separate from West Germany. He was ready for the sake of that understanding to suffer defeat at the hands of the Chinese in competition for the leadership among the Communists and radical nationalists in the underdeveloped continents. With his eyes fixed on Washington Khrushchev had time for considering only the British in their role of honest brokers between his country and America. He paid little attention to Paris, believing that de Gaulle was too deeply committed to the German policy.

If de Gaulle had wanted to improve French-Soviet relations at that time, he would have found a response in Moscow only on the condition that he abandon French friendship with Germany, which he would not do. After Khrushchev's "ultimatum" to the United States, Britain, and France in November 1958, asking for a modification of the status of West Berlin within six months, the French government imperturbably replied that it "was not willing to negotiate under the threat of an ultimatum."[70] De Gaulle was right in refusing to respond to Khrushchev's threats. Later developments demonstrated that Washington and London should not have taken the Soviet demands too seriously. Paradoxically, the French President, who was publicly doubtful regarding the validity of the American guaranty, must have thought that the Soviet government would not risk creating a more explosive situation either in West Berlin or on the roads of access to that city for fear of the American reaction. His stand was the closest to the West German.

He told the Russians on September 5, 1961: "Let the Soviets stop issuing threats. Let them help in reducing the tension instead of hindering the relaxation. . . . Then it will be possible for the three Western Powers to study with them all the problems of the world and, in particular, that of Germany."[71]

While the American and British press was racking its brains to find a new formula for the West Berlin regime, including the project of placing it under the United Nations protection, France retained her composure. By the same token, de Gaulle appeared to the Soviet government as the most difficult Western customer and to the Germans as their best friend.

As late as on October 29, 1963, while relations with Germany were already deteriorating, Foreign Minister Maurice Couve de Murville was still stiff in talking about the relations with Moscow:

> Now, detente happens to be a magic word for the Western peoples. Voicing it is enough for the immediate awakening of hopes and for the immediate display of eager intentions to negotiate. . . . Today's world is so made that the Soviet Union commands the situation. She is responsible for the cold war. She is also capable, and she alone is capable, of putting an end to it. Should she show the least sign in favor of detente, the entire world trembles with hope and declares itself eager to talk. . . . For the dialogue to become not only possible, but also useful, we think that a real

transformation is needed in the Soviet Union and its policy. Let this transformation appear, then all doors will be opened.[72]

Soon after, the President of the French Republic did not wait for a real transformation in the Soviet Union and in its policy to inaugurate his own new policy. He was pushed toward Moscow by his disappointment in West Germany.

Even earlier, at the time of cool French-Soviet relations, he did not abandon his vision of Big Europe including hopes for a Russian conversion, in a remote future, to a policy of improving relations with the West. These hopes were founded on the alleged Soviet fear of China. He told his press conference on November 10, 1959:

> Doubtless, Soviet Russia, although having helped Communism to become established in China, realizes that nothing can change the fact that she is herself Russia, a white European nation which had conquered part of Asia and that she is very well endowed with land, mines, factories and other wealth, while she is confronted with the yellow multitude which is China, numberless and wretchedly poor, indestructible and ambitious, building by dint of sacrifices a power which cannot be measured in advance and looking around at the expanses over which she must one day spread.[73]

According to him Russia was threatened by the hungry and rapacious China. His reference to the white race reminded one of William II's yellow peril. He was suggesting that the white Europeans, including the Russians, would have to unite to stem the aggressive outflow of yellow multitudes.

Of course, de Gaulle is not a Herodotus, a Hegel, a Karl Marx, or even an Arnold Toynbee, and is not obliged to be consistent in his philosophy of history. His grandiose views of the world change rather rapidly, depending on the requirements of his foreign policy. In 1959 China was a menacing, innumerable, miserable, and ambitious yellow multitude threatening the white race. In 1964, when diplomatic relations were established with the Communist government, his view of China was radically different:

> Who knows whether the affinities which manifestly exist between the two nations [France and China] with regard to intellectual matters, taking into account their mutual and deep sympathy and respect, will not lead them to a growing cultural cooperation? This is, in any case, sincerely hoped for here.[74]

The yellow multitude suddenly became culturally a sister-nation. In any event, Moscow did not resent the French recognition of the Peking government and even approved of it.

The Soviet government began to believe that perhaps some useful business might be done with France after de Gaulle's press conference of February 4, 1965. The French President's stand coincided almost completely with the Soviet. The problem of German reunification was a purely European question, dependent both on the conclusion of agreements concerning the recognition of present German Eastern borders, and on the limitation of German armaments. The only major divergence of views was the French refusal to recognize the Democratic Republic of Germany and to agree to any modifications in the status of West Berlin. Moscow probably hoped that, if French-German relations were to deteriorate further, the French President might come around and concede on these two points. What most interested Russia in de Gaulle's plan for German reunification was its unrealistic aspect. The Soviet Union did not wish anything more than to postpone the problem *ad calendas Graecas,* as de Gaulle suggested. *Le Monde* correctly described the Soviet reactions:

> At the same time [while the new Soviet Prime Minister A. Kosygin refused to pay a visit to Bonn promised by his predecessor], General de Gaulle's France initiates closer relations with the Kremlin. It is clear as daylight that the Soviets hope this French policy will lead toward the coordination of policies of both countries regarding Germany.[75]

The same commentator proved that he understood what was the main Soviet preoccupation:

> Since Yalta the preservation of this bastion [in Eastern and Central Europe] has been the primary objective of the Soviet Union. The Prague coup, the breach with Tito, the frantic purges in the people's democracies, the repeated attempts to obtain the recognition of the Oder-Neisse Line and of the Democratic Republic of Germany, the Geneva "summit" conference in 1955 and the intervention in 1956 in Hungary had no other purpose. Likewise, the incessant campaigns against Bonn, its "militarists" and its "avengers," can be, to a large extent, explained by the desire to prevent the reestablishment and rehabilitation of the only continental power who would have a true interest in, and, at the same time, a moral justification for questioning the *status quo,* and also a certain, at least potential, means of pressure to achieve a change in the *status quo.*[76]

Prime Minister Kosygin approved of the views which General de Gaulle expressed at his press conference of February 4, 1965. Talking to the French journalists in East Berlin he said:

> We agree with the views which General de Gaulle publicly expressed, in particular with his opinion that the German problem is a European problem. It should be resolved politically, not by military means. The question of frontiers must not be raised, because no one has ever seen the cession of a square inch of territory without war. . . . The *status quo* in Germany is, for the time being, satisfactory for us. Above all, it should not be modified.[77]

This is almost exactly what de Gaulle said.

Soviet Foreign Minister Gromyko, who visited Paris in May 1965, also noted that "the French and Soviet points of view coincided regarding the intangibility of frontiers and the prohibition of nuclear weapons for the Federal Republic."[78] In his conversations with the French government he failed only to obtain a revision of French policy regarding the nonrecognition of the German Democratic Republic. But he and his government could find a large consolation in discovering "a power at the other end of the Continent which publicly proclaims its intention to shake off the hegemony of the United States in Europe, in Asia, and even in South America."[79]

In 1964–65 the Germans were increasingly suspicious of ultimate French intentions. They noted the role of French firms as intermediaries in negotiations between American enterprises and Eastern Germany for the construction of a plant which would manufacture synthetic textiles, as well as the conclusion of a commercial agreement in January 1965 between France and the German Democratic Republic. They also reproached France for her occupation of first place among the Western nations at the Leipzig Fair. The French explanations did not appease the German suspicions. The French Embassy in Bonn declared that trade between France and the German Democratic Republic had been going on since 1956, that the total value of that trade had amounted in 1964 to only 12.5 million dollars, that the new commercial agreement would increase it to barely 22 million dollars, the equivalence of 0.25 per cent of the total external trade of France, and that in commerce with East Germany France occupied fifth place in imports (following Sweden, Austria, Britain, and Denmark) and seventh in exports (after Holland, Britain, Austria, Belgium, Sweden, and Denmark).[80] It was to no avail; France was no longer trusted in Bonn, where it was feared that her policy might eventually lead her to recognize the Democratic Republic of Germany.

At the same time, the Soviet Union manifested its new friendly feelings in selecting one of the top Soviet diplomats as its ambassador to Paris, the highest ranking party member to be the ambassador in any capital. Member of the Central Committee and first Vice Minister for Foreign Affairs until his appointment, Mr. Valerii Zorin was sent to Paris as the messenger bringing glad tidings from the Soviets. There was no other apparent reason for recalling his predecessor, Sergei Vinogradov, who had proved to be one of the most skillful ambassadors to Paris. Vinogradov had attached little importance to the public opinion polls which purported to show a very small percentage of Frenchmen believing in the possibility of the return to power of the old statesman who was brooding in retirement at Colombey-les-Deux-Eglises, and he had assiduously cultivated personal relations with the General. De Gaulle repaid him in kind after he had become President of the Republic. Vinogradov worked patiently, undeterred by the bad relations between his country and France. He was recalled at the moment of his diplomatic triumph; his successor was to gather the fruits of his labors.

Valerii Zorin could start his work from well-laid foundations: the low point of French-German relations, and the similarity of governments' views on many international problems, views which the United States radically opposed. He began to use the new Soviet propaganda slogan which proclaimed France and the Soviet Union as the only two great powers on the Continent. Raising France to the level of one of the Super-Powers certainly pleased General de Gaulle. The new ambassador was very optimistic in the lecture he gave in Paris on June 22, 1965:

> The Soviet Union and France, the great continental European powers, are called upon by their very location to play an important role in guaranteeing European security. The improvement in the French-Soviet relations is a natural process, I should venture to say, an unavoidable historical process.[81]

His French counterpart in Moscow, Ambassador Philippe Baudet, replied in no less warm words. Speaking at the opening of an exhibit of French paintings, he told the Soviet audience that the opening was taking place "at a time, which perhaps marks a date in history, when our relations begin to become lively again, and the expectation of a many-sided understanding points, more clearly than ever since the last war, to future close relations."[82] The French ambassador had a talk with his President two days before making this statement.

The amelioration in the relations with Russia could have given France the role of honest broker, traditionally played by Britain. The cool relations with Washington made this prospect rather unrealistic. Moreover, de Gaulle said many times that he feared a bilateral Soviet-American understanding; this would preclude his acting as an intermediary.

One of the symptoms of a new turn in French relations with the Soviet Union was the increase in mutual trade. On October 30, 1964 the two countries signed a new agreement for the regulation of their commerce from 1965 to 1969. It was planned that French exports during these five years should reach the value of 845 million dollars, while imports from the Soviet Union should amount to 712 million dollars. The annual increase was to be well over twice the former value of exchanges during the five years previous. The Soviet Union obligated itself either to pay half of the value of French imports in cash or to obtain French five-year credits. The other half was to be financed by French credits extending over seven years. This was another jab at the United States and West Germany, which had both tried to limit Western credits to the Communist countries to a maximum of five years. The main item of Soviet exports to France was to be oil; the French annual purchases were to increase from between the former 550,000 and 750,000 tons to 1,825,000 tons. These amounts would still be small by comparison to total French oil imports, which amounted to 43 million tons in 1963, including 16.4 million tons from Algeria. Finally, France took the obligation to supply Russia with wheat in case she needed it.

After the outbreak of the Common Market crisis with its menace to French agriculture, the Soviet Union concluded a contract in July 1965 for the purchase of 3 million quintals of wheat to be paid for in cash. Poland bought the same amount. Six million quintals were taken from the French surpluses. Of course, it was not much, if one knows that the total of those surpluses was expected to amount to 45 million quintals in 1965. The price offered by the two Communist countries was higher than France initially hoped for.

Another symptom of better relations was the signature on March 22, 1965, of a French-Soviet agreement on the joint exploitation of the French system of colored television. France won the competition in Eastern Europe against the American and German systems. The Soviet decision was probably dictated by political rather than technical considerations, but the net result was that Europe would not have a uniform system of colored television. In the summer of 1965 the two countries used the Soviet communication satellite *Molnya 1* for the experimental transmission of colored television.

In spite of the many symptoms of a thaw in French-Soviet relations, the French government was not yet ready to completely trust the Soviet intentions. Prime Minister Pompidou declared on June 18, 1965, during a great debate on foreign policy in the National Assembly, that "the Atlantic Alliance was conceived as an answer to a precise and clearly defined danger. As long as this danger does not disappear completely, the Alliance will remain necessary."[83] This *caveat* did not stop the Communist deputy, François Billoux, from paying a tribute to the official foreign policy in the usual Communist jargon: "Your policy is founded on the interests of monopolistic capitalism. . . . Although we never lose sight of this fundamental fact, nothing prevents us from taking note of realistic decisions which you sometimes happen to make."[84] The improvement in relations with the Soviet Union did not encounter reservations of principle in the opposition parties, but the Communist party was pleased the most, while persisting in its denunciation of domestic policies of the President of the Republic.

The French policy toward Eastern Europe develops along parallel lines with the American and British. All three governments want to improve their relations with the European Communist capitals, except for East Berlin. All three have the same hopes that the national self-assertion by the Eastern European governments might end in a sort of peaceful liquidation of the Soviet zone of influence. The future will tell whether these hopes do not overlook the fact that no great power sits with folded arms while its zone of influence disintegrates. Russia proved in November 1956 that there was a limit to her toleration of the emancipation of her vassal states, as the United States proved in 1965 by its intervention in the Dominican Republic.

It is undeniable that the trend toward greater autonomy, which began in 1956 in Poland, has been growing in importance and has possibly reached its maximum expression in the bold Rumanian policy. The Rumanians did not quit the Warsaw Pact, but rejected the Soviet plan for the economic integration of Eastern Europe which assigned them the modest role of producing agricultural products and oil. They have been looking toward the West for assistance in carrying out their industrialization plan, and have assumed a neutral position in the Peking-Moscow conflict. The question of what is the limit of Soviet forbearance remains unanswered. They told Eastern Europe in 1956 that the maximum limit of their patience was for their allies to stay in the Warsaw Pact and to keep the Communist party in power; the Hungarians transgressed this limit and brought Soviet military intervention on their heads.

In any event, the French government is careful to tell the Russians that its endeavors to ameliorate French relations with Eastern Europe are not directed against the Soviet Union but, on the contrary, are an integral part of the improvement in relations with the main Communist power. France has certain assets in that policy. Her cultural influence was dominant prior to the last war in almost all Eastern European countries. At that time France was an ally of Poland, Czechoslovakia, Yugoslavia and Rumania. No Communist government fears France, and all of them welcome the new course of French policy toward West Germany. The cultural exchanges between France and the Soviet Union as well as Eastern Europe are reviving old contacts which have not been forgotten. The French Ministers and deputies travel to Eastern European capitals, and the high dignitaries of Communist governments repay these visits. The agreements for mutual trade and for cultural cooperation have been concluded. The warm reception given to official and nonofficial French representatives is not limited to the governments; the people, who do not feel happy under the Soviet protectorate, are glad to renew contacts with a Western power which is not suspected of evil intentions either by the local Communist parties or by Moscow. France has the merit of helping to build bridges toward Communist Europe, a venture which is easier for her than for the United States and even Britain.

The Soviet attitude toward the Fifth Republic was defined in the clearest manner in an article *Pravda* published following de Gaulle's press conference of February 4, 1965. It is worthwhile to cite long excerpts from this Soviet comment, because it shows which French attitudes please Russia and on which points there remain divergent views. *Pravda* stated:

> The straightforward and realistic manner of formulating the most important matters, such as the fate of the United Nations, the tidying up of currency accounts, European security and the related German question, pleases an objective observer. . . . The President of France rightly remarked that the Charter, which had been calculated to ensure the balance of power between, and the security of, the United Nations, was grossly violated in 1950 when the General Assembly (under the pressure of the USA), ignoring the prerogatives of the Security Council, appropriated for itself the right to decide the question of the use of force and consequently transformed itself immediately into the field of "verbal battles." . . .
>
> The Soviet society entirely shares the French President's view that "the serious changes, which have taken place in the United Nations following those violations of legality, have indeed undermined its unity, prestige and functioning. . . ."

The French President equally realistically treated the problem of international currency accounts which had ripened a long time ago. He rightly pointed out that the system established as far back as 1922 which had bestowed on the dollar and the pound sterling the privilege of being considered equivalents of gold in external inter-state trade has become obsolete. . . . Not one man of common sense may disagree with de Gaulle's thesis that "it is difficult to imagine that there might be any other standard but gold. . . ."

How may one deny that European problems are, first of all, the concern of Europeans? . . . The French President was absolutely right when he declared that any solution of the German problem must include the settlement of the questions of German frontiers and German armaments through the agreement of all neighbors of the former Hitlerite Reich, both Eastern and Western neighbors. . . . Any solution of the German problem is inconceivable without due consideration of vital interests and security requirements of those countries which were victims of the aggression by Hitlerite Germany. De Gaulle's formulation of the problem of cooperation between the Western European and Eastern European States for peace and security is fully correct and comes at an appropriate time.

However, one cannot refrain from observing that the author of this correct conception was, at a certain moment, deserted by his sense of reality. He seemed not to notice the principal factor in the German problem of the sixties, the existence on the territory of the former German Reich of two independent German states, which have different economic and social foundations and which have developed in two diametrically opposed directions. To think that some external forces, but not they themselves, should settle the problem of their future fate, means to lose sight of the reality. In this respect one must stress that the problem of European security may and should be solved by all the European countries without any exception, including the two existing German states. There is no way to escape this elementary reality.

. . . In passing, one may not avoid remarking that the solution of ripe international problems would not be promoted by the President's observation that an effective settlement of the problem of European security within the framework of "Big" Europe would become possible only at a time when the social regime of the USSR and of the other Socialist countries of Europe have undergone a certain evolution according to Western taste.

The French President correctly pointed out that John Foster

Dulles, who had conceived the reckless plans "for pushing back communism in Europe," was finally compelled to abandon them. General de Gaulle said that "this was only a dream." Absolutely true! This justifies even less the unrealistic dreams of a somewhat different kind. . . .

On the whole, the French President's press conference, which was concerned with several ripe international problems and during which he brought forward a number of important and constructive ideas, had a not unimportant significance. It has, without doubt, opened interesting perspectives.[85]

The Soviet government agreed with the French President on several matters: the United Nations (see Chapter VII), the gold standard (see Chapter V), the German frontiers, and the international limitation of German armaments. It disagreed with him regarding the Democratic Republic of Germany. It restated its usual point of view that the German reunification was, in the first place, a problem to be solved in direct negotiations between the two existing German states. This is its way of saying that it opposes this unification under any circumstances. Two German states with opposite regimes, the fact duly stressed by *Pravda,* cannot agree on their merger, especially since the Soviet Union and the Communist government in East Germany never fail to insist that the "Socialist achievements" of the German Democratic Republic must not be lost in a union with the Federal Republic. Obviously, two opposite regimes, capitalist democracy and a one-party collectivist system, cannot dwell under the same roof. This Soviet stand underlines the unreality of de Gaulle's plan.

Pravda expressed regret that the French President ignored the existence of the Democratic Republic of Germany and, not without reason, qualified as a dream his expectation of an evolution of the Communist system in the Soviet Union and in Eastern Europe according to, as it said, "Western taste."

One can wonder what tangible profits de Gaulle expected to derive for France from his new policy toward the Soviet Union. His plan for German reunification is unacceptable to both West Germany and Russia, though for opposite reasons. In 1959 he abandoned one bargaining asset, the recognition of the Eastern German frontiers, without any Soviet *quid pro quo.* He cannot make the second concession, desired by Moscow, of recognizing the Democratic Republic of Germany, unless he wanted to end the prospect of any cooperation with Germany, which he needs in his Little Europe.

Except for the Communists, all French parties support General de

Gaulle's refusal to recognize the German Democratic Republic. However, the Federation of the Democratic and Socialist Left (headed by François Mitterand) seems unexpectedly to have taken a different stand in its program published on July 15, 1966 (*Le Monde,* July 14–20, No. 926). This program advocates the search for a solution of the problem of German reunification in a *confederation.* This is the very term currently used by all Communist governments and means some sort of organized cooperation between the two German states. It must have been self-evident to the Socialists, Radicals, and leftist clubs, which form the Federation of French Left, that the confederation would necessarily be founded on recognizing the existence of two German states, an anathema for the Western Germans for whom East Germany is a mere Soviet occupation zone.

The Federation accepted another Communist idea, namely a non-nuclear zone in Central Europe. This idea was launched several years ago by the Polish Foreign Minister and has been known by his name, the Rapacki Plan. This plan includes both parts of Germany, Poland, and Czechoslovakia within the zone. As the German Federal Republic emphatically rejects both the confederation with the Democratic Republic and the Rapacki Plan, the Federation of French Left has adopted for the first time an attitude toward Western Germany less friendly than de Gaulle. This attitude is hardly compatible with the full support voiced in the program for the European Community, which is unthinkable without French-German cooperation.

If the adoption of those two Communist concepts was meant to build a bridge toward the Popular Front, the affirmation in the same program of fidelity to the Atlantic Alliance and the European Community had nothing to commend itself to the French Communist party. The program seems to accept the French withdrawal from NATO as irreversible and admits the need for "a profound reorganization" of the Alliance. It asks only for the conclusion of new military agreements between France and her Atlantic allies. All in all, the Federation offers an alternative foreign policy which combines self-contradictory elements, some of them borrowed from the Communists and some others from de Gaulle. It is neither fish nor fowl.

It is difficult to imagine how Russia could recompense France for the princely gift of recognizing East Germany, except by laudatory articles which cost nothing. De Gaulle's importance in Soviet eyes is partly due to his nuisance value regarding the United States. The Russians do not need to make any concessions in exchange. The French President could do no better from their point of view if they prodded him; he needs no prodding.

In June 1966 General de Gaulle paid an eleven-day visit to the Soviet

Union. All commentators agreed that this was his personal triumph.[86]
The Soviet government, well briefed on his idiosyncrasies, did their best
to ensure a very pleasant sojourn to the distinguished French visitor.
They offered him a reception never before equalled in splendor and
honors on the occasion of former Western visits. The Soviet population
did not need any party directives to assemble on his way and to greet
him with a genuine and enthusiastic warmth.

For his part, de Gaulle demonstrated once again that he was a great
actor who knew to the minute detail how to perform his role and how to
charm his hosts. French journalists who accompanied him called this
"Operation Charm." He carefully memorized a few Russian sentences
and recited them without the slightest error to the delight of Soviet
crowds. In Leningrad he even quoted a few verses from one of Pushkin's
poems. This was his usual technique. In Germany and Latin America
he delighted other crowds with German or Spanish phrases skillfully
inserted in his French allocutions. For the sake of his Soviet hosts, he
made a half-concession by calling the country Russia and the Soviet
Union interchangeably.

He was taken by plane to Novosibirsk. From the high altitude he
could barely notice the low range of the Urals on his way to the fast-
expanding Siberian city with its important industries and even more
important research center. Perhaps the Russians hoped that he would
deduce a conclusion from that trip and would henceforth call for a Big
Europe from the Atlantic to the Russian Pacific instead of the Urals,
which hardly form any physical barrier between Europe and Asia.

The General was delighted to have the opportunity of, as Frenchmen
say, a "rejuvenating bath" by plunging into the vast crowds assembled
in every visited city to greet him, shaking hands with strangers or greet-
ing the onlookers with his long arms making the "V" sign.

The reception was supremely regal. De Gaulle was lodged in a Krem-
lin apartment and was invited to address the Moscovite crowd from the
historic balcony from which Lenin himself spoke to his followers. More
important, he was the only foreign guest to be invited to see the Soviet
Cape Kennedy at Baikonur in the Kazakh steppes, where he could
observe the launching of another Soviet "sputnik." His hosts wanted
to intimate to him that they would accept mutual cooperation in outer-
space exploration but also to impress him with Soviet might. They
certainly appreciated the honor of receiving the first Western Head of
State to come to Russia since the October Revolution. In Leningrad he
repaid their courtesy by calling the October Revolution the greatest
event in Russian history although he had never before hidden his distaste
for its consequences.

Everywhere he went, he was accompanied either by Aleksei Kosygin, the Soviet Prime Minister, or by Nikolai Podgornyi, the Chairman of the Presidium of the Supreme Soviet (the Soviet collegiate Head of State). However, his main interlocutor in Moscow was Leonid Brezhnev, Secretary General of the party. Frenchmen could convince themselves that Brezhnev was the leading Soviet statesman.

The Soviet press left in its warm comments no doubt why the French President was received with elaborate protocol and unusual hospitality. Their frequent references to the "West German militarists and avengers" were clear enough. It happened that de Gaulle came in the month of solemn commemoration of the twenty-fifth anniversary of the German attack on Russia. Soviet articles reminded him of the fact that France and the Soviet Union had fought the same enemy and acclaimed him as "one of the leaders of anti-Hitlerite coalition." The General diplomatically refrained from publicly recalling his wartime anti-German record. He was at his best. He indulged in no diatribes against the United States, no criticisms of the Atlantic Alliance, and no disobliging remarks about West Germany. This might have been disappointing for his hosts, but demonstrated that, once on the soil of the other camp, he knew how to preserve the balance of his foreign policy. Only a complete misunderstanding of that policy might have induced certain Western commentators to predict, in anticipation of his visit, the reversal of French alliances or at least the conclusion of a French-Soviet nonaggression pact in open defiance of the Atlantic allies.

Probably neither party to the conversations was unduly disappointed that the visit did not bring about spectacular results. This must have been expected both in Paris and in Moscow. However, it would be erroneous to dismiss the General's visit as an insignificant Soviet-French festival. One of the most perspicacious American commentators of French policies, C. L. Sulzberger, characterized de Gaulle in Moscow as an "icebreaker."[87] This is exactly what de Gaulle intended to accomplish. He did not go to Moscow as an authorized spokesman for Europe, as a British Cabinet Minister sourly remarked, but as a vanguard pioneer to help break the ice of the cold war. (The British Prime Ministers and Foreign Secretaries had not been authorized European spokesmen on their former frequent visits to Moscow either.)

In this respect he voiced the longing of the whole of Europe from the Atlantic to the Urals. The summer of 1966 witnessed the wave of high hopes in every European country for the stabilization of peace on the Continent, for a gradual reduction in mutual distrust, and for closer economic relations between the two parts of Europe. No one else but the former fierce Soviet opponent, Konrad Adenauer, told his amazed party colleagues shortly before de Gaulle's visit that the Soviet Union had become a "peace-loving nation," as witnessed by her mediation between India and Pakistan. This optimistic feeling that the cold war was over and that Europe was moving, after twenty years, toward a more normal condition, might or might not be a delusion, but it existed everywhere and was shared by the European governments.

The Soviet government expected that peace would rest on the petrified *status quo* in Central Europe. The Eastern European governments and populations hoped that the relaxation of tension would bring about greater independence from the Soviet Union. All Communist governments were inclined to welcome cooperation with Western corporations for the sake of more rapid economic development. The big Soviet contracts made with the Italian Fiat and the French Renault companies for the construction of automobile factories were taken by other Western corporations, including the German, as harbingers of a closer economic association between the Western surplus capital and superior technological know-how, and the Eastern surplus of manpower. The Western European governments welcomed the prospect of greater stability even if bought at the price of a divided Germany. The Germans hoped that the reduction of tension would eventually restore Soviet trust in their intentions and would persuade Russia to waive the veto against the reunification of the German nation in freedom and under one government.

General de Gaulle was speaking for all Europeans (including the Russian population who remembered the cost of the Second World War: 20 million dead) when he evoked in his speeches the Soviet slogan: "Peace to the world!" If his visit encouraged the Soviet government to seek a better understanding with the West, it would have been worthwhile for him to undertake that journey, which must have taxed his strength. He apparently intends to continue his crusade by going to the Eastern European capitals later. Big Europe has taken precedence for the time being over Little Europe. He had a glimpse of that vision in Moscow. Big Europe, if achieved, will not be what he dreams of: a harmoniously cooperating Continent; national interests will still be the source of divergent policies, but, if it were peaceful, the change would be welcome. One may only hope that unforeseen events do not shatter his and European expectations of the summer of 1966.

De Gaulle achieved modest results. The main problem, Germany, was discussed; but, as the General told his aides, both parties only played their old records. He adamantly refused to recognize the German Democratic Republic; his hosts no less adamantly repeated their thesis of the existence of two sovereign German states. The German question was barely mentioned in the final joint declaration.[88] This declaration stressed the need for a further reduction in international tension as the condition of restoring normal European relations; it expressed the pre-occupation with the situation in Vietnam (without any reference to the American policy) and recommended the settlement of that problem by the return to the 1954 Geneva agreement and noninterference by foreign powers; it assigned primary importance to preventing the proliferation of nuclear weapons, and promised mutual cooperation in color television, outer-space exploration, peaceful use of atomic energy, technology, and science. The declaration ended with a French invitation extended to Brezhnev, Kosygin and Podgornyi to visit France, which they gladly accepted.

The two Foreign Ministers signed French-Soviet agreements on outer-space exploration by combined efforts, including the launching of French satellites by Soviet rockets, and on scientific cooperation.

De Gaulle's visit did not modify the pattern of French relations with Germany and Russia as it had existed prior to his departure from Paris. Its significance for those relations may be fully appreciated by the juxtaposition of these two events, divided by less than four years: September 1962—a hero's welcome in Germany; June 1966—a truly royal reception in the Soviet Union.

Recognition of the Chinese Communist Government

General de Gaulle keeps several irons in the fire. There is nothing surprising in his adding the Chinese iron in January 1964. Rather, one can wonder why he waited until 1964. One of his French opponents is astonished that de Gaulle delayed the decision for five years:

> Certain indices allow one to guess that de Gaulle wished at the time of his return to power, as Bidault, Mendès-France, and Edgar Faure had wished, to normalize French relations with China. But it took him five years to make the decision either because, like his predecessors, he did not want to displease the American ally, who had to be treated considerately during the Algerian war, or because he did not yet exactly define his objectives.[89]

Unlike the United States, France has no vital interests to protect in the Far East. De Gaulle can say about China what he said about Russia: there are no conflicts between France and the other country.

The recognition would have come sooner or later, whatever French government were in power. Another of de Gaulle's adversaries, Paul Reynaud, admitted that: "No objection can be raised against the principle of recognition of a government which has ruled all continental China for the last fifteen years."[90] The French opposition criticized only the timing of de Gaulle's decision, which could have been interpreted as a deliberate challenge to the United States. Even so, this criticism was half-hearted and is now forgotten.

There were several reasons, all of them legitimate from the French point of view, for the establishment of diplomatic relations with Peking. Firstly, the open conflict between Russia and China guaranteed the independence of Chinese foreign policy. De Gaulle mentioned this particular reason on January 31, 1964:

> Doubtless there still remains, between the regimes in power in Moscow and in Peking, a certain doctrinal solidarity that may be manifested in the world rivalry of ideologies. Yet under a cloak that is torn a little more every day, appears the inevitable difference in national policies. The least we can say in this regard is that in Asia, where the frontier between the two states, from the Hindu Kush to Vladivostok, is the longest that exists in the world, Russia's interest, which is to conserve and to maintain, and China's, which is to grow and to acquire, cannot be considered identical. Consequently, the attitude and the action of a nation of 700 million inhabitants are effectively settled only by its own government.[91]

There is no reason whatsoever for France to take sides in the Sino-Soviet quarrel which provides her with an even greater freedom of movement in international politics. This movement is better assured by having diplomatic relations with the capitals of both Communist great powers whose disputes have repercussions on the attitudes of all Communist states and parties.

One may note marginally that only Germany among the American European continental allies could be tempted to sympathize with China rather than with Russia. The ancient political law that the enemy of my enemy is my friend might one day affect the foreign policy of West Germany. The other continental European allies have no more compelling reasons than France to take sides in the Sino-Soviet dispute.

Secondly, the French government considered it unrealistic to ignore the existence of a rising power with a growing influence in Asia. The particular reasons which precluded American recognition (such as the Chinese Communist mistreatment of American consuls toward the end of the Civil War, the Korean war, the commitment to the Taiwan regime, and the confrontation in Southeast Asia) did not exist for France. Even the United States has not been able to ignore the existence of the Communist government entirely. It took part with that government in the 1954 conference on Indochina and in the 1962 conference on Laos, and it maintains intermittent contact with that government through the American and Chinese ambassadors in Warsaw, who meet from time to time. Recognized or not, the Communist government exists.

The French President stressed one aspect of that problem in particular:

> In fact, there is in Asia no political reality, notably with regard to Cambodia, Laos, Vietnam, or to India, Pakistan, Afghanistan, Burma, or to Korea or Soviet Russia or Japan, etc., which does not concern or affect China. There is, in particular, neither a war nor a peace imaginable on this continent without China's being implicated in it. . . . But further, China's own mass, her value and her present needs, the scope of her future, cause her to reveal herself increasingly to the interests and concerns of the entire world. For all these reasons, it is clear that France must be able to listen to China directly and also to make herself heard.[92]

Several other European allies of the United States recognized the Communist government many years prior to de Gaulle's decision. Denmark, the Netherlands, Norway, and Britain did so in the first months of 1950, prior to the outbreak of the Korean war. Their recognition did not provoke any protests by the United States, which perhaps at that time was considering doing the same thing. China definitely became a villain in American eyes only after her intervention in the Korean war. French recognition came at an inconvenient time for the United States, but this consideration was without importance for the French President. Peking has diplomatic relations with some fifty states, European (including Sweden, Finland, and Switzerland), Asian and African, not to mention all the Communist states. France is not a spectacular exception. Trade is lively between China and most of the NATO allies (including Canada) in spite of the American embargo in U.S.-Chinese economic relations.

Third, the French President is convinced that the present distribution of power in the world is changing and that the *relative* weight of the Soviet Union and the United States is going to be reduced gradually because of the rise of new centers of power. He takes into account that China will be the most important of those future centers. His biographer notes:

> During that year [1963] de Gaulle did never stop paying attention to the deep trends which perhaps were going to transform the condition of the world. . . . For five years he has been announcing the coming of China to the rank of powerful and independent

states; nothing will prevent this from taking place anyhow, nor will anything prevent the multitudes of Latin America from contesting the North American hegemony. The Soviet hegemony is already being contested in several East European countries. Immense transformations will inevitably take place in Africa and in Southeast Asia. Hence, is it not in the French interest and thereby in the European interest to foresee these forthcoming changes and to plan one's game in the prospect of a completely new chessboard? De Gaulle is inclined to believe that France can and should do it.[93]

Fourth, there was an immediate reason for his extension of recognition, namely the situation in Vietnam and generally in Southeast Asia. He believed in 1964 and still believes that no solution for this situation can be found, whether by military or diplomatic means, while ignoring the existence of China. Foreign Minister Couve de Murville said it on April 28, 1964:

> We, for our part, cannot think that any of the problems of Asia can be settled without the participation of China in one way or another, and we know that China is going ahead in all respects, including in Indochina, with her own policy. . . . What we French, with the backing of ninety years' experience and, unfortunately, seven years' war in Indochina, can say is that it is useless to try to settle the fate of Vietnam without China.[94]

De Gaulle did not expect miraculous results from the establishment of diplomatic relations. He warned that "we must avoid nursing too many illusions in this regard."[95] He did not expect China to be guided by French advice or to see an impressive volume of mutual trade. He summarized his main argument in a short sentence: "France merely acknowledges the world as it is."[96] It is for this major reason that at his press conference of February 4, 1965, he advocated United Nations acceptance of the credentials of the representatives of the Communist government of China (see Chapter VII).

The results of the establishment of diplomatic relations have not been spectacular so far, as de Gaulle warned in advance. However, France enjoys the sympathy of Peking, while China is not on speaking terms with the United States, resents British support for American policy in Southeast Asia, and is on shouting terms with the Soviet Union. The political reasons for Chinese sympathy, which is reciprocated in Paris, are obvious. France recognizes that China has legitimate interests in Asia, opposes the American policy, and certainly is not thinking of any anti-Chinese understanding with the Soviet Union. The two countries occupy analogous positions within their respective ideological camps. Both have revolted against the predominant influence of their major allies, both suspect that these allies might one day come to an understanding at the expense of their friends, both aspire to wrest the leadership from them (France in Western Europe, China within the Communist camp), and both welcome the end of the bipolar world as a situation propitious for their own rise in international status. China, formerly an imposing empire and later a helpless object of international politics, and France, also a former world power later reduced to a lower position by her defeat in 1940, can very well understand each other's resentments and aspirations. France fights against one hegemony, the American, but talks about both hegemonies; this cannot help but please China, which is engaged in the actual struggle against both the American and the Soviet hegemonies, to use de Gaulle's vocabulary.

One could imagine a situation in which France could play in Asia the role of an honest broker between the United States and China. As is true of American-Soviet relations, the French President denies himself this role, which could be profitable for his country, not only by his disagreements with the United States (an honest broker cannot agree completely with either side) but even more by the pleasure which he visibly finds in jibing at the United States on every available occasion. An honest broker must be liked and somewhat trusted by both parties. In this respect de Gaulle again proves to have no diplomatic talent.

According to the French press:

> It is mainly the foreign policy of the Fifth Republic that is being approved by the Chinese leaders. Their representatives warmly cite the resolute independence of General de Gaulle regarding the United States; his opposition to the nuclear monopoly of "certain" powers; the French cooperation with the Socialist and neutralist countries such as Algeria and Cambodia, beneficiaries also of Chinese aid ("our mutual aid may exist simultaneously and without conflict"); the liquidation of French military bases in Africa ("let the Americans and the British do the same in Asia"); the French government's support for the proposal of a new conference on Laos and the facilities which it offered to the three Laotian factions for their meeting in Paris; finally, the French position regarding Vietnam.[97]

The economic results of diplomatic relations have been rather modest, although the trade, small as it is, is increasing. China imports French trucks and cars, tractors, cargo ships, equipment for the oil prospecting, steel, nickel, etc. The Chinese tell Frenchmen:

Good political relations between our two countries incline us to turn toward France, in the first place, rather than to other Western suppliers. Thus we should prefer to consider French offers rather than those coming from Great Britain or the Netherlands, both of which maintain diplomatic relations with us on the level of chargés d'affaires but whose external policies regarding Taiwan or Southeast Asia are tied too closely to the American policy. Only . . . the French prices are high and the conditions of payment often are less favorable than those offered by other countries. . . . Trade is regulated by the economic laws. It is impossible to substitute political for economic laws.[98]

This economic law inclined China to buy ten million quintals of French wheat in July 1964. This was not the first purchase, but in the three preceding years the amount bought each time was only one-third of the amount bought in 1964. The Chinese, being good businessmen, paid the international market price for the French wheat. France had to sell at a heavy loss of 48 million dollars. Fortunately for her, the EEC Agricultural Fund came to the rescue by taking over half of this loss. In effect, the five European partners subsidized the sale—another illustration, by the way, of the importance of Common Market for French agriculture.

The most visible results of the exchange of ambassadors have been in the realm of cultural relations, which consist in the exchange of university professors and students, of theatrical performances and films, as well as in travels by a small number of French tourists. The French benefit might prove to be important. In due time France will have a good number of qualified experts on Communist China; this might eventually be an asset for the whole West.

India and Japan

De Gaulle is not fascinated by China alone. He also takes into account the existence of an Asian triangle composed of three powers, one unfriendly to China and the other lukewarm. Speaking in June 1965 he duly noted the existence of these three powers:

China, who lives in a period of hard gestation but is aware of her immensity and rejects any foreign influence; India, who tries every day to overcome her misery; Japan, who rises, since her defeat, methodically and by an adequate effort to the first-rank economic power and who aspires to become the master of her destiny again.[99]

His remarks are interesting for their correct evaluation of the potential power of the three nations. He placed China and Japan very high on his scale but India rather low. However, France maintains friendly relations with all three. On July 24, 1965, for instance, Japan formally accepted French assistance in the peaceful exploitation of atomic energy. This is an interesting by-product of the French nuclear effort.

If Frenchmen were to glance in 1966 at the international thermometer, they would discover that it indicated different temperatures in each important capital: icy weather in Washington, frost in Bonn, warm sunshine in Moscow and Peking, and quite variable weather in the British Isles. General de Gaulle's reaction to these different temperatures might be to rely in the future on bilateral contacts rather than on his former Grand Designs, which have so far produced nothing but bitter frustrations. Bilateral contacts would provide him with a greater leeway for the independent course of action which he seems to cherish above anything else, and with the opportunity for quick adjustments of his foreign policy to "things as they are."

VII Hero of the Third World or a Member of a Collective Hegemony?

The hero

"Abébé Bikila, marathon victor at the last two Olympic Games, and General de Gaulle are the two most popular men in Africa. This is the conclusion of an enquiry carried out by the periodical *Jeune Afrique* among seven thousand of its readers."[1] The General received 65 per cent of the votes and was placed well ahead of the Olympic victor.

He is the most popular among Western statesmen in the Third World of underdeveloped countries. If a public opinion poll could be held in all the parts of the world, the curve of his popularity would probably be the highest in Africa, Asia and Latin America, fairly high in the Communist countries, much lower in Western Europe, and would fall down to the lowest level in the United States. This hypothetical curve would reflect the effects of his foreign policy, generous for the underprivileged Third World, conciliatory toward the Communist capitals, quarrelsome in relation to the Western European countries, and unfriendly toward Washington.

He is the hero of the Third World. To it he stands for the liberation of former French colonies in Africa, for the indefatigable apostolate of aid to the underdeveloped peoples and for nonintervention in their affairs.

His place in history will be marked forever by his creation, in 1940–45, of the myth of fighting and eventually victorious France and, in 1958–62, by his cutting of the Gordian knot of the Algerian war while preserving the democracy from the threat of a military putsch. It will be marked also by the liberation of colonial peoples in 1958–62 and by the generous aid given to the underdeveloped countries throughout his Presidency. His latter achievements and his personal greatness can be fully measured only by casting a glance at the record of the Fourth Republic, worn out and killed by the colonial cancer.

Myth of assimilation

The Third Republic, builder of the colonial empire, created the myth of assimilation. According to that myth, the colonial peoples of Southeast Asia and Africa were destined gradually to deserve the honor of becoming Frenchmen. The end of this process of cultural assimilation was to effect the solution to the depopulation problem in metropolitan France; sixty or more million people would join the ranks of white Frenchmen, and a nation of a hundred million men and women would rise strong enough to confront all the dangers on the European Continent. As unbelievable as this myth was, it was believed. The awakening of national consciousness among the Asian and Arab peoples was happily ignored, as was the fact that the national histories of the Vietnamese and of the Khmers were at least as ancient as that of France, or the other fact that North African Arabs belonged to the Moslem civilization.

This fantastic myth did not preclude the treatment of colonial peoples as mere subjects. Prior to the last war the natives were deprived of the political rights of French citizens and did not enjoy the benefits of social legislation; the sub-Saharan Africans were subject to a particularly severe criminal law and obligated to perform compulsory labor. Any association of more than twenty persons had to be licensed by the colonial administration, without whose permission no public assembly could be held. The natives could not emigrate from the colonial territory without a permit. Official posts were denied to them because they were not citizens.[2]

This flagrant contradiction between the myth and the actual colonial policy could escape the attention of Frenchmen, but not that of the natives. Those who were lucky enough to have been educated in France were the first to resent this bitter contradiction.

The Second World War undermined everywhere the prestige of the white man. The colonial empires began to disintegrate. In 1947 Britain retreated from India, Pakistan, Burma, and Ceylon; Holland was squeezed out of Indonesia. Threatening clouds were gathering on the French horizon. In the spring of 1945 nationalist demonstrations took place in Algeria, in particular in Setif; they were bloodily repressed. In March 1947 an insurrection broke out in Madagascar; it was ruthlessly quelled, and the nationalist deputies to the French parliament were imprisoned and tried for high treason. In 1949–50 the Ivory Coast was the scene of disorders. A French colonial specialist writes:

> The events in Setif in 1945 were never well known by the French public; the Malagasy revolt in 1947 and the trial in 1948 aroused only passing interest and did not provoke any serious reflection; the events in 1949 in the Ivory Coast are generally ignored even today.[3]

The average Frenchman was busy with his own affairs and happily continued to believe in the myth of assimilation. If he paid any attention to the disturbing news from the colonial possessions, he was sure that the disturbances were the work of a small minority of malcontents who were unable to appreciate the benefits that France was conferring on the colonial subjects by her civilizing mission; they suspected that the Communists and sometimes also the American anticolonialists were hiding behind the backs of those malcontents.

Even the leftist politicians preferred to remain blind to the awakening of colonial populations. Léon Blum, Socialist leader and the Prime Minister then, said on November 21, 1946, that he was opposed to both "the nationalist fanaticism and the colonial exploitation."[4] His colleague, Guy Mollet, echoed the same idea when he said ten years later that "the Socialists want to spare the dependent peoples the nationalist stage [of development]."[5]

These Socialist politicians, who would have desperately fought any foreign rule over their own country, were incapable of imagining that French rule might be resented by Asians and Africans. Only a nationalist fanatic could abandon, for the sake of remaining a Vietnamese or an Arab, the privilege of becoming a full-fledged Frenchman in a remote future. Can one be surprised that the politically less educated Frenchmen did not understand the significance of the Vietnamese struggle for independence and later of the Algerian revolt, "if the [colonial] conquest was the victory of civilization over barbarism, and if no school textbook ever told them of the atrocities committed in the nineteenth century or of the famines in the twentieth century?"[6]

Record of the Fourth Republic

The only answer, which the "nationalist fanatics" deserved, was military force.

> It was the unified Socialist government of Léon Blum that made the decision to wage war in Indochina in December 1946, and it was the government of Mendès-France that decided to put an end to this war in July 1954 and to repress the insurrection of the Algerian nationalists on November 1 of the same year.[7]

Even one of the Communist leaders, Roger Garaudy, succumbed to the prevailing view and wrote in 1947 in *Cahiers du Communisme*: "Any attempt to abandon the French Union could only result, together with an *illusory and short-lived pseudo-independence,* in the strengthening of imperialism."[8] Communists participated in the government of the time.

The war in Indochina ended with the French military disaster at Dien Bien Phou, where the French troops capitulated on May 7, 1954. The most capable politician of the Fourth Republic (disliked by his parliamentary colleagues) was given the thankless mission of terminating that costly war. Pierre Mendès-France did so by accepting the decisions of the

Geneva Conference in the same year, 1954. Shortly afterwards, on November 1, the revolt broke out in Algeria. One colonial war followed the other.

It is possible and even probable that the Fourth Republic would finally have accepted the evidence of hard facts in sub-Saharan Africa and would have granted independence to those colonies. The lesson of the Indochinese war and of the Algerian revolt was effective. Moreover, French national sentiments would not have been deeply hurt, as de Gaulle's later policy proved, by the departure of the colonial administration from sub-Saharan Africa, where no substantial French settlements existed. As a matter of fact, the first notable step toward the emancipation of that part of Africa was taken by the adoption of the so-called Framework Statute in June 1956. This statute granted the franchise to all French subjects. Europeans and Africans were placed on the same electoral roll. The colonial territories were allowed self-government in domestic affairs. France retained her exclusive control over foreign affairs, armed forces, internal security, and the judicial system for European Frenchmen. Other matters were transferred to the jurisdiction of locally elected assemblies and to the executives responsible to these assemblies. The French governors retained the ultimate veto and were ex officio presidents of the local executives, but the native vice presidents, elected by their compatriots and responsible to the assemblies, were already cutting the figures of political leaders in each territory. The assemblies became the training ground for native politicians. The statute did for sub-Saharan Africa what Britain had done after the First World War in India.

This statute was an admission that the policy of assimilation had failed. It was also the culmination of a progressively more liberal policy followed since the last war. Compulsory labor for natives was abolished on April 11, 1946. Discrimination against the natives regarding their civil rights was alleviated in 1946 by the extension of French citizenship to them. However, they were not granted equal electoral rights. Only certain categories of natives received the right to vote by virtue of the statute of October 6, 1946; the bill was sponsored by a government composed of Popular Republicans, Socialists, and Communists. The discrimination resulted in one-fifth of the overseas population having the electoral rights as against two-thirds in France herself.[9] Moreover, the overseas electors were grouped into two separate colleges, one for the natives and the other for French residents. The seats in the French parliament reserved for the overseas possessions were allocated in such a manner as to favor European France. This latter discrimination was maintained by the Framework Statute of June 23, 1956. The distribution of seats in the National Assembly was as follows:

> Forty-three million metropolitan Frenchmen were represented by 544 deputies, while 35 million inhabitants of the overseas departments and territories and 8 million Algerians were represented by 83 deputies, i.e., one metropolitan deputy represented approximately 79,000 inhabitants and one overseas deputy, 520,000. If the proportional representation were strictly observed, metropolitan France would have had about the same number of deputies as the overseas possessions.[10]

The conflict between the myth of assimilation and the fear of having half of the French parliamentary seats occupied by the African "Frenchmen" was self-evident. The veteran liberal politician of the Third Republic and the speaker of the National Assembly of the Fourth Republic, Edouard Herriot, when confronted with the prospect of electoral equality of overseas natives, exclaimed in horror: "France would become the colony of her own colonies." An African deputy and devoted friend of France (now the President of independent Senegal), Léopold Senghor, replied: "This is racism!"[11] This French-educated African did not lack "Latin logic"; if his compatriots were to become assimilated Frenchmen, was it only the color of their skin that frightened Herriot?

For sub-Saharan Africa the myth was exploded by this confrontation with the potential political results of assimilation. The Framework Statute of 1956 implicitly acknowledged the separate identity of African colonial possessions. The myth could not survive another of its potential logical consequences, the extension of French social legislation to the poor African masses. Their standard of living would have to be raised at the expense of the living standard of Frenchmen. Since the war France had abandoned her former policy of making each colony financially self-sufficient and had begun to spend money overseas. The colonies had started to cost.

The Constitution of the Fourth Republic named the former empire "the French Union." It created a consultative assembly of that union, which was evenly composed of French and overseas representatives. Its political role was nil; it was "a consultative chamber which was not consulted, which was or was not listened to, and whose debates and reports were more than often ignored by the National Assembly, which claimed to be all-powerful."[12] Members of that ghost assembly soon understood that it was a waste of time to attend its meetings. Finally, it disappeared in 1958 together with the Constitution of the Fourth Republic.

One should note two steps taken by the Fourth Republic to its credit. In July 1954 Prime Minister Mendès-France promised domestic autonomy to the protectorate of Tunisia. Prime Minister Edgar Faure conceded independence in March 1956 to Morocco and in June 1956 to Tunisia. These decisions were made after the failure of the former policy of repression which had only strengthened the national aspirations of both peoples. In 1954 Mendès-France transferred to India the French enclaves within that country.

In the 1950's, Frenchmen, even the most liberal, who could accept the end of war in Indochina, self-government for sub-Saharan Africa, and the independence of Tunisia and Morocco, rejected with horror any idea of self-government for the Algerian Arabs. With the characteristically legalistic bent of the French mind, Algeria seemed not a colonial possession but an integral part of metropolitan France. Legally, Algeria was a part of France in spite of its separation from Europe by the whole width of the Mediterranean Sea and its ethnic composition. French law was clear. What did it matter that nine million inhabitants were Moslems and only one million were Frenchmen of various extractions (French, Spanish, Italian, and Maltese)? Arabs were treated as subjects, but the myth of assimilation included them among prospective Frenchmen. Their high birth rate was expected to bring their number to 18 million by 1985, while it was forecast that the Europeans would reach only 1.2 million by that time.[13] Pro-French sentiments among the Arabs were certainly not promoted by the neglect in which they remained after the lapse of 130 years from the French conquest. The Europeans, who comprised 10 per cent of the population, earned 90 per cent of the Algerian national income. Algerian Arab per capita income was equivalent to one-twelfth of that in metropolitan France.[14] All European children went to school, while in 1954 (the year the insurrection broke out) only 19 per cent of Arab children received elementary education. The University of Algiers enrollment was 10 per cent Arab. While the Arab farmers had only 19 million acres to cultivate, twenty-five thousand European settlers exploited 6.67 million acres of the best land. Ninety per cent of the industries and the trade were in European hands.[15] In 1957, only 5.9 per cent of Moslem men and 1.6 per cent of Moslem women were literate.[16]

As long as it was possible to hold elections in Algeria, the results were falsified by the French administration, which carefully selected Frenchmen and loyal Moslems for the elective posts:

> The gerrymandering in the elections to the Algerian Assembly, the general and municipal councils, and the National Assembly resulted in depriving the Moslem population of any representation and in precluding the possibility of peaceful evolution in Algeria.[17]

Moslems, treated in their own homeland by European settlers as a docile labor force, had no legal recourse for their grievances. The French colonial administration sided with the settlers, and the government in Paris was deaf. For Arabs the assimilation was not even a myth; it was a bitterly ironical slogan of French propaganda. When the then Prime Minister Edgar Faure declared on September 25, 1955: "Our goal is the achievement of a complete integration of Algeria within the shortest possible period of time," the sixty-one Algerian Moslems who were at that time members of the French parliament, delegates to the Assembly of the French Union, or deputies to the Algerian territorial Assembly, replied:

> The policy of integration was never sincerely followed in spite of reiterated demands by the representatives of the second [Moslem] electoral college; now, it is overtaken by events. The immense majority of the population has accepted the idea of Algerian nationality.[18]

Other Algerians sought by that time to liberate their country by the force of arms. The Algerian rebellion came as an unexpected shock. The reaction of the Fourth Republic was unanimous: the revolt must be suppressed by force as would be an uprising in another French province.

> Whatever were their differences of view regarding other matters, all the governments of the Fourth Republic adopted, beginning with the end of 1954, an identical position regarding the uprising. This position was the official French point of view. Its main elements did not change, whoever was in power: Mendès-France, Pflimlin, . . . E. Faure, Guy Mollet, Bourgès-Maunoury or Gaillard. The Algerian uprising was considered an armed attack by French citizens on their own legal government, a rebellion by civilians who became thereby "outlaws."[19]

Mendès-France was Prime Minister when the news of the Algerian revolt reached Paris. He declared:

> Algeria is France. It is not a foreign country which we protect. . . . Let there be no expectation that we shall deal gently with this sedition or shall bargain with it. One does not compromise when the defense of national domestic peace and the integrity of the Republic are at stake. The departments of Algeria are parts of the Republic; they have been French for a long time. . . . There may be no conceivable Algerian secession from metropolitan France. . . . Neither France, nor any parliament, nor any government will ever make any concessions from this fundamental principle.[20]

His Minister of the Interior and now one of the leaders of anti-Gaullist leftist opposition, François Mitterand, took the same view: "Algeria is France."[21] The President of the Republic, Socialist Vincent Auriol, emphatically upheld the same attitude: "Do not expect me to sacrifice a new Alsace-Lorraine on the other side of the Mediterranean."[22] Guy Mollet adds his comment to these first reactions of the French government: "At the time when Mendès-France and Mitterand were uttering these statements, we not only refrained from protesting, but the unanimous Socialist group supported their government with its ballots."[23]

This quasi-unanimous French attitude was due mainly to the existence of one million Frenchmen in Algeria. The problem was somewhat similar to the one Britain had faced fifty and more years before when the Irish had asked for self-government; it was barely conceivable for the British people that Protestant Northern Irishmen could be sacrificed and placed under the rule of an Irish Catholic majority. The solution was found in the partition of Ireland. If one wants a more contemporary analogy: France had a problem somewhat similar to the one in Rhodesia, where the existence of a small but well-organized British minority prevents Britain from following her policy of decolonization and recognition of equal rights for the African majority.

All French governments pursued the policy of repression until the inglorious end of the Fourth Republic. The Republic "organized the most formidable military intervention that had ever been undertaken in an overseas territory."[24] The French Army, eventually half-a-million men strong and armed with modern weapons, was chasing in vain the Arab guerrillas who harassed the isolated outposts and terrorized the European settlements. The independence granted to Tunisia and Morocco further complicated the problem, because these two countries provided a safe sanctuary for the Arab rebels, who could enter and leave Algeria by crossing the frontier. Finally, electrified barbed wire sealed off communications between these two Arab countries and their revolted brethren in Algeria. The true problem of the French Army and administration was that of all guerrilla wars. The attitude of the population was the decisive factor. As 90 per cent of that population was Arab and as its sympathy for the rebels was growing, the French Army operated in a hostile environment where the guerrillas could find recruits, intelligence information, refuge, and material help. The war, which the generals were promising to terminate in another three months by a total victory, continued and in 1958 reached its fifth year.

The brutal means which the French Army had begun to use during the Indochinese war were applied on a large scale. One million Algerian peasants were being relocated in villages supervised by the Army. A French author writes:

Torture and murder of prisoners are currently practiced . . . everywhere where the struggle is going on. Certain military units and certain men become "specialists," in particular the paratroopers and the mobile units of rural police recruited among Algerian Europeans. . . . This system was installed without any amendment of Criminal Code which provides, for instance, capital punishment for persons guilty of inflicting tortures and defines as illegal confinement the holding of any individual under police arrest if he is not brought before a magistrate within twenty-four hours. It was installed although the principles of 1789 continued to be proclaimed the foundation of the State, although the governments did not stop to declare officially that torture was proscribed. It is true that they preferred to prosecute those who denounced torture rather than those who practiced it.[25]

The suspects were tortured in an inhuman manner, and many of them died during this process of investigation.

The war was costly in money and human blood, but its greatest risk was that it would subvert French respect for human rights. The government knew better than ordinary citizens what methods were used to suppress the rebellion. But the French population at home was gradually learning at least a part of the horrible truth through the tales of returning young soldiers. The depressing aspect of this was the lack of a mass revulsion. The progressive intellectuals protested, but the government denounced these protests as a slander against the French Army. Behind official denials the Fourth Republic was concealing the truth about the punitive expeditions against Arab villages suspected of giving assistance to the rebels, about the concentration camps where the disloyal or only the possibly disloyal Arabs were herded, about the resettlement of peasants, and about the tortures applied to men and women under arrest.

The two statutes passed in 1955 introduced a state of emergency in Algeria. They were confirmed by another statute passed in 1956. Their effect was to suspend civil rights: the administration was empowered to prohibit the circulation of persons and vehicles in certain areas, to forbid public meetings, to close access to public buildings, to censor the press and other mass media, to proceed with searches in daytime and at night, to assign people to forcible residence (this came to be interpreted as the right to confine to concentration camps), and all serious crimes were subjected to the jurisdiction of courts martial. Another statute of 1956 authorized the government to take all exceptional measures toward reestablishing order. Finally, a statute in 1957 allowed the government to proceed with administrative internment even on the metropolitan territory; this statute was directed against the sympathizers of rebellion among

Algerians residing in France. The administration of Algeria was in fact delegated to the Army.[26]

All the political parties bore the responsibility for this policy, because all of them participated, at one or another time, in the coalition governments. If the left had some scruples in the last years of the Fourth Republic, they did not change the policy for fear of the Army and the Algerian Europeans. In December 1955 the Socialist party adopted a plan for the Algerian Assembly to be composed of two chambers with equal powers; one chamber was to be elected by the Europeans and the other by the Moslems. The Socialist "liberalism" consisted in giving the same political power to one million Europeans and to the nine million Moslems. Guy Mollet, who had become Prime Minister in January 1956, intended to make some concessions to the Arabs, but quickly changed his mind after a visit to Algiers, where the Europeans received him with rotten tomatoes. He espoused their cause and decided to continue the policy of repression. In May 1956 Mendès-France resigned from his government in protest against the policy, which, as he wrote in his letter of resignation, would end in the loss of Algeria and eventually of all French Africa.[27] By that time Mendès-France favored a policy which would recognize the national aspirations of Algerian Moslems.

In October 1956 the French military authorities intercepted a plane of the Sultan of Morocco which transported the rebel leaders from Morocco to Tunisia. One of them was Ahmed Ben Bella, later President of the independent Algerian Republic. This act of lawlessness was covered up by Guy Mollet's government, and the rebels were transferred to a prison in France where they remained until the end of the Algerian War.

It was the same Socialist Prime Minister who decided in 1956 to fight his Algerian War—in Egypt. Angry at the assistance given to the rebels by President Nasser, he concluded that the elimination of the Egyptian leader would lead to the collapse of the revolt. This rather simplistic argument and the indignation at the seizure of the Suez Canal persuaded him to undertake, together with Britain, the military expedition in November 1956. The French public believed so strongly in the loyalty of the immense majority of Algerian Moslems that they also were sure that a victory over Nasser would bring an end to all difficulties in Algeria. A French author observes: "In the House of Commons, the Labor M.P.'s reacted violently, and the motion of confidence was adopted by only 270 votes against 218. In Paris, the deputies approved the governmental policy by 368 votes against 182 (Communists, Progressives and 28 Poujadists); the Council of the Republic offered the government a majority of 289 votes against 19."[28] Even after the failure of the Suez Canal expedition, public opinion was not against the government: "In March

1957, at a time when it was clear that the expedition had produced no positive result, 44 per cent retrospectively approved of it; Guy Mollet was right."[29] It was the United States that was blamed.

One of the last governments of the Fourth Republic, that of Félix Gaillard, sponsored a statute on Algeria (in November 1957) which characteristically opened with the emphatic statement: "Algeria is an integral part of the French Republic." This statute provided for an Algerian Assembly in which the European deputies would have the veto over all decisions. Mendès-France rightly observed that the statute would perpetuate "that unilateral domination which is incompatible with the condition of the twentieth-century world."[30]

The state of mind of the politicians of the Fourth Republic was best depicted by Félix Gaillard, who said: "It is difficult to keep Algeria. It is more difficult to lose it. Finally, the most difficult is to give it away."[31]

A Frenchman is best qualified for passing judgment on the Algerian policy of the Fourth Republic: "A regime that tolerates capital executions and tortures and violates its own principles by opposing the freedom of other peoples loses its own legitimacy even though the governments are elected by the majority of national representation."[32]

This was the deplorable heritage taken over by the Fifth Republic. It was accumulated more by the lack of civic courage than by conviction. Guy Mollet pointed out one of the main reasons of the policy that he and other Prime Ministers had pursued when he said in May 1958: "Independence, as it is desired by the F.L.N. [the nationalist Algerian organization], could not be realized even if it were the very best solution. Which government would survive its proclamation?"[33] The survival of ephemeral governments was more important than the ideological principles of French democracy.

In 1958 France faced not only the Algerian problem but the question of the future of her entire colonial possessions. The rebel organization proclaimed itself, soon after the fall of the Fourth Republic, the Provisional Government of Algeria in exile, with residence in Tunisia. The problem definitely ceased to be an internal French one; it became international.

Evolution of de Gaulle's views on colonial problems

It is improbable that de Gaulle would have been called by the Fourth Republic to return to power if the Algerian crisis had not reached its paroxysm in the spring of 1958. We do not need to enter into the intricacies of various intrigues which were plotted behind the scenes and in which Gaullists had their part. It suffices to say that de Gaulle came back by the will of the rebellious Army officers in Algeria who suspected that the Fourth Republic would finally inaugurate a policy of concessions to the Algerian rebels, and by the will of the political parties which feared an imminent military putsch. The officers expected de Gaulle to continue the war; the politicians hoped that he alone would have the courage to terminate it, and that he would then return quietly to Colombey-les-Deux-Eglises. He disappointed both parties.

His true views were an enigma. This was his asset, because each party could attribute to him the opinions which it wanted him to have. His former record was unclear. Prior to the war he did not make any statements relating to the colonial empire, but probably held the prevailing opinion that the empire should continue as it was. During the war he considered it his sacred duty to restore the colonial possessions to liberated France. His quarrels with Britain and the United States were, to a large extent, due to the suspicion that both great powers would have liked to undermine the French colonial empire. However, he understood that the war must have stirred up the natives, and that the former colonial regime could not be restored.

His views of the time were formulated at the Free French conference held in January 1944 in Brazzaville. The statement adopted by that conference rejected the idea of self-government for the French colonies:

> The goals of the French civilizing mission in the colonies cannot be reconciled with any idea of autonomy or with the prospect of an evolution outside the French empire. The self-government of the colonies even as a remote possibility is to be rejected. . . . We want the political authority of France to be exercised with precision and rigor in all the territories of her empire.[34]

However, another paragraph of the same statement contradicted this stern denial of self-government by promising the natives that they would be gradually involved in the colonial administration:

> We also want the colonies to enjoy great administrative and economic freedom. We want the colonial peoples to experience this freedom themselves, and we want their feeling of responsibility to be gradually formed and increased so that they might be associated in the public administration of their countries.[35]

De Gaulle himself has never explained this obvious contradiction. Retrospectively he likes to refer to the Brazzaville statement as a charter of colonial liberties, as though it did not contain the denial of self-government. In 1944 he might have wanted to reassure the French colonial administrators that they could rely on him to maintain the empire; in January 1944 France was not yet liberated, and his government rested on the loyalty of French troops and French administration in the colonial possessions. At the same time he could not have had any illusions that France could keep its colonial system intact; this explains his cautious promise to the natives. There were other promises, such as the pledge to extend French citizenship to certain categories of colonial subjects or even to whole "national blocs," a timid but logical deduction from the theory of assimilation. This privileged minority of native citizens was to be given representation in the French parliament, which representation "should correspond to the importance of the colonies within the French Community."[36] Whatever were de Gaulle's intentions in 1944, his "Free France was founded on the following principle: it intended to restore to the liberated France everything over which French sovereignty had extended."[37]

It would be disappointing to consult de Gaulle's *Memoirs* for clarification of his wartime ideas regarding the future of the colonial empire. All memoirs are self-written inscriptions destined to adorn the tombstone of the hero. De Gaulle's *Memoirs* are no exception; they were composed to carve a monument to the incarnation of "French legitimacy" and to be a testament and gospel for his followers. The last volume, published only in 1959, i.e., at a time when he, as President of the Republic, intended to emancipate the sub-Saharan Africa and to make concessions in Algeria, contains statements which reflect the ideas that he had in 1959; it is not absolutely certain that the same ideas dominated in his mind in 1945.

He says there that he told President Truman in August 1945:

> As to the more or less "colonial" countries of Asia and Africa, I declared that in my opinion the new era would mark their accession to independence, though the means would inevitably be varied and gradual. The West should understand and even desire this. But it was essential that these changes be made with, not against the West.[38]

Did he want to appease the American anticolonialists? In any event, he explains several pages later what he meant by "independence":

> If overseas territories cut themselves off from metropolitan France, or if our forces were engaged there, for how much would we count between the North Sea and the Mediterranean? Conversely, if those territories remained associated with us, our career on the continent would offer every opportunity for action. . . . Yet, after what had happened on the soil of our African and Asian possessions, it would be risky to attempt to maintain our Empire as it had been, particularly when the nationalities rise up from one end of the world to the other and Russia and America compete for their sympathy. If

the peoples for whom we were responsible are to remain with France tomorrow, we must take the initiative and transform their condition of subjects into autonomy, association replacing the present dependence.[39]

Whether these ideas were already his in 1945 or only at the time of his return to power, they depicted the future of the colonial possessions as having domestic autonomy though still in close association with France. He firmly rejected their complete independence and refused to see the French future within the confines of the national hexagon. These ideas were embodied in the Constitution of 1958.

For him, as for all other Frenchmen, Algeria was a different problem. It was an integral part of France. He said on August 18, 1947: "Sovereignty of France! This means, first of all, that we must not permit the fact that Algeria is part of our domain to be questioned in any way, either at home or abroad."[40] On October 12, 1947, he curtly told "those Frenchmen, Moslem or not, who are deluded by the dream of secession: 'You are deceiving yourselves and others.' " He added: "To lead the French Moslems to believe that they are warranted in separating their fate from that of France, any such policy would merely, in truth, open the door to decadence."[41]

After the outbreak of the Algerian rebellion, he had recourse in 1955 to a more flexible though unclear formula: "an integration within a Community larger than France, and an entire political participation by the Algerians, which participation is an element of sincere integration."[42] This Sybilline statement could be interpreted as a wish for the formation of a separate Algerian entity, associated with France, together with other overseas possessions, within a French Community, or as a grant of full political equality to the Moslems in recognition of their integration within the French nation, or both. What is certain is that his ideas were evolving during his long years of retirement. In 1958 he was ready to concede self-government or even independence to sub-Saharan Africa and to find a solution for Algeria which would take into account the fact that Moslems were not Frenchmen.

The decolonization of sub-Saharan Africa

De Gaulle's policy of decolonization must be examined under two separate headings: sub-Saharan Africa and Algeria. In 1958 the two problems seemed to him and all Frenchmen to be two different questions, although he ultimately conceded the same unrestricted independence to both areas. In 1958, or probably earlier, he conceived the concept of transforming the colonial empire into a French Community which would include autonomous countries closely associated with France. Algeria was to find an ill-defined place within that Community.

He did not expect to encounter any difficulty in carrying out this plan insofar as sub-Saharan Africa was concerned. The Framework Statute of 1956 prepared the ground. He was sure that French public opinion would not oppose the widening of the scope of self-government, and that the French-speaking Africans would not ask for more than domestic autonomy. His Grand Design was faithfully reflected in the Constitution of the Fifth Republic. Part XII (now a dead letter) of the Constitution changed the name of the former French Union (which had been the old colonial empire in disguise except for the reform contained in the Framework Statute, but not in the Constitution of the Fourth Republic) to the French Community. This French translation of the British Commonwealth marked the Fifth Republic's intention to inaugurate a new policy. Article 77 conceded to the colonial possessions the name of states and the autonomy in their domestic affairs. However, Article 78 reserved for the Community, in fact for France, jurisdiction over several matters: foreign affairs, defense, currency, economic and financial policies, strategic raw materials, justice, higher education, means of external transportation and telecommunications. This was a far cry from the true independence enjoyed by members of the Commonwealth, but it was a step forward in comparison to the Framework Statute. The French Community was to be a federation. The President of the French Republic was to be *ipso iure* the President of the Community. An Executive Council was to be composed of the President of the Community, the French Prime Minister, the heads of overseas governments, and the French Ministers in charge of matters reserved for the jurisdiction of the Community (in fact, for French jurisdiction). A Senate was to be formed of delegates designated by the French and African parliaments. Finally, a Court of Arbitration was to settle disputes between the member states. All in all, this was progress, but rather limited in scope. However, the most important provision was contained in Article 86, which conceded to each overseas possession the right to secede and proclaim its independence, if such were the wish of its legislative assembly confirmed in the local popular referendum.

In September 1958 France and her overseas possessions were asked to approve the new Constitution in a referendum. The rejection of the Constitution by any overseas possession was to be interpreted as a vote for an immediate independence. De Gaulle made it crystal clear that he expected all African possessions to accept the limited self-government the Constitution offered, but that he would reluctantly agree to an immediate independence if a territory rejected the Constitution.

He made a tour of African territories and was warmly received. He said in Madagascar: "This text [of the new Constitution] does not exclude any possibility—even, I say in passing, the most extreme, which is called secession."[43] However, he placed a stern alternative before the Africans: if they voted for independence, France would penalize them by cutting all the ties, including her aid, and they would be left to their own resources. He evoked the distant menace of an Asian imperialism against which Africa, left alone, would be defenseless; he said at Brazzaville: "Nobody ignores . . . the existence of great perils which are suspended over our heads and in particular over Africa. There are in the world, in the first place in Asia, immense human masses who think of expansion because they do not possess sufficient means of subsistence at home."[44] He was frightening the black Africans with the same vision of yellow peril which he cited elsewhere as a bond of solidarity among white Europeans.

In Guinea he met a man who refused to be frightened and who told him: "We prefer poverty in freedom to wealth in slavery. . . . We shall never renounce our legitimate right to independence."[45] This proud challenge by Sékou Touré, then the vice president of the executive council and later President of independent Guinea, brought a sharp rejoinder:

> Independence has been mentioned. I say here more loudly than elsewhere that independence is at the disposal of Guinea, who may take it. . . . I assure you that metropolitan France will raise no obstacles. Certainly, she will deduce the conclusions but will raise no obstacles.[46]

Soon after, he told African leaders assembled in Paris: "It is impossible to conceive of an independent territory that France would continue to aid."[47]

The referendum held in September 1958 brought a massive yes in all the African possessions, except for Guinea, which rejected the Constitution and opted for complete independence. Sékou Touré did not want to cut off all ties; rather he preferred to associate his country in some form with France. But de Gaulle remained true to his threat. He stopped all aid to Guinea and recalled the French personnel. Guinea was left to her own meager resources. De Gaulle's ultimatum misfired this time. Guinea turned toward the Soviet Union and immediately received its assistance. Later the United States came to the rescue.

The Guinean example proved to be contagious. During the following two years other African states asked for independence. The French President was wiser after the disappointing experience with Guinea; he readily acquiesced to their demands. Chapter XII of the Constitution of the Fifth Republic was discarded, and the French Community became a true Commonwealth of independent states that continued to cooperate with France.

The process of African decolonization was rapid. In September 1959 the Republic of Mali (at that time it was still the federation of what is now Mali and Senegal) chose independence, and France readily conceded it. In December of the same year Madagascar followed suit. All other African states did the same in 1960. By that time, de Gaulle fully understood the new reality: "At the time of the general liquidation of empires . . . could we claim to preserve our own? . . . These young states would have probably decided to rebel, following the examples of Indochina and Algeria, if we did not accept of our own volition their aspiration for emancipation."[48]

De Gaulle did not want to see the French influence disappear altogether, but he hoped that it would take a new form palatable to the independent states. France was to stay in Africa, but only because of her cooperation with the former colonies. His new philosophy is well formulated by a French specialist on colonial problems: "While relinquishing the external signs of our political sovereignty, we have tried to preserve in our former colonies an economic presence and a cultural influence which are, in the modern world, the only true realities."[49]

De Gaulle is not a man who would waste his time and effort on trying to ignore the changing realities of international life. He does not immediately yield if his policy encounters difficulties, but if his arguments and threats are to no avail, he adjusts his policy to the facts which he has not been able to change. His rather easy abandonment of the concept of French Community and his grant of independence to the former African possessions should be borne in mind by all his future adversaries. He concedes defeat if nothing else can be done and readjusts his world view in consequence. Then he immediately looks toward new successes along the road which he formerly refused to enter.

He, who had faced African leaders in September 1958 with a stern choice between independence or misery, was ready a year later, on November 10, 1959, to concede independence:

> Two facts are at the root of the policy France follows in relation to peoples with which she is linked. . . . The first fact is the concept of self-determination, which amounts to independence in the opinion of these peoples; this concept is their inspiration. . . . The second fact, which also has worldwide dimensions, is the growing desire of populations in contact with progress to raise their own living standards in a world where certain nations live in great prosperity. They

are increasingly less resigned to accept a situation where one does not eat enough, where one suffers from effects of bad weather, where one is the victim of epidemics, where one vegetates in ignorance. They want instead to have well-cultivated land, mines, factories, roads, railroads and bridges, airplanes, ships, schools and universities. How can they have all this without the administrative, financial, economic, and technological assistance of those who have the necessary means? Each step forward on the road of emancipation is accompanied by a growing need for aid by other nations.[50]

This time he did not offer French aid on the condition that dependent states must participate in the French Community. He completely reversed his position and told the Africans that they could have independence *and* French aid, but that he expected them to repay France with their friendship. On November 4, 1960, he took pride in the African independence:

This year thirteen African Republics and the Malagasy Republic, all of them former members of the French Union, have in their turn acceded, with our help, to international sovereignty; they cooperate with us in the most fruitful and most friendly way. This is the culmination of a transformation, in which we helped wholeheartedly, which involved no struggle or outrages, and which allowed us to transfer the jurisdiction to the authorities issued from regular and universal elections.[51]

In September of the same year he expressed his hopes: "The colonial era is over. . . . Madagascar and Africa have taken their destiny in their own hands. We hope that their road does not branch off from our own."[52]

On June 14, 1960 he told, with biting irony, of the last French Mohicans regretful of the old empire: "It is only natural that one feels nostalgic for what was the Empire, just as one can miss the sweet glow of oil lamps, the splendor of sailing boats and the charm of the horse-carriage era. But what? There is no worthwhile policy that ignores the reality."[53]

The grant of independence to thirteen African republics and to the Malagasy Republic was accompanied in 1960–61 by the signature of bilateral agreements on mutual cooperation. The main points of these agreements were as follows:

1. France assumed the diplomatic representation of those states in foreign capitals and international organizations, if they themselves did not intend to open their own embassies.

2. France and they promised to consult each other on matters of

foreign policy, but they retained complete freedom in formulating policies and in concluding international treaties.

3. They remained within the French monetary zone.

4. France and they conceded a preferential tariff treatment to each other. The French market was to remain open to their tropical products at prices higher than those prevailing on the international market. The commercial policies of African states were to be coordinated with French policy toward third states.

5. France promised to supply instructors and military matériel to the armed forces of African states. She and these states were to cooperate in matters of defense, while France was to retain her garrisons and military bases in some of them. The African governments were empowered to ask for French military assistance to maintain internal order and defend themselves against an external aggression.

At the present time France has reduced the number of African bases where her garrisons are concentrated to four: Dakar (Senegal); Abidjan (Ivory Coast); Diego-Suarez (Madagascar); and Fort-Lamy (Tchad), which is the most important because of its central geographical location.

6. French was recognized as the official language of the African states, while France promised to offer her assistance in developing the African school system by sending teachers and receiving African students at the French schools and universities. France also undertook the obligation to help found African universities.

7. Finally, France was given priority in buying strategic raw materials.

These agreements are not a heavy mortgage on the African independence. They may be denounced; if anything is sure, it is that de Gaulle would not try to reimpose them by force. Gabon excepted, France has never tried to maintain a pro-French government overthrown by domestic revolt. The French guaranty against external aggression might be useful in view of the ambitions of other African states, which would not mind enlarging their territory by encroachments on others, including those where French is spoken.

One of the African leaders most friendly to France, F. Houphouet-Boigny, President of the Ivory Coast, told France immediately after the grant of independence that his country did not intend to participate in the French alliances. Actually, all French-speaking African states opted for the policy of nonalignment. Each has its own preferences, including flirtation with the Soviet Union or China. Their neutralism between the West and the Communist powers has all sorts of variations. This does not irritate the French President, who himself vituperates against the two hegemonies. He, only half-committed, does not mind their noncommitment.

He has strong assets in his hands: preferential treatment for the African tropical products, financial assistance, and help in raising the cultural standards of French Africa. The colonial rule left a precious inheritance to both Britain and France: African elites educated at the British or French universities; and the English or French language as the only *lingua franca* for the Africans, who speak several different native tongues in each country. The French cultural influence, like the British, is there to remain. De Gaulle knows all this and has consistently done his best to strengthen further these economic and cultural ties, which, he hopes, will assure the permanence of French political influence. There is truth in this confident French statement: "France is today the power which awakes the least distrust among Africans."[54]

It is also true that other influences are infiltrating French Africa, which is now open to all powers who want to compete with France. It is equally true that the future elites, the rising generations of Africans, whether in British or in French Africa, might not feel the same attachment to the former colonial power as the present leaders do. A French specialist on colonial problems might be vindicated in his pessimistic prediction that "from one generation to the next, friendships are losing their former strength, and former attachments are felt less."[55] He adds a melancholic comment: "Neither French Canada nor Spanish America were active supporters of their former motherlands in world politics in spite of the common heritage of language, traditions, and culture."[56] This is a possible worry for future France, a long time after de Gaulle's demise. De Gaulle himself is not a pessimist by nature.

He who can be stern with the great powers takes great pains to make a show of exquisite courtesy regarding African leaders. Whenever they come to Paris, he offers them red-carpet hospitality. "Owing to this, close personal ties have been established between de Gaulle and the new African political personnel which perhaps will not survive him."[57] The same courtesy is shown to all the Presidents and Prime Ministers of countries of the Third World who personally meet the French President. Their hero never disappoints them.

The decolonization of Algeria

General de Gaulle liquidated the colonial regime in sub-Saharan Africa without encountering any resistance in French public opinion. The Algerian problem confronted him with the threat that his Fifth Republic would perish, like the Fourth Republic, at the hand of a rebellious Army. He surmounted the dangers owing to his sense of reality, the force of his will, his undaunted courage, and popular prestige. None of the Prime Ministers of the Fourth Republic had all these assets and qualities. Of the two ablest, Mendès-France lacked the prestige of de Gaulle, and Edgar Faure had neither prestige nor courage.

The problem was extremely difficult not only because the Army officers and Algerian Frenchmen rejected the prospect of liquidation of colonial rule, but also because de Gaulle himself was psychologically unprepared in 1958 to concede independence to the Arab rebels. This immensely proud man could not, at first, imagine that the rebels would in the end impose their own solution.

It is not easy to reconstruct the successive stages of his mental evolution, because initially he was unable to disclose his true thought. The Army officers who had brought him to the Elysée Palace did not trust him. The Algerian Europeans, whose revolt against the Fourth Republic also helped him return to power, hoped they could compel him to follow their wishes as they had done with the Prime Ministers of the Fourth Republic. He could count only on himself and on his popularity in France. It was impossible to be frank in that precarious situation.

On June 4, 1958, he went to Algeria. He immediately faced the Algerian Europeans with the logic of their own propaganda slogan that Arabs were patriotic Frenchmen. If this slogan were true, he told them, then "France believes that there is in all of Algeria only one category of inhabitants: full-fledged Frenchmen, all of them with the same rights and obligations."[58] Hence, he concluded, "All the privileges must disappear."[59] This was the last thing the Europeans wanted.

On his return to France he disclosed a bit of his real thought by beginning to talk about "the ten million Algerians," not "Frenchmen." If they were Algerians, their country was not simply another French province. The theory of assimilation of the Moslems was repudiated. De Gaulle replaced it by his concept of a "fraternal association" between France and Algeria. On his second visit to Algeria, in October 1958, he revealed his intention. He said: "In any event, the future of Algeria will be built up, this being in the nature of things, on a twofold foundation: its own personality and its solidarity with metropolitan France."[60]

In May 1959 he frankly acknowledged: "There is no one who ignores the fact that nothing will be accomplished by the struggle and that a reconciliation is the only solution. . . . Daddy's Algeria is dead."[61] The French tutelage and the privileges of French settlers were dead; the continuation of the war could not bring victory. He realistically conceded that even a military victory would not solve the Algerian problem: "Even if the pacification were complete, Algeria would soon be lost to us, because it would rise up again on the first occasion."[62]

From these premises he deduced the conclusion: "I do not prejudge the nature of the political status of the future Algeria. . . . We shall not have Algerians with us if they themselves do not want this."[63] This amounted to saying that the only solution was an agreement between France and the Algerians on the future political regime of Algeria. On September 16, 1959, he felt secure enough to proclaim the right of Algerians to "self-determination," the very word he used in his broadcast allocution. The self-determination was to be "the free choice of the future the Algerians wish to make."[64]

At this stage, he rejected the assimilation of Algerian Arabs as a sterile and naive slogan, but he did not hide his lack of sympathy for the secession. He threatened that, if the Algerians were to choose complete independence, he would not only cut off all French financial aid but would partition Algeria and move Europeans and loyal Moslems to a portion of the territory that would remain under French administration. Moreover, he did not intend in any event to abandon French sovereignty over the Sahara with its newly discovered oil and natural gas wealth.

He denied that the rebel organization was the only legitimate representation of Moslem Algerians. He firmly refused to allow

the Republic to bestow on them the privilege of negotiation regarding the destiny of Algeria; this would amount to their being elevated by the Republic to the status of Algerian government. There is no chance for France to consent to such an arbitrary act.[65]

Who could have predicted in September 1959 that a proud de Gaulle, who hated to bow to the will of others, would less than three years later conclude an agreement with the rebels which was to concede complete independence to their country?

On January 24, 1960, barricades were erected in the city of Algiers. The Europeans intended to overthrow the Fifth Republic as they had destroyed the Fourth less than two years before. The Army and the local authorities tolerated the rebellion, as they did in 1958. They ignored the orders coming from Paris. The President was in no mood to be blackmailed; on January 29 he renewed his pledge to grant self-determination to the Algerians. Finally, his will triumphed. The Army did not join the Europeans as it had done in May 1958; having to choose between mutiny and obedience to de Gaulle's orders, it opted for obedience after a week of uncertainty. On February 1 the Europeans were gently told to dismantle their barricades and to go home, which they did. The President won the first round in the undeclared war of will with the Army officers.

In March 1960 de Gaulle still thought that his will would compel the Arabs to accept his plan for a domestic autonomy in close association with France. He reiterated the threat of partition in case the Algerians were to choose complete independence, this time adding another, more serious, threat—that of expelling the Algerian workers from France. Those 400,000 Algerian workers were supporting their relatives in Algeria, approximately two million destitute Arabs. De Gaulle seemed to have forgotten what Sékou Touré had told him in 1958—that poverty in independence was preferable to wealth in servitude. The rebel organization was not frightened.

In June 1960 the first contacts took place between the French government and the rebels, unsuccessful because the two positions were too far apart. But de Gaulle was gradually approaching the time when he would understand that the rebel organization was the true voice of the Arabs. On September 5, 1960, he admitted that: "I am neither blind nor unjust enough to ignore the importance of the movement of wounded souls and of awakened hopes which has led so many Algerians to insurrection. I know very well what resonance the insurrection has found in a section of the population."[66] But he refused to negotiate solely with the rebel organization. The rebels were not yet in his eyes "the only representatives of the whole of Algeria."[67] He still hoped that negotiation would be conducted with several Arab organizations, the rebels being only one of them. The other Arabs, he thought, would be less demanding, and the rebels would be finally persuaded to accept a domestic autonomy in close association with France. He was to find out later that there was no serious substitute for the Algerian Provisional Government in exile as a valid interlocutor. When he exclaimed: "This I shall never do!" he forgot that "never" is a word missing from the political dictionary.

In the meantime, the President was doing his best to convince the Army officers, the only opposition he feared, that Algeria was not, as he said, another Lorraine or Provence. He soon learned that he had found no sympathy for his thesis. Then he decided to confront the officers with the will of the people. A popular referendum was to be held in France in January 1961. In December 1960 he extended his hand to the rebels:

> We are ready to receive at any time the delegates of those who fight against us. As soon as an end will be put to the last engagements and outrages the government will be able to define together with the various Algerian groups, in particular with the representatives of the rebellion, all the conditions under which a free self-determination will openly take place.[68]

The referendum held on January 8, 1961, proved that the French people supported de Gaulle's policy. Over seventy-six per cent of registered voters took part in the referendum. Over 15 million votes were cast for the Algerian self-determination as against less than 5 million.[69] The Algerian Europeans and a number of officers answered by forming a terroristic organization called the Organization of the Secret Army (O.A.S.).

On April 11, 1961, de Gaulle finally recognized the inevitable:

> France envisages in cold blood a solution whereby Algeria would cease to belong to her domain, although this solution would have appeared disastrous for us in former times. I say again that we now regard this solution with a perfectly calm heart. . . . It is difficult to pretend that the Algerian population as a whole desires to be a part of the French people. . . . France does not raise any objection or intend to erect any obstacles if the Algerian population decides to create a state which would undertake the mission of governing their country. . . . Insofar as I am concerned, I am convinced that this state will be sovereign at home and abroad.[70]

The die was cast. De Gaulle at last conceded complete independence. The will of the rebels had won a victory over him, but the test of wills with the Army was not yet over.

The Army officers in Algeria, led by the well-known generals, rose in revolt on April 22, 1961. De Gaulle, sure of popular support, was not frightened. After a few days the mutiny collapsed for lack of support among the military units in France and because the young conscripted soldiers threatened to disobey the officers' orders. The second round was won. Now the road was cleared for final negotiations with the representatives of the Algerian government in exile. In May the negotiations were opened. In vain, the O.A.S. tried to wreck the negotiations by its terrorist action in Algeria and in France. Neither their plastic bombs exploding in Paris nor their attempt at de Gaulle's life on September 8, 1961 could stop him once he had made his decision. He wanted to put an end to the war at almost any price; he conceded to the rebels that they would be invited to participate in the provisional administration which would supervise the referendum in Algeria, and that the Sahara would not be detached from an independent Algeria. No serious obstacles remained for a final settlement. On October 2, 1961, he publicly told the rebels that France was ready to reach an agreement for the restoration of peace, the definition of conditions of self-determination, and the determination of terms for future French-Algerian cooperation. In fact, he capitulated before a stronger will than his own.

In the meantime, the year 1961–62 looked like one of civil war in France with the continuous terrorist activity by the O.A.S. Many Frenchmen doubted that the Fifth Republic would be luckier than the Fourth and survive. They were wrong, because a true civil war would need the support of at least a large section of the French population; the immense

majority of Frenchmen were with de Gaulle, including his most resolute
domestic opponents. His Algerian policy was the policy of France. In
November 1961 he conceded what he had not believed in earlier years,
namely that the rebels had the support of "almost all Algerian Moslems."[71] The negotiations with the Provisional Algerian Government
dragged on, but were finally ended by the Evian agreements on March
19, 1962. Their main points were as follows:

1.   A cease-fire.

2.   Full independence for Algeria, if confirmed by the referenda held
in Algeria and in France.

3.   The Algerian guaranty of respect for the rights of the European
minority and for the economic interests of France, including the acquired
interests of French corporations in the exploitation of Saharan oil and
gas resources. This was a major item for de Gaulle who wanted to ensure
France a certain independence of the foreign (in fact, mainly "Anglo-
Saxon") supplies of oil.

4.   France pledged herself to give Algeria financial and technical aid
in proportion to its justification by the existence of French interests in
Algeria.

5.   A preferential treatment in the mutual trade.

6.   Algeria would remain within the French monetary system.

7.   The French obligation to indemnify French citizens who would be
expropriated in consequence of the Algerian agrarian reform.

8.   Algerian workers in France would enjoy the same benefits of the
French social legislation as French workers.

9.   French troops in Algeria would be reduced to 80,000 men and
would be garrisoned at places fixed by common agreement. France would
retain her naval base at Mers-el-Kabir for fifteen years, and would have
the use of seven airfields.

10.   France would have the nuclear testing grounds in the Sahara at
her disposal for five years.[72]

This was a total victory for the rebels. It was even greater than they
believed possible in March 1962. Their cooperation with France could
have been endangered by the existence of the French minority of one
million people. This problem was "solved" by the unbelievable stupidity
of the Europeans. Their answer to the Evian agreements was an indis-
criminate reign of terror against all the Moslems—men, women, and
children—and a scorched-earth policy. They were murdering defenseless
Arabs in the streets of Algerian cities, the same Arabs whom they
claimed in 1958 to be loyal Frenchmen. They wantonly destroyed public
buildings, schools, and public utilities. When the time had come for the
French troops' evacuation, the Europeans knew that they had to depart.

The European minority was quickly reduced from one million to less than 80,000.

The French settlers felt that France had let them down. A large part of them refused to be repatriated to the country whose language they spoke but where they had not been born, and emigrated to Spain, Canada, or Latin America. Most, however, settled in France, where they increased the number of de Gaulle's irreconcilable enemies. If one adds the repatriates from other African colonies, in particular from Morocco and Tunisia, France had to receive well over one million people on her territory. On the one hand, it was a difficult adjustment for France and the repatriates. On the other hand, French manpower was increased by these enterprising and skilled people who are now being quickly absorbed by the expanding French economy. The problem was certainly not small but incomparably lesser than that which West Germany faced in the aftermath of the last war with the influx of some ten million refugees from Eastern-Central Europe and from East Germany. In Germany over 20 per cent of the population are those refugees or their descendants; all of them found jobs and helped in the rapid expansion of West German economy. By comparison, over one million repatriates in the French population, which nears the mark of 50 million, do not represent an insolvable economic problem; the true difficulty consists rather in their assimilation to the political atmosphere of the country.

The rebels did not expect that France would rapidly evacuate almost all her troops (except for the small garrisons at the testing grounds in the Sahara and the naval base at Mers-el-Kabir) well ahead of the date fixed in the Evian agreements. The nuclear testing grounds eventually became useless after France had reached the stage of thermonuclear tests for which other testing grounds in the Pacific were needed.

The French referendum for the approval of the Evian agreements was held on April 8, 1962. De Gaulle's main argument in the appeal to his countrymen was: the restoration of peace after the intermittent hostilities which France had to wage since 1939 in Europe, in Indochina, and in Algeria. The French approval was overwhelming: 17,866,423 positive votes against only 1,809,074 nays.[73]

Guy Mollet was only fair when he said:

> I want, first of all, to explain what we owe de Gaulle concerning Algeria. Whatever his reasons and intentions were, his policy helped in the evolution that took place in public opinion. The ideas of self-determination or even of ultimate independence, which are today generally accepted, could not have been even mentioned as recently as a few years ago. He also took a courageous stand against

the outrages committed by factious persons. We have no right to forget it.[74]

The Algerian chapter was closed, except for the small minority represented by the O.A.S. who almost succeeded in murdering de Gaulle in August 1962 and have never renounced their intention to get revenge on the man who liquidated the colonial empire.

The Algerian story not only shows de Gaulle at one of his greatest moments, but especially proves that he is not a statesman who never retreats. He may be compelled to accept the point of view of others, if the other party demonstrates clearly to have an equal will and adequate means for overcoming his resistance.

The colonial career of France was terminated in 1962. Free of that burden which had been absorbing the French energies and had been paralyzing her foreign policy in the world, the French vessel could take any course its bold captain selected. The ocean of the Third World was at last open to its navigation. The colonialist stigma was effaced from the French forehead.

It is true that small odds and ends of the former empire remain under French sovereignty: Martinique, Guadeloupe, Guyane in the Caribbean area, the tiny islands of St. Pierre and Miquelon, French Somaliland, Reunion and the Comoro Islands, New Caledonia, New Hebrides held in condominium with Britain, Wallis and Futuna Islands, the Society Islands (including Tahiti) and the Marquise Islands. These odds and ends in the Western Hemisphere, Africa, and in the Indian and Pacific oceans, have a total population of 1,200,000. This is a minor problem. There is an autonomist movement in the French Caribbean possessions and on the Reunion. It is due to various factors: the low living standards, a very high natural increase which hinders the improvement of the living condition of the population, the frustration of being governed by officials sent from France while the other colonies had been liberated and the British possessions in their neighborhood had attained independence, and the attraction of Castro's Cuba. The autonomists do not ask for independence; culturally they are assimilated by long French influence. Economically, they do not see any hope except in increased French assistance. Their aspirations are modest: to have their own legislative assemblies and the executives responsible to those assemblies, i.e., domestic autonomy. The population of Martinique is 276,000; Guadeloupe has 263,000 people. It is difficult to guess why de Gaulle presently refuses to grant autonomy after having emancipated millions of Arabs and Africans. This minor problem of remnants of the former empire cannot disturb his relations with the Third World, whose eyes are riveted on the more weighty questions of Rhodesia, South Africa, and the Portuguese African colonies. In October 1963 he liquidated the last issue which could have cast a shadow on his reputation; the French base at Bizerte, Tunisia, was removed.

The moral duty of developed nations

The termination of the Algerian war suddenly transformed the image of France. From one of the main colonial powers, vehemently denounced in the Third World, she became a trusted partner. General de Gaulle has built his policy toward the underdeveloped countries on the following triple foundation: economic and technical aid with priority given to former colonial possessions; the denunciation of external intervention in the domestic affairs of those countries; and propaganda against the two hegemonies.

He and most of his countrymen fully enjoy pointing out the reversal of roles between France and the United States. Until 1962 the American public castigated France for her colonial rule and colonial wars. Now Frenchmen are free to denounce the American actions in Vietnam and in the Dominican Republic. They do it to their hearts' content, because:

> The French public . . . almost constantly believed that the secret objective of American diplomacy was to expel Frenchmen from Indochina and North Africa. The rightist and leftist papers, each for its own reasons, were spreading this story, liked by many who refused to believe that any people could of its own volition revolt against France.[75]

De Gaulle's motivation in consenting to a massive aid program for underdeveloped countries is complex. Partly, it is due to his belief that the rich nations have a moral obligation to help their underprivileged brethren. The other stronger motivation is the conviction he shares with the American, Soviet, and even Chinese governments, that the most effective way to be present in Asia, Africa, and Latin America is to pay for it. The underdeveloped countries themselves expect foreign governments to bring aid if they want to participate in the competition for influence. France has no choice under the present conditions. If she stopped her aid, she would be quickly replaced by other powers, and finally her influence would be removed from her former colonies.

Her best investment in the future is the educational assistance which perpetuates French influence by training new generations in the spirit of French culture. These cultural bonds might prove stronger than anything else, including passing political divergencies which might appear in the future between France and French-speaking Africa.

After the termination of the decolonization process in 1962, France had a free choice between two policies. She could have decided that her obligations toward the former colonial possessions had come to an end, and that she would invest all her means in the economic development of her own hexagon. This policy would have strengthened her position on the continent. The other policy, chosen by de Gaulle, was to continue to aid the former colonies and, if possible, even other underdeveloped countries, thus retaining a worldwide influence.

In this respect the President of the Fifth Republic continues the tradition of the Fourth Republic which had demonstrated its sympathy for the problems of underdeveloped countries. For instance, in 1956 Christian Pineau, Socialist Minister of Foreign Affairs, submitted a plan to the United Nations where he proposed the stabilization of prices for raw materials and tropical products, organized purchases of surpluses, financial assistance in economic development, and the founding of an international agency to coordinate aid granted to underdeveloped countries.[76]

General de Gaulle has intensified the French campaign in favor of international assistance and has dramatized the issue by his incomparable eloquence. He confronted all the developed nations with their moral obligation at the press conference held on March 25, 1959:

> We, who live between the Atlantic and the Urals; we, who are Europe, and who possess, together with Europe's daughter, America, the principal sources and resources of civilization; we, who have the means to feed, clothe and house ourselves and to keep warm . . . why do we not found together a fraternal organization which will assist the others? Why do we not pool together a part of our raw materials, our manufactured goods, our foodstuffs, a certain number of our scientists, technologists, and economists, a certain quantity of our trucks, ships and aircrafts, in order to vanquish misery, develop the resources and help in the work of the less developed peoples? Let us do this, not that they be the pawns of our policies, but to improve chances of life and peace. How much more worthwhile that would be than the territorial demands, ideological claims and imperialist ambitions which lead the world to its death?[77]

This was not a demagogue who spoke to win over the sympathies of the Third World, because he had himself decided to make a generous contribution from French resources. In April of the same year he reminded his own countrymen that:

> We live in a difficult world harsh for all but especially for the peoples who have not reached the level of development of France.

However, those countries also have the right to life and progress. A country such as ours has the obligation to help them. There should exist an international fraternal organization, because the earth is round, because there is only one earth, and because all men are like us.[78]

In July 1960 he pointed out that the problem was not only that of human solidarity but also of international politics:

There are on our earth two billion men who do not eat enough. Peace, true peace is inconceivable as long as this situation lasts with all that it entails as the source of troubles, upheavals and wars. This is an evil, a world's evil, and it must be remedied. All the well-endowed countries must agree to help those who have nothing.[79]

He has never tired of these appeals for aid to the underprivileged majority of mankind. At his press conference of January 31, 1964, he said that the time was over when the developed countries could look at the underdeveloped areas only as at "exotic markets and lands to colonize." Then he emphasized that today's aspiration of "two billion men to progress, better life and dignity," was "a fact whose importance and scope have never been equalled since the world has existed."[80]

Very few people would contest this view. Mankind has never before seen anything like the present gulf which separates its wealthy northern one-third from the miserable southern two-thirds. The conflict between relatively rich Russia and poor China demonstrates that the opposition between the prosperous and underdeveloped nations is stronger than the ideological community of views. The problem is further aggravated by the fact that prosperity is an almost exclusive privilege of white nations, and poverty, the scourge of predominantly colored peoples. Never before was a great majority of mankind aspiring at one and the same time to modernize its economic and social structures, and never before did it have to cope with the gigantic difficulties which accompany this revolution of modernization. The political uncertainties and social unrest are integral parts of that vast transformation. De Gaulle is right that this is the main problem facing the world.

Yet his reiterated appeals for a concerted effort by the developed nations have so far remained without echo. The prosperous nations help but help in a bilateral and uncoordinated manner, competing with each other for the influence which they hope to win or retain.

On September 9, 1965, he again made the appeal for a coordinated assistance: "How much this aid, which is scattered and often conflicting, would gain if it were combined on a large scale."[81] His sincerity may not be questioned as long as other powers have not responded to his invitation to coordinate action on a universal scale. However, there is doubt concerning the exact meaning of his concept: does he want to replace bilateral by multilateral aid, or does he wish only for an international coordination of bilateral aids? France has been as reluctant as the other Western powers to support the concept of a United Nations Capital Development Fund. This concept is dear to all the underdeveloped nations which have tried in vain to have it accepted by the assisting nations. Does it mean that France prefers, like other assisting nations (Western and Communist alike), the bilateral aid which offers notable advantages to the assisting state? Bilateral aid provides the opportunity for direct supervision over the use of resources placed at the disposal of the underdeveloped country, ties the credits to the purchases of goods on the market of the assisting state, and clearly bears the mark of its national origin. It strengthens the political influence of the assisting state. If this is de Gaulle's preference, his appeals should not be understood in the sense of multilateral aid, where dollars, francs, rubles, and other currencies would be pooled together and woud lose their national identity, but rather in the sense of international coordination of bilateral aids to avoid waste, unnecessary duplication, and rivalry between assisting states. Even this coordination would be useful.

Arguments in favor of foreign aid

The aid granted to the underdeveloped countries is as controversial in France as in the other developed nations. There can be hardly any doubt that the ordinary Russians and Chinese, if they could publicly express their views, would join the chorus of many Westerners, including Frenchmen, who object to the "waste" of money which should have been used at home. The French opposition is not yet strong but it does exist.

De Gaulle uses not only moral arguments, the least effective in any country, but also utilitarian ones to justify his policy in the eyes of his countrymen. For instance, he pointed out on January 31, 1964, that foreign aid was in the French national interest:

> It is true that this cooperation is not only a one-way affair. The maintenance of active commercial relations with the Arab States [he referred to Algeria, Morocco and Tunisia] and the States of Africa south of the Sahara which have signed agreements with us, and the concessions granted us with regard to certain raw materials, particularly a share of the Algerian oil, are not without value to us. . . . It is obvious that we would be little inclined to furnish much to those who would furnish us nothing in return.[82]

Quite rightly, he conditions French aid on its rational use by the former French colonies, and threatens to take the aid to other states if this condition is not observed:

> If they waste themselves in sterile agitations and contests, at home and abroad, then the world will soon see them as nothing more than areas of competition and possible battlefields for the great imperialist ambitions of today and tomorrow. As for France, it is evident that such a conclusion would lead her to take her aid and her hopes elsewhere.[83]

In any event, French aid should also be extended to countries other than former French overseas possessions: "the undertaking goes beyond the African context and actually constitutes a world-wide policy."[84] We shall see later that French aid is increasingly directed to other underdeveloped countries, but that the priority for the former colonies is being preserved. At the same time, de Gaulle realizes that: "No doubt the effort which we Frenchmen are capable of making materially in this regard is limited by our resources, which are not vast."[85]

At the press conference of January 31, 1964, he pointed with justified pride to the French record:

> It is, quite naturally, to the overseas nations which, starting from our administration, have become sovereign states, that we are above all lending our aid. Of course, this is costly to us. . . . Public aid, that is, the aid furnished from one state to another, in economic, financial, technological, cultural and military areas, amounts to about $1 billion a year. As for the many forms of private aid, it amounts to some $400 million. The 1.4 billion that we thus draw annually from our resources are equivalent to more than 2 per cent of our national revenue and more than 10 per cent of the investments we make in France. There is not a single nation in the world that dedicates to the progress of others a similar proportion of what it is doing for her own. After us, the next, from this point of view, is America. Doubtless America offers a great number of countries various forms of aid whose total, in absolute value, is much larger, but in relation to its means, the aid America furnishes is not, in percentages, half of our own.[86]

Again and again he has recourse to the most convincing argument of national interest in order to rally Frenchmen to his policy:

> As for putting an end to the friendly, reciprocal and planned cooperation that we practice with regard to a number of developing states, that would mean, first, moving away from them and leaving our place to others. That would lead us also to closing immense

fields of economic, technical and cultural action instead of opening them up to ourselves. Last but not least, that would be tantamount to denying the role which is ours as regards the evolution which is bringing so many peoples of Africa, Asia and Latin America to develop themselves, in their turn, without surrendering to one or the other of the two hegemonies which are tending to share the world so long as Western Europe is not able or does not have the will to organize itself so that the balance may be found.[87]

France should give aid in order to be present in the non-European parts of the world which she protects against the threat of being vassalized by one or the other hegemony. France appears here in the role of defender of the liberties of the Third World.

The French government does not use one particular argument in favor of aid, namely that this would stem the advance of Communist influence. Its policy friendly to the Communist powers would anyhow prevent it from mentioning this argument. Moreover, a commission of study, which submitted its report to the government in July 1963, refuted it by pointing out two aspects of the question. Firstly, the Communist countries' present needs for raw materials and tropical products are relatively small. Secondly, the underdeveloped countries must export these primary products in order to pay for their own imports; only the Western advanced countries provide a wide-open and solvent market.[88]

The French assistance takes various forms: financial, technical, military, support of unbalanced budgets, preferential trade, purchase of primary products at prices higher than the international market prices, etc. French preferential tariffs for products imported from the former colonies find their counterpart in the markets of these countries which are also preferentially open to French exports. The mutual exchanges are greatly stimulated by the membership of former colonial possessions in the French monetary zone which includes France and her remaining overseas possessions, fourteen French-speaking sub-Saharan African states, Morocco, Tunisia and Algeria. Guinea is not a member but has her own account at the Bank of France. This arrangement allows France to buy raw materials, tropical products and a large portion of oil she needs by paying in francs and thus safeguarding her reserves in gold, dollars, and pounds.

One of the French authors has calculated that France makes a net gain annually of some 250 million dollars in her preferential trade within the French monetary zone; she buys at prices higher than the international market prices but she also sells her industrial products at higher prices.[89]

However, the proportionate place of the franc zone in the total French trade has been steadily declining. The proportion of exports to the zone in the total French exports fell from 36 per cent in 1954 to 20 per cent in 1962 and to 18 per cent in 1963. The proportion of imports from the zone declined from 27 per cent of the total French imports in 1954 to 21 per cent in 1962 despite the simultaneous growth in imports of Algerian oil. This decline is due mainly to the global increase in the volume of French trade owing to much livelier commercial relations with countries other than those of the franc zone, in particular the other developed nations. An opponent of aid could say that the primary products, which France buys from her former colonies, could be easily purchased from other countries at a lower price, and that her industrial exports to those former colonies are largely due to the French credits or grants which are used for buying French goods. The trade of countries of the franc zone with third states ends in a deficit, i.e., France must use her gold and dollar reserves to restore the balance. She has been constantly increasing this reserve owing to her own exports to the third countries, but her former colonies have been in this respect a burden rather than asset.[90]

One benefit derived from the French aid is the favorable climate for French private enterprises installed on former colonial territory. Still another is the profits which France makes on having the priority in supplying maritime and air transportation, as well as banking, insurance, and similar services. Finally, the French government expects to be repaid by the African states' support of its foreign policy, and by the privilege of retaining its military bases on the African Continent.

Arguments against foreign aid

Those Frenchmen who oppose foreign aid have a series of arguments familiar to any Western ear. These arguments are all tantamount to saying that France cannot afford to face all the responsibilities of her national defense and domestic development and at the same time spend great amounts of money on foreign countries. One of the critics sums up all these arguments in one sentence:

> She [France] will realize at her own expense that it is impossible to continue a costly military policy, an independent nuclear policy, a policy of aid to the overseas countries, and, at the same time, to develop her own national territory, to modernize her economy, to train the adequate number of her technologists and to renovate her educational system.[91]

This is a powerful argument and raises the whole problem of national priorities. The question whether France can afford all the priorities selected by her President cannot be now answered, especially since the future cost of nuclear armaments remains uncertain.

What is certainly true is the urgent need at home for large public investment. During the years 1950 to 1960 the growth of the French gross national product was lower than that of Germany, Italy, and Holland. Proportionately France exports more primary commodities and semi-finished goods and a lesser proportion of manufactured products than either Germany or Britain. Yet the existence of the Common Market compels her to compete with industries of the five other partners; the export of manufactured goods to other countries also is needed. The greatest profits of any developed country are realized by exports of industrial goods.[92]

She needs renovation after the former period of stagnation: 43 per cent of rural communes, where nine million people live, had no running water in 1963. In the same year the total lengths of French automobile throughways was 240 kilometers, while it was 3,000 in Germany, 210 for small Belgium, 792 for small Holland, 302 for Britain, and 1,341 for Italy.

The rhythm of housing construction is not very rapid. In 1963 only 10 per cent of apartments had a bathroom, while the percentage was 30 for Holland, 43 for Germany, and 62 for Britain.[93] In the same year, the national education budget amounted only to 3.5 per cent of the gross national product.[94] Teachers sent to foreign countries would find full employment in France, where they are needed.

Another French critic points out the irritation among French peasants. Many of them see their own often outmoded agricultural implements, the decrepit housing, the lack of irrigation where it is needed or of running water in the villages, and they "find it difficult to understand why important aid is given to countries which have broken off from France and do not always support her international policy."[95]

Those are weighty arguments, which could be repeated *mutatis mutandis* in other developed countries. De Gaulle disregards them for the two reasons which have been indicated: worldwide French policy, and the moral obligation of the prosperous to help the poor.

The size of French financial assistance

French assistance takes almost exclusively the bilateral form as is true of other developed nations. It is expected to bring political profits, which would have been lost in the anonymity of multilateral aid, and compels the receiving countries to purchase French products for the francs which are placed at their disposal.

The former colonial possessions enjoy priority:

> At present, taking only percentages, the countries of the franc area received more than 85 per cent of the public and private bilateral aid granted by France, and more than 95 per cent of public aid

alone in 1961 and 1962. This aid was distributed within the franc area in the following way: in Algeria-Sahara—48 per cent in 1961, 42 per cent in 1962, in Black Africa and Madagascar—25 per cent in 1961, 30 per cent in 1962.[96]

However, the trend in the last few years has been toward a greater share for other underdeveloped countries. In 1963 the proportion of total French aid, public and private, given to the countries of the franc zone fell to 79 per cent, and in 1964 it was further reduced to 76.7 per cent. The French Minister of National Economy, Giscard d'Estaing, commented in July 1965 that this was the result of a deliberate policy to increase the proportion reserved for other underdeveloped countries. This new policy reflects de Gaulle's ambition to extend French influence to all three underdeveloped continents and in particular to Latin America. It represents also a reassurance against possible political disappointments in French Africa, and helps in diversifying French exports; the extension of credits to such underdeveloped countries, which have a greater capacity than French sub-Saharan Africa to absorb industrial imports, would provide a stimulus for French industrial production.

One obvious area where France may extend her aid is that part of French-speaking Africa which had been under Belgian administration. In 1963 agreements for technical assistance were concluded with Burundi and Congo-Leopoldville. In the same year France seemed to have reached the first stage in a reconciliation with her prodigal son, Guinea; cultural cooperation agreements were signed on May 22, terminating the long period of mutual resentment which had followed the Guinean option for independence in 1958. But the reconciliation did not last long. In November 1965 Guinea accused France of having participated in a plot to overthrow Sékou Touré's regime. Diplomatic relations between the two countries were broken off. This new quarrel with France did not greatly affect the situation of Guinea. She had not been among the recipients of French aid. The mutual trade was insignificant. The only sanction that France was able to apply was the recalling of 140 technical assistants (mostly teachers). The two French corporations which exploited the Guinean iron-ore deposits and produced aluminum from local bauxite quietly continued their operation, paying no attention either to the breach in 1958 or to the quarrel in 1965. For trade Guinea relies mostly on the Soviet Union and for development mostly on rather generous American aid.[97]

The other areas where France offers or intends to offer her assistance —financial, and, above all, technical—are Latin America, Cambodia and Laos, and the Near East.[98]

One can appreciate the size of French aid if one glances at the actual figures. The French government includes within the totals of financial assistance not only public aid but also investments, loans, and short-term (shorter than five years) commercial credits granted by French private institutions such as banks and industrial corporations. The percentages of foreign aid in the gross national product and in the national income are calculated without deducting that portion of aid which never leaves France: one-third of the salaries of the technical assistance personnel which must be left in France as a sort of compulsory saving, and the credits which are granted with the stipulation that the assisted state will purchase French goods (other governments also include these credits in their total foreign aid). Like other assisting countries, France never deducts the amount of repatriated French capital from the annual total aid. As a result, the assisted countries receive less foreign exchange for purchases abroad than one would believe from looking at the totals of foreign aid. Hence the official French figures are higher than they would be if they included only the net amount of French public and private capital transferred to the assisted states.

The official figures (in millions of dollars) are as follows for the years 1962, 1963, and 1964:[99]

	1962	1963	1964
Public aid	995.0	855.8	849.0
Private aid	407.0	393.2	524.6
Total aid	1,402.0	1,249.0	1,373.6

The component parts of the above totals were:[100]

	1962	1963	1964
Public subsidies to budgets and the consolidation of former public and private loans	12%	15%	10%
Cost of technical and cultural assistance	20%	25%	25%
Economic investments	68%	60%	65%

The proportionate growth of expenditure geared to technical-cultural assistance and to investment in the economic development of underdeveloped countries, combined with the proportionate reduction in nonproductive subsidies to balance the budgets of those countries and with the consolidation of their former debts to France, marked the beginning of a healthy trend in 1964 which the French government intends to promote. In 1964 this trend was principally due to a 30 per cent decrease in subsidies granted to support the Algerian budget.

Another interesting trend is the reduction in total public aid and the corresponding increase in 1964 of the total of private loans and investments. This not only proves that the French banks and industrial corporations now have a greater confidence in the future of underdeveloped countries, but it also reflects the new attitude of the French government, which now believes that technical-cultural assistance is relatively more important than financial aid. This is a reasonable surmise only if it does not become a general rule. The truly undeveloped countries cannot usefully absorb large quantities of foreign capital because they lack the necessary skilled personnel to make a productive use of that capital. However, even these countries need a certain amount of financial aid to build their socioeconomic substructure (such as roads, harbors, hospitals, and schools). Other developing countries have a larger pool of skilled personnel and are able to use greater amounts of financial aid productively.

As we said, in recent years France has been paying growing attention to developing nations other than her former colonies which belong to the franc monetary zone. The proportional distribution of French public and private aid was as follows in the years 1962, 1963, and 1964:[101]

	1962	1963	1964
Franc zone	85%	79%	76.7%
Other countries	12%	15%	22.0%

The remainder of French aid was channelled through multilateral organizations such as the EEC and the United Nations organizations. The totals of multilateral aid have constantly remained low: 117 million dollars in 1962, 28.1 million in 1963, and 16.7 million in 1964. The French government intended to do better in 1965.

The official French estimates of the proportionate relation between the total aid, both public and private, and the gross national product or the national income are higher than if they were calculated otherwise (see the observations above). Even so they show a proportional decline of foreign aid. The figures are as follows:[102]

	1962	1963	1964
Foreign aid in:			
Percentage of gross national product	1.92%	1.56%	1.56%
Percentage of national income	2.51%	2.07%	2.07%

If one were to deduct the amounts made up of the one-third of salaries paid to the French technical-assistance personnel, the money which may be used only for the purchase of French goods, and the capital repatriated to France, the net percentage of gross national product spent in 1964 on foreign aid would fall to 1.35. If one did not deduct those items but used the system of computation adopted by the Organization for Economic Cooperation and Development, he would eliminate the credits granted for periods shorter than five years. Then the comparative figures of proportion of national income spent on foreign aid in 1964 would look as follows:[103]

France	1.94%
Belgium	1.13%
Britain	1.09%
USA	0.96%
Germany	0.94%

Whatever the manner of calculation, France always remains, percentagewise, at the head of large Western nations insofar as foreign aid is concerned. Of course, absolute figures tell a somewhat different story. The United States' assistance amounted to 57 per cent of the total Western aid which, in 1964, reached the figure of almost 9 billion dollars. (The aid offered by the Communist states was much smaller, amounting only to 1.3 million dollars.) France occupied second place even regarding the absolute amount of financial assistance.

This aid has produced satisfactory results in sub-Saharan Africa, where the growth rate of the gross national product has been on the average 6.6 per cent annually during the years 1958–63. Gabon, the Ivory Coast, Senegal, Mauritania and Cameroons were the most successful in this respect. The exports from the former French sub-Saharan Africa have increased by 33 per cent, twice the average for all the underdeveloped countries. It is only fair to add that the stimulating factor other than French assistance has been the EEC aid and preferential trade (see below).

On September 29, 1965, Foreign Minister Maurice Couve de Murville proudly told the UN General Assembly that his government considered that foreign aid "should be subordinate to a formal condition, which is abstention from linking aid, whatever its form, to any political condition whatsoever, and abstention from any intervention in this respect in the affairs" of recipient states.[104] The calm with which the French government observed the changes of government and the variety of foreign policies in its former colonial possessions, especially in Algeria, confirms the truth of his statement. Except for Guinea and Tunisia, France has never retaliated by suspending her aid.

Algeria: keystone of relations with the Third World

France gives the first place in foreign aid to Algeria.

For France, the success of cooperation with Algeria will be the keystone in her relations with the other countries of "the Third

World." Moreover, the French government wants to preserve its interests in the Sahara regarding both oil and gas and the atomic test grounds.[105]

Algeria has been receiving well over 40 per cent of the total aid given to the franc zone. She is definitely General de Gaulle's spoiled child. In his relations with the Algerian government since 1962, he has displayed an unusual degree of patience and forbearance, which are not his outstanding virtues. For instance, he could not control his temper in 1963 when Brazil interfered with the French fishing boats that were looking for lobsters too close to the Brazilian coast. He sent a destroyer, but Brazil was quick in meeting it with a battleship and an aircraft carrier. The French destroyer had no choice but to retreat. The lobster war was fortunately avoided, and de Gaulle's Latin-American policy was not compromised by this rather ridiculous outburst of anger.

Algeria has repeatedly and grossly violated many provisions of the Evian agreements. The French President has patiently borne these infractions, which hurt French interests. Algeria entered into friendly relations with other powers, in particular the Soviet Union. De Gaulle did not insist on an exclusive friendship for France. The Algerian government, which had signed the Evian agreements, was soon after overthrown by the combined efforts of Ben Bella and Colonel Boumedienne, the commander-in-chief of Algerian armed forces. De Gaulle established the most cordial relations with Ben Bella, who became the favorite son of both Paris and Moscow. In June 1965 Ben Bella was overthrown in turn by the military coup of his former friend, Colonel Boumedienne. Moscow hardly concealed its dissatisfaction, but the French government took the change in stride, especially as the first declarations of the new Algerian government assured France of its intention to continue the most friendly cooperation. The French President received the new Algerian ambassador on July 3 and told him: "I beg you to believe that the French Republic has the greatest sympathy for the Algerian Republic."[106] A few days later he sent a cordial message to the new government. Finally, on July 29, 1965, France and Algeria signed a new agreement on the exploitation of oil and natural gas resources of the Sahara; France made important concessions.

Briefly, in that agreement France committed her financial and technical resources for at least fifteen years which might, however, bring unexpected changes in the oil market. The cost of exploitation in the Sahara is three or four times higher than that in the Near East. The advantages are the good quality of Algerian oil and the proximity of European ports. The price France pays for that oil is higher than the world price; gasoline costs 50 per cent more in France than in Germany or Italy where the oil market is open to free foreign competition. The French companies are allowed to export only half of their profits on the exploitation in Algeria. The new agreement significantly increased the Algerian government's share in the profits. Moreover, France took on the obligation to assist in the industrial development of Algeria, which depends mainly on her resources in oil and natural gas.

The oil agreement has a significance much wider than the French-Algerian relations. It introduced the concept of mutually fruitful cooperation between the underdeveloped country, producer of oil, and a Western country. France was guaranteed the supply of Algerian oil, but she also agreed to aid in Algerian industrialization. The mutual interests of both partners were happily harmonized at no small cost to France.

The Algerian production of oil has rapidly increased from 1.2 million tons in 1959 to 26.2 million tons in 1964. In 1964 the French oil imports reached a total of 49 million tons, of which 17.1 million came from Algeria. The reserves of Algerian natural gas are calculated to amount to 1,000 billion cubic meters.[107]

Why is it that the Fifth Republic has chosen to commit itself to the exploitation of Algerian natural resources at a high cost to itself and at the risk that a future Algerian government might tear down the present agreement? Probably the most plausible explanation is that the French President wants to be as independent as possible of oil supplies which are controlled by the "Anglo-Saxon" corporations. In any event, the French privileged aid to Algeria is conditional, in the first place, upon the possibility of exploiting these resources.

The generous financial and technical aid is not the only French asset in the relations with Algeria. The other is the presence of several hundred thousand Algerian workers in France who support their families in Algeria and whose expulsion would be a major disaster for that country. Finally, Algerian trade relies heavily on exports of wine to France.

The other reason for pampering the Algerian government is losing its importance: the testing grounds are being replaced by the new ones in the Pacific better suited for thermonuclear tests.

A final reason is probably the most important in de Gaulle's eyes. Algeria is conceived of as a gateway leading to the other underdeveloped countries. France is demonstrating there what her policy is toward the whole Third World. It is not only that her aid to Algeria is very impressive and free from any political strings. France has proved, throughout the short but turbulent history of the Algerian Republic, that she does not interfere in the domestic affairs of underdeveloped countries. She is prepared to cooperate with any government, whatever its political and social complexion and whatever its other international friendships, as long as she is repaid with sympathy. This aspect of the French policy toward Algeria represents an invaluable asset regarding the whole Third World.

A policy of noninterference

Prime Minister Pompidou stressed France's policy of noninterference in the domestic affairs of other countries in his speech on June 18, 1965, in the National Assembly, while voicing the disapproval of American actions in Vietnam and the Dominican Republic. He said:

> We are criticised for allegedly compromising the [Atlantic] Alliance and even acting against its spirit by refusing to support the policy of the United States in Vietnam or in Santo Domingo. Nobody on the opposition benches has approved of that policy. But they say that the French government and the President of the Republic are wrong in publicly expressing disagreement. I hope that no one here has lost his memory. Did the United States hesitate to disagree publicly with the French policy at the time of Suez or of the bombing of Sakiet? The comparison with Suez is particularly convincing, because in that case France and Britain took military measures, without informing the United States, for the defense of what they considered their vital interests. Likewise, the United States recently sent troops to Santo Domingo, without informing us, to defend what it considered its vital interests there. What did Mr. Dulles say on November 2, 1956, at the famous meeting of the United Nations Assembly? "Our disagreement with our friends has made us reconsider and reexamine our position . . . , but our disagreement continues to exist even after this reexamination. And because it seems to us that this disagreement involves principles of an importance which transcends by far the importance of the question before us, we feel that it is our duty to make our point of view known to members of this Assembly and, by their intermediary, to the entire world." The French government can adopt these words integrally as its own. They define our own attitude perfectly . . . because, when we defend not only our independence but the independence of all nations, when we denounce all foreign interventions whatever their origin, we only defend what is at the root of our democratic traditions, of our traditions of freedom, I want to say, the right of peoples, of all the peoples to self-determination.[108]

These eloquent words were addressed not so much to the National Assembly as to the Third World. Foreign Minister Couve de Murville upheld the same principle on September 29, 1965, in his speech at the UN

General Assembly: "An essential condition [of international coopera-
tion] is respect for each one by each other, respect for independence,
non-interference in the affairs of others, establishment of world-wide
cooperation on the basis of strict equality."[109]

The EEC and French African policy

The picture of French economic relations with her former colonial
possessions would be incomplete if one overlooked the benefits France
derives in this respect from the existence of the European Economic
Community. She twice overcame the resistance of her partners and persuaded them to share to some extent the cost of maintaining French
influence in Africa. The Treaty of Rome established a fund of financial
assistance to the colonial dependencies of France, Belgium, Holland, and
Italy. Out of the total of 581 million dollars derived from the contributions of the Six, 511 million dollars were earmarked for the French
colonial possessions. As the French contribution to the fund amounted
to 200 million dollars, the net French gain was 311 million. This fund
was spent in five years. France fought for its renewal and won the battle.

A new treaty, the so-called Treaty of Yaoundé, was signed in 1963
between the six members of the EEC, and the following underdeveloped
countries: Mauritania, Senegal, Mali, the Ivory Coast, High Volta, Togo,
Dahomey, Niger, Tchad, Cameroon, the Central African Republic,
Gabon, Congo-Brazzaville, Madagascar (former French colonies);
Congo-Leopoldville, Ruanda, Burundi (formerly under the Belgian administration); and the former Italian Somaliland. On November 14,
1961, the same benefits were extended to the Dutch Caribbean possessions.

This treaty created for another five years a fund of financial assistance
to the amount of 800 million dollars; 620 million dollars are to be grants
and 180 million will be lent. These sums are being used to promote
economic and social development and for the diversification of production. Seventy million dollars are reserved for colonial possessions not yet
emancipated. The contributions of the Six are as follows: France and
Germany, 246.5 million each; Italy, 100 million; Belgium, 69 million;
Holland, 66 million; and Luxembourg 2 million dollars. As Germany
had lost her colonies after the First World War and the share of territories
formerly administrated by Italy, Belgium, and Holland is very small, the
main beneficiaries of the fund are France and her former colonial possessions. Eighty-seven per cent of the fund established by the Treaty of
Rome was spent on assistance to former French possessions. The same
was true during the first year of the operations of the Yaoundé Treaty
fund; for instance, by July 1965, 90 per cent was spent on former French
possessions and only 10 per cent on Dutch Caribbean dependencies.[110]

The Treaty of Rome established a preferential tariff for the imports of the Six coming from the colonial dependencies of Common Market members, principally France. The Treaty of Yaoundé extended this system in spite of a strong German and Dutch opposition. Germany and Holland trade mostly with British Africa and are reluctant to antagonize their customers, who compete with French Africa in exports of tropical products. Moreover, they did not want to displease their Latin-American customers who export coffee and bananas. Finally, France won the battle after making some concessions to her partners. The Yaoundé Treaty granted preferential treatment to tropical imports from French-speaking Africa; these imports are not subject to any EEC customs duties or domestic taxes. However, the external tariff of the Common Market regarding tropical imports from other countries was lowered (a French concession compensated by the increase in the amount of financial assistance to French-speaking Africa), but maintained.

African states repaid this preferential treatment by promising to eliminate all customs duties on imports from the Common Market. They retained the right to have tariffs if this were required as a source of national revenue, to protect their new industries, or to keep their economies diversified. All enterprises of the Six operating on the territories of the underdeveloped countries, parties to the treaty, are guaranteed the same equal treatment; they cannot be discriminated against in favor of enterprises of the former colonial powers.

Finally, the EEC gives technical assistance by providing scholarships for young Africans, geological surveys, and demographic studies. It also helps carry out the projects it finances. In effect, France shares a good part of the burden of assistance to her former colonies with her partners in the Common Market. This is another reason why the termination of this Market would be costly to her.

French technical assistance

The French effort in providing technical assistance is as impressive as it is in giving economic assistance. This aid is principally directed toward those twenty-one non-European countries where French is the official language. In 1962 the total of French personnel serving abroad was over 46,000. Seventy per cent of them were teachers, 12 per cent economic advisers, 10 per cent public administrators, and 10 per cent were experts in various other fields, including postal and telecommunications.[111] The priority of French Africa is observed also regarding technical assistance. Out of the 46,121 technical assistants (including teachers) 32,928 worked in North Africa, principally in Algeria; 10,399 in the former sub-Saharan African colonies; and 312 in various other African countries. The remaining 2,492 were scattered all over the world: about 1,000 in the three countries of Indochina, 450 in the Near East, and 563 in Latin America.[112]

The most lasting French investment is cultural. Thirty-two thousand French teachers serve abroad. Five thousand of them work in the sub-Saharan countries, 12,000 in Algeria, a very large part of the remaining 15,000 in Morocco, Tunisia (over 11,000 in these two countries), Lebanon, Congo-Leopoldville, Cambodia, Laos, and Vietnam. Twenty-seven thousand in all serve in the countries where French is the official language or the language of educated elites.[113] This investment in the future cultural ties is supplemented by the studies in France; the number of African students from the former colonial possessions, including the Arabs, each year exceeds 10,000. (The total of foreign students in France was 38,000 in 1964–65.) France has helped in another way by founding universities in Tunis, Rabat, Dakar, Tananarive, Abidjan, and Brazzaville, and schools of public administration in Congo (Leopoldville), Burundi, Morocco, Tunisia, Vietnam, Cambodia, Laos, Turkey, Lebanon, Colombia, and Paraguay.[114]

The most recent data on French technical assistance to the former overseas possessions are as follows. There are now 8,300 teachers (formerly 12,000) and 4,000 other technical aides personnel (formerly 14,000) in Algeria; 7,000 teachers work in Morocco. Teachers also remain in Tunisia in spite of a bitter quarrel which broke out in 1964 over the Tunisian nationalization of French-owned land. However, all financial aid to that country was cancelled and preferential treatment in trade refused.

There are 9,000 Frenchmen, including over 5,000 teachers, who work in sub-Saharan Africa.[115]

French technical aid, like the financial, is predominantly bilateral. France lent the services of her 1,350 experts in 1964 to the international technical-cooperation agencies. Although this figure is small in comparison to the large personnel engaged in the bilateral aid, France occupies, even in this respect, a second place in the world, immediately following the United States.[116]

It is the French view that technical assistance is more important than financial. The Foreign Minister said on April 28, 1964:

Training of men is the true, the only means of putting the underdeveloped countries in a position to carry out the main body of the task themselves, as is indispensable, since everything in the final analysis depends for each of these countries on the individual effort that it will be able to make. . . . I personally think that, in accord with our spirit and within our means, it is above all the training of men that should be stressed. . . . This means a much greater increase in our technical aid.[117]

A French high official in charge of French cultural programs abroad quoted the saying of Confucius: "If you are making plans for one year, grow rice. If you are making them for a century, train men."

From the domestic point of view technical assistance has the notable advantage of involving France in comparatively small expense; this is why it has not met with any serious opposition.

Stabilization of prices for primary commodities

France has another asset in her relations with the underdeveloped countries. They constantly insist on the international stabilization of prices for primary commodities which are the main source of the income they derive from foreign trade. The trend observed for a long time has been toward the decline in these prices and the parallel rise in the prices of industrial goods which the underdeveloped countries have to import. Moreover, the frequent fluctuations in the prices for primary commodities (due to the variable demand of developed countries) sometimes reduce the income from exports and the reserves of foreign currencies so rapidly that, in a bad year, they cancel the benefits which should be derived from foreign aid. The currencies placed by the developed countries at the disposal of the underdeveloped countries might, in such a year, not even compensate the loss of profits which were expected to be realized in the exports of primary products. The French study committee observed in its report submitted to the government that France was "on this point the natural ally of the underdeveloped countries."[118] Being herself an important exporter of agricultural surpluses, she advocates the international stabilization of prices for primary commodities.

However, she parts ways with the exporters of tropical goods from British Africa and Latin America insofar as she grants preferential treatment to French Africa and is responsible for the Common Market preferential system. In fact, this particular grievance has temporarily lost its impact on French relations with British Africa and Latin America because of a general decline in prices for tropical goods such as coffee. The French-African prices are higher than those prevailing on the international market, and the competitors from British Africa and Latin America sell their products on the Common Market in spite of discriminatory tariffs.

France adopted a sympathetic attitude to the underdeveloped countries at the United Nations Conference on Trade and Development held in Geneva from March to June 1964. The French position included the following points:

1. A market organization for individual primary commodities, combined with a reasonable limitation on production, guaranteed outlets, and stable, remunerative prices, would be established.

2. Regional economic unions would be promoted among the underdeveloped countries to provide them with a large scope for joint and coordinated development. France did not object to the fact that such unions would have, on the one hand, an internal free circulation of goods, and, on the other hand, external tariffs to protect the union's market against undue foreign competition. She saw the model of these unions in the European Common Market.

3. She favored the industrialization of underdeveloped countries.[119]

Wooing of all Africans

Like St. Peter, de Gaulle is a fisher of men. His net is cast in all the oceans and seas. Whenever he pulls it out, he finds there only a few Americans, a lesser number of West Europeans than he has hoped for, a good many European and Asian Communists, but above all his catch is rich in the underdeveloped countries. He casts his net without paying any attention to the complaints of other powers that he is a poacher who fishes in their waters.

His cultivation of excellent relations with sub-Saharan Africans is no longer restricted to the former French Africa. The pilgrims come now from other parts, including British Africa and the Belgian Congo. In the summer of 1965 it was President Nyerere, formerly the American favorite son in Africa, who paid a visit to the French President; a French newspaper remarked that the two men could find at least one common denominator in "Mr. Nyerere's neutralism and General de Gaulle's refusal of automatic alignment."[120] During the same summer seven Presidents of the former French colonial possessions and the Congolese Prime Minister Tshombé came to pay homage to their hero. At the reception given them by the French President, one of them, the President of the Ivory Coast, Houphouet-Boigny, enthusiastically exclaimed:

> Thanks to you we have been able to lead our peoples along the road of freedom and happiness. We who are gathered here and all the others, whether they speak French or English, turn their eyes toward Paris, knowing that you are the guaranty of our peace and security. . . . We should like to welcome you in each of our states where our good people are impatient to see you and to give

you a reception such, I do not want to exaggerate, as you have had nowhere, not even in France.[121]

North Africa did not remain behind. The Moroccan Ambassador in Paris told a French audience that:

> Between the two colossi who confront each other with all the might of their frightening power in order to settle the problem of the world's hegemony, has emerged a man who thinks that other peoples might have a common denominator other than material wealth and the non-peaceful use of the atom, who understands that it is necessary to rally all those underdeveloped peoples under a banner, no doubt, less spectacular than the missiles and the outer-space satellites, but how much more exalting, how much more becoming to human dignity: freedom, the self-determination of peoples, their right to live and survive in respect for their own genius. This catalyst of the world, which should be called Third, is General de Gaulle.[122]

The propaganda against the two hegemonies has visibly paid rich dividends. It brought dividends also in Peking where the French Minister André Malraux was received in the summer of 1965 with the marks of friendship rarely given to other foreign guests. Mao Tse-tung, who now seldom sees foreign visitors; Liu Shao-tsi, the head of the Chinese Republic; Chou En-lai, its Prime Minister; and Chen Yi, the Foreign Minister, all found time to have talks with him. This hospitality was a tribute paid to the French foreign policy and certainly not personally to André Malraux, whom the Chinese leaders could have regarded as a traitor to the Communist cause; his early literary fame originated in the recollections of his participation in the twenties in the Communist struggle against Kuomintang. To the Chinese, Malraux was the trusted man of the French President.

Arab Near East

The Arab Near East, formerly one of the main areas of French-British competition and the zone of strong French cultural influence, was practically closed to France during the six years of the Algerian war. She was denounced as the number one Western enemy. Her diplomatic relations with Egypt had been severed since the fall of 1956. The settlement of the Algerian question entirely changed the scenery. In April 1962 the Council of the Arab League expressed hope that the Evian agreements would open a new era of fruitful French relations with the whole Arab world.

France has greater freedom to maneuver in the Near East than Britain with her Persian Gulf protectorates and her base at Aden or even the United States with its vested interests in the Near Eastern oil and its close friendship with Israel. The only difficulty France encounters is her own sympathy for Israel which she has so far refused to sacrifice for the sake of the Arabs.

Diplomatic relations with the United Arab Republic were restored in April 1963. The mutual exchange of visits by the French and Egyptian V.I.P.'s, including Edgar Faure, the unofficial roving ambassador for the French President (he prepared the ground in 1964 for the establishment of diplomatic relations with China and in February 1965 paid a visit to President Nasser), and Marshal Abdel Hakim Amer, Vice President of the United Arab Republic who came to Paris in October 1965, demonstrated the warmth of relations between Paris and Cairo. It is said that President Nasser considers France the Western power closest to the orientation of Egyptian foreign policy. He welcomes the French principle of nonintervention in the domestic affairs of other countries, the opposition to the United States, the recognition of Peking, the propaganda in favor of the neutralization of Vietnam, the French position regarding the Cyprus affair, and even de Gaulle's Latin-American tour. No doubt, the two philosophies of international politics are not too far apart. The Egyptians dislike only the Israeli aspect of French policy, but do not make a major tragedy of it and interpret the recent French moves as a desirable evolution: the vote in the United Nations in favor of the return of Arab refugees to Israel, and the French refusal to extend military cooperation with Israel to include nuclear armaments. French is again taught in the Egyptian schools. Only trade is no longer what it used to be prior to the Suez Canal affair; France, which was the second best customer in 1956, now occupies thirteenth place. Since 1963 France granted 100 million dollars in credits to the U.A.R.

The Egyptians set de Gaulle's "true France" in opposition to the "France of Guy Mollet" that invaded their country in 1956. They know that Couve de Murville, now French Foreign Minister, was opposed to that invasion and believe that at that time de Gaulle had no sympathy for the Suez venture.

Vietnam and SEATO

Farther afield, General de Gaulle has completely parted ways with the United States. His views differ radically from the American regarding the three states of the Indochinese peninsula. He obviously does not believe in the domino theory, according to which the loss of South Vietnam would bring about the fall of Laos and Cambodia, of Thailand

and Burma, possibly also of Malaysia, and the extension of the Chinese influence throughout the whole of Southeast Asia to the borders of India. He has never publicly disclosed the details of his own plan for the settlement of the Vietnamese question. His slogan, "neutralization," might mean many things. It certainly means the departure of American troops from Indochina. A free guess is permitted. Those Frenchmen who know Vietnam stress the traditional animosity of the Vietnamese toward the Chinese, who had held them under their power for a thousand years. They say that these feelings are shared in Hanoi, where the Communist government least desires a Chinese reoccupation. Perhaps de Gaulle's analysis develops according to the following scheme. If American actions did not compel the North Vietnamese to look for help anywhere, including China, and if the Americans departed, the two Vietnams would soon be united under the Communist administration. The fact that it would be a Communist unified Vietnam does not worry the French President, for whom ideologies are passing phenomena in the life of the only realities, nations. A united Vietnam, no longer fearing the West but suspicious of Chinese intentions, would turn to Russia as the most trusted and geographically remote friend. The Soviet Union, who has no territorial ambitions in Southeast Asia, would acquire an ally there. Vietnam would occupy a position in that part of Asia somewhat similar to that of Albania, the Chinese friend in Europe. The distrust of the closest Communist power would have for effect in both cases friendship with the rival Communist power. If this is what de Gaulle has in mind, it is impossible either to prove that he is right or to refute him. There are many if's in this view of the future. The main if's are the Chinese assent to the situation which would be prejudicial to Chinese interests and the American willingness to engage in a gamble which de Gaulle perhaps has in mind.

De Gaulle publicly dissociated himself from American policy in several statements. One of them was made on August 29, 1963:

> The French government is following with attention and emotion the grave events occurring in Vietnam. . . . France's knowledge of the merits of that people makes her appreciate the role they would be capable of playing in the present situation in Asia for their own progress and in furthering international understanding, once they could go ahead with their activities independently of the outside, in the domestic peace and unity and in harmony with their neighbors. Today more than ever, this is what France wishes for Vietnam as a whole. Naturally it is up to the Vietnamese people and to them alone to choose the means of achieving it, but any national

effort that would be undertaken in Vietnam with this objective in view would find France ready, to the extent of her own possibilities, to organize a cordial cooperation with that country.[123]

The French President was no more specific when he made another statement on September 9, 1965, relating to Vietnam:

We believe that in Asia the end of fighting now going on, then the satisfactory development of peoples, can be obtained only by establishing relations, by opening negotiations and by achieving a *modus vivendi* among the powers whose direct or indirect responsibility has, since the end of World War II, been committed to the events of the southeast of that continent, that is, China, France, America, Russia and Britain. But we also believe more firmly than ever that the primary condition for such an understanding would be the effective end of all foreign intervention, and therefore the complete and controlled neutralization of the zone in which there is fighting. That is what France, for her part, subscribed to in 1954. . . . This is what she considers necessary since the United States intervened in Indochina after the departure of French forces.[124]

He left unanswered a few self-evident questions: How can China and the United States be brought to a conference table and to a mutually acceptable agreement? How can Southeast Asia be neutralized effectively and future Chinese encroachments prevented? What kind of guaranties would be required to defend this neutrality? Should the status of neutrality allow North Vietnam to unite the whole country and overthrow the Southern regime, if this took place without any foreign assistance?

Conversely, the two statements made other aspects of the French stand clear: an independent and neutral Vietnam should be free of any foreign intervention (presumably both Chinese and American) and eventually united under one government. The procedure to be followed for the settlement of the Vietnamese problem should be, according to General de Gaulle, a new Geneva Conference attended by the five great powers and Vietnamese representatives. This conference should find a solution based on the decisions of the former Geneva Conference of 1954.

The elimination of the American and Chinese influences would reopen the French prospect of returning to the Indochinese peninsula owing to her economic and cultural cooperation. She still retains strong influence in Cambodia, who trusts her more than any other great power, Western or Communist. France is no prospective threat to the independence of the Indochinese states for the simple reason that her means are too modest for such ambition.

Saigon's rupture in 1965 of diplomatic relations with France did not make de Gaulle unhappy. He might have been relieved to see his obligations toward that government terminated; he would anyhow sacrifice it for the sake of the unification and neutrality of the whole of Vietnam. President Sukarno, another pilgrim to Paris in 1965, correctly presented the French President's views when he said on his return to Indonesia that General de Gaulle did not believe in the American victory in Vietnam.[125]

In 1966 de Gaulle continued to take steps which further widened the gulf between his stand and American policy. The commercial missions of North Vietnam and France were raised in early 1966 to the status of delegations, a level not much lower than that of embassies. On February 8, 1966 the French President sent a personal letter to Ho Chi Minh, President of North Vietnam.[126] He recalled in this letter France's strict observance of the 1954 Geneva agreements and the noninterference in Vietnamese affairs. He assured the North Vietnamese *government* (he actually used this word to convey a sort of informal recognition) that France desired a return to the general and full implementation of the Geneva agreements (probably including the elections in both parts of the country promised in these agreements for 1956 but never held in South Vietnam), that she was opposed to intervention (this could have been interpreted as a disapproval not only of the American but also of the Chinese and Soviet policies), and that she wanted Vietnam eventually unified to enjoy the status of neutrality under international guaranty. He also called for the formation of a truly representative government in South Vietnam, i.e., of a government in which presumably the National Liberation Front would at least participate if not dominate. Finally, he excluded the possibility of reaching any solution by military action; he probably meant that neither the United States nor the North Vietnamese and Vietcong could win a decisive victory. He expressed the French opposition to the present hostilities and strongly protested against a further escalation of war. In conclusion, he promised Ho Chi Minh that he would use French influence to pursue those objectives.

This stand, at variance with official American policy, seems to have the support of French public opinion. One of the fiercest domestic opponents of de Gaulle, the editor-in-chief of *Le Monde,* added the following comment to the President's letter: "There is practically no single Frenchman who is not in deep agreement [with de Gaulle] on this problem."[127]

The problem of Southeast Asia divided France from the United States as deeply as the French withdrawal from NATO. In February 1966 the United States requested the Security Council of the United Nations to place the Vietnamese problem on its agenda. France joined the Soviet Union in opposing this request. Both claimed that this question should be discussed outside of the United Nations, at a conference in which China and Vietnam could be represented, since neither of them was a UN member. The Soviet delegate cast a nay vote, while the French representative abstained in disapproval.

The President of the French Republic again had the opportunity to mention the Vietnamese problem at the press conference held on February 21, 1966.[128] He reiterated his known views. According to him, the only practical way out was to reach an agreement among the five world powers (the United States, the Soviet Union, France, China, and Britain). The substance of that agreement should be composed of two elements: the prohibition of any foreign intervention in Vietnamese affairs, and the neutrality and independence of Vietnam presumably guaranteed by the same five powers.

One may guess that General de Gaulle's policy regarding Vietnam is strongly influenced by his own experience in Algeria. Once he had been convinced that almost all Algerian Moslems (nine-tenths of the population) sympathized with the rebel guerrillas who were at home in that sympathetic environment, he realized that France could not win a decisive military victory in spite of her imposing armed superiority over the rebels. His own country had enough of that long and frustrating war. He himself conceded that even a decisive military victory would not put an end to the Algerian problem, because France could eliminate the rebels for a time only and a new revolt would break out again if the vast majority of the population was alienated from France and was ready to give support to the rebellion. If this reminiscence influences his stand on Vietnam, he overlooks one difference: France did not face other great powers in Algeria. The problem was limited to a French-Algerian dispute, while the United States believes that it indirectly contains the expansion of China, its main competitor in the Far East.

Prince Shihanouk, a frequent visitor to Paris, took the opportunity of the inauguration of the first deepsea port in Cambodia, Shihanoukville, built thanks to French assistance, to call France the most constant and the most faithful friend of his country.[129] In spite of her surviving influence in Indochina, France has no means, except persuasion, for imposing her own solution. She is only a pale shadow there; the decision belongs to the United States, China, and the Soviet Union.

Her lack of commitment is hardly compatible with her participation in SEATO. General de Gaulle recently took a step in the direction of disengaging France from her SEATO and other Asian commitments. He did not send his Foreign Minister, as it was usual before, to the SEATO meeting held in London in May 1965. France was represented only by an observer, her ambassador in Thailand, who declared that no joint policy and, furthermore, no common action was possible between France and the other members of SEATO. This statement once more dissociated France from American policy in Vietnam and from British, Australian, and New Zealander policy in Malaysia. The next logical step would be to quit the organization, which the Fourth Republic had joined in 1954, paradoxically after the French retreat from Vietnam. The French government entertains the most cordial relations with Indonesia and was the only Western power to side with it quite openly against Malaysia. In June 1965 the French liaison officer attached to the so-called United Nations command in Korea was recalled home; this was another sign that France wanted to remain uncommitted to the American position in Asia.

India and Pakistan

One of the fascinating aspects of French foreign policy is de Gaulle's ability to use as an asset the French weakness in the areas remote from Europe. No doubt, France is one of the principal European powers and, as such, may strongly influence the course of events. Her stand cannot remain without effect on the relations between Western Europe and either the United States or the Soviet Union, on the fate of the European Community and its relation to Britain, and on the future of NATO. She has a strong position in Africa and might recover her former influence in the Near East. However, her means are extremely feeble for any truly significant action in Asia or Latin America. De Gaulle exploits the paucity of French means. A power that cannot even try to impose its will inspires confidence. It might be pleasant to shed tears with it over the villainy of the hegemons. An emotional common denominator is created. Perhaps France does not gain much from this game in real or lasting benefits, but de Gaulle's personal popularity has been growing.

This game extends to India and Pakistan. France cannot replace the American or Soviet aid or usefully act as a mediator between India and her two enemies, China and Pakistan, but her general philosophy is as attractive there as it is in the United Arab Republic. In February 1965 Prime Minister Pompidou went to India and Pakistan. He and the Indian Prime Minister Shastri agreed to periodical consultations between the two governments on matters of common interest and found out that India and France held similar views on Vietnam. The French Prime Minister promised to increase technical assistance to India.

The next visit was to Pakistan. Faced with a pressing request for long-term credits, the French Prime Minister was unable to promise anything. He, like other foreign guests, was in both capitals, noncommittal on Kashmir. However, he reminded the Pakistanis that France planned to sell three submarines to their government. If anything seriously interested both governments it was their trade relations with the Common Market. Pakistan and India expected France to defend their interests within the EEC.

Those Indians who favor the acquisition of nuclear armaments in response to the Chinese tests hope that France, the non-signatory of the Moscow Treaty on the suspension of nuclear tests, would be prepared to assist. They found comfort in an interview granted by General Pierre Gallois to the Indian *Statesman* in which the French theoretician of nuclear problems strongly advised India to acquire nuclear weapons, because, as he said, China would otherwise be able to impose her will on all her neighbors in five years.[130] Unfortunately General Gallois is not a spokesman for the French government, which might be embarrassed if approached by India. Any aid given to India in this particular field would immediately disturb the friendly relations with both China and Pakistan.

In 1965 General de Gaulle learned the truth of the saying that one may not be the friend of all the people. The outbreak of hostilities between India and Pakistan embarrassed him just as much as the other Western powers and the Soviet Union. France adopted the same neutral position as they did. She tried to do her best to avoid spoiling her friendship with either belligerent. She fully supported the mediating efforts by the United Nations Security Council and by its Secretary General. For once the Security Council was unanimous. However, the French position in favor of bringing fighting to an end was no more liked in Peking than the similar stand by the United States, Britain, and Russia.

Latin-American brothers

General de Gaulle has hoped in recent years to make a rich catch in Latin America, where his anti-Yankee attitude finds many favorable echoes. It is there more than anywhere else that his diatribes against the hegemony are best understood. He pictures himself in the role of the Latin elder brother. Nearer home, he is not particularly successful with the other big Latin nation, Italy. He finds her constantly on the other side of the barricade within both the Common Market and NATO.

He entertains cordial relations with the two Latin dictatorial regimes in the Iberian peninsula, but this might prove to be not the best legacy after the disappearance of Franco and Salazar, who are not immortal.

His neat division of peoples into Gauls, Anglo-Saxons, Latins, and Slavs is disarmingly simple. The Slavs have very little in common except linguistic affinity. The American "Anglo-Saxons" descend from forebears who had lived all over Europe, Africa, and in the Near East. He forgets that many American "Latins" have had colored—Indian and African—ancestors. But his poetic images do not suffer such refined shades of color.

An old man, he did not hesitate to undertake two long tours in 1964 which took him to most of the Latin-American capitals. He went there as an errant knight to find new admirers for his "princess in the fairy tales." He was warmly applauded everywhere, but, as one of his French critics remarked, he was acclaimed not so much for his own sake but against someone else, the United States.[131] He was well briefed on what the Latin-Americans wanted to hear. In his speeches he emphasized Latin cultural unity, foreign aid (which France cannot offer there in any large amounts) without political strings attached, opposition to any hegemony, the economic diversification and industrialization of developing nations, and the stabilization of prices for primary commodities. In Mexico he paid homage to the "vast potential and the growing realities in Latin America." These verbal effusions did not change the actual situation. The United States remained the dominant power in the Western Hemisphere. Latin-American resentment against the Yankees did not wait for his visit to be born. The social and political problems of the turbulent continent were not solved. The only tangible result was a few credits, including 150 million dollars granted to Mexico; an increase in French technical assistance; and the pleasant recollection of his eloquence.

If his relations with the United States were better, he could have done something more beneficial for Latin Americans than paying them compliments. He would have been able to mobilize the resources of Western Europe for a large grant to supplement United States aid. From the American point of view the increase in the not unfriendly Western European influence in the Western Hemisphere would be an alternative much more attractive than the growth of Soviet or Chinese influence.

As it is, the French policy in Latin America is based on the easy exploitation of anti-Yankee resentment. Relations with Cuba are cordial. A group of French parliamentarians (the majority of them Gaullists) paid a visit in January 1965 to Havana. France occupies fifth place in the Cuban trade among the non-Communist States following Canada,

Spain, Holland, and Morocco. She sells trucks, tractors, locomotives, and other railroad equipment. The Cuban press hails, of course, every statement which de Gaulle makes against the hegemonies. The French government is planning to conclude an agreement with Cuba on cultural cooperation.

Those Latin Americans who are particularly dissatisfied with the existing relations between their countries and the United States are sure to find warm hospitality in Paris. They repay de Gaulle's compliments with their own. The former Brazilian President Juscellino Kubitschek took the opportunity of the visit to France to declare that Brazil and all other Latin-American countries expected much from France, to which they were linked by a deep friendship.[132] Eduardo Frei, the President of Chile, got red-carpet reception in the same month, July 1965, probably because of his well-known reservations concerning the policies of the United States in the Western Hemisphere. He had several conversations with the French President, who gave that guest from a distant country more time than he ever had given a European statesman. The joint communiqué of the two Presidents stressed a principle dear to Latin Americans and strictly observed by France: "the principle of non-intervention in domestic affairs, and the right of peoples to determine their fate."[133] They both agreed on the desirability of closer economic and cultural relations between the two countries, and on the need to stabilize prices for primary products and to facilitate exports of finished and semifinished goods from the developing nations. The French President expressed his sympathy for the economic integration of Latin America, while President Frei formulated his wish for closer economic cooperation between Latin America and Europe. Both envisaged a future entente between the two great communities, Europe and Latin America. This did not leave much room for the Organization of American States, for which President Frei had no tender feelings. On the last day of his visit he made statements to the press which could not displease his host. He said: "We cannot recognize the hegemony or the dominance by any people. . . . We want an inter-American system without any hegemony. . . . Cuba is a part of Latin America. Chile voted against her expulsion from the O.A.S." He finally expressed the hope that Western Europe would offer its own "Alliance for Progress."[134]

The French President was consistent when he instructed his representative in the United Nations to dissociate France from American intervention in the Dominican Republic. At the meeting of the Security Council the French delegate expressed France's disapproval of the dispatch of American troops as contrary to the principle of nonintervention in the affairs of other countries. He equally denounced the intervention by the Organization of American States. Whatever one may think of the wisdom of the American intervention, France, an ally, did her best to increase the embarrassment of the United States by joining the chorus of uncommitted and Communist nations.

De Gaulle's creed

General de Gaulle formulated his creed in a speech broadcast on April 27, 1965:

> With respect to the problems in the rest of the world, our independence leads us to act in accordance with our present concept, which is: no hegemony exercised by whomsoever, no foreign intervention in the domestic affairs of any State, no prohibition made to any country regarding peaceful relations maintained with any other country, are justified. On the contrary, in our view, the supreme interest of mankind dictates that every nation be responsible for herself, free from encroachments, aided in her progress without being compelled to obey. Hence, our reprobation of the war which is spreading in Asia day by day and more and more, our favorable attitude toward the efforts of human liberation and national organization undertaken by various countries of Latin America, the assistance we are giving to the development of a good number of new African States, the relations we are forging with China, and so on.[135]

This creed corresponds to the deepest aspirations of the Third World. It reflects the best liberal traditions of the West. It is unfortunate that it is being preached mainly against the United States.

United Nations

De Gaulle is at his greatest when his beloved France is confronted with a grave and immediate danger. He then quickly and clearly grasps the meaning and the implications of the problem and finds a solution. He did it from 1940 to 1945 and from 1958 to 1962. He is quick in detecting the great trends which shape the world and does not waste his time trying to halt the torrent of change. But his fertile mind is too mobile. It produces at one and the same time not one Grand Design but several that are not necessarily in harmony. Some of his major foreign policies are thwarted by other policies of his own. His policy toward the Third World, intelligent and generous, is contradicted by his aristocratic concept of international order. He is convinced that the world of medium-sized and small nations should be governed by a concert of great powers. He, who displays the zeal of a medieval Franciscan friar in denouncing the two hegemonies, at the same time advocates the collective hegemony of great powers. This collective hegemony acquires respectability in his eyes, because, of course, France would be one of the five hegemons.

He has not hidden his preference for this aristocratic form of international government (this urge to talk is one of his weaknesses); he has disclosed it each time he has fired a salvo at the United Nations. Yet this organization is the favorite forum of those medium-sized and small nations to whom he addresses his philippics against the two hegemonies. There and only there they fully enjoy the illusion of being equals of the strongest nations. Each of them has one vote in the General Assembly; the great powers have also only one vote each. A two-thirds majority decides which resolutions will be adopted. These resolutions seldom influence the course of events, but the great powers appreciate their propaganda value and sweat in the lobbies to collect the necessary votes. Each small nation can ventilate her grievances from the tribune of the United Nations and cannot be silenced. The publicity of that world forum is an impediment in the too cynical pursuit of power politics and acts as a feeble brake—but a brake nevertheless—on the Big Brothers.

General de Gaulle's publicized strictures against the United Nations could have been understood until the settlement of the Algerian question. France was often in the dock; many fingers in the General Assembly were accusingly pointing at her as an oppressor of colonial peoples. The debates in the General Assembly irritated both de Gaulle and his countrymen. Their national pride was hurt when they heard the representatives of small nations denounce France, and the delegates of the Soviet Union, herself a colonial power in a modern form, join the chorus of indignant protests; their resentment was further embittered by the visible embarrassment of their Atlantic allies, who could not and did not want to defend the French colonial policies.

Gone was the time when the French public opinion enthusiastically supported the League of Nations. This enthusiasm had died in the late thirties and was never revived for the benefit of the United Nations. The League was the child of France as well as of the United States and Britain. Its Covenant was drafted with an active French participation. The United Nations Charter was essentially the fruit of a compromise among the Big Three, France not having been one of them. The permanent seat on the Security Council, unlike on the League of Nations Council, was not due to the foremost place of France among the principal victors. It was bestowed on France, thanks to Sir Winston Churchill's successful pleadings at the Yalta conference, as a gift of the Big Three. Frenchmen do not seem to appreciate the fact that they were luckier than the three other holders of permanent seats in the League's Council: Germany, Japan, and Italy.

France, which has not been able to influence the deliberations of the United Nations greatly, was one of the two pillars of the League, the other being Britain. The League was adjusted to the environment of the time. Medium-sized and small nations respected the authority of their Big Brothers. Colonial questions could not be debated. The assumption was that the Big Brothers were the only judges competent to decide the morality or immorality of international behavior. In the United Nations each small nation claims to be as competent as the great powers to pass judgment.

General de Gaulle is not, in this respect as in many others, an isolated voice in France. Public opinion polls taken during the last years of the Fourth Republic revealed that:

> Overall judgment on the activities of the United Nations is not favorable. Its work is not considered satisfactory. The dominant trend in the public opinion is that the United Nations has not really justified its existence.[136]

French sentiments have not much changed since. Since 1962 resentment has given place to indifference.

It is strange that the French President did not seem until very recently to notice that the United Nations would be a perfect instrument in his hands for the apostolate of aspirations of the Third World. His delegates could denounce the two hegemonies from the most resonant tribune and defend the concepts dear to medium-sized and small nations: their independence, noninterference by the Big Brothers in their affairs, the right of each people to have any government it likes, and the obligation of the rich to help the poor. The full use of the United Nations tribune would have helped France to be the voice of the Third World, the ambition of General de Gaulle. France could rely on the support of small nations, among whom her own former colonies represent over twenty votes in the General Assembly. But for years General de Gaulle could not overcome his aversion.

He likes, however, contact with anonymous crowds and never resists the temptation to plunge in their midst to shake hands with unknown individuals. This might be his psychological compensation for the self-imposed solitude. He, who has fervent admirers but hardly any intimate friends, delights in the sight of crowds. These may be crowds in a capital or in a tiny French town; they may be French, German, Italian, Latin-American, African, or Soviet crowds; he is always happy to have mass audiences for his eloquent monologues,

This is his way of maintaining contact with human beings without incurring the compulsion involved in personal relations which necessarily consist in dialogues. But he dislikes one crowd, that of the delegates to the United Nations General Assembly.

One of the reasons is his impatience with the parliamentary procedures which seem to him an unnecessary waste of time. He, who does not have an excessive respect for the French National Assembly, cannot be expected to show a predilection for the international parliament. His definite preference is for the old-style diplomacy and businesslike bargaining across the table. In his *Memoirs* he noted his skeptical attitude in 1945 toward the future United Nations at the time of the San Francisco Conference.[137] We have already seen his aversion to the European Parliament and his preference for the Council of Ministers. We have also seen his antipathy for the international "technocrats" of the EEC Commission. He displays the same antipathy for the "technocrats" of the Secretariat of the United Nations. He particularly disliked Dag Hammarskjöld, who seemed to him an ambitious man who wanted to give himself the power of decision that legitimately belonged only to governments. Supranationality is the enemy de Gaulle fights not only in Little Europe but also in the United Nations. Any international organization must remain an association of sovereign states who may consent to cooperate but whom no one and nothing, neither an international official nor a majority vote, should compel to act in a way they dislike.

He defined his attitude at the press conference held on April 11, 1961. His contempt for the United Nations was indirectly revealed by his errors in interpreting the Charter. Usually, he comes to a press conference very well briefed; his phenomenal memory easily retains figures which he recites without notes. He did not take this trouble when he subjected the United Nations to severe criticism. He seemed to think that it was not worth the trouble to memorize the provisions of the Charter of that *"machin"* (what's-its-name) as he called the United Nations on another occasion.[138]

He said:

[Initially] there was an executive council, the Security Council, which was a sort of government composed of the five great powers, that is to say, the United States, the Soviet Union, Great Britain, China and France. And then there was a kind of non-legislative but deliberative parliament, the General Assembly. This General Assembly, at that time, was supposed to debate only on subjects which the Security Council would submit to it. [The Charter did

not restrict the agenda of the General Assembly to matters submitted by the Security Council] . . . In the Security Council each
of the great powers had the right of veto. . . . Today it must be
said that the United Nations really does not in any way resemble
what it was or ought to have been at the start. First of all, the
Security Council no longer comprises, it is far from comprising,
only great powers; it includes also several powers elected in turn
[the Charter fixed the composition of the Security Council: five
permanent members and six non-permanent members elected by
the General Assembly for a three-year term of office], and then
there is an undetermined number of other delegations attending
all debates of the Security Council, depending on the subjects under discussion. [The Charter provided for the invitation of states
concerned to take part in the deliberations of the Council without
the right to vote.] As for the General Assembly, it has assumed
at the present time all powers. It can deliberate on everything,
without and even against the advice of the Security Council which
is thus dispossessed of its essential prerogative. This General Assembly now includes the delegates of more than a hundred States
—soon they will number one hundred twenty—most of which,
at least many of which, are improvised States and believe that it
is their duty to stress grievances or claims with regard to the old
nations rather than ideas of reason and progress. . . . So that now
the meetings of the United Nations are no more than riotous
and scandalous sessions where there is no way to organize an objective debate and which are filled with invectives and insults, a
behavior in which the Communists and those who are allied with
them against the West excel. And then as the United Nations becomes the scene of disturbance, confusion and division, it acquires the ambition to intervene in all kinds of matters. This is
especially true of its officers. It is anxious to assert itself, even
by force of arms, as it did in the Congo. The result is that it
carries to the local scene its own global incoherence, the personal
conceptions of its various agents and the individual partiality of
each of the States which send their contingents with their own
orders, send them and then withdraw them. Under these conditions, France does not see how she can adopt any attitude toward
the United, or disunited, Nations other than that of the greatest
reserve. In any case, she does not wish to contribute her men or
her money to any present or future undertaking of this organization or disorganization.[139]

There was a grain of truth in his diatribe in spite of his misreading of the Charter and the violence of his language. The voting system in the General Assembly, where a two-thirds majority might pass resolutions over the protest of great powers, if the small nations were unwise enough to do so, does not alter international reality. Power cannot be exorcised and told to disappear as an essential factor in international politics because of any voting formula. However, he overlooked the main reason for the ineffectiveness of the United Nations and the paralysis of the Security Council: the discord among the great powers. The crisis of the United Nations is due not to the "tumultuous and scandalous" debates in the General Assembly, but to the fierce competition between the great powers to which General de Gaulle, as President of the French Republic, has also contributed.

He had a good point in his implicit criticism of the Uniting for Peace Resolution which transferred, in violation of the Charter, the prerogatives of the Security Council regarding matters of peace and security to the General Assembly. This resolution, an opportunist device invented in the Korean crisis to circumvent the Soviet veto and for which France voted with other Western powers, does no longer enjoy the enthusiastic support in the Western capitals that it had in the fifties. The enormous increase in the United Nations membership does no longer guarantee that a pro-Western majority will always be found in the General Assembly. The restoration of the former powers of the Security Council, de Gaulle's and the Soviet thesis, now finds supporters in London and Washington.

His criticism of the political initiatives of the former Secretary General was not ill founded. The United Nations is an association of states; its policies should be decided by governments, not by individuals, even those with the best intentions.

De Gaulle's opposition to the United Nations intervention in Congo was not entirely unjustified. In view of the geographical location of Western Africa, where the Soviet Union could not directly interfere, he favored a concerted action of Western powers. The chaos in Congo was not terminated by the United Nations intervention. De Gaulle's opposition to armed United Nations action against the Katanga might be viewed as wise or unwise. However, the United States, which had fully backed this action against Tshombé, later supported him in his capacity of Congolese Prime Minister. The intervention in the Congo brought about a financial crisis in the United Nations which threatened to paralyze it. The great American-Soviet quarrel over the payment of the cost of the Congo intervention finally resulted in 1964 and 1965 in the rather scandalous impossibility for the General Assembly to vote and to hold a regular session. France has made her own "contribution" to this crisis by refusing to pay her assessed part of the cost, but de Gaulle, opposed to the intervention, was as logical as the Soviet Union. Finally, the crisis was resolved by the United States abandoning its former position on the Soviet and French contributions; the General Assembly was thereby allowed to resume normal activities in the fall of 1965.

The most illogical part of de Gaulle's statement was his contemptuous reference to the "improvised" states. He not only "improvised" many of them by liquidating the French colonial empire, of which he is rightly proud, but he wants to be the spokesman of those newly independent states who form the great majority of the Third World. No less illogical was his nostalgia for the international government of great powers, although he has never tired of denouncing the "hegemonies" to the thunderous applause of the "improvised" peoples, some of which have had a history at least as long as, if not longer than, France's.

He came to a conclusion that France would adopt a policy of reserve. In 1959, he was in the United States, but refused to pay a visit to the Secretary General whom he considered to be only an employee of the members of the United Nations. The Secretary General had to come to his headquarters in New York in order to enjoy the benefit of a conversation with de Gaulle. In September 1960 he refused to take part in the General Assembly attended by almost all Heads of State, including the American President and the Soviet Prime Minister. In 1961 he forbade his Foreign Minister to participate in the deliberations of the United Nations; France was represented by her permanent delegate. Even that delegate was not allowed to make a speech in the general debate in which all the other states took part. The tribune of the United Nations was not used by France as it could have been.

There is a certain coincidence of views between France and the Soviet Union. Russia also defends the rights of the Security Council but is clever enough not to castigate the General Assembly. She realizes the value of the United Nations forum for her own propaganda and the need to respect the susceptibilities of smaller nations whom she wants to cultivate. She refuses, like France, to pay for the cost of executive actions of the United Nations, of which she has disapproved. While the United States threatened to insist on strict observance of the Charter, which deprived members of the right to vote as a penalty for nonpayment of their share of expenses, the net effect would have been to deny that right not only to the Soviet Union but also to France. The United Nations would have probably lost two permanent members of the Security Council and perhaps would not survive because the un-committed nations could hardly have remained in it.

In 1962 the General Assembly asked the International Court of Justice to give its advisory opinion regarding this controversial question of the obligation of member states to contribute toward the cost of the United Nations' executive actions although these members had disapproved of them. The majority of judges supported the thesis that such an obligation existed. The French judge, together with his Soviet and Polish colleagues, was opposed. In December 1962 the General Assembly approved this advisory opinion against seventeen votes, which included the Communist bloc and France. In 1963 the General Assembly again adopted the resolutions with the same kind of financial responsibility for all member-states in aiding executive actions; the French delegate voiced his opposition, using arguments analogous to those of his Soviet colleague. General de Gaulle did not want to spend a single French cent on actions of which he disapproved.

France contributes to the cost of another peace-keeping operation, the United Nations Emergency Force in the Near East, but she has initially approved of this operation. The French position, like the Soviet, consists in asking for two preliminary conditions: (1) every peace-keeping operation must be decided by the Security Council alone; (2) the mode of financing the operation should also be determined by the Council. The jurisdiction of the General Assembly in these matters is not conceded by either of the two great powers.

Another consistent attitude of the French President is his firm opposition to any UN interference in the domestic affairs of its members. His strict interpretation of the Charter has never varied. For him, the problems of colonial possessions are internal problems of the colonial power concerned. This view was understandable from 1958 to 1962, when France was one of the countries denounced in the United Nations. Since her colonial empire was relinquished, this is no longer so. He places France in opposition to the Third World, which attaches enormous importance to emancipation of the remaining colonial possessions. France is not only prevented from joining the indignant voices of delegates of the Third World when they denounce the Portuguese colonialism or the racialism of Rhodesia and South Africa; she actually tells these delegates that they have no right to interfere in what she considers an internal matter. This legalistic attitude of the General is politically illogical; one cannot aspire to be a spokesman of the Third World and at the same time oppose the flow of its indignant eloquence against the survivals of colonialism, which he himself considers a relic of a bygone age. President de Gaulle is no more consistent in his policies with Portugal and South Africa, both of which are the *bêtes noires* for the former colonial peoples. France even sells military matériel to those two states.

The picture of French policies toward the United Nations would be incomplete without mentioning two other matters. The skeptical attitude of General de Gaulle has never prevented the French delegates from taking a very active part in the social activities of the United Nations. Conversely, France has boycotted the eighteen-power Geneva conference on disarmament. Her seat has remained empty. The French government holds that the conference has too many members by far, and that fruitful disarmament negotiations should be restricted to the five nuclear powers, including China. It believes that a large conference, attended by several smaller powers, is bound to become a propaganda forum, while the absence of China precludes the conclusion of any meaningful agreement on the limitation of armaments.

The general lines of de Gaulle's position remain today as they were in his statement of 1961. But his attitude has not been static. The emancipation of Algeria had its effect. France now very rarely hears any criticism from the tribune of the United Nations. The activities of the United Nations no longer give the General any particular reason to be irritated. The organization is no longer referred to as that "what's-its-name." Prime Minister Pompidou told the National Assembly in December 1962 that: "Henceforth, the United Nations, if it refrained from interventions, which are not its vocation and which were for it a source of many frustrations, could play its role by becoming the meeting place where peoples can better acquaint themselves with each other and better understand each other."[140] The French government thus recognized that there was some usefulness in the existence of the United Nations; for instance, their meetings provide an opportunity to pursue traditional diplomacy in the lobbies, behind the screen of "tumultuous" public debates. The permanent French delegate attended the solemn celebration of the twentieth anniversary of the foundation of the United Nations which took place in San Francisco in June 1965. He was allowed to say in his speech that: "The Charter, although imperfect as are all human creations, is and will remain, undoubtedly, for a long time to come the best instrument of international cooperation that the world may have."[141] He did not fail to point out the danger of hegemony by one power or a group of powers and insisted on the need for universality; the latter remark was interpreted as a hint at the need of accepting the credentials of Communist China.

The French Foreign Minister headed his country's delegation to the session of the General Assembly in the fall of 1965 and took part in the general debate. It was the proof that the French President at last discovered that the forum of the Assembly might be useful for France. The Foreign Minister was allowed to pay a tribute to the present Secretary General and to say that the General Assembly "is the expression of international public opinion and should consequently be the world's highest political forum."[142] He asked that the Communist Chinese representation be admitted to both the General Assembly and the Security Council, because, among other things, the problems of Asia could not be settled "without the direct participation of the largest Asian power." At the same session of the General Assembly France cast her vote for Communist China.

The French parliament, controlled by the progovernmental majority in the National Assembly, approved in June 1965 the amendments to the Charter which increased the membership in the Security Council and the Economic and Social Council. The Security Council will have not six but ten elective members. General de Gaulle, however, was not happy as recently as 1961 that six smaller nations were allowed to sit there in the august company of great powers. Prior to the parliamentary approval, the Foreign Minister told the National Assembly that France had consented to this increase in the number of elective seats in order to provide a better representation to the Asian and African states although she would have desired a lesser increase. He then referred to his President's favorite thesis that the UN crisis was due to "the divergent interpretations of the Charter relating to the distribution of powers between the Security Council and the General Assembly. Certain countries, like the United States, want to increase the powers of the Assembly against the view of other countries, in particular of France."[143] He should have been better informed and should have known that there was already a disillusionment in Washington with the functioning of the General Assembly and greater willingness to restore its former prerogatives to the Security Council.

Collective hegemony of the five great powers

The main concept developed in 1961 has remained unchanged. The tone, however, has been altered; it is no longer contemptuous. Before holding his press conference on February 4, 1965, the President took the trouble this time to read the Charter. But his fundamental views have remained the same:

> The idea re-appeared, before even the guns were silenced, to offer to nations a framework within which they could be equally represented, discuss the problems of the world, express the consensus of peoples concerning these problems, disapprove of warlike in-

tentions of the ambitious governments, gather at one place the information relating to the material, social and moral condition of all countries, and organize a collective assistance for their development. . . . Everyone knows that the Charter of the United Nations instituted, on the one hand, a Council which was to safeguard the international security and was empowered to take the necessary measures to enforce the respect for that security; and, on the other hand, an Assembly whose deliberations would lead to recommendations. But the right to take action was, however, vested in the Council alone. The latter Council included among its eleven members five permanent, namely the victorious great powers, each having the veto power. . . . This Charter was reasonable. Owing to this arrangement, the Assembly was to be the place of regular and periodical meetings and confrontations of almost all the States of the world. It was to be a sort of a forum where an international opinion could emerge and where the equality of all of its Members bestowed on each of them, in particular on those who only recently acquired their independence and sovereignty, a highly recognized dignity. Moreover, the five powers who had a world-wide responsibility, owing to their policies, economies, armed forces and influence, were to meet in the Council and, if possible, to cooperate in maintaining the peace. These provisions corresponded to what was possible and at the same time prudent. . . . Under the pressure of events . . . the so-called "united" Nations, which were so no more, permitted themselves to exceed their nature and their possibilities. They deviated from the Charter. Disregarding the jurisdiction of the Security Council, the General Assembly arrogated to itself in 1950 the right to decide on the use of force; this made it the scene of quarrels between the two rivals. Helped by the disorder thus created, the then Secretary General was led to set himself up as a supreme and excessive authority. Continuing these abuses, the Organization involved itself directly in the internal situation of the Congo, sent there at great cost military contingents furnished by States which mostly were interested—which State is not?—and political, administrative and economic missions which, in fact, followed the intentions of one great power [United States]. To be sure, this intervention has been stopped thanks to the wisdom of the present Secretary General and because of its cost. Let it be said in passing that France could not assume a part of this cost, since she has never ceased to disapprove of that unjustified venture and of the procedure contrary to the San Francisco Treaty. . . . I will say frankly that, in my opinion, it is by returning to prudence and to the Charter that the United Nations can regain its equilibrium. In the present circumstances, it would clearly be necessary for Washington, Moscow, London, Peking and Paris to agree to return to the point of departure, as they had once agreed to found the United Nations.[144]

In four years the tone has changed. No more castigations of "tumultuous and scandalous" debates in which the "improvised" states participated. The organization was recognized as a useful institution, in particular for the dignity of those newly independent nations. The present Secretary General received a courteous compliment due not only to his political discretion but also perhaps to the fact that he was Asian. In the spring of 1966 the French President went so far in displaying his friendship for U Thant that he gave him a warm reception in Paris and even asked him to remain the Secretary General of the United Nations for another term of office. This stood in sharp contrast to the General's antipathy for Dag Hammarskjöld.

But the main concept of the central role of the Security Council and of the five great powers in it remained unchanged. This concept of world government by the five nuclear powers had nothing to commend itself to the Third World. From their point of view the competition between the two "hegemonies" and the denunciation of these "hegemonies" by the two other great powers (France and China) was much better than a collective hegemony of the five. Could they trust General de Gaulle, who spoke with two voices? Was he to be believed when he defended the democratic concept of an international community, or when he proposed to rule the small countries by a directorate of great powers and claimed one of the five seats on that directorate for France? His friends, Germany, Japan and Italy, could ask him why only France should have that privilege.

The circumstances were unfavorable for the consideration of his suggestion of a five-power conference for the reform of the United Nations. The United States was engaged in a confrontation with China. American-Soviet relations were deteriorating. Moreover, China was less willing to consider membership in the United Nations and was undertaking a propaganda program for a new international organization of the Third World from which not only the two "hegemons" but also France would be excluded.

General de Gaulle is caught in a dilemma: either to make a common front with the Third World or to claim for France a place on the directorate of great powers, to be the leader of the medium-sized and small nations or be one of their five rulers?

Conclusion

It would be repetitious and superfluous to impose on the reader a re-hash of the comments which he has read all through this book. He is able himself to evaluate the merits and demerits of General de Gaulle's foreign policy. In doing this, he would be well advised not to dismiss all de Gaulle's ideas and policies because they contradict his own favorite concepts. He should remember that a nonconformist (de Gaulle is certainly this in international politics) is not always wrong and has the merit of compelling others to reexamine critically their own inveterate thinking habits. The net result might be to continue to disagree with the General regarding several issues while following his bold lead on other matters.

The depressingly long roll of false political prophets is not encouraging in predicting either the next move the General might make or the future course of French foreign policy. As long as he remains at the helm, certain elements of his policy are bound to be associated with his fundamental outlook: the national nuclear force; opposition to the delegation of sovereign French rights to any international organization, including the European Community; sympathy for the Third World; and his anti-American bias. For the rest, his fertile and flexible mind might in the future take an unexpected direction. Only he may answer these questions: How will France play her game between Britain and the Five, between Germany and Russia, between China and the Soviet Union? If asked today, he would wisely answer: "It will depend on international circumstances." One may be sure that he will be guided as usual by "things as they are" or, rather, as he thinks they are.

The post-Gaullist future is shrouded in the thickest fog. Who can be sure that the Gaullists will remain in power or, conversely, that they will be replaced by a coalition of traditional parties? If the latter, what kind of coalition? The French multi-party political system, which stubbornly refuses to die, makes all forecasts liable to error. This uncertainty regarding the nature of post-Gaullist regime in France vitiates all predictions as to her future foreign policy.

The style is his own. It will disappear with him. But will the main policies be abandoned? One is tempted to say that his nuclear policy will be continued even by his present domestic opponents if only its cost does not prove prohibitive. The reservations regarding the dominant American influence in Western Europe will not evaporate because they are expressed by the opposition parties also. But the present policy of going it alone might be replaced by attempts to counterbalance the American influence by a French effort to accelerate European integration. This new policy, if the opposition parties took over de Gaulle's succession, would not object to a measure of supranationality in European institutions or to the enlargement of the European Community by including Britain and other members of the EFTA. France's European partners would find cooperation with her less difficult. If the potential Soviet threat were to continue, France would remain in the Atlantic Alliance, and the traditional parties, if they formed the government of France, might perhaps reintegrate French armed forces within NATO. In other words, certain decisions of the present President are not necessarily irreversible.

Correct and perhaps cordial relations with the Communist powers will probably be maintained, as no vital French interest necessitates a change. De Gaulle's policy toward the Third World is not threatened by a reversal after his demise. However, it might become less generous regarding financial assistance as opposed to technical aid. His denunciation of the hegemonies seems to be a foible which his successors will not inherit.

On the whole, it would be unwise to expect a total reversal of his policies. Men, even great men, come and go; governments take and relinquish power; regimes change, but the foreign policy continues. De Gaulle would be the first to agree with this statement. External policy is modified radically by a sensible nation only if international circumstances are also radically altered by unexpected developments.

What lasting benefits will de Gaulle's foreign policy bring to his country? A few years ago Edgar Faure gave a wise answer by quoting one of the French queens: "God rewards only at the end."[1]

Notes to Chapters

I. THE CHARISMATIC LEADER

1. Alfred Grosser, *La Politique Extérieure de la Ve République*, p. 25.
2. Press conference of September 9, 1965. *Le Monde*, September 9–15, 1965, No. 882.
3. Léo Hamon and Albert Mabileau (eds.), *La Personnalisation du Pouvoir*, p. 275.
4. Charles de Gaulle, *The War Memoirs of Charles de Gaulle*, III, 7.
5. Press conference held on September 5, 1961; French Embassy, *Major Addresses, Statements and Press Conferences of General Charles de Gaulle*, p. 150.
6. Charles de Gaulle, *op. cit.*, I, 3.
7. Alfred Fabre-Luce, *Le Plus Illustre des Français*, p. 17.
8. Quoted in Jean Lacouture, *De Gaulle*, pp. 69–70.
9. François Mauriac, *De Gaulle*, pp. 44 and 106.
10. Jean Lacouture, *op. cit.*, p. 90.
11. Quoted in François Mauriac, *op. cit.*, p. 68.
12. Charles de Gaulle, *op. cit.*, I, 84.
13. André Siegfried, *De la IIIe à la IVe République*, p. 126.
14. Charles de Gaulle, *op. cit.*, I, 83.
15. Charles de Gaulle, *op. cit.*, III, 327.
16. French Embassy, *Major Addresses*, p. 74.
17. *Ibid.*, p. 128.
18. *Ibid.*, p. 112.
19. *L'Année Politique 1962*, p. 688.
20. French Embassy, *Major Addresses*, p. 190.
21. Jean-Raymond Tournoux, *Sécrets d'Etat*, p. 343.
22. *Ibid.*, pp. 345–46.
23. Charles de Gaulle, *op. cit.*, III, 132.
24. Paul-Marie de la Gorce, *De Gaulle Entre Deux Mondes*, p. 519.
25. François Mauriac, *op. cit.*, p. 191.
26. French Embassy, *Major Addresses*, pp. 248–49.
27. François Mauriac, *op. cit.*, p. 60.
28. Quoted in Alfred Fabre-Luce, *op. cit.*, p. 20.
29. Charles de Gaulle, *op. cit.*, I, 57.
30. Georges Izard, "Le passé: impérialisme de la politique française," *La Nef*, December 1949–January 1950, p. 34.
31. Paul-Marie de la Gorce, *op. cit.*, pp. 7–8.
32. Jean-Raymond Tournoux, *op. cit.*, p. 343.
33. Alfred Grosser, *La IVe République et Sa Politique Extérieure*, p. 19.
34. Charles de Gaulle, *op. cit.*, III, 136.
35. Association Française de Science Politique, *Le Référendum de Septembre et les Elections de Novembre 1958*, p. 224.
36. André Siegfried, *De la IVe à la Ve République*, p. 268.
37. Guy Mollet, *13 Mai 1958–13 Mai 1962*, p. 124.
38. Jacques Duclos, *Gaullisme, Technocratie, Corporatisme?*, p. 164.

39. Paul-Marie de la Gorce, *op. cit.*, p. 34.

40. François Goguel and Alfred Grosser, *La Politique en France*, p. 245.

41. *Ibid.*, p. 246.

42. The speech on May 31, 1960. French Embassy, *Major Addresses*, p. 78.

43. Jean-Raymond Tournoux, *op. cit.*, p. 173.

44. Jean Lacouture, *op. cit.*, pp. 31 and 73.

45. François Mauriac, *op. cit.*, p. 99.

46. Jean-Raymond Tournoux, *op. cit.*, p. 327.

47. *L'Année Politique 1962*, p. vii.

48. Alfred Fabre-Luce, *Le Couronnement du Prince*, p. 59.

49. *Ibid.*, p. 90.

50. Alfred Fabre-Luce, *Le Plus Illustre des Français*, pp. 183 and 41.

51. Pierre Mendès-France, *La Politique et la Vérité*, p. 305.

52. French Embassy, *Major Addresses*, p. 104.

53. Eugène Mannoni, *Moi, Général de Gaulle*, p. 132.

54. Jean Baillou and Pierre Pelletier, *Les Affaires Etrangères*, pp. 1–2.

55. President de Gaulle's press conference of September 9, 1965. Ambassade de France, *Speeches and Press Conferences*, No. 228, p. 6.

56. Jean Baillou and Pierre Pelletier, *op. cit.*, pp. 209–10.

57. Ambassade de France, *Speeches and Press Conferences*, No. 203, pp. 2–3.

58. Jean Baillou and Pierre Pelletier, *op. cit.*, p. 3.

59. *Ibid.*, p. 219.

60. Jacques Bloch-Morhange, *Le Gaullisme*, p. 98. The Palace of Matignon is the residence of the French Prime Minister; the Palace of Elysée, the residence of the President of the Republic.

61. The broadcast speech of December 31, 1963. French Embassy, *Major Addresses*, p. 244.

62. François Mauriac, *op. cit.*, p. 58.

63. *Ibid.*, p. 187.

64. Michel Debré, *Au Service de la Nation*, pp. 161, 274–75.

65. Paul Reynaud, *La Politique Etrangère du Gaullisme*, pp. 15–16. President de Gaulle does not disagree with Paul Reynaud and others concerning the present power of France as compared with other periods of history. Using almost the same words as Reynaud, he said on September 9, 1965: "Doubtless, France no longer appears to be the gigantic nation that she was in the times of Louis XIV or of Napoleon I." Ambassade de France, *Speeches and Press Conferences*, No. 228, p. 7.

66. Quotation from his *La France et Son Armée*, cited in Alfred Fabre-Luce, *Le Couronnement du Prince*, p. 137.

67. Charles de Gaulle, *op. cit.*, III, 58–60.

68. Roger Massip, *De Gaulle et l'Europe*, p. 173.

69. Charles de Gaulle, *op. cit.*, I, 104.

70. He said in 1951 no less categorically: "America is not a part of Europe." (Quoted in Roger Massip, *op. cit.*, p. 188.)

71. Roger Massip, *op. cit.*, p. 174.

72. *Ibid.*, p. 173.

73. *Ibid.*, p. 183.

74. *Ibid.*, p. 184.

75. *Ibid.*, p. 192.

76. *Ibid.*, p. 185.

77. Charles de Gaulle, *op. cit.*, III, 205. This volume was published in France in 1959 when he was already the President of the Republic.

78. Paul Reynaud, *La Politique Etrangère du Gaullisme*, p. 30.

79. Ambassade de France, *French Affairs*, No. 166.

80. Cf. his statements made on May 15, 1962, and on December 31, 1962, both printed in French Embassy, *Major Addresses*, pp. 173–75 and 207.

81. Georges Pompidou's speech before the National Assembly on December 13, 1962, *L'Année Politique 1962*, p. 695.

82. François Mitterand, *Le Coup d'Etat Permanent*, pp. 112–13.

83. Paul Reynaud, *La Politique Etrangère du Gaullisme*, pp. 258–59.

84. See Chapter II.

85. François Mitterand, *op. cit.*, p. 81.

86. *Ibid.*, p. 32.

87. Jean-Raymond Tournoux, *op. cit.*, p. 211.

88. François Mitterand, his irreconcilable political enemy, paid, perhaps unwittingly, a tribute to de Gaulle. Speaking to journalists on September 21, 1965, in his capacity as the leftist candidate for the Presidency of the Republic, Mitterand said that he would mention de Gaulle during the electoral campaign "with care not to overlook either his signal merits which have assured him of the lasting gratitude of the country or his exceptional prestige beyond our frontiers." (*Le Monde*, September 23–29, 1965, No. 884.)

89. *Esprit*, Année 30, No. 303, February, 1962, p. 279.

90. François Mitterand, *op. cit.*, p. 279.

91. The speech broadcast January 6, 1961. French Embassy, *Major Addresses*, p. 112.

92. Charles de Gaulle, *op. cit.*, III, 263.

93. Quoted in Paul-Marie de la Gorce, *op. cit.*, p. 707.

94. Michel Debré, *op. cit.*, p. 202.

95. Alexander Werth, *La France depuis la Guerre*, p. 355.

96. François Goguel in Stanley Hoffmann *et al.*, *In Search of France*, p. 363.

II. HIS PEOPLE

1. Charles de Gaulle, *op. cit.*, III, 270.

2. Eugène Mannoni, *op. cit.*, p. 80.

3. François Mauriac, "Le Bloc-notes," *Le Figaro Littéraire*, March 26–April 1, 1964.

4. The best description of France today is Stanley Hoffmann *et al.*, *In Search of France*.

5. François Goguel and Alfred Grosser, *op. cit.*, pp. 20–21.

6. Léon Noël, *Notre Dernière Chance*, pp. 112 and 131–32.

7. Alfred Sauvy, *La Montée des Jeunes*, p. 153.

8. Pierre Pflimlin, former Prime Minister and one of the leaders of Popular Republicans, in René Rémond *et al.*, *La Démocratie à Refaire*, p. 210.

9. Stanley Hoffmann *et al.*, *In Search of France*, p. 99.

10. Herbert Lüthy, *A l'Heure de Son Clocher*, p. 60.

11. Pierre Mendès-France, *op. cit.*, p. 240.

12. His speech made on December 27, 1954, at the National Assembly and quoted in Louis Rougier, *L'Erreur de la Démocratie Française*, p. 120.

13. *Sondages, Revue Française de l'Opinion Publique*, 26-e Année, 1964, No. 3, p. 6.

14. Poll taken in December 1962. *Sondages*, 25-e Année, 1963, No. 2, p. 107.

15. See, e.g., Club Jean Moulin, *L'Etat et le Citoyen*, p. 188; Jacques Rigaud, *Débat Sur la France de Demain*, p. 119; Alexandre Sanguinetti, *La France et l'Arme Atomique*, p. 120; Georges Vedel (ed.), *La Dépolitisation*.

16. *Sondages*, 25-e Année, 1963, No. 2, p. 111.

17. François Goguel and Alfred Grosser, *op. cit.*, pp. 30–31.

18. See, e.g., René Rémond *et al.*, *op. cit.*

19. Stanley Hoffmann *et al.*, *op. cit.*, p. 110; also, Herbert Lüthy, *op. cit.*, pp. 113–14, and Jacques Fauvet, *La France Déchirée*, p. 80.

20. Léo Hamon (ed.), *Les Nouveaux Comportements Politiques de la Classe Ouvrière*, p. 172.

21. *Sondages*, 26-e Année, 1964, No. 3, p. 44.

22. *Ibid.*, p. 45.

23. *Ibid.*, pp. 45–46.

24. *Ibid.*, p. 46.

25. *Ibid.*, p. 45.

26. An excellent study of current politics in France and of emerging habits is P. Viansson-Ponté, "Vacances et veillée d'armes," *Le Monde*, July 1–3, 1965, Nos. 6364–6366.

27. Raymond Aron, *Immuable et Changeante*, pp. 13–14.

28. René Rémond *et al.*, *op. cit.*, p. 73.

29. François Mauriac, *op. cit.*, p. 58.

30. Jean-Raymond Tournoux, *op. cit.*, pp. 176 and 375.

31. Jean Barets, *La Fin des Politiques*, p. 208.

32. Club Jean Moulin, *L'Etat et le Citoyen*, p. 79.

33. Jacques Fauvet and Jean Planchais, *La Fronde des Généraux*, p. 249.

34. Julien Cheverny, *Le Carnaval des Régents*, p. 70.

35. Raymond Aron, *op. cit.*, p. 188.

36. Alfred Grosser, *La IVe République et Sa Politique Extérieure*, p. 26.

37. René Rémond *et al.*, *op. cit.*, p. 50.

38. *Sondages*, 26-e Année, 1964, No. 3, p. 13.

39. Club Jean Moulin, *op. cit.*, pp. 200–201.

40. Louis Rougier, *op. cit.*, p. 17.

41. François Goguel and Alfred Grosser, *op. cit.*, p. 253.

42. Alfred Sauvy, *op. cit.*, and *Le Monde*, December 24–30, 1964, No. 845.

43. Michel Debré, *op. cit.*, p. 17.

44. Ambassade de France, *French Affairs*, No. 186A.

45. *Sondages*, No. 4, 1965.

46. Ambassade de France, *French Affairs*, No. 186A.

47. Ambassade de France, *Speeches and Press Conferences*, No. 239.

48. Jacques Fauvet, "Le 'Troisième Tour,'" *Le Monde*, February 10–16, 1966, No. 904.

49. Association Française de Science Politique, *La Politique Etrangère et Ses Fondements*, pp. 85 and 89.

50. Léo Hamon in Georges Vedel (ed.), *La Dépolitisation*, p. 118.

51. *Sondages*, 26-e Année, 1964, No. 3, p. 51.

52. *Ibid.*, p. 52.

53. *Ibid.*, p. 31.

54. *Ibid.,* p. 52.
55. *Ibid.,* p. 74.
56. *Ibid.,* p. 53.
57. *Ibid.,* p. 66.
58. *Ibid.,* pp. 54–55.
59. *Ibid.,* p. 68.
60. *Ibid.,* p. 55.
61. *Ibid.*
62. *Ibid.*
63. *Ibid.,* p. 57.
64. *Ibid.*
65. *Ibid.,* p. 30.
66. Michel Debré, *op. cit.,* p. 11.
67. Charles de Gaulle, *op. cit.,* III, 271.
68. French Embassy, *Major Addresses,* p. 137.
69. André Passeron, *De Gaulle Parle,* p. 518.
70. *Cartierisme* is derived from Raymond Cartier, publisher of the popular *Match,* who opposes French aid to underdeveloped countries.
71. J. B. Duroselle in Stanley Hoffmann *et al., op. cit.,* p. 356.
72. Cahiers de la Fondation Nationale des Sciences Politiques, *Le Référendum du 8 janvier 1961,* p. 85.
73. Raymond Aron, *op. cit.,* p. 262.
74. F. L'Huillier, *Histoire de Notre Temps,* p. 32.
75. Charles de Gaulle, *op. cit.,* III, 268.
76. J. Basdevant *et al., Les Affaires Etrangères,* p. 158.
77. *Ibid.*
78. J. Baillou and P. Pelletier, *op. cit.,* p. 212.
79. Alexander Werth, *op. cit.,* pp. 10–11.
80. Laurence Wylie, *Village in the Vaucluse,* p. 207.
81. Stanley Hoffmann *et al., op. cit.,* p. 19.
82. René Viard, *La Fin de l'Empire Colonial Français,* pp. 132–33.
83. Jacques de Lacretelle, "L'age adulte," in *Le Figaro Littéraire,* No. 1000, June 17–23, 1965.
84. André Siegfried, *De la IIIe à la IVe République,* p. 256.
85. *Ibid.,* p. 265.
86. Club Jean Moulin, *op. cit.,* p. 408.
87. Alexandre Sanguinetti, *La France et l'Arme Atomique,* pp. 40–41.
88. Pierre Mendès-France, *op. cit.,* p. 122. Three French doctors received the Nobel prize in medicine in the fall of 1965.
89. Herbert Lüthy, *op. cit.,* pp. 157 and 18.
90. Jean Baillou and Pierre Pelletier, *op. cit.,* p. 311.
91. J. Basdevant *et al., op. cit.,* p. 153.
92. Guy Mollet, *op. cit.,* p. 50.
93. René Rémond *et al., op. cit.,* p. 93. This proud statement leads to the questions: Why was the Fourth Republic misruled, and why are the political parties unable to adjust to modern conditions if the French political personnel is superior to the British and American?
94. Jacques Rigaud, *Débat Sur la France de Demain,* p. 30.
95. *Ibid.,* p. 245.
96. Club Jean Moulin, *op. cit.,* p. 340.

97. *Ibid.,* p. 341.

98. Alfred Grosser, *La Politique Extérieure de la Vᵉ République,* p. 167.

99. Stanley Hoffmann *et al., op. cit.,* pp. 265–66.

100. Maurice Duverger, "Nationalisme français et 'nationalisme européen,' " *Le Monde,* May 13–19, 1965, No. 865.

101. François Mauriac, *op. cit.,* p. 46.

102. Maurice Duverger's interview with *L'Express* on March 5, 1964, quoted in Alfred Grosser, *La Politique Extérieure de la Vᵉ République,* p. 168.

103. Alfred Grosser, *La IVᵉ République et Sa Politique Extérieure,* p. 176.

104. Alexander Werth, *op. cit.,* p. 394.

105. Club Jean Moulin, *op. cit.,* p. 338.

106. André Siegfried, *De la IIIᵉ à la IVᵉ République,* p. 48.

107. Alfred Sauvy, *op. cit.,* p. 55.

108. André Siegfried, *De la IIIᵉ à la IVᵉ République,* p. 64.

109. Georges Bernanos, *Français, si Vous Saviez,* p. 198.

110. *Ibid.,* p. 198.

111. *Le Monde,* May 14–20, 1964, No. 813.

112. J. B. Duroselle in Stanley Hoffmann *et al., op. cit.,* p. 321.

113. Alfred Sauvy, *op. cit.,* pp. 77–78.

114. J. B. Duroselle in Stanley Hoffmann *et al., op. cit.,* p. 322.

115. Robert Aron, *Histoire de Vichy,* p. 23. The present author was an eyewitness of that confusion.

116. *Ibid.,* p. 13.

117. *Ibid.,* p. 61.

118. *Ibid.,* p. 12.

119. *Ibid.,* p. 93.

120. Léon Noël, *op. cit.,* p. 157.

121. Robert Aron, *op. cit.,* pp. 60–61.

122. *Ibid.,* p. 41.

123. *Ibid.,* pp. 90–91.

124. *Ibid.,* p. 25.

125. André Siegfried, *De la IIIᵉ à la IVᵉ République,* p. 72, and J. A. Laponce, *The Government of the Fifth Republic,* p. 51.

126. Robert Aron, *op. cit.,* p. 33.

127. *Ibid.,* p. 36.

128. J. B. Duroselle in Stanley Hoffmann *et al., op. cit.,* p. 325.

129. André Siegfried, *De la IIIᵉ à la IVᵉ République,* pp. 68 and 79.

130. J. B. Duroselle in Stanley Hoffmann *et al., op. cit.,* p. 328; also Alfred Fabre-Luce, *Le Plus Illustre des Français,* p. 74.

131. Robert Aron, *op. cit.,* p. 668.

132. Robert Aron, *Histoire de la Libération de France,* p. 102.

133. Paul-Marie de la Gorce, *op. cit.,* p. 197.

134. Robert Aron, *Histoire de Vichy,* p. 585.

135. Robert Aron, *Histoire de la Libération de la France,* p. 716.

136. J. B. Duroselle in Stanley Hoffmann *et al., op. cit.,* pp. 319 and 327.

137. Robert Aron, *Histoire de la Libération de la France,* p. 318.

138. J. B. Duroselle in Stanley Hoffmann *et al., op. cit.,* p. 331.

139. *Ibid.,* p. 35.

140. Robert Aron, *Histoire de la Libération de la France,* pp. 30, 32 and 33.

141. *Ibid.,* p. 394.

142. *Ibid.,* p. 430.

143. *Ibid.,* p. 680.

144. *Ibid.,* p. 664.

145. Charles de Gaulle, *op. cit.,* III, 159–60.

146. Robert Aron, *Histoire de la Libération de la France,* p. 83.

147. *Ibid.,* p. 84.

148. Charles de Gaulle, *op. cit.,* III, 202.

149. Paul-Marie de la Gorce, *op. cit.,* p. 418; see also Jean Lacouture, *De Gaulle,* pp. 134–35.

150. Charles de Gaulle, *op. cit.,* III, 101–2.

151. The quotation was written by a Swiss writer and reproduced in Alfred Fabre-Luce, *Gaulle Deux,* pp. 64–65.

152. Jacques Bloch-Morhange, *op. cit.,* p. 27.

153. Robert Aron, *Histoire de la Libération de la France,* p. 442.

154. André Passeron, *op. cit.,* p. 355.

155. *Le Monde,* August 13–19, 1964, No. 826.

156. Georges Bernanos, *op. cit.,* p. 33.

157. F. L'Huillier, *op. cit.,* p. 13.

158. Herbert Lüthy, *op. cit.,* p. 71.

III.   THE NUCLEAR DETERRENT AGAINST WHOM?

1. Alfred Grosser, *La IVe République et Sa Politique Extérieure,* p. 20.

2. *L'Année Politique 1959,* p. 633.

3. For instance, François Mitterand, the leftist candidate in the Presidential election, emphatically declared on September 21, 1965, that he would convert the French nuclear plants to peaceful use only. *Le Monde,* September 23–29, 1965, No. 884.

4. *L'Année Politique 1959,* p. 632.

5. French Embassy, *Major Addresses,* p. 173.

6. His address of November 3, 1959, at the French Center of High Military Studies. *L'Année Politique 1959,* p. 631.

7. French Embassy, *Major Addresses,* p. 216.

8. *Ibid.,* p. 217.

9. Ambassade de France, *Speeches and Press Conferences,* No. 244A.

10. French Embassy, *Major Addresses,* p. 219.

11. Ambassade de France, *Speeches and Press Conferences,* No. 208, p. 8.

12. *Ibid.,* pp. 8–9.

13. De Gaulle's other statements concerning his nuclear policy may be found in French Embassy, *Major Addresses,* and in Ambassade de France, *Speeches and Press Conferences.*

14. *Pour ou Contre la Force de Frappe,* p. 44.

15. *Ibid.,* p. 260. See also General Pierre-M. Gallois' identical view in Claude Delmas *et al., L'Avenir de l'Alliance Atlantique,* p. 118.

16. *Pour ou Contre la Force de Frappe,* pp. 252–53.

17. *Ibid.,* p. 63.

18. Ambassade de France, *Speeches and Press Conferences,* Nos. 243A and 245A.

19. *Pour ou Contre la Force de Frappe,* p. 27.

20. Maurice Faure, "Les Choix de la France," in *Le Monde*, February 20–26, 1964, No. 801.

21. *Pour ou Contre la Force de Frappe*, p. 88.

22. *Ibid.*, pp. 249–50.

23. *Ibid.*, p. 78.

24. Club Jean Moulin, *La Force de Frappe et le Citoyen*, p. 111.

25. André Fontaine, "Histoire de la force multilatérale," *Le Monde*, November 12–18, 1964, No. 839.

26. *L'Année Politique 1962*, p. 87.

27. Claude Delmas *et al.*, *L'Avenir de l'Alliance Atlantique*, p. 127.

28. Jacques Bloch-Morhange, *op. cit.*, p. 107.

29. Ambassade de France, *Speeches and Press Conferences*, Nos. 243A and 245A.

30. *L'Année Politique 1958*, p. 292.

31. *Pour ou Contre la Force de Frappe*, pp. 48–49; Raymond Cartier, the publisher of *Match*, frequently supports the same view. *Ibid.*, p. 75.

32. *Ibid.*, p. 118.

33. Raymond Aron, *Paix et Guerre entre les Nations*, p. 474, footnote, and his *Le Grand Débat*, pp. 96 and 236.

34. Raymond Aron, *Le Grand Débat*, p. 96.

35. *Ibid.*, p. 90.

36. André Fontaine, *L'Alliance Atlantique à l'Heure du Dégel*, p. 26.

37. *Pour ou Contre la Force de Frappe*, p. 266.

38. *Ibid.*, p. 267.

39. *Le Monde*, March 24–30, 1966, No. 910.

40. *Pour ou Contre la Force de Frappe*, p. 251.

41. *Ibid.*, p. 47.

42. Quoted in Jean Planchais, "Riposte Adaptée ou Riposte Massive?" *Le Monde*, January 28–February 3, 1965, No. 850.

43. Coral Bell (ed.), *Europe without Britain*, p. 16.

44. *Pour ou Contre la Force de Frappe*, p. 119. See also Club de Grenelle, *Siècle de Damoclès*, p. 58.

45. Club Jean Moulin, *La Force de Frappe et le Citoyen*, p. 59.

46. Paul Reynaud, *La Politique Etrangère du Gaullisme*, p. 101.

47. *Le Monde*, December 26–January 1, 1963–64, No. 793.

48. *Ibid.*

49. Club Jean Moulin, *La Force de Frappe et le Citoyen*, p. 54.

50. *Le Monde*, November 19–25, 1964, No. 840.

51. Even an enthusiastic advocate of French nuclear armaments admits that the French force will amount only to 2 per cent of the power of either the American or Soviet force. Alexandre Sanguinetti, *La France et l'Arme Atomique*, p. 29.

52. Club de Grenelle, *op. cit.*, p. 83.

53. Michel Debré, *op. cit.*, p. 151.

54. *Pour ou Contre la Force de Frappe*, p. 39.

55. Club de Grenelle, *op. cit.*, p. 16.

56. Raymond Aron, *Paix et Guerre entre les Nations*, p. 614.

57. André Fontaine, *op. cit.*, p. 63.

58. Paul Reynaud, *La Politique Etrangère du Gaullisme*, p. 98. See also Club Jean Moulin, *La Force de Frappe et le Citoyen*, p. 38.

59. *L'Année Politique 1960*, p. 545.

60. *Le Monde,* December 26–January 1, 1963–64, No. 793.

61. *Ibid.*

62. Raymond Dronne in *Pour ou Contre la Force de Frappe,* pp. 196–97.

63. Club Jean Moulin, *L'Etat et le Citoyen,* p. 309.

64. Club Jean Moulin, *La Force de Frappe et le Citoyen,* p. 40.

65. Raymond Aron, *Le Grand Débat,* p. 133.

66. Club de Grenelle, *op. cit.,* p. 50.

67. References to this hypothesis, relating to the military officers, are to be found, e.g., in Stanley Hoffmann *et al., In Search of France,* p. 85; Alexandre Sanguinetti, *op. cit.,* p. 63; Raymond Aron, *Le Grand Débat,* p. 119, footnote.

68. See Raymond Aron, *Paix et Guerre entre les Nations,* pp. 482–83, Jacques Bloch-Morhange, *op. cit.,* p. 107, and *Pour ou Contre la Force de Frappe,* p. 192.

69. Michel Debré, *op. cit.,* p. 152.

70. Raymond Aron, *Le Grand Débat,* pp. 125 and 271.

71. *Le Monde,* January 28–February 3, 1965, No. 850.

72. Sirius, "La Bombe," *Le Monde,* November 26–December 2, 1964, No. 841.

73. Raymond Aron, *Le Grand Débat,* p. 104.

74. Michel Debré, *op. cit.,* p. 155.

75. *Pour ou Contre la Force de Frappe,* pp. 101–4.

76. *L'Année Politique 1962,* p. 573.

77. *Ibid.,* p. 694.

78. Alfred Grosser, *La Politique Extérieure de la Vᵉ République,* p. 126.

79. See *The Economist,* February 2, 1964, p. 588.

80. Raymond Aron, *Le Grand Débat,* p. 131.

81. The various arguments pro and con are to be found, among others, in Alexandre Sanguinetti, *op. cit.,* Club de Grenelle, *op. cit.,* Club Jean Moulin, *La Force de Frappe et le Citoyen,* and Raymond Aron, *Le Grand Débat.*

82. Raymond Aron, *Paix et Guerre entre les Nations,* p. 613.

83. *Pour ou Contre la Force de Frappe,* p. 29. See also the statement by the Minister of Information. *Ibid.,* pp. 253–55.

84. See, e.g., *Pour ou Contre la Force de Frappe,* pp. 239–40.

85. Paul Reynaud, *La Politique Etrangère du Gaullisme,* p. 89.

86. *Le Monde,* April 22–28, 1965, No. 862.

87. *Pour ou Contre la Force de Frappe,* p. 28.

88. Michel Debré, *op. cit.,* p. 153.

89. *Pour ou Contre la Force de Frappe,* pp. 128–40.

90. *Ibid.,* pp. 38, 106–7, 234–35.

91. Club Jean Moulin, *La Force de Frappe et le Citoyen,* p. 77.

92. *Le Figaro Littéraire,* January 30–February 5, 1964.

93. French Embassy, *Major Addresses,* p. 171.

94. *L'Année Politique 1963,* p. 85.

95. *Sondages,* 25-e Année, 1963, No. 3, and 26-e Année, 1964, no. 3.

96. *L'Année Politique 1962,* p. 90.

97. Club de Grenelle, *op. cit.,* p. 95.

98. Alfred Grosser, *La Politique Extérieure de la Vᵉ République,* p. 130.

99. *L'Année Politique 1958,* p. 290.

100. *Ibid.,* p. 461.

101. The sources for the nuclear history of the Fourth Republic are to be found in, among others, Alfred Grosser, *La IVᵉ République et Sa Politique Extérieure; La Politique Extérieure de la Vᵉ République* by the same author; Alfred Fabre-

Luce, *Le Couronnement du Prince*; Club de Grenelle, *op. cit.*; Michel Debré, *op. cit.*; and *L'Année Politique.*

102. French Embassy, *Major Addresses,* pp. 27–28.

103. *Ibid.*, p. 238.

104. *Ibid.*, p. 237.

105. *Ibid.*, p. 122.

106. *Ibid.*, p. 60.

107. Ambassade de France, *Speeches and Press Conferences,* No. 210, p. 3.

108. André Fontaine, *op. cit.*, p. 59.

109. *New York Times,* February 14, 1964.

110. Coral Bell (ed.), *op. cit.*, p. 15.

111. *Pour ou Contre la Force de Frappe,* p. 80.

112. Michel Debré, *op. cit.*, p. 156.

113. *Le Monde,* January 21–27, 1965, No. 849.

114. Alexandre Sanguinetti, *op. cit.*, p. 33.

115. Club Jean Moulin, *La Force de Frappe et le Citoyen,* p. 65.

116. The French arguments regarding the nuclear armament of Germany are to be found, e.g., in *Pour ou Contre la Force de Frappe;* Alexandre Sanguinetti, *op. cit.*; Club Jean Moulin, *La Force de Frappe et le Citoyen;* Raymond Aron, *Le Grand Débat.*

117. French Embassy, *Major Addresses,* pp. 216–19.

118. *Ibid.*

119. Michel Debré, *op. cit.*, pp. 157–58.

120. *Le Monde,* November 5–11, 1964, No. 838.

121. Maurice Duverger, "Une solution fausse," *Le Monde,* December 10–16, 1964, No. 843.

122. A brief but penetrating French version of the history of the MLF is André Fontaine, "Histoire de la force multilatérale," *Le Monde,* November 12–18, 1964, No. 839; November 19–25, 1964, No. 840; and November 26–December 2, 1964, No. 841.

123. Maurice Faure, "Les Choix de la France," *Le Monde,* February 20–26, 1964, No. 801.

124. Club Jean Moulin, *La Force de Frappe et le Citoyen,* pp. 119–21.

125. *Pour ou Contre la Force de Frappe,* p. 241.

126. *L'Année Politique 1962,* p. 90.

127. *Pour ou Contre la Force de Frappe,* p. 262.

128. *L'Année Politique 1963,* p. 89.

129. Quoted in André Fontaine, *op. cit.*, p. 117.

130. Michel Debré, *op. cit.*, p. 158.

131. *L'Année Politique 1962,* p. xii.

IV. THE ATLANTIC ALLIANCE AND THE AMERICAN
"PROTECTORATE"

1. Raymond Aron, *Paix et Guerre Entre les Nations,* p. 439.

2. *Le Monde,* December 31–January 6, 1964–65, No. 846.

3. *Ibid.*, April 29–May 5, 1965, No. 863.

4. Ambassade de France, *French Affairs,* No. 163, p. 6.

5. Ambassade de France, *Speeches and Press Conferences,* No. 208, pp. 4–5.

6. Michel Debré, *op. cit.*, p. 174.
7. French Embassy, *Major Addresses*, p. 142.
8. *Ibid.*, p. 141.
9. *Ibid.*, p. 61.
10. Quoted in Jacques Bloch-Morhange, *op. cit.*, p. 95.
11. *Le Monde*, November 5–11, 1964, No. 838.
12. French Embassy, *Major Addresses*, p. 233.
13. *Ibid.*, pp. 95–96.
14. *Ibid.*, p. 124.
15. Coral Bell (ed.), *op. cit.*, p. 20.
16. French Embassy, *Major Addresses*, p. 233.
17. *Pour ou Contre la Force de Frappe*, p. 267.
18. Ambassade de France, *Speeches and Press Conferences*, No. 228, p. 7.
19. *Le Monde*, September 23–29, 1965, No. 884.
20. *New York Times*, October 17, 1965.
21. *L'Année Politique 1960*, p. 562.
22. *L'Année Politique 1958*, p. 453.
23. André Fontaine, *op. cit.*, p. 94.
24. *L'Année Politique 1958*, p. 498.
25. *L'Année Politique 1960*, p. 549.
26. *Ibid.*, p. 577.
27. *L'Année Politique 1962*, p. 375.
28. *Ibid.*, p. 483.
29. French Embassy, *Major Addresses*, p. 124.
30. *L'Année Politique 1961*, p. 382.
31. *L'Année Politique 1960*, p. 578.
32. French Embassy, *Major Addresses*, pp. 87–88.
33. Michel Debré, *op. cit.*, p. 171.
34. André Fontaine, *op. cit.*, p. 131.
35. André Passeron, *op. cit.*, p. 357.
36. Raymond Aron, *op. cit.*, p. 468.
37. Michel Debré, *op. cit.*, p. 172.
38. *Ibid.*, p. 173.
39. French Embassy, *Major Addresses*, p. 236.
40. André Fontaine, *op. cit.*, p. 88.
41. Claude Delmas *et al.*, *L'Avenir de l'Alliance Atlantique*, p. 299.
42. Guy Mollet, *op. cit.*, pp. 43–46.
43. Jean-Raymond Tournoux, *op. cit.*, p. 363.
44. Alfred Grosser, *La IVᵉ République et Sa Politique Extérieure*, p. 30.
45. *Le Monde*, June 17, 1965, No. 6352.
46. *L'Année Politique 1959*, p. 479.
47. Alfred Grosser, *La Politique Extérieure de la Vᵉ République*, pp. 17 and 150.
48. *Sondages*, 20-e Année, 1958, Nos. 1 and 2, p. 23.
49. For French reactions at that time, see Alfred Grosser, *La IVᵉ République et Sa Politique Extérieure* and *L'Année Politique*.
50. André Fontaine, "Une candidature européenne?," *Le Monde*, August 4, 1965, No. 6393.
51. *Le Monde*, May 6–12, 1965, No. 864.
52. *L'Année Politique 1959*, p. 632.
53. *L'Année Politique 1960*, p. 658.

54. Raymond Aron, *op. cit.*, pp. 461–62.

55. Coral Bell (ed.), *op. cit.*, p. 18.

56. Ambassade de France, *Speeches and Press Conferences*, No. 187.

57. *Le Monde*, March 10–16, 1966, No. 908.

58. *Süddeutsche Zeitung*, February 23, 1966.

59. *Le Monde*, March 10–16, 1966, No. 908.

60. *Le Monde*, March 31–April 6, 1966, No. 911.

61. *New York Times*, April 17, 1966.

62. *Le Monde*, April 14–20, 1966, No. 913.

63. *Ibid.*

64. *Le Monde*, April 21–27, 1966, No. 914.

65. *Ibid.*

V. WESTERN EUROPEAN UNION VERSUS FRENCH INDEPENDENCE

1. A competent Belgian commentator says: "Doubtless, Europe of the Six has never been for the Head of the French State a goal in itself." Henri Brugmans, *L'Idée Européenne: 1918–1965*, p. 234.

2. This leitmotiv of preserving national sovereignty within the united Little Europe constantly reappears in de Gaulle's speeches; for instance, he referred to it in April 1965. *Le Monde*, April 29–May 5, 1965, No. 863.

3. His speech of July 18, 1965, in the National Assembly. *Le Monde*, June 19, 1965, No. 6354.

4. Charles de Gaulle, *op. cit.*, III, 53.

5. *Ibid.*

6. *Ibid.*, p. 205.

7. Quoted in Roger Massip, *op. cit.*, p. 192.

8. *Ibid.*, p. 193.

9. French Embassy, *Major Addresses*, p. 159.

10. *Ibid.*, p. 109.

11. *Ibid.*, p. 78.

12. Quoted in Roger Massip, *op. cit.*, p. 150.

13. *Ibid.*

14. French Embassy, *Major Addresses*, p. 77.

15. *Ibid.*, p. 244.

16. Ambassade de France, *Speeches and Press Conferences*, No. 210, pp. 10–11.

17. Press Conference of July 23, 1964. Ambassade de France, *Speeches and Press Conferences*, No. 208, p. 5.

18. French Embassy, *Major Addresses*, p. 172.

19. Statement of May 31, 1960, *ibid.*, p. 78.

20. Roger Massip, *op. cit.*, pp. 184–85.

21. Statement made in October 1960, *ibid.*, p. 193.

22. *Le Monde*, January 30–February 5, 1964, No. 798.

23. Ambassade de France, *French Affairs*, No. 175, pp. 2–3.

24. Paul Reynaud, *op. cit.*, p. 51.

25. Alfred Grosser, *La IVe République et Sa Politique Extérieure*, p. 346.

26. Roger Massip, *op. cit.*, p. 33.

27. *Ibid.*, p. 143.

28. Henri Brugmans, *op. cit.*, p. 209.

29. French Embassy, *Major Addresses*, pp. 92–93.

30. *Ibid.*, p. 176.

31. *Ibid.*

32. *Ibid.*

33. Raymond Aron, *Paix et Guerre Entre les Nations*, pp. 730–33.

34. Pierre Drouin, *L'Europe du Marché Commun*, p. 129. For an identical view expressed by another expert on the Common Market, see Nicola Catalano, *Manuel de Droit des Communautés Européennes*, pp. 52–53.

35. Pierre Drouin, *op. cit.*, p. 133.

36. Professor Maurice Byé in J. Basdevant *et al.*, *op. cit.*, p. 269.

37. *Ibid.*, p. 363.

38. French Embassy, *Major Addresses*, p. 253. He expressed the same view on January 14, 1963. *Ibid.*, p. 213.

39. Pierre Drouin, *op. cit.*, p. 137.

40. Jean Lecerf, *Histoire de l'Unité Européenne*, pp. 108–10.

41. French Embassy, *Major Addresses*, p. 176.

42. Pierre Drouin, *op. cit.*, p. 107.

43. French Embassy, *Major Addresses*, pp. 176–77.

44. Georges Elgozy, *La France Devant le Marché Commun*, p. 76.

45. French Embassy, *Major Addresses*, p. 177.

46. The press conference of July 23, 1964. Ambassade de France, *Speeches and Press Conferences*, No. 208, p. 5.

47. Pierre Uri, "Bruxelles et l'intérêt français," *Le Monde*, July 14, 1965, No. 6375.

48. Pierre Drouin, "Une dangereuse incertitude pour l'industrie," *Le Monde*, September 16–22, 1965, No. 883.

49. *Ibid.*

50. French Embassy, *Major Addresses*, p. 254.

51. Pierre Drouin, "Si le pire arrivait . . . ," *Le Monde*, November 5–11, 1964, No. 838.

52. François-Henri de Virieu, "Une lourde note à payer par le Trésor et les producteurs agricoles," *Le Monde*, September 16–22, 1965, No. 883.

53. Pierre Drouin, "Une dangereuse incertitude pour l'industrie," *Le Monde*, September 16–22, 1965, No. 883.

54. Ambassade de France, *Speeches and Press Conferences*, No. 228, pp. 5–6.

55. *Le Monde*, September 23–29, 1965, No. 884.

56. French Embassy, *Major Addresses*, pp. 239–40.

57. Jacques de Montalais, "Vocations," *Le Monde*, July 8, 1965, No. 6370.

58. *The Economist*, May 14, 1966, p. XI.

59. *Ibid.*

60. French Embassy, *Major Addresses*, p. 254.

61. Jean Meynaud, *La Révolte Paysanne*, p. 208.

62. *Ibid.*, p. 210.

63. *L'Année Politique 1962*, pp. 404–5 and 574–75.

64. Mentioned in Alfred Grosser, *La Politique Extérieure de la V*e *République*, p. 111.

65. One of the best studies of the agricultural problem of the Common Market is François Clerc, *Le Marché Commun Agricole*.

66. Ambassade de France, *French Affairs*, No. 187.

67. Ambassade de France, *French Affairs*, No. 188.
68. *Le Monde*, May 12–18, 1966, No. 917.
69. *Le Monde*, June 18, 1965, No. 6353.
70. Roger Nathan, "Une crise profonde," *Le Monde*, July 10, 1965, No. 6372.
71. Maurice Duverger, "La grande explication," *Le Monde*, July 8, 1965, No. 6370.
72. French Embassy, *Major Addresses*, p. 93.
73. *Ibid.*, p. 174.
74. Roger Massip, *op. cit.*, p. 130.
75. *Ibid.*, pp. 91–92.
76. John Pinder, *Europe against de Gaulle*, p. 77.
77. *Ibid.*, p. 80.
78. *The Economist*, May 14, 1966.
79. *L'Année Politique 1961*, p. 504.
80. *Le Monde*, December 31–January 6, 1965, No. 846.
81. Ambassade de France, *Speeches and Press Conferences*, No. 244A.
82. *Le Monde*, February 20–26, 1964, No. 801.
83. Ambassade de France, *Speeches and Press Conferences*, No. 239.
84. Charles de Gaulle, *op. cit.*, I, 163.
85. French Embassy, *Major Addresses*, p. 215.
86. John Pinder, *op. cit.*, p. 49.
87. Coral Bell (ed.), *op. cit.*, pp. 30, 110–11.
88. French Embassy, *Major Addresses*, p. 147.
89. Guy Mollet, *op. cit.*, p. 40.
90. *Le Monde*, February 20–26, 1964, No. 801.
91. *L'Année Politique 1963*, p. 9.
92. *Ibid.*
93. *Ibid.*, p. 7.
94. *Ibid.*
95. *L'Année Politique 1962*, p. 542.
96. *L'Année Politique 1961*, p. 476.
97. *L'Année Politique 1963*, p. 244.
98. Pierre Drouin, *op. cit.*, p. 260.
99. These apprehensions are echoed in Michel Debré, *op. cit.*, p. 168.
100. Coral Bell (ed.), *op. cit.*, pp. 24–25.
101. Henri Brugmans, *op. cit.*, p. 226.
102. *L'Année Politique 1962*, p. 694.
103. Coral Bell (ed.), *op. cit.*, p. 28.
104. Roger Massip, *op. cit.*, p. 181.
105. *Ibid.*, p. 181.
106. French Embassy, *Major Addresses*, pp. 213–15.
107. *Ibid.*, p. 215.
108. Roger Massip, *op. cit.*, p. 49.
109. Michel Debré, *op. cit.*, p. 167.
110. Jacques Nobécourt, "Intégration de l'Europe des Six et intégration allemande," *Le Monde*, April 1–7, 1965, No. 859.
111. *The Economist*, May 14, 1966, pp. i–xxxii. This supplement to the weekly issue offers an excellent though somewhat optimistic analysis of problems related to the British membership in the Common Market.
112. *Ibid.*, p. xix.

113. *Ibid.,* p. xix.

114. *Ibid.,* p. viii.

115. French Embassy, *Major Addresses,* p. 232.

116. An excellent history of the early wartime quarrels between the United States and Free France is Dorothy S. White, *Seeds of Discord* (Syracuse: Syracuse University Press, 1964).

117. Coral Bell (ed.), *op. cit.,* p. 19.

118. Pierre Drouin, *op. cit.,* pp. 322 and 324.

119. *Ibid.,* p. 327.

120. *L'Année Politique 1962,* p. xiii.

121. *Le Monde,* February 20–26, 1964, No. 801.

122. René Mayer, "Nouvelle hégémonie ou solidarité," *Le Monde,* November 19–25, 1964, No. 840.

123. Henri Brugmans, *op. cit.,* pp. 240–41.

124. *Ibid.,* p. 248.

125. *L'Année Politique 1959,* p. 307.

126. One may mention in passing two other alarmist voices warning against the "colonization" of France by American capital: (1) the former President of Euratom, Etienne Hirsch, "Réponse d'un jean-foutre," *Le Monde,* June 16, 1965, No. 6351; and (2) the speech by François Mitterand in the National Assembly on June 18, 1965, reported in *Le Monde,* June 19, 1965, No 6354. Mr. Mitterand, the leftist candidate in 1965, and Mr. Hirsch are both implacable enemies of de Gaulle. This topic must be a propaganda goldmine in France, if Socialist Gaston Defferre and conservative Valéry Giscard d'Estaing agree on this matter. Defferre reaffirmed his fear of the "colonization" of France by American capital in an article he published in *Foreign Affairs,* April, 1966. Giscard d'Estaing said on April 23, 1966, that he, so long as he was Minister of National Economy, had firmly opposed the sale of French enterprises to American corporations, and expressed his regret that his successor in Pompidou's government, Michel Debré, was more tolerant regarding such sales. Both criticized the government for its unduly liberal attitude toward the implantation of American capital. In the light of this criticism de Gaulle looked insufficiently suspicious of Americans!

127. Alfred Grosser, *La Politique Extérieure de la Ve République,* p. 164.

128. *Ibid.,* p. 165.

129. Pierre Uri, "Pour une politique européenne des investissements américains," *Le Monde,* February 25–March 3, 1965, No. 854.

130. Professor Maurice Byé in J. Basdevant *et al., op. cit.,* p. 270.

131. See a scholarly study of American investments, Gilles-Y. Bertin, *L'Investissement des Firmes Etrangères en France.*

132. *Le Monde,* March 25–31, 1965, No. 858.

133. Henry Brugmans, *op. cit.,* pp. 232–33.

134. *Le Monde,* July 15, 1965, No. 6376.

135. *Ibid.*

136. Ambassade de France, *Speeches and Press Conferences,* No. 216, p. 6.

137. Michel Debré, *op. cit.,* p. 167.

138. *Le Monde,* July 23, 1965, No. 6383.

139. Paul Reynaud, *op. cit.,* p. 126.

140. Guy Mollet, *op. cit.,* p. 33.

141. Alfred Grosser, *La Politique Extérieure de la Ve République,* p. 117.

142. *Ibid.,* p. 183.

143. *Sondages,* 25-e Année, 1963, No. 3, pp. 88–89.
144. Henri Brugmans, *op. cit.,* pp. 256–57.
145. *Ibid.,* p. 245.

VI.   SEVERAL IRONS IN THE FIRE: GERMANY, RUSSIA, AND CHINA

1. Quoted in Roger Massip, *op. cit.,* p. 155.
2. Robert Aron, *Histoire de Vichy,* pp. 511–12.
3. Charles de Gaulle, *op. cit.,* III, 51–52.
4. Roger Massip, *op. cit.,* pp. 46–47.
5. *Ibid.,* p. 48.
6. Association Française de Science Politique, *La Politique Etrangère et Ses Fondements,* p. 104.
7. Charles de Gaulle, *op. cit.,* III, 61.
8. *Ibid.,* III, 201.
9. *Ibid.,* III, 235.
10. Roger Massip, *op. cit.,* pp. 52–53.
11. *Ibid.,* pp. 54–55.
12. Alfred Grosser, *La IVᵉ République et Sa Politique Extérieure,* p. 196.
13. *Ibid.,* pp. 319–320.
14. J. B. Duroselle in Stanley Hoffmann *et al., In Search of France,* pp. 347–48.
15. *Sondages,* 20-e Année, 1958, Nos. 1 and 2, pp. 49 and 22.
16. *Sondages,* 25-e Année, 1963, No. 1, pp. 99–100.
17. French Embassy, *Major Addresses,* p. 43.
18. Paul-Marie de la Gorce, *op. cit.,* pp. 712–13.
19. *L'Année Politique 1958,* pp. 432–33.
20. *Ibid.,* p. 433.
21. *L'Année Politique 1962,* p. 672.
22. *Ibid.,* p. 673.
23. *L'Année Politique 1960,* pp. 425–26.
24. Alfred Grosser, *La Politique Extérieure de la Vᵉ République,* p. 92.
25. *L'Année Politique 1962,* p. 544.
26. The text of the treaty can be found in *Journal Officiel de la République Française, Lois et Décrets,* September 2–3, 1963, No. 206, pp. 8028–29.
27. French Embassy, *Major Addresses,* p. 220.
28. *L'Année Politique 1959,* p. xix.
29. *L'Année Politique 1963,* pp. 406–7.
30. *Ibid.,* p. 47.
31. *Ibid.,* p. 48.
32. *Ibid.,* p. 280.
33. Ambassade de France, *Speeches and Press Conferences,* No. 208, pp. 6–7.
34. *Le Monde,* June 12, 1965, No. 6348.
35. *Ibid.,* June 15, 1965, No. 6350.
36. Ambassade de France, *Speeches and Press Conferences,* No. 228, p. 9.
37. One of the frankest German presentations of divergent views that exist between the Federal Republic of Germany and the United States is Kurt Birrenbach's "The Federal Republic and America: Problems of an Alliance," published in

Aussenpolitik, No. 2, 1966, and reproduced in *The German Tribune, A Selection from German Periodicals,* April 30, 1966.

38. *Bulletin de l'Office de Presse et d'Information du Gouvernement Fédéral,* October 28, 1964.
39. *News from the German Embassy,* IX, no. 5, May 7, 1965, p. 1.
40. *Ibid.,* p. 4.
41. *Ibid.*
42. *L'Année Politique 1963,* p. 254.
43. Paul Reynaud, *op. cit.,* p. 151.
44. Ambassade de France, *Speeches and Press Conferences,* No. 212, p. 3.
45. French Embassy, *Major Addresses,* p. 178.
46. Ambassade de France, *Speeches and Press Conferences,* No. 216, pp. 9–11.
47. *Ibid.,* p. 12.
48. Jean-Raymond Tournoux, *op. cit.,* p. 351.
49. Jacques Bloch-Morhange, *op. cit.,* p. 121.
50. Ambassade de France, *Speeches and Press Conferences,* No. 239.
51. French Embassy, *Major Addresses,* p. 43.
52. *L'Année Politique 1959,* p. 525.
53. French Embassy, *Major Addresses,* p. 42.
54. André Passeron, *op. cit.,* p. 396.
55. Michel Debré, *op. cit.,* p. 162.
56. René Lauret, *Notre Voisin Allemand,* p. 7.
57. *Le Monde,* September 23–29, 1965, No. 884.
58. Guy Mollet, *op. cit.,* p. 63.
59. Coral Bell (ed.), *op. cit.,* p. 21.
60. *Pravda,* March 30, 1966.
61. *Ibid.,* April 3, 1966.
62. André Passeron, *op. cit.,* p. 396.
63. *Le Monde,* June 13–14, 1965, No. 6349.
64. *Ibid.,* May 13–19, 1965, No. 865.
65. *News from the German Embassy,* IX, No. 7, May 12, 1965, p. 2.
66. *Le Monde,* January 21–27, 1965, No. 849.
67. Quoted in Alfred Grosser, *La IVᵉ République et Sa Politique Extérieure,* p. 18.
68. Charles de Gaulle, *op. cit.,* III, 378. French edition.
69. André Passeron, *op. cit.,* p. 417.
70. *L'Année Politique 1958,* p. 497.
71. French Embassy, *Major Addresses,* p. 142.
72. Ambassade de France, *French Affairs,* No. 163, p. 3.
73. French Embassy, *Major Addresses,* p. 58.
74. Ambassade de France, *Speeches and Press Conferences,* No. 201, p. 14.
75. André Fontaine, "L'Europe et l'Asie," *Le Monde,* March 4–10, 1965, No. 855.
76. *Ibid.*
77. *Le Monde,* May 6–12, 1965, No. 864.
78. *Ibid.,* April 29–May 5, 1965, No. 863.
79. *Ibid.*
80. *Ibid.,* January 7–13, 1965, No. 847.
81. *Ibid.,* June 23, 1965, No. 6357.
82. *Ibid.,* July 25–26, 1965, No. 6385.

83. *Ibid.*, June 19, 1965, No. 6354.
84. *Ibid.*
85. Obozrevatel, "Nazrevshiye problemy," *Pravda*, February 14, 1965.
86. The fullest description of the visit was given by *Pravda* and *Le Monde*.
87. C. L. Sulzberger, "Foreign Affairs: The Icebreaker Cometh," *New York Times*, July 3, 1966.
88. *Pravda*, July 1, 1966.
89. François Mitterand, *op. cit.*, p. 107.
90. Paul Reynaud, *op. cit.*, p. 229.
91. Ambassade de France, *Speeches and Press Conferences*, No. 201, p. 13.
92. *Ibid.*, pp. 13, 14.
93. Paul-Marie de la Gorce, *op. cit.*, pp. 734–35.
94. Ambassade de France, *Speeches and Press Conferences*, No. 206, pp. 4, 5.
95. *Ibid.*, No. 201, p. 14.
96. *Ibid.*
97. *Le Monde*, February 11–17, 1965, No. 852.
98. *Ibid.*
99. *Le Monde*, June 17, 1965, No. 6352.

VII. HERO OF THE THIRD WORLD OR A MEMBER OF A COLLECTIVE HEGEMONY?

1. *Le Monde*, July 28, 1965, No. 6387.
2. François Borella, *L'Evolution Politique et Juridique de l'Union Française Depuis 1946*, pp. 173, 177, 178 and 179.
3. *Ibid.*, p. 65.
4. Alfred Grosser, *La IVᵉ République et Sa Politique Extérieure*, p. 116.
5. *Ibid.*
6. *Ibid.*, p. 173.
7. J. B. Duroselle in Stanley Hoffmann *et al.*, *op. cit.*, p. 342.
8. Guy Mollet, *op. cit.*, p. 141.
9. François Borella, *op. cit.*, p. 185.
10. *Ibid.*, p. 188.
11. Alfred Grosser, *op. cit.*, p. 250.
12. René Viard, *La Fin de l'Empire Colonial Français*, pp. 52–53.
13. Alfred Sauvy, *op. cit.*, p. 243.
14. *Ibid.*, p. 238.
15. Thomas Oppermann, *Le Problème Algérien*, pp. 41–60.
16. Alfred Grosser, *op. cit.*, p. 389.
17. François Borella, *op. cit.*, p. 160.
18. Alfred Grosser, *op. cit.*, p. 378.
19. Thomas Oppermann, *op. cit.*, p. 135.
20. Alfred Grosser, *op. cit.*, p. 332.
21. *Ibid.*
22. *Ibid.*, p. 48.
23. Guy Mollet, *op. cit.*, p. 146.
24. François Borella, *op. cit.*, p. 59.
25. Pierre Vidal-Naquet, *La Raison d'Etat*, pp. 20, 25. This is the best documented study of that sad chapter of history of the Fourth Republic. It is confirmed in Thomas Oppermann, *op. cit.*, pp. 151–54.

26. François Borella, *op. cit.,* pp. 259–261.
27. Pierre Mendès-France, *La Politique et la Vérité,* pp. 184–86.
28. Alfred Grosser, *op. cit.,* p. 371.
29. *Ibid.,* p. 373.
30. *Ibid.,* p. 383.
31. *L'Année Politique 1961,* p. x.
32. Alfred Grosser, *op. cit.,* p. 188.
33. Guy Mollet, *op. cit.,* p. 104.
34. René Viard, *op. cit.,* p. 14.
35. *Ibid.,* p. 18.
36. *Ibid.,* p. 23.
37. Paul-Marie de la Gorce, *op. cit.,* p. 426.
38. Charles de Gaulle, *op. cit.,* III, 242.
39. *Ibid.,* p. 253.
40. François Mauriac, *op. cit.,* p. 198.
41. *Ibid.,* pp. 198–99.
42. Alfred Grosser, *op. cit.,* p. 139.
43. André Passeron, *op. cit.,* p. 453.
44. *Ibid.,* p. 457.
45. *Ibid.,* p. 458.
46. *Ibid.,* p. 459.
47. René Viard, *op. cit.,* p. 85.
48. *Ibid.,* pp. 148 and 156.
49. *Ibid.,* p. xvi.
50. André Passeron, *op. cit.,* pp. 465–66.
51. *Ibid.,* p. 478.
52. *Ibid.,* p. 481.
53. French Embassy, *Major Addresses,* p. 82.
54. Philippe Herreman, "La Carte française," *Le Monde,* November 26–December 2, 1964, No. 841.
55. René Viard, *op. cit.,* p. 152.
56. *Ibid.,* p. xvi.
57. Paul-Marie de la Gorce, *op. cit.,* p. 610.
58. André Passeron, *op. cit.,* p. 151.
59. *Ibid.,* p. 154.
60. *Ibid.,* p. 170.
61. *Ibid.,* pp. 191 and 193.
62. *Ibid.,* p. 195.
63. *Ibid.,* pp. 197 and 200.
64. *Ibid.,* p. 202.
65. *Ibid.,* p. 206.
66. *Ibid.,* p. 251.
67. *Ibid.,* p. 252.
68. *Ibid.,* p. 280.
69. Fondation Nationale des Sciences Politiques, *Le Référendum du 8 janvier 1961,* p. 115.
70. André Passeron, *op. cit.,* p. 287.
71. *Ibid.,* p. 327.
72. The full text of the Evian agreements is in *L'Année Politique 1962,* pp. 631–46.

73. *L'Année Politique, 1962,* p. 701.

74. Guy Mollet, *op. cit.,* p. 134.

75. J. B. Duroselle and J. Meyriat, *La Communauté Internationale Face Aux Jeunes Etats,* p. 87.

76. Edouard Bonnefous, *Les Milliards Qui S'Envolent,* p. 155.

77. French Embassy, *Major Addresses,* p. 45.

78. André Passeron, *op. cit.,* p. 438.

79. *Ibid.,* p. 441.

80. French Embassy, *Major Addresses,* p. 250.

81. Ambassade de France, *Speeches and Press Conferences,* No. 228, pp. 8–9.

82. Ambassade de France, *Major Addresses,* p. 251.

83. *Ibid.,* p. 252.

84. *Ibid.,* p. 252.

85. *Ibid.,* p. 252.

86. *Ibid.,* p. 251.

87. De Gaulle's televised speech of April 16, 1964. Ambassade de France, *French Affairs,* No. 166, p. 4.

88. Ambassade de France, *French Cooperation with Developing Countries.* Summary of the report drawn up by the Special Commission presided over by Jean-Marcel Jeanneney, p. 16.

89. Edouard Bonnefous, *op. cit.,* p. 47.

90. Ambassade de France, *French Cooperation with Developing Countries,* pp. 14–16.

91. Edouard Bonnefous, *op. cit.,* p. 7.

92. *Ibid.,* pp. 84–85.

93. The above data are given in *ibid.,* pp. 84–87.

94. *Ibid.,* p. 87.

95. Jean Meynaud, *op. cit.,* p. 34.

96. Ambassade de France, *French Cooperation with Developing Countries,* p. 26.

97. *Le Monde,* November 25–December 1, 1965, No. 893.

98. De Gaulle's press conference of September 9, 1965. Ambassade de France, *Speeches and Press Conferences,* No. 228, p. 8.

99. Ambassade de France, *French Cooperation with Developing Countries,* and *Le Monde,* March 10–16, 1966, No. 908 (An analysis of the report submitted in December 1965 by the French Ministry of Finances to the O.E.C.D.)

100. *Ibid.*

101. *Ibid.*

102. *Ibid.*

103. *Ibid.*

104. Ambassade de France, *Speeches and Press Conferences,* No. 229, p. 8.

105. *L'Année Politique 1963,* p. 193.

106. *Le Monde,* July 4–5, 1965, No. 6367.

107. The text of the French-Algerian agreement and interesting comments in *Le Monde,* July 30, 1965, No. 6389.

108. *Le Monde,* June 19, 1965, No. 6354.

109. Ambassade de France, *Speeches and Press Conferences,* No. 229, p. 9.

110. *Le Monde,* August 1–2, 1965, No. 6391.

111. Ambassade de France, *French Cooperation with Developing Countries,* pp. 22–23.

112. *Ibid.*, pp. 26–27.

113. *Le Monde*, February 4–10, 1965, No. 851.

114. *Tiers Monde*, 1962, pp. 25–27. Also, Ambassade de France, *French Affairs*, No. 182.

115. *Le Monde*, November 25–December 1, 1965, No. 893.

116. Ambassade de France, *French Affairs*, No. 182, p. 2.

117. *Ibid.*, p. 2.

118. Ambassade de France, *French Cooperation with Developing Countries*, p. 34.

119. Ambassade de France, *French Affairs*, No. 178, pp. 9–10.

120. *Le Monde*, June 30, 1965, No. 6363.

121. *Ibid.*, July 4–5, 1965, No. 6367.

122. *Ibid.*, July 2, 1965, No. 6365.

123. French Embassy, *Major Addresses*, p. 241.

124. Ambassade de France, *Speeches and Press Conferences*, No. 228, p. 9.

125. *Le Monde*, August 3, 1965, No. 6392.

126. De Gaulle's letter to Ho Chi Minh, *Le Monde*, February 17–23, 1966, No. 905.

127. Sirius, "Pour l'honneur du navire," *Le Monde*, February 17–23, 1966, No. 905.

128. Ambassade de France, *Speeches and Press Conferences*, No. 239.

129. *Le Monde*, July 18–19, 1965, No. 6379.

130. *Ibid.*, July 11–12, 1965, No. 6373.

131. Paul Reynaud, *op. cit.*, p. 200.

132. *Le Monde*, July 2, 1965, No. 6365.

133. *Ibid.*, July 11–12, 1965, No. 6373.

134. *Ibid.*, July 14, 1965, No. 6375.

135. Ambassade de France, *French Affairs*, No. 175, p. 2.

136. *Sondages*, 20-e Année, 1958, Nos. 1 and 2, p. 192.

137. Charles de Gaulle, *op. cit.*, III, 227–29.

138. In September 1960. André Passeron, *op. cit.*, p. 477.

139. French Embassy, *Major Addresses*, pp. 119–21.

140. *L'Année Politique 1962*, p. 695.

141. *Le Monde*, June 29, 1965, No. 6362.

142. Ambassade de France, *Speeches and Press Conferences*, No. 229, p. 2.

143. *Le Monde*, June 12, 1965, No. 6348.

144. Ambassade de France, *Speeches and Press Conferences*, No. 216, pp. 7–9. President de Gaulle reiterated the same view at the press conference held on September 9, 1965. Again he suggested that international order and peace could be ensured only by the concerted action of the five permanent members of the Security Council who were at the same time the only nuclear powers. (See *ibid.*, No. 228, p. 10.)

Conclusion

1. *L'Année Politique 1962*, p. viii.

Bibliography

OFFICIAL SOURCES

Journal Officiel de la République Française
    Lois et Décrets
    Débats de l'Assemblée Nationale
    Débats du Sénat
    Documents de l'Assemblée Nationale
    Documents du Sénat
    Conseil Economique et Social
La Documentation Française
    Articles et Documents
    Notes et Etudes Documentaires
    Chroniques Etrangères
    Problèmes Economiques
    Les Cahiers Français
Ambassade de France, Service de Presse et d'Information
    Major Addresses, Statements and Press Conferences of General Charles de Gaulle: May 19, 1958–January 31, 1964.
    Speeches and Press Conferences
    French Affairs

BOOKS

L'Année Politique, Economique, Sociale et Diplomatique en France. Years 1944–1945 to 1965. Paris: Presses Universitaires de France.

Aron, Raymond. *Immuable et Changeante: de la IVe à la Ve République.* Paris: Calmann-Lévy, 1959.

———. *L'Algérie et la République.* Paris: Plon, 1958.

———. *La Tragédie Algérienne.* Paris: Plon, 1957.

———. *Le Grand Débat: Initiation à la Stratégie Atomique.* Paris: Calmann-Lévy, 1963.

———. *Paix et Guerre Entre les Nations.* Paris: Calmann-Lévy, 1962.

Aron, Robert. *Histoire de la Libération de la France: Juin 1944–Mai 1945.* Paris: Librairie Arthème Fayard, 1959.

———. *Histoire de Vichy: 1940–1944.* Paris: Librairie Arthème Fayard, 1954.

Association Française de Science Politique. *La Politique Etrangère et Ses Fondements.* Paris: Librairie Armand Colin, 1954.

———. *L'Etablissement de la Cinquième République: Le Référendum de Septembre et les Elections de Novembre 1958.* Paris: Librairie Armand Colin, 1960.

Baillou, Jean, and Pierre Pelletier. *Les Affaires Etrangères.* Paris: Presses Universitaires de France, 1962.

Barets, Jean. *La Fin des Politiques.* Paris: Calmann-Lévy, 1962.

Basdevant, Jules, *et al. Les Affaires Etrangères.* Paris: Presses Universitaires de France, 1959.

415

Bauchet, Pierre. *La Planification Française: Quinze Ans d'Expérience*. Paris: Editions du Seuil, 1962.

Bell, Coral (ed.). *Europe Without Britain*. Melbourne: F. W. Cheshire, 1963.

Bernanos, Georges. *Français, Si Vous Saviez: 1945–1948*. Paris: Gallimard, 1961.

Bertin, Gilles-Y. *L'Investissement des Firmes Etrangères en France: 1945–1962*. Paris: Presses Universitaires de France, 1963.

Bloch-Morhange, Jacques. *Le Gaullisme*. Paris: Plon, 1963.

Bonnefous, Edouard. *Les Milliards Qui S'Envolent: L'Aide Française Aux Pays Sous-Développés*. Paris: Fayard, 1963.

Borella, François. *L'Evolution Politique et Juridique de l'Union Française Depuis 1946*. Paris: R. Pichon and R. Durand-Anzias, 1958.

Bourrinet, Jacques. *Le Problème Agricole Dans l'Intégration Européenne*. Paris: Editions Cujas, 1964.

Bouvier-Ajam, Maurice, and Gilbert Mury. *Les Classes Sociales En France*. 2 vols. Paris: Editions Sociales, 1963.

Brugmans, Henri. *L'Idée Européenne: 1918–1965*. Bruges: De Tempel, 1965.

Burdeau, Georges. *Les Libertés Publiques*. 2nd ed. Paris: R. Pichon and R. Durand-Anzias, 1961.

Cahiers de la Fondation Nationale des Sciences Politiques. *Le Référendum du 8 Janvier 1961*. Paris: Librairie Armand Colin, 1962.

Catalano, Nicola. *Manuel de Droit des Communautés Européennes*. Paris: Dalloz and Sirey, 1962.

Césaire, Aimé. *Discours Sur le Colonialisme*. 4th ed. Paris: Présence Africaine, 1955.

Charnay, Jean-Paul. *Les Scrutins Politiques en France de 1815 à 1962*. Paris: Librairie Armand Colin, 1964.

Cheverny, Julien. *Le Carnaval des Régents*. Paris: René Julliard, 1963.

Clement, Marcel. *Enquête Sur le Nationalisme*. Paris: Nouvelles Editions Latines, 1957.

Clerc, François. *Le Marché Commun Agricole*. Paris: Presses Universitaires de France, 1964.

Club de Grenelle. *Siècle de Damoclès: La Force Nucléaire Stratégique*. Paris: Pierre Couderc, 1964.

Club Jean Moulin. *La Force de Frappe et le Citoyen*. Paris: Editions du Seuil, 1963.

———. *L'Etat et le Citoyen*. Paris: Editions du Seuil, 1961.

Collège d'Europe. *Intégration Européenne et Réalité Economique*. Bruges: De Tempel, 1964.

Colliard, Claude-Albert. *Libertés Publiques*. Paris: Dalloz, 1959.

Debeauvais, Michel, Jean-Claude Sournia, and Emile Valin. *Tiers-Monde: L'Assistance Technique*. Paris: Presses Universitaires de France, 1962.

Debré, Michel. *Au Service de la Nation*. Paris: Stock, 1963.

De Gaulle, Charles. *Mémoires de Guerre*. 3 vols. Paris: Librairie Plon, 1954-1956-1959.

———. *War Memoirs of Charles de Gaulle*. Translated from the French by Richard Howard. 3 vols. New York: Simon and Schuster, 1955-1959-1960.

Delmas, Claude. *L'Alliance Atlantique*. Paris: Payot, 1962.

———. *La Stratégie Nucléaire*. Paris: Presses Universitaires de France, 1963.

Delmas, Claude, Général Marcel Carpentier, Général Pierre-M. Gallois, and

Maurice Faure. *L'Avenir de l'Alliance Atlantique*. Paris: Berger-Levrault, 1961.

Deschamps, Hubert. *La Communauté Française* (mimeographed). Paris: Institut d'Etudes Politiques de l'Université de Paris, 1958–1959.

Dollot, Louis. *La France Dans le Monde Actuel*. Paris: Presses Universitaires de France, 1964.

D'Ormesson, Wladimir. *Les Vraies Confidences*. Paris: Plon, 1962.

Drouin, Pierre. *L'Europe du Marché Commun*. Paris: René Julliard, 1963.

Ducattillon, J. V. *Patriotisme et Colonisation*. Paris: Editions Desclée et Cie, 1957.

Duchet, Roger. *Pour le Salut Publique: Les Indépendants Devant Les Grands Problèmes Nationaux*. Paris: Plon, 1958.

Duclos, Jacques. *Gaullisme, Technocratie, Corporatisme?* Paris: Editions Sociales, 1963.

Dumon, Frédéric. *La Communauté Franco-Afro-Malgache: Ses Origines, Ses Institutions, Son Evolution*. Bruxelles: Université Libre de Bruxelles, 1960.

Duquesne, Jacques. *L'Algérie ou la Guerre des Mythes*. Paris: Desclée de Brouwer, 1958.

Durand-Réville, Luc. *L'Assistance de la France Aux Pays Insuffisamment Développés*. Paris: M–Th. Génin, 1961.

Duroselle, J.-B., and J. Meyriat. *La Communauté Internationale Face Aux Jeunes Etats*. Paris: Armand Colin, 1964.

Duverger, Maurice. *La Cinquième République*. Paris: Presses Universitaires de France, 1963.

———. *Les Régimes Politiques*. 2nd ed. Paris: Presses Universitaires de France, 1965.

Echanges Franco-Allemands. Le Problème de Berlin. Paris: Presses Universitaires de France, 1962.

Ehrhard, Jean. *Le Destin du Colonialisme*. Paris: Editions Eyrolles, 1958.

Elgozy, Georges. *La France Devant le Marché Commun*. Paris: Flammarion, 1958.

Etudes Economiques de l'OCDE. France. Paris: Organisation de Coopération et de Développement Economique, 1962.

Fabre-Luce, Alfred. *Gaulle Deux*. Paris: René Julliard, 1958.

———. *Le Couronnement du Prince*. Paris: La Table Ronde, 1964.

———. *Le Plus Illustre des Français*. Paris: René Julliard, 1960.

Faucher, Jean André. *La Cinquième République*. Paris: Editions Galia, 1962.

Fauvet, Jacques. *La France Déchirée*. Paris: Librairie Arthème Fayard, 1957.

——— and Jean Planchais. *La Fronde des Généraux*. Paris: Arthaud, 1961.

Figueras, André. *Les Origines Etranges de la Ve République*. Paris: Les Presses du Mail, 1962.

Fontaine, André. *L'Alliance Atlantique à l'Heure du Dégel*. Paris: Calmann-Lévy, 1959.

Fontaine, François. *La Nation Frein*. Paris: René Julliard, 1956.

Fougeyrollas, Pierre. *La Conscience Politique Dans la France Contemporaine*. Paris: Denoël, 1963.

Garçon, Maurice. *Plaidoyer Contre la Censure*. Paris: J. J. Pauvert, 1963.

Giscard d'Estaing, Edmond. *La France et l'Unification Economique de l'Europe*. Paris: Editions M.-Th. Génin, 1953.

Goguel, François, and Alfred Grosser. *La Politique en France*. Paris: Armand Colin, 1964.

Gorce, Paul-Marie de la. *De Gaulle Entre Deux Mondes: Une Vie et Une Epoque.* Paris: Fayard, 1964.

———. *La France Pauvre.* Paris: Grasset, 1965.

Grosser, Alfred. *La IVe République et Sa Politique Extérieure.* Paris: Librairie Armand Colin, 1961.

———. *La Politique Extérieure de la Ve République.* Paris: Editions du Seuil, 1965. English translation: *The Foreign Policy of the Fifth Republic.* Boston, Massachusetts: Little, Brown and Co., [1967].

Guichard-Ayoub, Eliane, Charles Roig, and Jean Grange. *Etudes sur le Parlement de la Ve République.* Paris: Presses Universitaires de France, 1965.

Hamon, Léo. *Les Nouveaux Comportements Politiques de la Classe Ouvrière.* Paris: Presses Universitaires de France, 1962.

——— and Albert Mabileau (eds.). *La Personnalisation du Pouvoir.* Paris: Presses Universitaires de France, 1964.

Hoffmann, Stanley *et al. In Search of France.* Cambridge: Harvard University Press, 1963.

Lacouture, Jean. *De Gaulle.* Paris: Editions du Seuil, 1965.

———. *Cinq Hommes et la France.* Paris: Editions du Seuil, 1961.

Laponce, J. A. *The Government of the Fifth Republic: French Political Parties and the Constitution.* Berkeley and Los Angeles: University of California Press, 1961.

Lauret, René. *Notre Voisin Allemand: Deux Peuples S'Affrontent.* Paris: Nouvelles Editions Latines, 1960.

Lecerf, Jean. *Histoire de l'Unité Européenne.* Paris: Gallimard, 1965.

Leites, Nathan. *Du Malaise Politique en France.* Paris: Librairie Plon, 1958.

L'Huillier, F. (ed.). *Histoire de Notre Temps: Politiques Nationales et Conflits Internationaux, 1945–1962.* Paris: Sirey, 1964.

Lüthy, Herbert. *A l'Heure de Son Clocher: Essai Sur la France.* Paris: Calmann-Lévy, 1955.

Macridis, Roy C., and Bernard E. Brown. *The De Gaulle Republic: Quest for Unity.* Homewood, Ill.: The Dorsey Press, 1960.

Mallet, Serge. *Les Paysans Contre le Passé.* Paris: Editions du Seuil, 1962.

Mannoni, Eugène. *Moi, Général de Gaulle.* Paris: Editions du Seuil, 1964.

Marcus, John T. *Neutralism and Nationalism in France: A Case Study.* New York: Bookman Associates, 1958.

Massigli, René. *Sur Quelques Maladies de l'Etat.* Paris: Plon, 1958.

Massip, Roger. *De Gaulle et l'Europe.* Paris: Flammarion, 1963.

Mauriac, François. *De Gaulle.* Paris: Bernard Grasset, 1964. English translation cited in the present work: *De Gaulle.* New York: Doubleday and Co., 1966 (copyright by Doubleday and Co. and The Bodley Head Ltd., London, England).

Mendès-France, Pierre. *La Politique et la Vérité: Juin 1955-Septembre 1958.* Paris: René Julliard, 1958.

Meynaud, Jean. *La Participation des Français à la Politique.* Paris: Presses Universitaires de France, 1965.

———. *La Révolte Paysanne.* Paris: Payot, 1963.

———. *Les Groupes de Pression.* 2nd ed. Paris: Presses Universitaires de France, 1965.

——— and Alain Lancelot. *Les Attitudes Politiques.* Paris: Presses Universitaires de France, 1964.

Mitterand, François. *Le Coup d'Etat Permanent.* Paris: Plon, 1964.

Mollet, Guy. *13 Mai 1958—13 Mai 1962*. Paris: Plon, 1962.

Noël, Léon. *Notre Dernière Chance*. Paris: Librairie Gedalge, 1956.

Oppermann, Thomas. *Le Problème Algérien*. Paris: François Maspero, 1961.

Passeron, André. *De Gaulle Parle*. Paris: Plon, 1962.

Pénicaud, Jean Philippe. *La Doctrine du Néo-Nationalisme Français*. Paris: L'Avenir de la France, 1963.

Pinder, John. *Europe Against de Gaulle*. London: Pall Mall Press, 1963.

Plumyène, J., and R. Lasierra. *Les Fascismes Français: 1923-1963*. Paris: Editions du Seuil, 1963.

Pour on Contre la Force de Frappe. Paris: Les Editions John Didier, 1963.

Rémond, René (ed.). *Forces Religieuses et Attitudes Politiques Dans la France Contemporaine*. Paris: Librairie Armand Colin, 1965.

————. *La Droite en France: De la Première Restauration à la Vᵉ République*. Paris: Aubier, 1963.

————, et al. *La Démocratie à Refaire*. Paris: Les Editions Ouvrières, 1963.

Reynaud, Paul. *Et Après?* Paris: Plon, 1964.

————. *La Politique Etrangère du Gaullisme*. Paris: René Julliard, 1964.

Rigaud, Jacques (ed.). *Débat sur la France de Demain*. Paris: René Julliard, 1961.

Robertson, Arthur Clendenin. *La Doctrine du Général de Gaulle*. Paris: Librairie Arthème Fayard, 1959.

Rougier, Louis. *L'Erreur de la Démocratie Française*. Paris: Editions l'Esprit Nouveau, 1963.

Saint Marc, Michèle. *Zone Franc et Décolonisation*. Paris: Sèdes, 1964.

Sainte Lorette, L. de. *Le Marché Commun*. Paris: Armand Collin, 1963.

Sanguinetti, Alexandre. *La France et l'Arme Atomique*. Paris: René Julliard, 1964.

Sauvy, Alfred. *La Montée des Jeunes*. Paris: Calmann-Lévy, 1959.

Savary, Alain. *Nationalisme Algérien et Grandeur Française*. Paris: Plon, 1960.

Siegfried, André. *De la IIIᵉ à la IVᵉ République*. Paris: Grasset, 1956.

————. *De la IVᵉ à la Vᵉ République*. Paris: Grasset, 1958.

Soustelle, Jacques. *Le Drame Algérien et la Décadence Française: Réponse à Raymond Aron*. Paris: Plon, 1957.

————. *L'Espérance Trahie*. Paris: Editions de l'Alma, 1962.

Thiam, Doudou. *Les Politiques Etrangères des Etats Africains*. Paris: Presses Universitaires de France, 1963.

Tillion, Germaine. *Les Ennemis Complémentaires*. Paris: Les Editions de Minuit, 1960.

Tournoux, Jean-Raymond. *Secrets d'Etat*. Paris: Plon, 1960.

Varin d'Ainvelle, Madeleine. *La Presse en France: Genèse et Evolution de Ses Fonctions Psycho-Sociales*. Paris: Presses Universitaires de France, 1965.

Vedel, Georges (ed.). *La Dépolitisation: Mythe ou Réalité?* Paris: Cahiers de la Fondation Nationale des Sciences Politiques, Librairie Armand Collin, 1962.

Viansson-Ponté, Pierre. *Les Gaullistes: Rituel et Annuaire*. Paris: Editions du Seuil, 1963.

Viard, René. *La Fin de l'Empire Colonial Français*. Paris: G. P. Maisonneuve and Larose, 1963.

Vidal-Naquet, Pierre. *La Raison d'Etat*. Paris: Les Editions de Minuit, 1962.

Werth, Alexander. *La France Depuis la Guerre: 1944-1957*. Paris: Gallimard, 1957.

Wylie, Laurence. *Village in the Vaucluse*. Cambridge: Harvard University Press, 1961.

PERIODICALS

Le Monde, daily or weekly
Cahiers de la République
Ecrits de Paris
Esprit
La Nef
La Nouvelle Critique
L'Ordre Français
Politique Etrangère
Preuves
Revue de Défense Nationale
Revue des Deux Mondes
Revue Française de Science Politique
Revue de l'Action Populaire
Revue Politique et Parlementaire
Revue Socialiste
Sondages, Revue Française de l'Opinion Publique

Index of Persons

General Index

Afghanistan, 316
Africa, 1, 22, 23, 32, 33, 35, 75, 121, 133, 134, 155, 156, 160, 161, 168–70, 172, 174, 278, 296, 316–18, 321, 323, 333, 348, 353, 374, 378, 387; English-speaking, 247, 364, 366, 367; French-speaking, 1, 18, 19, 25, 127, 128, 212, 240, 321, 324, 325, 333–40, 348, 351, 353, 356, 359, 363, 364, 366, 367; North, 82, 85, 91, 250, 322, 348, 364, 368
Agreements, *see* Treaties
Albania, 21, 122, 370
Algeria, 1, 7, 15, 16, 19, 50, 65, 69, 175, 305, 318, 322, 325–31, 333, 334, 340–47, 351, 353, 354, 356, 359–62, 364, 365, 373, 379, 386; French in, 7, 56, 57, 326, 330, 341–43, 345, 373; Moslems in, 326, 327, 330, 334, 341–43, 345, 373; *see also* Wars
Alliances, 20, 23, 95, 99; *see also* Atlantic Alliance
Alsace, 15, 86, 87, 261, 262, 269
Anti-Americanism, 67, 77–79, 174, 249–57
Arabs, 322, 323
Argentina, 134, 218, 219
Army, 37, 38, 51, 52, 82, 120, 121, 125–28, 328–32, 341, 342, 344; Generals' Rebellion (1961), 38, 51, 52, 69, 344; revolt against Fourth Republic (1958), 50, 51, 52
Asia, 18, 22, 23, 32, 33, 35, 75, 105, 133, 156, 161, 162, 168, 170, 172, 278, 296, 303, 315–18, 321–23, 333, 348, 353, 371, 372, 374, 378, 387; Southeast, 19, 21, 168, 179, 251, 278, 317, 319, 321, 348, 365, 369, 370, 371, 373
Atlantic Alliance, 19, 20, 22, 30, 31, 34, 35, 36, 62, 67, 95, 98–105, 110, 118, 137, 142, 147, 148, 152–89, 193, 231, 232, 258, 271, 272, 276, 277, 281, 288, 296, 298, 306, 310, 312, 362, 379, 392; *see also* NATO
Australia, 31, 134, 218, 236, 240, 374
Austria, 15, 81, 181, 236, 249, 257, 283, 303

Belgium, 18, 33, 55, 71, 125, 145, 166–69, 182, 193, 195, 197, 199, 205, 208, 210, 211, 215, 216, 220, 225, 227, 231, 232, 264, 303, 355, 356, 359, 363
Berlin, *see* Germany
Bizerte, 85, 348
Brazil, 134, 360, 377
Burma, 316, 322, 370
Burundi, 356, 363, 365

Cambodia, 316, 318, 322, 356, 365, 369, 373
Canada, 71, 134, 145, 166, 181, 184, 218, 219, 236, 240, 316, 340, 346, 376
Ceylon, 322
China, 1, 14, 18, 20, 21, 22, 23, 24, 25, 33, 36, 76, 105, 120, 122, 131–34, 153–56, 159, 162, 168, 174, 175, 209, 257, 261, 278, 279, 295, 296, 298, 299, 301, 302, 306, 314–20, 339, 348, 350, 351, 368–78, 381, 386, 387, 389, 391
Chile, 377
Colonies (French), 10, 12, 13, 19, 32, 69, 321–47
Common Market, 25, 28, 30, 32, 34, 53, 55, 56, 60, 63, 66, 68, 122, 124, 143, 148, 149, 152, 166, 178, 180, 182, 185, 190, 191, 195, 198, 200–203, 206, 230, 234, 251, 252, 255, 257–59, 270, 275, 280, 282, 288, 296, 305, 319, 355, 358, 367, 374, 375, 391, 392; and agriculture, 39, 190, 191, 197, 203, 207–11, 213–15, 217–21, 223–26, 237, 238, 240, 241, 243, 244, 248, 249, 252, 279, 280; British accession to, 121, 141, 191, 215, 225, 231, 232, 234–49, 257, 275–77; Commission, 190, 197, 200, 201, 203, 205–10, 213, 214, 220–24, 229, 239, 240, 243, 254, 255, 259, 381; Council of Ministers, 190, 197, 204–207, 209, 213, 214, 219–24, 231, 258, 381; European Fund for Agricultural Orientation and Guaranty, 207, 208, 212, 220, 225, 226, 319; European Fund for Overseas Development, 212, 359, 363, 364; European Par-

423